CATHOLICS IN COLLEGE

CATHOLICS IN COLLEGE

Religious Commitment and the Intellectual Life

JAMES W. TRENT
with
JENETTE GOLDS

With a Foreword by
JOHN TRACY ELLIS

THE UNIVERSITY OF CHICAGO PRESS
CHICAGO & LONDON

Library of Congress Catalog Card Number: 67-25518

THE UNIVERSITY OF CHICAGO PRESS, CHICAGO & LONDON

The University of Toronto Press, Toronto 5, Canada

FOREWORD

Since many Catholic youth want to obtain a higher education to become physicians, attorneys, or priests, it has long been the ambition of the bishops to erect such higher institutions of learning and to supervise them in order that these young men, who otherwise would attend the public state schools, might not go astray.[1]

Such was the observation made by Canon Josef Salzbacher of Saint Stephen's Cathedral, Vienna, following a tour of the United States in the spring and summer of 1842. At first reading, this comment of a century and a quarter ago on the motives for higher education among American Catholics might appear to be very much out of date. But Trent's book will disabuse the reader of that idea, for it demonstrates that only within the last decade has there emerged in the American Catholic community a clearly discernible emphasis on college and university education as a goal apart from its relation to students' religious training. Thus if Canon Salzbacher were to have returned to the United States a century after his first visit, he would have found a system of Catholic higher education tremendously larger than the one he had seen in 1842, but generally speaking, he would have discerned scarcely more than occasional suggestions of a radically different motivation for Catholic education. And, at either date, few highly placed in the church—whether among the diocesan or religious clergy—would have fully comprehended or been prepared to accept Cardinal Newman's answer to the question: "What Is a University?"

It is a place where inquiry is pushed forward, and discoveries verified and perfected, and rashness rendered innocuous, and error exposed, by the collision of mind with mind, and knowledge with knowledge. . . .[2]

Few aspects of Catholic life have elicited more widespread and sustained attention on the part of Americans, regardless of religious affiliation, than the state of higher education under the church's aus-

[1] Salzbacher (1967), 1: 261.
[2] Newman (1872), p. 16.

v

pices. For more than a decade it has been submitted to the closest scrutiny by Catholics themselves, as well as having been made the object of study and criticism by an increasing number outside the church. In some instances this scrutiny has done a disservice to Catholic colleges and universities, either because writers, Catholic or non-Catholic, have exaggerated the weaknesses of these institutions, or because Catholics, prompted by their defensive attitudes, have falsified the true situation in the mistaken view that any criticism was a manifestation of hostility. Trent has shown an awareness of both extremes, and he has sought—with a good measure of success in my opinion—to remedy their defects by resting his case on the solid ground of demonstrable facts. Although fully cognizant that the picture that emerges from his research is in a number of respects anything but flattering to the Catholic colleges and universities, Trent is also keenly aware of the rapid pace of improvement that is now current on the best Catholic campuses. For that reason he is frank to acknowledge that many of his findings may, indeed, be rendered out of date within the next decade or two.

Meanwhile, as the effort to attain quality and excellence grows in Catholic academic circles, and as Catholics move farther into the more sensitive and delicate area of academic freedom in the generally accepted meaning of that term—as they are now doing—those connected with the church's colleges and universities will wish to avail themselves of all the reliable data they can find, especially in those sectors of their commitment where weaknesses have been most pronounced. For no one who is serious about the future of Catholic higher education will gainsay the relevance here of Pierre Teilhard de Chardin's remark, even when applied to the immediate past, that historical research teaches one that "there is only one real road . . . it is to build the future." In that regard the same Catholic educators have no desire to be numbered among those who "behave as though the past were interesting in itself, and treat it as only the future deserves to be treated."[3]

No people can escape from their past, and American Catholics have been no exception to this general law of life. It is in terms of the past, in terms of what Trent calls their subculture within the American framework, that Catholics' weaknesses in higher education begin to become comprehensible. Given their immigrant background and the closure of certain church policies and personnel, it should come as no surprise that the Catholic college and university students possess a distinctly lower intellectual disposition than that found among non-

[3] De Chardin (1962), p. 209.

Catholic students, and lower, in fact, than their own level of ability would suggest. This might be surprising only in the face of the argument that Catholics have now had time to become acculturated in American society. True, the Catholic college seniors in the author's sampling demonstrated a significant intellectual development over what they had shown as freshmen. Yet it is evident that the only way in which students in Catholic institutions can overtake the distance between themselves and their peers in the secular colleges and universities is to outrun their secular counterparts in fostering intellectual growth on their campuses.

On another front this book will have immediate relevance for Catholic educators. It is obvious that the present generation of college and university students in this country, including those in Catholic institutions, has taken a far more sceptical attitude toward religion and the churches than did their predecessors. This fact has raised a number of questions in Trent's mind, questions to which administrators and faculties of Catholic colleges and universities are going to have to address themselves with increasing frequency in the years immediately ahead. Are Catholic institutions prepared to have their Catholic students openly express doubt and disagreement with what have hitherto been regarded as traditional and fixed articles of Catholic belief? Can the students do this and still retain their faith in the accepted Catholic sense? Can the church, in turn, permit this kind of challenge to her teaching magisterium by her youthful members? And will the church's colleges and universities allow this type of dissent, and if they will not, what are the alternatives?

One of the services that books of this kind render to the learned fraternity is to raise the right questions and to provoke serious thought concerning their answers. Questions such as those mentioned above will do just that, and there is, in my judgment, no more critical area awaiting those involved in Catholic higher education than that surrounding the complicated terrain of religious commitment and its relation to academic freedom. Yet beyond posing questions to which there is no immediate and precise answer, Trent also provides the evidence for a number of other questions. For example, those who are still facing the problem of coeducation in the church's institutions may derive some helpful guidelines from the superiority of women's Catholic colleges in intellectual awareness and disposition over the Catholic colleges that restrict enrollment to men, a fact that may offer an additional argument, if any is still needed, for coeducation in the latter type of institution.

Trent's detailed analysis of the religious commitment and intellectual life of over 4,000 students in 5 Catholic colleges, 1 public college, and 1 public university on the Pacific Coast, and approximately 2,500 students across the country enrolled in 74 Catholic colleges and around 600 secular institutions located principally in the Middle West, California, and Pennsylvania, contains many arresting conclusions other than those I have mentioned. Yet in spite of the uncomplimentary evidence the book uncovers, the author has not been led to despair of the future of Catholic higher education, nor does he call in question, as some have done, the possibility of achieving the accepted goals of higher learning within the juridical framework of the church. Those who hold that position must explain how the Catholic University of Louvain has for over 500 years occupied a proud position in the world of learning, while at the same time operating under the auspices of the Belgian hierarchy.

After reading this book it occurred to me—and I wonder if it might not occur to others, Catholics and non-Catholics alike—that Trent has himself unconsciously demonstrated in this volume the possibility of the reconciliation of objective scholarship and a questioning but loyal approach to religious faith. In other words, he manifests the opposite of what Dom Leclercq had in mind about a Catholic who is heedless of either one of these two high ideals when he said:

If he performs his task poorly, he compromises his reputation and also the cause he serves, the truth he should manifest, and the Church whose honor he hopes to enhance.[4]

John Tracy Ellis

[4] Leclercq (1961), p. 321.

PREFACE

This study assesses the intellectual and religious values expressed by Catholic college freshmen and seniors and by Catholics and non-Catholics enrolled in public and private colleges between 1959 and 1966. In a sense this study began during my undergraduate years at a Catholic university. I was active in a branch of the Jocist movement known in America as the Young Christian Students. The object of this movement is the continual examination and implementation of the role of Christian and student, or better, the implementation of the Christian ideal in the student world. This means, primarily, trying to be a student while helping others to be students, not just college attenders.

Out of this spirit, I, together with fellow members of the Young Christian Students, had occasion to observe what it meant to be a student, a seeker of knowledge and wisdom, or a Christian intellectual. This observation included an inquiry into the nature of our colleges and what they had to contribute to the student vocation. Dissatisfaction arose as we continued to compare the reality around us with models we viewed as the ideal. However, this dissatisfaction was not the source so much of a youthful rebellion against our church and its educational institutions as it was the source of an earnest desire to see change and improvement take place within the church.

Over ten years have passed since I first began to inquire into the intellectual life in a Catholic context. But neither the need for, nor the interest in that original inquiry have diminished. The present study issues from wider interests and concerns than that of my original inquiry, but it may certainly have been partially motivated by my earlier concerns. Of course, there would be reason enough for undertaking the study if it should somehow help illuminate the nature of intellectual commitment in a religious subculture and the relationship of intellectual and religious orientations. But if such an exploration should also assist in any small way a fuller realization of the student vocation, then so much the better. It is my hope that the present study will represent to some degree a means toward both these ends among Catholics and non-Catholics alike.

Catholic intellectuality, or its lack, in America remains both intriguing and problematical. Consequently, I see no value in glossing over unflattering material uncovered in the course of the study. Theory and speculation about the source of the problem of Catholic intellectuality are openly included, together with data which probe into and illustrate the problem. Had I not tried to be as objective and forthright as possible, I would have been doing a disservice to my academic discipline, to the church, and particularly to those Catholic colleges which generously participated in this study. Thus, both the limitations and implications of the data are frankly discussed.

In general, the Catholic college students comprising the cross-country samples in this study have been found to be relatively uncommitted intellectually and to be more docile, close-minded, and unimaginative than the non-Catholic college students observed. Catholic students who do manifest an intellectual orientation are also much more critical or liberal in religious orientation when compared with their less intellectual peers. This phenomenon is apparent in reference to a variety of reported activities and carefully measured attitudes. This phenomenon is also apparent among both Catholic college freshmen and seniors and among those planning on post-baccalaureate education.

Nevertheless, there is evidence that the character of American Catholic intellectuality is changing. Indeed, I would not be surprised to see many of the findings of the present study made passé within the next decade or two. A number of signs of intellectual development within the church are presented in chapter 11. Not the least of these signs, perhaps, is the courage and interest of a number of the administrators of Catholic colleges participating in this study, indicated by their willingness to undergo the exposure and soul-searching that this study was bound to represent for them. One administrator's comment was that the study probably would not be very complimentary, but that it would be better for all concerned to "let the chips fall where they may." The nature of the falling chips prohibits the mentioning of these administrators or their colleges by name, other than in the list of participating colleges in Appendix B. But they are individually assured of my immense gratitude and admiration. I use the word "admiration" with deliberate meaning. In the last few years, I have watched the administration and faculty in many of the participating colleges make seemingly Herculean efforts to improve the intellectual quality of their institutions.

Sincere acknowledgment is also due others who assisted in the realization of this study. A grant from the Committee on Research of the University of California made it possible to assemble and prepare much of the data for computer processing. Those friends and clerical assistants who worked tirelessly and meticulously on coding the instruments and transcribing the data already know my great gratitude. Jeffrey Koon took a diligent interest in the preparation of the final manuscript. Terry Berge, Jean Goodman, Marilyn Hillesland, Deborah Jones, Robert Miller, Barbara Neuberger, David Rose, and particularly Janet Ruyle gave their time and extremely helpful efforts beyond the ordinary limits of employment and friendship. Dr. Manford Ferris assisted in the design of the statistical analyses of the study.

It is only fitting that Monsignor John Tracy Ellis of the University of San Francisco should write the foreword to this book. His critical insights and scholarship contributed greatly to the inspiration for the book, and the interest he showed in it is appreciated. Sincere appreciation is also extended to David Riesman of Harvard University. His own scholarship as well as the direct and generous interest he took in my research not only contributed to the inspiration for this book but also to its publication. Drs. Paul Heist, T. R. McConnell, and Leland L. Medsker of the Center for Research and Development in Higher Education, University of California, Berkeley, graciously allowed me the use of the Center's Omnibus Personality Inventory and supplementary data. They also provided research and clerical assistance necessary for the coding, scoring, and tabulation of the instruments and data used in the study.

Dr. Elwin D. Farwell, presently of Luther College, Iowa, Dr. Heist, Dr. McConnell, Dr. Medsker, Mrs. Ruyle, and Dr. George D. Yonge have been at once cherished colleagues, critics, and inspiring teachers, through the course of the author's graduate studies and his career at the Center for Research and Development in Higher Education. I also wish especially to acknowledge the assistance of Mrs. Jenette Golds, who reviewed the literature and assembled relevant data, and whose constant, unequaled efforts and exceptional talents both enhanced the book and made possible its completion in the face of competing activities. Above all, my wife Gretchen Anne has coura-

CONTENTS

CONTENTS

CHAPTER ONE

American Catholic Intellectual Life

The call for renewal and reform reverberating throughout the Catholic world brings with it possibilities of change at all levels and in all areas of Catholic life. A church that for centuries has been regarded as unchanging is now being challenged by its own members and by its leaders as well. The church has never been the monolithic structure it has superficially appeared to be, but the diversity within it has been limited in nature and is seldom obvious. Although its members have always had differences in religious interpretation and practice, the church has been seen as having only one answer to every question and as having an answer to all possible questions. Now, however, new questions are being asked, not only about the teachings and practices of the church but about its relevance to modern life. These questions, which were initiated primarily in Europe before the start of Vatican II, are openly asked, and the different responses to them are widely publicized.

The results of this questioning are already clearly visible in some areas of church life. Most evident have been the changes in the church liturgy, as well as in the newly generated spirit of cooperation with other religions. Change is also discernible in the discussion within the church on a wide range of social and moral issues, from birth control to priestly celibacy. Change may even be anticipated in the training and requirements of the clergy.

Pope Paul has emphasized that "reform cannot concern either the essential concept of the church or its basic structure,"[1] but once we accept this reservation, all other areas of church life become proper subjects for discussion and debate, and the possibilities for change become virtually limitless. Not all areas will be equally affected, nor will the extent or permanence of change become immediately evident. It may be many years before we can know whether the existing potential for change will be realized, but at last the church is attempting

[1] *Catholic Voice,* August 14, 1964, p. 6.

1

to modify many immobile features which have characterized it in the past.

Much of the discussion and debate taking place has concerned an area of life long neglected in the church, particularly in America: that is, the lack of intellectual commitment among Catholics. Despite its intellectual tradition, the church has throughout much of its history failed to encourage in its members an appreciation for the intellectual side of life.

Catholicism is a religion founded upon reason and upon belief in a rational universe, and many of the most revered and respected leaders in the church have been men of great learning and independent thought. For centuries, the church has insisted upon an educated clergy. The origin of the modern university can be traced to the medieval church, and the church has theoretically been an advocate and supporter of universities and of creativity in the arts since the Middle Ages. Yet the church has not in practice greatly encouraged independent intellectual activity among its members. Typically it has encouraged them, instead, to be devout, docile, and obedient to all of its teachings, but not to engage in the critical evaluation of their faith. Acceptance of the authority of the church, as represented by the local clergy, has been emphasized rather than intellectual questioning and scholarly endeavor.

Instead of fostering intellectual commitment, certain practices of the church have tended to inhibit intellectual freedom. Two well-known examples are the Index of Forbidden Books and the Imprimatur. The Index lists books which may not be read by Catholics without special permission, since they are considered a threat to faith or morals. The Imprimatur is required for approved books written by Catholics, again on matters concerned with faith and morals, and signifies that the book is free of doctrinal or moral error.

The European theologian Hans Küng, in his lecture tour of America in 1963, expressed the hope that Vatican II would "take those repressive institutions—which the church got along very well without for fifteen hundred years and which are unquestionably out of date today —and boldly and confidently abolish them."[2] To date, these institutions have not been abolished, but, since Vatican II, there are indications that the Index has been quietly shelved; and if the Imprimatur has not been eliminated, at least it does not appear as restrictive as it once was. The fact that the Imprimatur was recently granted to the Revised Standard Version of the Bible, a book long used by Protes-

---

[2] Küng (1963), p. 351.

tants but forbidden to Catholics, is a sign of a greater openness and intellectual awareness within the church.

This easing of restrictive practices, added to the increased discussion and participation with non-Catholics in social issues, and the increased questioning of the church itself, all evince the possibility of a long-overdue intellectual awakening for Catholics. This awakening is already well underway in Europe and is gaining momentum in this country.

The lack of Catholic contributions to the intellectual life of the United States is one indication that such an awakening is needed. For reasons that will be explored later, there have been comparatively few Catholics in the scholarly community, regardless of how that community is defined. There have also been comparatively few Catholics attending college, when college attendance might be considered the first step toward entrance to the scholarly community. Moreover, the colleges Catholics have attended have been relatively lacking in intellectual excellence.

Concern about this particular situation has been growing in recent years. As questions have been asked about the church as a whole, so critical appraisals of the schools and colleges that the church supports have also been undertaken. Catholic educators since 1955 have been engaged in candid self-criticism, and students and their schools have been surveyed by psychologists and sociologists seeking evidence of intellectual awareness and productivity. These studies preceded the official start of Vatican II and were set in motion in part by the searching questions about Catholic intellectualism that were raised by such Catholic scholars as Ellis, O'Dea, and Weigel.[3]

Many of the questions about Catholic intellectualism pertained to the Catholic colleges as institutions primarily charged with the responsibility of developing intellectual engagement and concern. Taking note of the paucity of intellectual productivity among Catholic college graduates, Ellis and others leveled a variety of criticisms against Catholic colleges. They objected that these colleges failed to develop a love of scholarship for its own sake among their students, that they overemphasized their roles as agencies for the moral development of their students, and that they failed to foster in their students respect for the scholarly achievements of non-Catholics, consideration of the ideas of others, and a sense of objectivity. In addition, criticism has been that too many competing schools have been maintained, that the colleges neglected the fields of study in which they should be especially

[3] Ellis (1955, 1956a, 1956b); O'Dea (1958, 1959); Weigel (1957).

strong, and that the lay graduates who did gain renown did so almost exclusively in law.

These criticisms began to gain widespread public attention in 1955; in the years since, critical questions remain without satisfactory answers. Has the intellectual life of Catholic college students changed during these years? Have the conditions that were criticized become a thing of the past? Some discussions of Catholic intellectual life, and of Catholic colleges in particular, give the impression that this is so. But it is difficult to bring about radical and pervasive changes in a human culture and its institutions in so short a time; in fact, ten years from now these changes may still be far from accomplished. That the changes will be given impetus by Vatican II is to be hoped, but it is far too early to tell what the exact effect will be.

The present book is written within the framework of this continuing concern about the extent and quality of Catholic intellectualism and about the possibilities and repercussions of an intellectual awakening actuated by Vatican II. The book deals primarily with the nature of American Catholic intellectual life, as represented by Catholic students attending both Catholic and non-Catholic colleges. Attention is given to these students on the assumption that they represent the greatest potential source of Catholic intellectual leaders.

Information about these students is drawn from many recent studies. These studies have covered a variety of Catholic and public colleges and have examined the values, attitudes, abilities, and goals of these students. The primary data are drawn from two of our studies: an intensive comparative study of students in 5 Catholic and 2 public, "secular" colleges on the West Coast; and a study of 10,000 high school graduates in 16 communities between California and Pennsylvania, almost half of whom entered nearly 700 colleges.[4] Both studies were conducted under the auspices of the Center for Research and Development in Higher Education, University of California, Berkeley. Both studies were longitudinal in nature; that is, they followed the development of the students under consideration for four to five years, between 1959 and 1964. Pertinent materials are also drawn from other studies conducted within and without the Center.

In the following pages the distinction is usually made between Catholics attending Catholic colleges (termed "Catholics" in the tables), Catholics attending secular colleges ("secular Catholics"), and non-Catholics attending secular colleges ("non-Catholics"). Most

[4] Trent (1964); Trent and Medsker (1967).

of the secular colleges are public, but they also include private sectarian and nonsectarian institutions. The term secular is applied to colleges only to denote that they are outside of the control of the Catholic church. Similarly, Catholic students are referred to as secular only to make clear that they are attending colleges outside of the control of the church.

The focus of this book will be upon the intellectual disposition of Catholic students, but since we are concerned with intellectualism in a religious context, we will also consider the relationship between intellectual and religious disposition. Although our emphasis will be on Catholics, we will also include relevant findings about other religious groups, since Catholics have not been alone in their failure to stimulate intellectual achievement, and certain other groups, primarily Protestant fundamentalist groups, have been found to be equally lacking in intellectual values.

In chapters 1 through 9 we will concentrate upon the intellectual development of Catholics, both as the situation has existed historically and as it exists today. To present a full picture of contemporary Catholic students, we will be concerned with the proportions and characteristics of Catholics who go to Catholic and non-Catholic colleges and graduate schools. We will consider intellectual and religious development in particular, as well as the effect of intellectual commitment upon the religious life of students. Ensuing discussion is directed toward two additional questions: What does it mean to be a Catholic intellectual? What is the effect of a high degree of intellectual development on the individual and on his church?

In chapters 10 through 12 our discussion will center on the American Catholic system and the ways in which it has inhibited intellectual development. This "system" includes not only the church but also the families, individuals, schools, and colleges affiliated with it. Our concern is with the way the generally closed church-family-self system has affected Catholics in the past, how the system is changing, and what changes may be anticipated in the future.

Since the primary concern of this book is the psychodynamics of Catholic intellectual life, we must first define the meaning of intellectual disposition as we perceive it. We must also consider the importance of intellectual development in a time of radical change such as the present and look at some of the reasons for the anti-intellectualism that has been pervasive in America in the past, especially those religious sources of anti-intellectualism shared by Protestants and Catholics.

Intellectualism may be defined in the simplest sense as devotion to the exercise of intellect or to intellectual pursuits. But such a definition in itself means very little. To some people, intellectualism means learning: the man who has acquired a vast fund of knowledge would thus be called an intellectual, or the man who has obtained good grades in school. To others intellectualism simply implies interest in matters of a theoretical rather than a practical nature: a man who scorns practical considerations in approaching problems would by this definition be considered an intellectual.

The term intellectual as used in this book refers to much more than academic achievement or lack of interest in practical concerns. Intellectualism also implies not only an interest in but a commitment to a wide range of scholarly and cultural pursuits. The term intellectual is used here to distinguish the person who exhibits a consistent, creative devotion to understanding and appreciating a wide variety of ideas and forms of expression in the arts and sciences. It does not refer to a mind but a state of mind, a state of mind that is open to and actively seeks out the mysteries and beauties of life.

It can be said that the intellectual is one who makes questions out of answers, and it is this constant questioning that characterizes the intellectual. Intellectualism does not only depend on what a man knows, but on his attitude toward learning and what he does with his knowledge. The intellectual is not content to accept the answers that come to him, but is always seeking new questions and facing the conflict of opposing answers.

Intellectualism cannot be equated with erudition in an adult, and neither can it be equated with intelligence, nor with academic aptitude or achievement in a student. Thus a student cannot be assumed to be an intellectual simply because his ability scores are high or his grades are good, or because he is planning to enter graduate or professional school, or because he has won a scholarship. Similarly, intellectualism cannot be assumed to exist because a person is a member of a certain profession. There are lawyers whose vision of life is bounded by the codifications of their legal texts, and doctors who know the individual parts of the anatomy but never see life as a whole. And there are professors who look at life only from the standpoint of their own specialty and never seek to learn what other specialties may add to their conception of life. There are, of course, many intellectual doctors, lawyers, and college professors, but membership in the professions does not guarantee intellectualism. A certain amount of mental ability is a necessary precondition for the exercise of intellectualism, and many professions require a high degree of such ability, but intelligence alone does not constitute intellectual disposition.

The distinction between intelligence and intellect has been discussed in detail by Hofstadter. He defines intelligence as ". . . an excellence of mind that is employed within a fairly narrow, immediate, and predictable range: it is a manipulative, adjustive, unfailingly practical quality. . . ." Intellect is the "critical, creative, and contemplative side of mind" which "looks for the meanings of situations as a whole."[5]

This critical and creative approach to life is urgently needed today. The individual must be able to look at situations in all their complexities and consider all the implications and consequences involved in possible courses of action. It is not enough, for example, to think of birth control in terms only of historical Catholic teachings. Birth control is an issue that exists in the worldwide context of the population explosion, where there are changing attitudes toward marriage and evolving concepts of natural law.

Of course, Catholics are not the only ones who need a comprehensive and creative approach to life. It is an approach needed by all men in all walks of life. America is facing a time of extreme change, when technological advances may automate large segments of the population out of the employment market. It is a time of great social change, when groups that have previously not participated fully in society have become full voting members who want the education, housing, and other rights and privileges to which most members of society already have access. It is a time when men are being sent to fight in a war in which they may not believe, and in which there is the constant threat of international holocaust.

It is also a time when established religious values are being challenged. Even the existence of God is being seriously questioned, and questioned not only by philosophers, but by theologians as well, to the point where a popular magazine carried the question "Is God Dead?" emblazoned across its cover.

Apart from the religious question, much of the population is beset by anxiety, although often unable to name the source of concern. This anxiety is revealed not only in student discontent and in feelings of alienation within the nation's colleges and universities, but in unrest in many other aspects of life. It is also shown by increasing demands for psychological help. These demands come not only from those who are afflicted with serious mental illness, but from those who simply feel lost and unsure of where they are going in this world. Part

[5] Hofstadter (1964), p. 25.

of this growing need for psychological help can be explained by the decreased importance of religion in the lives of many people. As old values have been swept away, the psychiatrist, psychologist, or counselor has for many people taken the place of the priest or minister as a person with whom to discuss problems.

In such a period of radical upheaval as the present, the need for independent, flexible thinking is paramount. The rigid conformist who is used to simple answers will no longer be able to find them, for such answers will no longer exist. He will not be able to say what we have heard so often, that his religious beliefs are simply "all that the church teaches," for many of the traditional teachings of the church are being challenged or are undergoing change. He will no longer be able to say that he wants to be a printer because "it looks like a good job," for there may come a time when there is no need for printers.

To prepare the individual to cope with changing conditions, many schools have adopted as a primary objective, education for change. The individual can no longer be educated for a specific role in life, since so many of these roles are changing; education must now be designed to prepare the individual to accept change, whether it involves moving from one job to another, from one city to another, or from one way of life to another—in short, to give him an intellectual, or at least a flexible, open attitude toward life and learning. There is a very practical value, then, to encouraging the growth of intellectual disposition, quite apart from the fact that intellectuality represents the highest order of human endeavor.

The problem may be posed this way: What will life mean to people as they search for a kind of security and stability that will no longer be possible? How can they avoid a feeling of futility if they cannot plan ahead and see order in their lives and results from their labors? If individuals and the nation are to transcend the turbulence ahead, the country needs intellectual leaders who will consider these questions and who will look at the long-range effects of change. The nation needs thinkers who will be concerned about the question of how life can be meaningful to people when so many of the old props and guideposts are gone. There is an urgent need for such creative, intellectual leaders in all areas of endeavor—political, economic, social, spiritual, educational, and cultural. They must be men and women who will be willing to take risks with new ideas and willing to search out unique ways to solve new problems.

Of course, the need for open, independent thinking is not limited to a few intellectual leaders. It permeates the whole society. Just as simple skills will not be enough to guarantee a job, so common sense will not be enough to enable the individual to chart his course through the years ahead. Each individual must develop his intellectual faculties to the fullest, and not simply by cramming knowledge, useful or otherwise, into his head. Even if he is not an intellectual leader, he still must be able to think critically and creatively and to be flexible in meeting new ideas and new situations so that he will not be overwhelmed by them. And if he is not only to meet life but to master it, he must find new ways to fulfill and enrich his life.

This kind of independent and creative approach to life has not often been esteemed in America in the past, but perhaps it has never been needed so desperately as it is now. Perhaps the anti-intellectualism that has been pervasive throughout American history could be considered an unfortunate characteristic of a restless, expanding nation. But anti-intellectualism in a time of extreme upheaval such as the present represents an acute and menacing problem which the nation cannot overlook, and which organized religion can no longer be a party to, however unwittingly.

Many sources, religious and otherwise, have contributed to America's anti-intellectual tradition. Ironically, among these have been some of the most basic and cherished ideals of American life, particularly the ideal of egalitarianism upon which the country was founded. Men who accepted the doctrine that all men are created equal often looked with suspicion upon those who sought more education than their fellows and who might be considered members of an intellectual elite. They distrusted those who thought and acted in ways different from their own; they respected the common man, not the intellectual.

Another source of anti-intellectualism has been the romanticism which has characterized the nation. Americans romanticized the life of the frontier and idealized the natural man, untrained and untutored, who conquered the wilderness. His natural abilities, his innate goodness, his reliance upon his impulses and emotions, rather than upon logic and learning, all contributed to a lack of interest and respect for the intellectual life. The strength of a man's will and the strength of his back counted far more than any amount of learning.

American emphasis upon business, an emphasis which has been reinforced by Calvinist beliefs in the significance of hard work, has also contributed to the anti-intellectual spirit in American life. Although its most successful businessmen have frequently contributed part of the fruits of their labors toward the improvement of education, charitable institutions, and cultural foundations, a nation which honors its businessmen more than its scholars, as the United States does, is not sufficiently encouraging intellectual commitment.

Religion may not be considered the primary source of anti-intellectualism in America, but the churches, too, have certainly contributed greatly to this condition. Despite the diversity of religious groups within the country, there has been a peculiarly American approach to religion, and it has not been one conducive to the development of a vigorous and stimulating intellectual life. Just as Americans have emphasized the practical rather than the theoretical aspects of life in general, so have they regarded religion. They have not been interested in discussions of theology and of doctrine but have looked for practical results from religion in the form of happiness, security, and a better life in this world. As Herberg points out, American religion tends to be actively occupied with the things of this world.[6] Americans place their faith in religion, whatever religion they have been born into or fallen into, and expect their lives to be better because they have "a religion."

This practical approach to religion has been reflected in the typical American's attitude toward education. Commager comments, ". . . as he expected his religion to be practical and pay dividends, he expected education to prepare for life—by which he meant, increasingly, jobs and professions."[7] As the interest has not been in religion for its own sake, so there has not been interest in learning for the sake of learning but for the practical results that could be achieved from it.

This is not to say that the churches have made no positive contributions to American intellectual life. The early New England clergy were renowned for their broad interest in learning and were responsible for the founding of such church colleges as Harvard, which even in its beginnings did not limit education to narrow theological concerns. One writer has summed up Puritan contributions with the comment, "Puritan founders had their terrible faults, but they had at least the respect for mind and the intensity of spirit which are necessary to distinguished intellectual achievement."[8]

Despite the distinctive contributions to American intellectual life of many Puritan leaders and many Protestant clergymen who followed them, there has consistently been a distinctly anti-intellectual tendency within American Protestantism. This tendency has stemmed primarily from the Calvinist emphasis upon the preeminent importance of hard

[6] Herberg (1960a).
[7] Commager (1950), p. 10.
[8] Hofstadter (1964), p. 399.

work, since it was deemed that through man's devotion to hard work he proved he was one of the elect, chosen by God for salvation.[9] Hard work was a virtue, but idle intellectual speculation was not, and devotion to business and commerce was honored far above interest in abstract ideas, or specifically, in theology and philosophy. The tiller of the soil and hewer of wood were inordinately revered, but the scholar was held suspect.

But the rise of the fundamentalist evangelical movement was probably the Protestant religious influence that contributed most to the development of anti-intellectualism in the United States. The established churches were already torn by conflicts over whether religion should be based upon an appeal to reason or an appeal to emotion. With the expansion of the evangelical movement across the land, emotion predominated. For the Protestant fundamentalists, religion was primarily a matter of the heart, not the head, and it was what a man felt in his heart that counted, not what he happened to know.

It is not surprising that with this emphasis upon emotion, the whole idea of a need for a learned clergy was attacked. This attack resulted partly from the jealousies and fears of the circuit riders, who often had little respect for their educated eastern contemporaries, but it can also be attributed to the difficulty of finding enough educated preachers to fill the needs of ministering to the frontier. Moreover, the frontier Protestant fundamentalist was seldom educated and generally represented a relatively low socioeconomic group opposed to learning and mistrustful of authority.

Still, the frontier fundamentalist sects were usually eager that children be taught to read, since if the Bible was depended upon for religious truth, children had at least to be able to read that truth. These sects also came to accept education as training that would help them earn their way in the world, but they had little use for impractical higher education, for themselves, or for their clergy. The uneducated clergy contributed to and shared the prejudice against learning that was predominant among the fundamentalists. Such groups as the Baptists early maintained very strong prejudices against advanced education, and it was to be a long time before they established colleges of their own, particularly ones which emphasized the intellectually oriented liberal arts.

The evangelical movement led to internal divisions in the three major established Protestant churches—the Presbyterian, Congrega-

[9] Weber (1963), for example, has discussed the relationship between religion and business activity, particularly in pp. 246–61.

tional, and Episcopal. Hofstadter describes the leaders of the more evangelical branches of these churches as "the heirs to the New England intellectual tradition," but adds that "their culture was exceptionally narrow; their view of learning was extremely instrumental; and instead of enlarging their intellectual inheritance, they steadily contracted it."[10]

As the intellectual horizons of these congregations diminished, so did their size. Thus, a steadily smaller proportion of the population belonged to the religious groups that championed whatever intellectualism there was in whatever reduced form. At the end of the Revolution, Anglicans, Presbyterians, and Congregationalists were the largest and strongest religious groups. By the middle of the next century, Roman Catholics, Methodists, and Baptists claimed the most adherents. The anti-intellectualism of the Protestant fundamentalists was soon to be equaled, if not exceeded, by members of what had become by 1850 the largest single religious denominational group in the country, the Roman Catholics.

It is not surprising that Catholics as a group should have little interest in intellectual pursuits. Various historical and religious factors account for this situation. To start with, the increase in the American Catholic population resulted primarily from an influx of Polish, German, Latin, and especially Irish immigrants, who were predominantly underprivileged and uneducated. They neither valued nor had an opportunity to gain education; they immediately became a part of the lower socioeconomic strata in America and were slow to improve this situation.

Between 1820 and 1865 almost two million Irish immigrants entered the country. With them came members of the Irish clergy, who assumed positions of authority in the American church. Earlier, the American Catholic church had had much of a French and English laissez-faire attitude about it. Under such a system of "trusteeism," Catholic congregations were to a great extent autonomous and under lay direction. Around 1850, however, multiple internal struggles led to a take-over of the official church by the Irish clergy, who substituted strong autocracy for moderate autonomy. From this time on, the American Catholic church was an Irish Catholic church, and the Irish pastor was the last word on almost all things to his parishioners.

Because of this Irish domination, the American Church "absorbed little of the impressive scholarship of German Catholicism or ques-

[10] Hofstadter (1964), p. 91.

tioning intellectualism of the French church, and much more of the harsh Puritanism and fierce militancy of the Irish clergy."[11] Harshness and militancy may have been characteristics of the clergy; certainly an interest in intellectual pursuits was not, and this lack of interest was clearly communicated to parishioners. O'Dea has identified the one-sided power possessed by the Irish pastor as clericalism and sees it as a continuing force.[12] Thomas and Kane express a similar view.[13] The pastor was usually the only one who had any education at all, and, consequently, the immigrant Catholic became completely dependent upon him for representation and guidance in a strange and alien land.

A disregard for intellectual concerns has also often been fostered by attitudes within the Catholic family. Evidence of this has been provided by Strodtbeck in his study of Jewish and Italian Catholic families, by Whiteman in a study of Catholic, Baptist, and Jewish parents, and by Donovan in his study of family characteristics of faculties at Catholic colleges.[14] Strodtbeck identified in Italian Catholic families a pattern of emphasizing dependency among their children, of failing to recognize individual merits among their children, and of being fatalistic about their ability to achieve. In addition, the Italians were found to be more autocratic in their relationships than were Jews.

Similarly, Whiteman found that Catholics and Baptists were more dogmatic, authoritarian, and stereotyped in their beliefs and interactions than Jews, and were less likely to interact flexibly and democratically with their children. The Catholic and Protestant parents were both found to be more overprotective and constrictive toward children than were the Jewish parents and more inclined to foster dependency.

Although Strodtbeck studied only Italian families, Whiteman's study was not limited to any particular national group. That such findings are typical of more than one national group within Catholicism is indicated also in Donovan's study. In his extensive 1958 survey of Catholic college faculty members, Donovan found that most of them came from Irish families that maintained strict, unpermissive, authoritarian, dependent, and mother-centered family patterns. The consistent discovery of an autocratic-dependency pattern among Catholic families is particularly relevant, since it can be seen to inhibit

[11] *Ibid.,* p. 138.
[12] O'Dea (1958).
[13] Kane (1955); Thomas (1956).
[14] Donovan (1964); Strodtbeck (1958); Whiteman (1962).

the development of intellectualism, which requires free, open, and independent thought.

The anti-intellectualism displayed historically by American Catholics can thus be traced to many sources, including lack of education, low socioeconomic status, the influence of an anti-intellectual clergy, and lack of intellectual attitudes in the family. Moreover, these were Catholic immigrants arriving in a Protestant land, which became increasingly hostile to them as their numbers increased. Catholics were subjected to an immense amount of bigotry and prejudice and even physical persecution.[15] The resultant defensiveness of Catholics has lasted to this day. Catholics who were faced with a hostile, pluralistic society and who were sometimes forced into physical ghettoes formed a long-lasting mental ghetto.

Many of the Catholic church's objectives, policies, and practices reinforced the ghetto mentality of its membership. In particular, the mental ghetto of Catholicism was immediately fostered through a quickly growing school system. The subsequent lack of intellectual excellence in Catholic schools was probably inevitable. In fact, Ward has remarked that there should be no surprise over the lack of quality education within Catholic schools.[16] Their primary purpose was not to educate but to provide for the protection and reinforcement of the Catholic faith from grammar school through college.[17] The fact is that education, whether lower or higher, has been second to catechism and character formation in Catholic schools.

But the problem has not been religious training so much as an accompanying defensiveness. For the permeation of Catholic defensiveness throughout the educational system has led to Catholic isolation from the secular world of knowledge and ideas. An "outsider," Robert Cross, has stated:

Because men, caught up in the search for knowledge, sometimes abandoned truths vital to their faith, it was prudent for the faithful to insulate themselves

---

[15] See Handlin (1951); Myers (1960).

[16] Ward (1958).

[17] An interesting departure from this aim of protection of the faith occurred in the original intents of the establishment of Catholic University of America. Bishop Keane, under Cardinal Gibbons' tutelage, had in mind the flourishing of a Catholic intellectual life in his first faculty, and he apparently chose his faculty well for the purpose (Maynard, 1960). But as intellectualism now seems to breed controversy, so it did then, and critical church leaders kept Catholic University from implementing its original purpose until decades afterwards, and, if Victor's (1963) article is valid, it has yet a long way to go. (See also: *Time*, 1963 and *National Catholic Reporter*, April 26, 1967, p. 1 and May 3, 1967, p. 1.)

as far as possible from those inside or outside the Church who dabbled in new ideas.[18]

Personal intellectual inquiry has not been held up by the church as being of any particular virtue. Typically, a few able churchmen would become aware enough of a new field of knowledge or thought only to keep its "errors" apart from church doctrine. Indeed, defensive isolationism has consistently led to negation and ridicule of all secular systems, innovations, and thinkers to such a degree that Ong has suggested that it has affected the Catholic's attitude not only toward the intellectual life, but toward any phase of culture not specifically Catholic:

> This fact is manifest in orientation not only at the scientific level, but also at the level of practical sociology. Scouting, for example—in its various forms, certainly a product of romanticism, was accepted by American Catholics with great reluctance, and then for negative reasons—to keep Catholic youth away from troops operated under non-Catholic sponsorship. The American Catholic, like all Americans, enjoys scenery. But he is not a promoter of the Great Outdoors which to him, in some mysterious way, seems to have been turned over by its Creator to the Protestants.[19]

Out of a spirit of intellectual isolationism, the Catholic has been "invited to minimize real intellectual development" and accept instead "carefully worked out explanations with which 'informed' Catholics are familiar."[20] Hence, Bland's lament that the Catholic student has been generally confined to "carefully expurgated, Catholic-authored books" which have been, at best, second-rate and incomplete.[21] Moreover, if many great non-Catholic thinkers and researchers were studied at all, typically only their "bad points" were presented, and then for the sake of devastating criticism. John Dewey is a classic case in point; or Locke, who is known among many Catholics for his divergence from Thomism, rather than for his many contributions to psychology or his brilliance as an essayist.[22]

Apart from the fact that the educational system in the church has been intellectually isolated, the leaders and educators in the church have not brought to this system an enriched educational attainment among themselves. Not one American Catholic bishop in the church is known to have had a father with a baccalaureate degree.[23] Further-

---

[18] Cross (1958), p. 146.
[19] Ong (1956), p. 407.
[20] *Ibid.*, p. 401.
[21] Bland (1959).
[22] McGlade (1953).
[23] Wright (1956).

more, what educational attainment does exist among the hierarchy is often inbred. Religious members receive their higher education in their own seminaries and novitiates, or—at best—in their own college, which is often on a special "campus" of the college, meaning their own seminary. And the quality of seminary education, in the past little discussed, is itself open to grave question.[24] These people, in turn, educate the new members in their religious communities. Higher degrees have also typically been obtained from Catholic universities; there is the annual summer surge to Catholic University of America or to Fordham or to St. Louis University. Increasingly those obtaining doctorates now receive them in private or public universities such as the University of Chicago or the University of California, but the numbers are minimal in any event. Although comprehensive statistics on the question are not readily available, according to Dunne, only a negligible proportion of teaching sisters hold doctorates.[25]

Teachers in the elementary and high schools very likely will not even possess bachelor's degrees or teaching credentials. In the comprehensive survey of Catholic schools recently completed at the University of Notre Dame, it was found that in 1962 approximately 50 per cent of the elementary school teachers and over 7 per cent of the high school teachers had not yet obtained their bachelor's degrees. A greater proportion of the religious teachers than the lay teachers had baccalaureate degrees, but still close to half the sisters were teaching without having completed college. And as recently as 1965, 55 per cent of the Catholic elementary school teachers and 60 per cent of the high school teachers were reported to have had either no college degree or no certificate for teaching.[26]

Two earlier surveys of teaching sisters' institutions revealed that only half or less of them maintained sister teacher-training programs.[27] Another survey of a majority of teacher-sister communities revealed that less than 6 per cent maintain a full bachelor's program.[28] Such training, when taken, is often taken part-time at neighboring Catholic colleges over a period of ten to twenty years, while the sisters are expending already overdrawn energies in teaching full-time in over-

[24] Donovan (1964); Drummond (1956); Halton (1961); Lee and Putz (1965); Poole (1965); *San Francisco Chronicle,* June 8, 1962, p. 2; Sloyan (1960); Weigel (1956a, b).
[25] Dunne (1960).
[26] *National Catholic Reporter,* February 23, 1966, p. 3; Neuwien (1966).
[27] Highbaugh (1961); Velardi (1959).
[28] McDonald, D. (1956).

crowded classrooms and in keeping up with their religious exercises.[29] Problems of this kind had become so acute that the Sister Formation Movement was inaugurated in 1953 to press for fuller education for all sisters in all respects, as well as to help develop a richer spiritual life among them.[30]

But it is evident that if the teaching sisters in Catholic schools are undereducated and untrained for teaching, so are the majority of lay teachers in parochial schools. Several surveys indicate that in addition to the fact that most lay elementary school and many high school teachers do not hold bachelor's degrees, they also receive substandard mean annual salaries compared to public school teachers, seldom work under written contracts, and are frequently treated as subordinates rather than colleagues.[31] These are conditions that are surely intolerable to any qualified teacher, no matter how dedicated.

Few Catholic college faculty members hold doctorates in comparison to their non-Catholic college colleagues, and many Catholic colleges make a practice of assigning full professorships to faculty members holding only master's degrees (to say nothing of the inbred source of these degrees), a practice seldom heard of in major public and private universities.[32] There are also problems of lay-religious relationships and of the frequently observed lack of educational and intellectual commitment by Catholic college lay and religious faculty members.[33]

The problem of a lack of educational resources has been intensified by the poor distribution of these resources. For example, some religious orders make it a practice to shift their members from community to community at regular intervals, making it more difficult to build up strong departments and for the religious faculty members to keep up with their fields of knowledge. And at least one major order, the Jesuits, generally has its members teach three or four years as part of their religious training without prior teacher training. Naturally enough, some of these members are not inclined toward teaching, and might have difficulties obtaining certification through a regular public teacher-training program. If these practices are convenient for the reli-

---

[29] Fleming (1963); McDonald, D. (1956, 1960); McDonald, G. E. (1959); Shuster (1962); Star (1963); Voight (1962).

[30] The Sister Formation Movement is discussed further in chapter 11.

[31] Fleming (1963); Glass (1961); McDonald, D. (1960); McDowell (1960); Nale (1961); Neuwien (1966); Ryan (1960); Star (1963); Trapani (1960); Voight (1962).

[32] Kennedy (1961); Mills (1964).

[33] Donovan (1964).

gious body, they often are not for the student who must therefore settle for inadequate teaching.

There has also been the highly criticized matter of policy and administration characteristically remaining entirely in the hands of the clergy. Obviously, the highly qualified lay faculty member will not move into an institutional setting where he cannot contribute to the purpose of the institution, where he cannot receive a fair and open hearing on disciplinary matters, where he is told what to teach without consultation—and where, moreover, he still is likely to be underpaid.[34] A number of Catholic universities have recently recognized this problem, so much so that McCluskey sees an actual partnership between religious and lay faculty taking place in several Jesuit universities (which, however, is adamantly denied by the possibly partisan voices of Coffey and Keating).[35] This partnership has yet to be fully realized on the college level, however, and apparently has much farther to go at the lower levels of education.

A third practice in distribution of educational resources has also fallen under much criticism. This is the continued wasteful proliferation of small, fragmented colleges.[36] These institutions may be destined to remain inadequately staffed and equipped because of the "professional jealousy" of the numerous different orders, which are just beginning to combine efforts in mutual enterprises and only to a minimal extent. The result is the duplication of innumerable small libraries and laboratories and the recruitment here and there of one outstanding faculty member in a single field, instead of having fewer, but outstanding, libraries housed on a campus where there exists a faculty of high-caliber scholars in every department. Further, many of these colleges are attempting to maintain graduate departments in the same inadequate manner.

But it is not just a matter of the lack of education of Catholic teachers or the poor distribution of educational resources. Before this lack stand the rules and spirit of many religious groups whose religious detachment has led, willingly or unwillingly, to an attitude of anti-intellectualism.[37] Many religious writers and leaders consider intellectual pursuit not bad in itself, perhaps, but a serious or frivolous distraction from religious pursuit. Such deemphasis of intellectual

---

[34] Ederer (1960).

[35] McCluskey (1958); Coffey (1963); Keating (1963).

[36] Ellis (1956a, 1960, 1962); Herberg (1960b); Litzinger (1961); *San Francisco Chronicle*, June 8, 1962, p. 2; Weigel (1957, 1963).

[37] Cf. Lawler (1959).

pursuits has kept sisters now teaching in colleges from attending national and regional academic and research conferences designed for professional educational growth. For the same reason, most sisters have been kept from corresponding activities, such as evening lectures, or from reading and research that would add to their intellectual life but take them away from spiritual contemplation, under the assumption that the two pursuits could not complement each other.

Another aspect of the spirit of religious members is the emphasis that has been put on obedience, discipline, and authority. This emphasis has discouraged individual research by the religious member who is faced with an unpermissive superior or has led the student to accept just as uncritically every word of this same religious member, who is his teacher. This peculiar brand of displaced authoritarianism has encouraged intellectual docility instead of free intellectual inquiry. Thus, there has existed a "Yes, Sister" (or "Yes, Father") mentality which caused one Catholic critic to ask, "Are Catholic students encouraged to think for themselves, or are they reprimanded for 'having the nerve' to disagree with Sister?"[38] Novak's observation offers a forceful answer:

The main tragedy of American Catholic education is that it is excruciatingly difficult to be perfectly honest with nuns, priests, or over-protected students. [No one] is so easy to scandalize as American Catholics; new ideas, new approaches, new criticisms make them distinctly, if not vocally, uncomfortable. Catholic students need clear means of showing vigorous disagreement—which will sometimes appear disrespectful, skeptical, frightening—to no matter whom.[39]

This kind of dissent, "based upon understanding," as Novak puts it, provides for an intellectual thrust into an awareness of reality. But as long as the student's questioning of his instructor is to be interpreted as disrespect for God-given authority or lack of discipline, then any attempt at intellectual inquiry will be frustrated. No less a person than Pope Pius XII has taken notice of the Catholic's tendency toward "mute servility." In criticizing this trait, he concluded:

The Church is a living body, and something would be lacking in her life if expression could not be given public opinion within her ranks. For such a lack, both pastors and faithful might be to blame.[40]

The prevalent confusion over the role of hierarchical authority as exercised by the teacher or administrator has not ended with the sup-

[38] Lee (1961), p. 10.
[39] Novak (1962), p. 108.
[40] McDonnell (1960), p. 14.

pression of free, honest intellectual inquiry. Stress of rigid discipline for the sake of character formation has increased the problem. Discipline is a subject that has been much discussed and that is much respected among Catholic educators, as witnessed by numerous descriptions and even studies of its various practices and functions in Catholic schools.[41] It has taken various forms—insisting that high school students observe absolute silence between classes, or refusing to allow Catholic college women to wear tennis shoes in class, or insisting that resident college students study at a certain hour and turn their lights out at a certain hour. Whatever the form, and there have been many, the purpose of this kind of discipline is very probably not being realized. In two studies so far conducted on the subject, Catholic students have been found to be the least responsible and least mature of students.[42]

We are not questioning the objective of character formation but the method used to encourage this formation, especially since it appears to lead to lack of independence and responsibility. Moreover, the apparent ill effect of this type of training appears to be compounded by yet another and perhaps more serious practice common among many Catholic educators. This is the application of a dogmatic approach to all fields of knowledge, resulting in the presentation of all material through a set of ready, predigested answers, precluding any alternative or any further question. O'Dea identifies this practice as "formalism."[43] On the same subject, Weigel made it clear that, for the most part, the American Catholic does not even know what scholarship is.[44]

Although emphasis is placed on reason, the student is discouraged from using his own reasoning ability. Any new situation is ignored, in Weigel's words, for "a scheme of questions carried over from the past. . . ." Questions are treated mechanically, all by a priori definition. There is no intellectual discovery, but instead, ". . . deep freeze technique gives the students the impression that there really are no new questions." Ideas are often reduced to "timeless verbalism" and then "pigeon-holed" to be forevermore ignored. The student need only recognize that a man is a materialist, which allows him immediately to categorize him and correspondingly judge that ". . . he is no good

---

[41] Gallagher (1957); Gremma (1959); Holland, H. (1959); Justin (1957); Kastner (1958); Kelley, D. (1959); Long (1956); Phillips (1956); Tyrrell (1957).

[42] Brown, F. (1959); Farwell and Warren (1959).

[43] O'Dea (1958).

[44] The entire article by Weigel (1957) is highly recommended.

and his doctrine is absurd. There is no scholarly task to be done now. It was done long ago." It is thus that:

This kind of training leads away from scholarship. The postulate of all scholarly investigation is the nagging existence of mystery. The training of not a few Catholics makes them believe there is no mystery. It is all objectively clear and the category schemes of the past make it manifest. If that is so, there is nothing more to be done. It has been done already and why waste time doing it over again? Better to dedicate one's life to something more rewarding.[45]

In Weigel's words, again, intellectual scholarship ". . . is a matter of creative love. To love you must be acquainted. To look for new acquaintances, there must be dissatisfaction with what is at hand." Similarly, Novak speaks of a need for dissent. Its lack brings about the intellectual laziness of the Catholic, who need make no new acquaintances, who need not pursue the life of intellectual inquiry, since he already has the answers.

Perhaps this situation, more than anything else, explains why the psychologist finds the Catholic dogmatic, uncreative, stereotyped in thinking, and authoritarian. And if the Catholic is taught that there is a certain limited scheme of ready-made answers for everything, then the diversity, ambiguity, and "mystery" of the intellectual world may very well threaten him. If one's hold on reality is based on the possession of all-inclusive absolutes, then all security is lost in the face of the changing, the new, the vague, the inconclusive, and the unknown. Intellectual inquiry deliberately seeks out the unknown and unsettled, leaving the dogmatic person fearful of his hold on reality and anxious about his security. The consequence may be a quick retreat into a yet deeper dogmatic system and, thus, a further manifestation of authoritarianism and anti-intellectualism.

There should be little wonder about the existence of this phenomenon, however. As Lawler commented:

. . . considering the historical circumstance of the development of American Catholic schools, the poverty of the peasant background of many Catholic immigrants, the existence frequently of language barriers, the demand for clerical training, and the isolation of Catholics, as a result of all these factors, from the intellectual life of the nation—considering these circumstances, it is cause neither for surprise nor for recrimination that it is only in the past three decades that concerted attention should be directed toward the less utilitarian bases of Catholic education.[46]

Indeed, one may wonder that Catholic education has progressed as much as it has under the circumstances. But extenuating circumstances

[45] Weigel (1957), p. 305.
[46] Lawler (1959), p. 36.

of the past are best left there, and the current attention given the intellectual life of the changing church is surely justified, particularly in view of the factors summarized above and the history of the Catholic in America. These historical details may be recapitulated as:

1. an immigrant Catholic population whose tradition has been to place little value on education;
2. a population which has shown overdependency on an autocratic, predominantly Irish clergy;
3. the quick and fixed establishment of an intellectually isolated, ghetto-minded population and ministry;
4. the perpetuation of this isolation through a poorly educated, defensive ministry which has characteristically operated inadequate schools under a religious spirit often incompatible with intellectual endeavor.

Such are the salient aspects of the background of the American Catholic's intellectual life which may serve as a framework for deeper investigation into the intellectual life of the Catholic. Catholics have moved up the economic ladder and have moved out to the suburbs, but they have all too often taken with them minds conditioned to a strictly Catholic world, made up of Catholic schools, friends, publications, activities, and beliefs. The suburban Catholic school built before the church itself is built may be not a testimonial to faith, but a testimonial to a lack of open and critical thinking. It may represent an automatic, protective response to historical conditions that no longer exist and not a thoughtful and considered action based on finding the best way to educate children in a pluralistic society in a turbulent time.

In such a society and at such a time there is a need to develop intellectual potential to the fullest, beyond a single religious denomination or subculture. The questioning and critical appraisal going on in the Catholic church now, and the signs of change already occurring in the church, bring hopes that such intellectual development will be encouraged in the future. It has not been encouraged in the past, however, and some evidences of the result will be discussed in chapter 2. Succeeding chapters will deal with a consideration of the contemporary Catholic college students who should make such intellectual contributions in the future.

CHAPTER TWO

The Background and Sources of the Study

The inevitable lack of intellectual productivity resulting from the history, traditions, and tenets of the American Catholic church was empirically documented as early as 1933 in Fry's study of the religious affiliation of American leaders.[1] This documentation was to be repeated in the next three decades by such researchers as Davis, Kenniston, Rogoff, and especially Knapp and his associates.[2] To be sure, some Catholics were aware of the problem; but although Catholics have criticized their own educational process throughout the history of the Catholic church in America, the criticism has characteristically been levied by a few laymen and ignored or denied by the church's hierarchy.[3] The church has fostered, instead, the myth that a good general education was to be had only in Catholic schools.

This condition existed until Ellis, one of the church's leading historians, took candid stock of the evidence in 1955 and emphatically indicted his church for its meager contribution to American intellectual life.[4] Pleasants and Bauer, among others, made a similar accusation ten years before Ellis, but without equal effect.[5] Ellis wrote as a member of the clergy, as a sincere scholar, and as a man capable of forceful rhetoric. Perhaps he also addressed his criticism of the church at a ripe moment in history when the church was able to put aside its other problems long enough to listen to him. Interest was also unquestionably increased and sustained by the whole spirit of reform amplified a few years later by Vatican II. In any event, whereas earlier criticism of Catholic intellectual life had been largely ignored, the

[1] Fry (1933).

[2] Davis, B. (1953); Kenniston (1957); Knapp and Goodrich (1952); Knapp and Greenbaum (1953); Rogoff (1957). See also Kunkel and Prentice (1951) and Traxler (1957).

[3] Christ and Sherry (1961).

[4] Ellis (1955).

[5] Pleasants and Bauer (1946).

23

impact of Ellis' criticism was immediate and great; he started waves
of self-criticism that have yet to ebb.

Much of the discussion of Catholic intellectualism since 1955 has
been divorced from fact, but an impressive amount of research has
also accumulated that currently, in a variety of ways, verifies Ellis'
concern. This research makes evident two prevalent conditions among
American Catholics: (1) there is a disproportionate lack of scholarly
endeavor in Catholic schools and colleges; and (2) there is a disproportionate lack of scholarly attitudes among Catholic college students
and faculty members.

In this chapter we will briefly review some of the major findings
bearing upon the issue of Catholic intellectual disposition and productivity and will indicate how we anticipate going beyond them. It
is not enough simply to survey the intellectual scene and count the
number of Catholic heads that are found there. It is necessary to delve
more deeply into the problem, to study the psychodynamics of the
Catholic mentality through the use of more precise research instruments, more comprehensive methods of analysis, and more broadly
based samples than have been used previously. Our objective is to
ascertain how Catholics in church colleges and in secular colleges
compare intellectually with other students. To accomplish this objective we intend to explore some of the reasons for the disparities that
exist. We will go beyond discussion of the historical and social factors
that may have influenced the intellectual life of American Catholics
and concentrate on such psychological factors as attitudes, values, and
disposition. We will also consider some of the changes that may lie
ahead in the church, in its colleges, and in its intellectual life.

There is abundant evidence that Catholics, and specifically Catholic college graduates, have been underrepresented in the scholarly
community. This holds regardless of whether the criteria are the educational quality of a college, the number of doctoral degrees granted,
scholarly and creative contributions in the arts and sciences, or the expression of certain attitudes believed to be associated with scholarship.

Looking first at the amount of scholarly endeavor undertaken by
Catholics, we can see that Catholics begin at a disadvantage, since
scholarly output depends in great part upon the potential scholars
who enter college, and American Catholics have, historically, been
less likely than Protestants to attend college. Although the situation
has recently improved somewhat, statistics that we will present in
chapter 3 indicate that Catholics are still not sending their share of
potential scholars to college.

But what about the intellectual productivity of the Catholics who do attend college? There are several ways to measure scholarly endeavor. One is to ascertain the number of doctoral degrees graduates of various colleges obtain. One can also compare the institutions where graduates listed in such annals as *Who's Who in America* or *American Men of Science* received their bachelor's degrees. A third measure is the pooled assessment of leading educators. Some studies are simply tabulations of the number of doctorates earned by graduates of each college and lose validity inasmuch as they do not take into account the size of the colleges' student bodies. Most studies follow some form of the Productivity Index first established by Knapp and Goodrich, however, which measures scholarly attainment, or the attainment of the doctorate, by the number of potential scholars from any given institution.[6]

But no matter what the measure or index of the intellectual productivity of their graduates, Catholic institutions invariably appear inferior to other liberal arts colleges and universities. In 1953, Catholic colleges without exception placed in the bottom 10 per cent on the production of scientists, and there is little difference in the arts and humanities.[7] Furthermore, more recent research shows that the situation has not changed, even when considering the ability and differing numbers of the students enrolled in the nation's colleges.[8]

Catholics who do obtain higher degrees and who, therefore, could be expected to make intellectual contributions to scholarship, appear to be in the same intellectual position. In 1946, Pleasants and Bauer, publishing in the Jesuits' *America* noted that there was not only a great lack of Catholics on college and university faculties, but that disproportionately few published scholarly contributions compared to their non-Catholic faculty colleagues.[9] As for faculty members on Catholic campuses, only 18 per cent had ever published. Although it is likely that only a minority of all persons who hold doctoral degrees publish, Pleasants and Bauer concluded that there was only one-fourth as much productive scholarship among Catholics as might be expected in comparison with non-Catholics. Carrying similar analyses up to 1960, Berelson, Donovan, and Lazarsfeld and Thielens found no change in this tendency, even when reviewing graduates of the better

[6] Knapp and Goodrich (1952).

[7] *Ibid.*; Knapp and Greenbaum (1953).

[8] Astin (1962); Heist and Yonge (1962); Holland, J. L. (1957); Rogoff (1957); Thistlethwaite (1959*a, b*).

[9] Pleasants and Bauer (1946).

Catholic universities who attained doctoral degrees.[10]

Catholic graduate students, too, appear to fall below the level of their fellows. Heiss found, in a study to be discussed in detail later, that proportionately very few Catholics were among the doctoral candidates at the University of California, one of the largest doctoral degree-granting institutions in the country.[11] When comparing graduate school plans of students at Fordham, Columbia, and Cornell universities, McNamara found that Catholics were less likely to be seeking doctoral degrees.[12]

Several arguments have been raised in defense of Catholic intellectual productivity, taking a positive view of certain observable signs of increased productivity. Sheehan found that half of the women's colleges above the median in the proportionate attainment by alumnae of their doctorates between 1936 and 1950 were Catholic colleges.[13] On this basis, she concluded that although the primary purpose of Catholic colleges is not the production of doctorates, they are contributing their fair share to this "organized pursuit of knowledge."

Sheehan, however, apparently failed to take into account the fact that considerably more than half the Catholic colleges on her list would have to be above the median in production of "scholars" if their alumnae were to be adequately represented among the relatively few women obtaining doctoral degrees. This is the case, since two-thirds of the type of women's colleges surveyed were Catholic colleges. Furthermore, Newcomer conducted a study of the scholarly productivity of women's colleges through 1957, using a variety of sources and of criteria of scholarship, and found that Catholic women's colleges possessed the lowest scholarly productivity ratios of all private women's colleges.[14]

Evidence has also been presented recently that suggests extenuating circumstances for or even changes in the Catholic intellectual condition. One argument is that Catholic schools could produce "at the rate of the best of them" if only they had more money. There is evidence, although not at all clear-cut, that the monetary assets of a school are to some extent associated with its quality.[15] But some of the most

[10] Berelson (1960); Donovan (1964); Lazarsfeld and Thielens (1958).

[11] Heiss (1964).

[12] McNamara (1963). This was not true of graduating students at the University of Notre Dame. However, the Notre Dame sample was a small voluntary one rather than a scientifically drawn representative one. Therefore it is difficult to generalize about it.

[13] Sheehan (1957).

[14] Newcomer (1959).

[15] Astin and Holland (1962).

highly productive colleges in the country are small liberal arts colleges, without lavish laboratories or even graduate schools. These are the very colleges that are rated the highest by Knapp and Greenbaum.[16] Moreover, in the words of an *America* editorial, ". . . a Catholic institution, when it possesses a very high proportion of unpaid clergy on its faculty, enjoys an immense hidden endowment."[17] And yet, it must be said, in fairness, that this hidden endowment is decreasing, since there is an increasing dependence upon lay teachers in all Catholic schools, including Catholic colleges and universities. Also, when all the costs of training and maintaining the clergy are considered, these faculty members represent a considerable expense to the church, if not directly to the college.

More recently, Greeley has argued that Catholic college students are the intellectual equals of their non-Catholic peers.[18] He bases his generalization upon data obtained by the National Opinion Research Center from college seniors in 1961. Greeley concluded that Catholics are represented in college in proportion to their representation in the national population, that Catholic college seniors as often as non-Catholics plan to enter graduate school, and that Catholic students as often as non-Catholics identify themselves as intellectuals. Greeley's findings are of interest, but they are not corroborated by a variety of other research to be discussed in this book. Problems of sampling, methodology, and interpretation frequently affect research of this kind, and therefore the various findings should be evaluated with these problems in mind.

We have been concerned thus far with intellectual productivity. But the problem is not one just of poor schools or poor teachers. It goes much deeper than that. The lack of scholarly endeavor that has been revealed has been matched by, and in large part undoubtedly stems from, lack of scholarly or intellectual attitudes among Catholic college students and faculty members. A body of psychological research that has accumulated particularly in the last ten years has probed into the attitudinal set of the Catholic mentality. A consistent picture of anti-intellectualism or lack of intellectual disposition among Catholics has resulted, characterized by authoritarianism, dogmatism, and dislike for ideas and critical thinking. This evidence has been virtually ignored by almost all Catholic publications, however. Therefore, it is

[16] Knapp and Greenbaum (1953).

[17] *America* (1958), 98:590. In a more recent article Seidl (1965) discussed the expenses involved in maintaining lay and religious teachers in Catholic schools.

[18] Greeley (1962*a, b*, 1963).

important to note the personality patterns delineated by this research and to understand the implications of the pronounced authoritarianism and lack of critical, creative thinking found among Catholics as a group.

Since the authoritarian personality is characterized by a rigid and intolerant approach to life, and since intellectualism, as the term is used in this book, implies an openness to the ideas of others and a tolerance for other points of view, one would expect to find little appreciation for intellectualism among those who display a high degree of authoritarianism. Of course, a low degree of authoritarianism does not in itself indicate intellectualism, since a person may be extremely tolerant and yet have no interest in the life of the mind. In addition, since there are degrees of authoritarianism as well as degrees of intellectualism, the same person may display a certain amount of authoritarianism coupled with some interest in scholarly and creative activity.

There are also individuals who are extremely open, flexible, and creative in certain areas of life but have rigid and uncompromising attitudes in other areas. It is possible for an artist or a scientist to be intensely flexible in his work but rigid in his political views, or for a statesman to be creative in attempts to resolve a labor dispute but be completely lacking in appreciation for art. Thus it is possible to conceive of intellectuals who are also authoritarian in certain respects. But despite these qualifications and reservations our assertion holds that one would expect to find little intellectualism where there is much authoritarianism. Since research has indicated that Catholics are the most authoritarian of all religious groups, one would thus expect to find that Catholics display a disproportionate lack of interest in the intellectual life.

The characteristics of the authoritarian, as identified by Adorno and others in 1950, would seem in fact to be highly related to the characteristics associated with anti-intellectualism.[19] The authoritarian is described as intolerant, opinionated, stereotyped in thinking, unquestioningly submissive to authority, compulsively conventional, conservative, suspicious of members of the out-group, and particularly ethnocentric. The authoritarian has also been found to be anti-democratic, punitive, condescending toward perceived inferiors, power-minded, fixated on the immoral behavior of others—and yet, usually

[19] Adorno *et al.* (1950).

religious.[20] This combination of rigidity and religiosity clearly indicates that, as Sanford has pointed out, joining or identifying with a religious body in America does not mean that the person has assumed all the traditional Christian values, if one considers tolerance, brotherhood, and equality to represent such values.[21]

Subsequent research in the 1950's, examining unselected populations as well as college students, reinforces these conclusions. The results of this research indicate that: (1) there is a definite and positive relationship between religious orthodoxy and authoritarianism; (2) Catholics are consistently the most authoritarian when compared with other groups; (3) fundamentalist Protestant sects, such as Pentecostals, Baptists, Mormons, and Lutherans, are nearly as authoritarian as Catholics and are radically different from other Protestants in this respect; (4) these relationships hold, even with socioeconomic background held constant.[22]

Since the more fundamentalist Protestant sects in this country have been found to display the same characteristics as Catholics—that is, to be highly authoritarian and to have a low degree of intellectual productivity—there is an indication that conservative religiousness, authoritarianism, and lack of intellectuality are interrelated. The factors accounting for this relationship thus may operate across and issue from similar religious and social conditions. A comparatively low socioeconomic status, lack of emphasis upon education, and the

[20] Although authoritarianism has not been disputed as a psychological entity, the early work on the trait did not pass without criticism, primarily on the basis of measurement technique, confinement to a psychoanalytic, political, or ethnocentric framework, and disregard for intervening and interacting variables clouding the "pure" notion of authoritarianism. (See Hyman [1955] as an example of the criticism levied against Adorno.) Much subsequent research has controlled for interacting variables; the trait's theoretical basis has long since been expanded beyond psychoanalysis by Stewart and Hoult (1959), among others, and Rokeach (1960) has devised an instrument which takes into account authoritarianism on the "left" as well as on the "right." A variety of other research and theory has probed the authoritarian personality as just described, for example: Allen (1955); Davids (1955); Freedman, Webster, and Sanford (1955); Goldberg and Stern (1952); Gregory (1952, 1955a, b); Honingmann (1954); Jackson, et al. (1957); Leavitt, Hax, and Roche (1955); Plant (1958, 1959, 1962); Rokeach (1960); Stotsky (1955); Struening (1957, 1958); Wallach and Kogan (1959); Wayman (1955); Webster (1958).

[21] Adorno et al. (1950), p. 219.

[22] Broen (1955); Dreger (1952); Foster, Stanek, and Krassowski (1961); Gregory (1952, 1955a, b); Khanna (1957); Lehmann (1960); Levinson and Schermerhorn (1951); Plant (1958, 1959, 1962); Ranck (1955); Rokeach (1960); Struening (1957, 1958).

authoritarian attitudes often unconsciously fostered by these churches may together contribute to an authoritarian attitude and a lack of interest in intellectual concerns among the church's membership. Although this book concentrates on the Catholic culture, we suggest that the findings presented have much bearing on Protestant fundamentalism as well.

An examination of particular attitudinal traits associated with authoritarianism shows results similar to those summarized above. Lehmann and Dressel and Dressel surveyed students at Michigan State University between 1958 and 1962 and found that Catholics as a group, particularly those who graduated from Catholic high schools, were more stereotypic, uncritical, and dogmatic in their thinking and attitudes than all other students.[23] Baptists were very similar.

When Rokeach surveyed contemporary students in eastern and midwestern public universities, he found that Catholic students as groups were the most opinionated of all students, although in one instance they were no more dogmatic in their thinking than other students.[24] In none of this research, however, are other factors, such as ethnicity or social class, examined for their possible influence on the data. There has, similarly, been no examination of the attitudes of Catholics in Catholic colleges as opposed to those of Catholics in secular schools. It is important to find out whether the personality characteristics of these students vary; that is, to see whether students who are less exposed to the total system of church and school are different intellectually from those who have been more encompassed by it.

Within the limits of Rokeach's and Lehmann and Dressel's research, however, even Catholics who attended secular colleges were found to differ from non-Catholics in aspects of intellectual disposition. The scales used in this research measure a general tendency toward rigidity and close-minded thinking; they are not devoted specifically to religious attitude and so cannot be considered simply a measure of religious orientation or to be biased against students who are more religiously oriented than others. The differences also do not appear to be attributable to differences in ability.

Stark's analyses of a sample of graduate students that was considered representative by the National Opinion Research Center indicated that Catholic graduate students, compared with others, were disproportionately lacking in exposure to scientific scholarship.[25] In their

[23] Dressel (1959); Lehmann and Dressel (1962, 1963).
[24] Rokeach (1960).
[25] Stark (1963).

assessment of certain personality patterns of the 1956 National Merit Scholarship winners and runners-up, Farwell and Warren found that when high-ability students enrolled in Catholic colleges were compared to students of equal ability enrolled in all other colleges, those in Catholic colleges were the most superficial in their perceptions, the least interested in abstract thought and the interplay of ideas apart from their practical consequences, and the most authoritarian of all groups of students.[26]

A self-study of a West Coast Jesuit university in the 1960's also bore out this pattern.[27] The Catholic university students were found to be decidedly more authoritarian, more dogmatic, more ethnocentric, and less prone to critical thinking than students at Michigan State University and at a neighboring state college. Thus, compared with students at a major state university and with those at a state college in their own geographic region, these students had a much less open and critical approach to life. The Catholic students also showed the least change in personality toward nonathoritarianism after two years of college. Therefore, these Catholic students, too, clearly could not be considered as a group to be as open and flexible in their thinking as their fellow students at secular schools.

Studies have not been limited to the characteristics of students in a particular group or institution. They have also examined the comparative environmental characteristics, impact, or press across a large number of institutions. Riesman and Jencks, in their institutional case studies, have found an emphasis upon utilitarian rather than intellectual interests in Catholic colleges.[28] Astin and Holland assessed over 300 colleges, using the Environmental Assessment Technique, and found Catholic colleges, and particularly large Catholic universities, to be the most "conventional" of all colleges, a trait negatively related to intellectualism, objectivity, and understanding, as measured by correlations with the College Characteristics Index.[29]

The implications of such conventionality are suggested in a study by Thistlethwaite, which found that flexibility of curriculum and the energy and controversiality of instruction were positively related to how much students studied and to the extent of their intellectual endeavors.[30] However, closeness of supervision, lack of controversiality,

---

[26] Farwell and Warren (1959).
[27] Foster, Stanek, and Krassowski (1961).
[28] Riesman and Jencks (1962).
[29] Astin and Holland (1962).
[30] Thistlethwaite (1959*b*).

and the directiveness of teaching methods, greatly espoused by Catholic colleges, were negatively related to amount of study and intellectual endeavor.

A number of other studies have assessed the intellectual orientation of college faculties. In 1958 Lazarsfeld and Thielens completed a major survey of an extensive sample of college faculties throughout the country.[31] An important secondary analysis of these data was conducted by Neel.[32] In analyzing the attitudes and opinions of Catholic and non-Catholic social-science faculty members, Neel found that the Catholic faculty group was almost exclusively "fact-oriented," preferring "to give students a basic grounding of facts in the subject." In contrast, the non-Catholic faculty group was more "problem-oriented," preferring to "get the students thinking about the problem areas in the subject." Correlative to their fact orientation, the Catholic faculty members tended much more to avoid controversial issues, to show a lack of interest in civil liberties, and to show the least interest in the creative preparation of their courses.

This same tendency has been shown by Donovan in his survey of a national random sample of Catholic college faculty members.[33] Donovan also found that many of the Catholic college faculty entered their profession without any particular motivation or intellectual commitment. They regarded their jobs primarily as a comfortable niche that would provide them a lifetime of security, and they were not, as a rule, dedicated or creative thinkers, teachers, or researchers.

The lack of a generally creative and intellectual atmosphere in Catholic colleges, and some indication of the tensions that result from such a lack, have been uniquely dramatized in a heated exchange that took place among several faculty members in the alumni magazine of a Jesuit university. One faculty member wrote: "Students are too used to being told what to do, thus will not do it on their own. We (as teachers) must make sure they are told—with assignments that force them to do it. It will help them to develop a new habit they did not have."[34] The chairman of the theology department countered with a plea for independent thinking and controversy, considering them essential to learning and the intellectual development of students, and concluded that his university ". . . had better decide beforehand if it wishes its dominant pattern of action to be reaction—with the fore-

---

[31] Lazarsfeld and Thielens (1958).
[32] Neel (1962).
[33] Donovan (1964).
[34] *Santa Claran* (1961), 10(1): 8.

gone conclusion that despite its label as an institution of higher learn-ing it will reflect external opinion vastly more than it will form it."[35]

This argument was attacked by a fellow faculty member and Jesuit who stated that controversy is not to be tolerated on campus, especially in theological issues, where truth is so fully possessed that no more argument is needed.[36] He added, "Students are taught to think, to judge, to reason, to arrive at their own conclusions, to embrace their own convictions by the gentle if sometimes subtle leadership and inspi-ration of their teachers." Having made this broad assumption, he concluded categorically that the student's "most important virtue [is] docility." The student is to listen respectfully and alertly to the teacher, but is never to question him, for the teacher ". . . has far more train-ing and wisdom in the area in which he is a teacher than the student. . . ."

Here is an unabashed call for a directed spirit of docility instead of intellectual controversy, illustrating the nonintellectual and even anti-intellectual attitude too often found on Catholic college cam-puses. If students show authoritarianism, dependency, conformity, and lack of interest in other groups and ideas, as research has indicated, they have shared these traits with many of their faculty. But a sign of change is also apparent: it is noteworthy that a senior member of the faculty urged intellectual controversy as a stimulus of enriched education. Perhaps it is even more remarkable that this faculty mem-ber was chairman of the theology department, which might be expected to be the most conservative and defensive.

There is a sequel to the story, however. The articles created so much interest among the alumni that they wrote an unusually large number of letters to the editor expressing their reactions. Almost without exception, they favored docility rather than controversy, and this was just as true of the more recent graduates as it was of the older alumni.

In spite of all evidence substantiating a lack of Catholic intellectual productivity in America and a lack of intellectual stimulation in Catholic colleges, this has been frequently and vigorously disputed. One of the clearest examples of this kind of apologetics may be found in the heated National Catholic Educational Association Meeting of 1961, where the president of the University of Notre Dame rose to speak of the "abysmal mediocrity" of Catholic education. In reply, the superintendent of Chicago's Catholic schools rose to lament this sort

[35] Mackin (1961), p. 7.
[36] Sweeters (1962), p. 9.

of "public breast-beating" and added that in his view it was "time to call a moratorium on all this exaggerated self-criticism." The principal of California's School of Greenbrae hastened to add that "people line up ten deep" to get into California's Catholic schools, many of them non-Catholics who care only that their children "get in for the general education."[37]

Since 1961 there have been indications that although the grounds for concern may have changed somewhat, the attitudes of many Catholic educators have not. Reports from the 1966 National Catholic Educational Association Meeting indicate that participants felt that Catholic education was being criticized "rashly and unfairly by the press." Much of the concern expressed centered on the issue of academic freedom in Catholic colleges. Bishop James P. Shannon, president of the College of St. Thomas in St. Paul, Minnesota, commented: "Educators in Catholic colleges are running scared, quite unnecessarily."[38]

In contrast to Bishop Shannon, at the same conference Dr. Manning Patillo, associate director of the Danforth Foundation, called the need for guidelines to maintain academic freedom "the most urgent problem facing Catholic education today," and said he was "greatly disturbed by glib denials of the existence of this difficulty in many quarters." Patillo's comments about academic freedom evidently generated little concern, as did his comments about the intellectual quality of Catholic education. He contended that "many of the Catholic men's and coeducational colleges have a strong pragmatic tone about them—an emphasis on specialized and occupational training which belies their professional dedication to liberal education." Other participants, with the major exception of John Cogley, were evidently primarily concerned with contradicting or softening Patillo's remarks, with little awareness that even, or perhaps especially, in this age of reform such remarks might be justified and worthy of the most serious consideration by all Catholic educators.

The research that has been carried out gives a fairly comprehensive picture of the lack of Catholic intellectual development up to recent times, but it is not without its shortcomings. Much of it was conducted with limited samples and inadequate controls for such "contaminating" variables as intelligence and social class, and it was frequently based on relatively crude research instruments. But the many extensive findings reported have been too recent, and have resulted in too much consensus for them to be ignored, as they have been in most of the

[37] *Newsweek* (1961); *San Francisco Chronicle* (1961); *Time* (1961).
[38] *National Catholic Reporter,* April 20, 1966, p. 5.

publications on the subject of Catholic intellectualism. And even without the intensive research to be reported in the next chapters, the above findings compel us to dismiss the contention that this problem ceased to exist twenty or thirty years ago.[39]

Nor, as will be seen, can the problem be said to stem from a lack of mental potential among Catholic college students, since Catholic colleges are recruiting students academically above average compared to public and Protestant colleges. This suggests that factors other than ability must account for the fact that so few Catholic college graduates have made scholarly and creative contributions compared with graduates of other colleges.

Care must be taken not to assume that the lack of scholarly attitude and endeavor is the result solely of Catholic college education. Presumably the student forms most of his basic values and attitudes before entering college. Thus, even an optimum college environment should not be expected to change the values of its students greatly, as has been argued by Jacob and others.[40] Some value change can be anticipated, however; we found indications in data published elsewhere that college students increased significantly more in intellectual disposition and autonomous thinking than their contemporaries who did not attend college.[41]

There are conflicting conclusions about the intellectual values of students, in general, and about the values of Catholic college students, in particular. Therefore, it is important to examine the methodology used in the research leading to these conclusions. Discussions of the education, personal values, and intellectual outlook of Catholics is likely to evoke strong emotional reactions among some persons. Such discussion is liable to be regarded as an attack on cherished beliefs by others. For still others, it may suggest serious repercussions or represent the impetus for action. For this reason, especially, we must make generalizations and inferences only within the limits allowed by the methodology of the research that is to be interpreted.

Social-science research reports are not a set of unequivocal answers to a list of simple questions. The answers themselves often do not solve the original problems of the research. Often the data are not exact or inclusive enough to provide the answers desired or claimed

[39] Greeley, for example (1962*a, b;* 1963, p. 19) has argued that the research that indicates a lack of intellectual scholarship among Catholics pertains only to conditions as they existed two or three decades ago.

[40] Jacob (1957, 1958).

[41] Trent and Medsker (1967).

from them. Sometimes the answers are not sufficiently understood or presented; the data may be misused and thus distort the findings obtained.

Some misuses of data occur when they are not evaluated and reported precisely. For example, sample limitations are common: the persons tested or surveyed may not be sufficiently diverse or representative to justify broad, sweeping generalizations about the population they are supposed to represent. It must be determined that students in particular colleges are representative of a larger group, or conclusions must be restricted to those institutions.

Another research abuse is to report a finding out of context or in the wrong frame of reference. For example, it may be momentarily dazzling to report, as has been done, that parochial school children achieve at a higher level than other children, as determined by national norms (the achievement level on a particular test reported for the students in the country as a whole).[42] Catholic schools (and colleges) select students on the basis of ability; also, there are relatively few Catholics who are not Caucasian and few who live in the South, where the educational achievement level is considerably lower than in the rest of the country. Therefore, the only meaningful comparison of Catholic and public school achievement levels would have to control for race, region, and ability at the least. That is, public and Catholic school children of the same level of ability, who live in the same area, and who are all Caucasian would have to be compared before one could begin to comment on the meaning of the differences in level of measured achievement between the two groups.

Yet another example of imprecision yielding misleading results occurs when the investigator neglects to acknowledge the limitations, or even the characteristics, of his research instrument or techniques. This is crucial because there are many different ways of asking a basically similar question, or, at least, what one assumes to be a similar question. For example, two investigators may be interested in assessing the intellectual potential and performance of Catholic college students as compared with their non-Catholic peers. One may approach this problem in survey fashion, inquiring through a questionnaire the extent to which Catholic college students go to graduate school, how well they do in their courses, how much they say they like the

---

[42] It is commendable in this respect that the Neuwien (1966) report, *Catholic Schools in Action,* carefully specifies that the superior academic ability of contemporary students in Catholic schools compared with students nationally may be attributable to the selectivity of these schools.

school, and how much they claim that they themselves are "intellectual," whatever this term may mean to them. Such data must be evaluated entirely differently from most of those in this book. Here an attempt is made to account for the underlying personality dynamics of intellectuality, based upon the consistency of numerous responses to functional scales.

Superficial demographic and questionnaire data are often treated as if they dealt with underlying personality factors and are even labeled as such. This can be a grave error. A phenomenon may appear one way on the surface, when the subject involved is giving a direct or socially acceptable "answer"; yet it may appear entirely opposite when it is examined through more subtle instruments that attempt assessment with more depth, such as the more sensitive projective devices or the more reliable inventory techniques providing validated "scales" in fact, and not just in name. Thus, it is possible that Catholic students may say they are "intellectual" and that they fully intend to pursue graduate work. Yet on an instrument which taps psychodynamics, it can be found that these same students possess a mentality that stresses authoritarian ways of thinking and a general restrictiveness antithetical to what is considered to be "intellectuality" or intellectual disposition. In fact, as will be seen in chapter 9, we have found that Catholic college students at a low level of measured intellectual disposition as a group reported themselves on a questionnaire item to have developed intellectually in as great a proportion as their classmates who actually had a high level of intellectualism.

How do such contradictory findings exist in a group, and what do they signify? In the light of their personality structure, as much as psychological instruments can measure this, the students' questionnaire responses must be critically examined. Although Catholic students are identified on psychological scales as more authoritarian, uninventive, restricted, cautious, and docile than other students, they of course are not likely to describe themselves in a way that can be construed so negatively. A number of other reasons may also account for inaccuracies in the self-descriptions of the students. These include the tendency to respond according to what is deemed as socially acceptable; or from unrealistic self-concepts or notions about themselves; or simply, from a lack of awareness of what intellectualism, for example, really means.

Selection of criteria and their proper interpretation also enter here. To illustrate, like other investigators we found that a majority of Catholic college men plan at some time to attend graduate or professional school. But this does not automatically mean that there will be a commensurate number of Catholic scholars now or even five or ten years from now. There is a large gap between planning on or entering graduate school and obtaining the more scholarly oriented doctoral degree—not to mention the questions that may be asked about the intellectual worth of the degree itself. There are also many reasons for entering graduate school that have little or nothing to do with intellectual interest. One may conceivably enter graduate school to increase his earning power, or to keep up with his peers, or to fulfill expectations of parents, or to gain prestige, or for any one of a number of reasons that do not necessarily denote a desire for searching out, questioning, and discovering.

Another reason for more knowledge about the research instruments used is that often their items are described as "scales," when in reality these scales may consist of responses to only one or two questions. But to call something a scale implies that it has reliability, validity, and a good bit of solidity—the lack of which would lead the discerning reader to question the scale. If the investigator makes it very clear that what he is for convenience, perhaps, calling a scale is really a very loose assortment of questions, then that opens the door to questioning about the very nature of this scale. This questioning may lead to greater accuracy and less confusion.

A further imprecision in reporting data is the incorrect manipulation of findings once they are obtained. An author can state that 40 per cent of Catholic college students report an interest in reading books, compared with 50 per cent of Protestant students. But all too often, such differences are presented as if they were meaningful differences when they are not. Some differences could be explained as occurring by sampling error, by chance, by a number of extraneous factors other than the one the investigator is interested in—the literary bent of the students. This is where tests of significance, correctly used, are important. Not all differences between groups of students are great enough to base any conclusions on, and therefore it is necessary to find out which ones are.

For this reason, comparative differences in scores or responses between the groups of students under consideration in subsequent chapters will be tested for statistical signficance through the use of chi square, multivariate analysis, and other techniques. When we report a difference to be significant at least at the 5 per cent level of probability ($p \leq .05$), this means that only five times out of a hundred could this difference have occurred by chance; if we report a difference to be at the one per cent level or better ($p \leq .01$), we mean that no more than one time out of a hundred could it have been expected to occur by chance.

Regardless of statistical technique, however, no finding can be more significant than the source of information upon which it is based. The primary way of understanding just what an instrument measures, and how well, is by looking at the reliability and validity information available to see to what extent it measures the traits or behavior with which it claims to deal, and with what consistency and effectiveness.

One of the major instruments used in the research to be described, the Omnibus Personality Inventory (OPI), is an important contribution to this kind of understanding. Developed by the Center for Research and Development in Higher Education at the University of California, the Omnibus Personality Inventory is an attitudinal inventory with scales that measure intellectual, emotional, and dispositional personality traits. The inventory includes twelve scales, comprising nearly 400 items that are to be marked true or false as they apply to the respondent and that have been carefully selected for their reliability and functional value. In format the Omnibus Personality Inventory resembles the Minnesota Multiphasic Personality Inventory and the California Psychological Inventory. Most of the scale reliabilities, both internal consistency and test-retest, are in the high seventies and eighties, indicating a very acceptable degree of reliability. The scales have been validated against such factors as known criterion groups, faculty ratings, correlations with scales in other reputable instruments, and observed performance such as prize-winning endeavors or intellectual performance.

The Omnibus Personality Inventory is especially valuable for the present study since, to our knowledge, it is one of the few personality inventories that has been designed particularly to assess a variety of attitudinal traits constituting intellectual disposition and that has been found to reflect observed intellectual behavior. Moreover, it was designed primarily for research on college students and has shown an impressive capability of distinguishing differences in intellectual and emotional behavior among a variety of student groups.

The various Omnibus Personality Inventory scales may be distinguished according to whether they deal with intellectual disposition or with other characteristics, such as affective and religious disposition. The intellective scales include Thinking Introversion, Theoretical Orientation, Complexity, Estheticism, Autonomy, Social Maturity and Nonauthoritarianism. The affective and religious scales include

Lack of Anxiety, Impulse Expression, and Religious Liberalism. Additional scales have been added to the Omnibus Personality Inventory since 1962 but were not part of this study. The scales will be described as they are discussed in later chapters; technical details of the scales are described in Appendix A of this volume and in the Omnibus Personality Inventory Manual.[43]

In addition to data from the Omnibus Personality Inventory, extensive but less reliable information about the students examined in the present volume is available from questionnaires given to them as freshmen and seniors. The questionnaires cover such characteristics as family background and relationships, cultural awareness, intellectual and social interests, personal values, religious practices and attitudes, institutional images, and vocational, educational, and life goals. Academic aptitude scores for these students were obtained from the colleges and were converted to the School and College Ability Test (SCAT), Form 1A.[44] These scores make it possible to analyze responses by ability level where variables might be presumed to be affected by a student's ability. We developed two special measures of religious attitude in addition to the Religious Liberalism scale of the Omnibus Personality Inventory. These are the Religious Concepts Inventory and the Religious Practices Index, which will be described in detail later.

The primary data to be considered in this book are drawn from two studies carried out through the facilities of the Center for Research and Development in Higher Education at the University of California, Berkeley. The first source of data is a study of West Coast Catholic college students, entitled "The Etiology of Catholic Intellectualism—Development of Intellectual Disposition within Catholic Colleges."[45] This study began with a doctoral dissertation completed in 1964. The second study, which concerned nationwide high school graduates, was directed by the author and financed by the U.S. Office of Education.[46] It followed high school graduates of 1959 through five post-high-school years, ending in 1964. For brevity these studies will be referred to as the West Coast Sample and the National Sample.

The purpose of the West Coast Sample study was to compare the intellectual values of students in Catholic colleges with the values of Catholics and non-Catholics in public institutions. The original

---

[43] Center for the Study of Higher Education (1962).
[44] Conversion tables are found in Darley (1962).
[45] Trent (1964).
[46] Trent and Medsker (1967).

sample included over 4,000 freshmen and seniors at five West Coast Catholic colleges, San Francisco State College, and the University of California, Berkeley. Freshmen and seniors in the Catholic colleges and the University of California freshmen were surveyed in the academic year 1959–60. The California state-college students were surveyed in 1958–59. Other groups of students were included for additional selective comparisons.

In each case, the entire freshman class participated in the study. The senior classes of 1959 and 1960 constituted either random or representative samples based upon such criteria as sex and major; in no case was less than one-fourth of any Catholic college senior class included. All the 1959 freshmen who remained in college were surveyed again as seniors in 1963.

West Coast men's, women's, and coeducational Catholic colleges were included in an attempt to survey a representative cross-section of types of Catholic colleges. The average enrollment of the colleges was 1,000 students, identical to the figure reported as the average enrollment nationally in Catholic colleges in 1961. Four of the Catholic colleges were primarily residential colleges, and all were primarily liberal arts institutions. Four of the schools offered a limited graduate program, and one granted the doctorate in one field only. The state college data were included to provide a comparison or point of reference in reviewing the characteristics of the Catholic college students, under the assumption that the state college students would represent an average public college in such criteria as the socioeconomic status of the students, their academic qualities, and the quality of the institution they attended. The University of California students were considered to compare Catholics and non-Catholics in a relatively select, large public university. (Students who enroll at California must rank in the upper 12 per cent of their high school classes.) Colleges included in the study are listed in Appendix B.

Extensive information concerning students was obtained in the West Coast Sample, but regardless of the comprehensiveness of the research instruments and design, there was a major limitation inherent in the study. Certainly no claim can be made to a "broad, national representation" of Catholic colleges. This limitation is mitigated by two factors, however: first, in terms of size, sex, and curricular offerings, the schools included present more of a sampling of the "average" Catholic college than do a number of other surveys; second, Astin, in his book, *Who Goes Where to College,* has found that when the same types of institutions are being compared, there are, essentially, no regional differences between colleges on variables of this kind.[47] Although we do not entirely agree with Astin on this issue, indications are that conclusions from the West Coast college sample have implications for other regions as well.

The second major source of data, the National Sample, afforded a broader representation of students. Nearly 10,000 high school graduates were studied in 16 communities in the Midwest, California, and Pennsylvania. (The communities are listed in Appendix B.) These communities were all multi-industrial cities, with populations ranging from about 35,000 to 800,000. The sample covered 9 states and included 37 high schools. Over 25 per cent of the students in this sample were Catholics, approximating the proportion of Catholics in the general population. The students in the National Sample comprised the entire senior class in the public high schools in these communities, as well as the senior class of all private schools that enrolled an appreciable proportion of the community's students.[48] The sample was primarily Caucasian, with Negroes accounting for approximately 4 per cent of the population studied.

This study was designed to show the relationship between intellectual and nonintellectual characteristics of high school graduates and their subsequent pursuits and educational development. Scales from the Omnibus Personality Inventory were administered to these students in 1959 and again in 1963 when those who attended college were seniors. In addition, several detailed questionnaires were administered between 1959 and 1964. A sample of over 500 students was interviewed, carefully chosen to be representative of the entire sample originally surveyed in 1959. The interviews lasted an average of two hours each and were devised to provide more comprehensive and direct information than could be obtained from questionnaires.

Forty per cent of the high school graduates entered college full time the semester after graduation. More than 70 Catholic institutions were included among the colleges they attended. The University of Notre Dame, Marquette University, and Dominican College of Wisconsin drew the greatest number of Catholic students; however, most Catholic students attended non-Catholic colleges. Data are available for 2,500 Catholic and non-Catholic students who entered college and completed at least one year and for 1,400 of these students who per-

[47] Astin (1965).

[48] In the one large city, which had a population of 800,000, seniors were surveyed in three high schools representing a demographic cross-section as determined by the superintendent of schools.

sisted in college for four years. Relevant data are also available for the entire National Sample.

As in the West Coast Sample, it is again possible to compare students in Catholic colleges with Catholics at secular colleges and with non-Catholic students on a variety of dimensions. The presence of longitudinal data is of importance in both samples, so that we can see not only what all freshman and senior students are like, but what the same students are like as freshmen and as seniors. We are thus able to see how students in different types of colleges change during their college years, even though we cannot say that college is completely responsible for the change.

Data to supplement that of the West Coast and National samples are available from two other studies conducted at the Center for Research and Development in Higher Education. One of these is a study of National Merit Scholarship winners, conducted by Fred T. Tyler; the other is a study of selected institutions, conducted by T. R. McConnell, Paul Heist, and associates.[49]

The first study concerns 900 students who were winners or runners-up in the National Merit Scholarship competition of 1956. Although the proportion of Catholics in this group is small, it is especially interesting to look at the intellectual characteristics of these very bright and achieving students to see how they compare to equally bright and achieving non-Catholic students. The National Merit Scholarship Study was designed to describe these scholarship winners in terms of a large number of psychological traits, to study their distribution among various institutions and fields of study, and to learn what changes occurred in their attitudes and values during the college years. Questionnaires and tests were used, including an early version of the Omnibus Personality Inventory, and a sample of 200 was interviewed.

The second contributive study concerns differential recruitment and institutional impact in selected institutions. This study of eight rather distinct colleges and universities, which differ from each other in a variety of ways, began with freshmen in 1958 and 1959. The investigation centered on the intellectual and academic development of students in these institutions, with emphasis upon variations in policies and patterns of recruitment among the schools, the types of students the institutions attract, and changes in characteristics of students during college years. This study provided the information on

[49] Further descriptions of these studies may be found in the 1960–61 Annual Report, Center for the Study of Higher Education, University of California, Berkeley. Reports of both studies are in preparation.

44   BACKGROUND AND SOURCES

the University of California students and also the entering students in a Lutheran college. The data from the Lutheran college allowed us to compare the intellectual and religious characteristics of students in a Catholic college with those of students in a church-related college of another denomination.

Supplementary data have been made available to us from a third, ongoing study of primary importance directed by C. Robert Pace at the University of California at Los Angeles.[50] Through his college and University Environment Scales (CUES), Pace has sought to identify the intellectual, social, and cultural climate of colleges and universities throughout the country. Pace has supplied us with the scores of students at 31 Catholic institutions, collected mostly between 1964 and 1966, together with normative data for his sample as a whole. These data have been subjected to several distinctive analyses of our design and are an important adjunct to our original data. Information from CUES is especially valuable since it is in the form of five validated and reliable scales, rather than being a collection of simple self-report items, and is obtained from another broad, contemporary sampling of Catholic colleges across the country.

Although we draw most of the data from the West Coast and National samples, supplemented by other studies at the Center for Research and Development and the CUES data, we will also consider information from at least a dozen additional studies relevant to the issue of Catholic intellectuality. These studies will be described in greater detail as they are discussed in succeeding chapters. Thus information about Catholic students is available on a variety of issues and from many different sources. Most of the studies present a dramatic consensus in their general findings in important areas; some others provide conflicting results; and a few reach conflicting conclusions, based upon similar results. For this reason the problem of methodology discussed above must be kept in mind. This is true for the past research which has been cited on the lack of intellectual disposition and endeavor among American Catholics, as well as the materials in succeeding chapters on the general characteristics, religious behavior, and intellectual life of contemporary Catholic young adults.

[50] Dr. Pace is gratefully acknowledged for his contribution by allowing us access to the CUES data he has been collecting for the last several years.

The Entering Catholic College Student

Before we attempt to assess the intellectual disposition of Catholic college students, we shall consider some of the general characteristics of these students. Who are the Catholic students who go to college? What do we know about their socioeconomic level, educational background, and ability? What kinds of colleges do they attend? And are they attending college in the same proportion as non-Catholic students? Answers to these questions provide information about the background of Catholic college students basic to an understanding of their intellectual development.

Considering first the kinds of colleges that Catholics attend, we find that a majority of Catholic students do not attend Catholic colleges. Out of over one million Catholics estimated to be attending college in 1965 only about a third were enrolled in church colleges.[1] Sixty-one per cent of the Catholic colleges are located in the northeastern and north central parts of the United States. The majority of students in Catholic colleges in 1966 were attending institutions with enrollments of less than 2,700. The average enrollment in Catholic colleges was 1,043. Of the 368 Catholic colleges listed in the *Education Directory* in 1966, 20 per cent enrolled less than 100 students and 25 per cent enrolled over 1,000.[2] Thirty-six per cent of the Catholic college students were enrolled in colleges of over 5,000 students, although colleges of this size represent only four per cent of the total number of Catholic colleges.

The majority of women are found in the women's colleges, which make up almost half (178) of all Catholic colleges. Only 17 per cent of Catholic colleges are coeducational. All but 3 of the largest institutions, with enrollments of over 5,000 students each, are coeducational, but women are vastly outnumbered in most of these schools, so that

[1] Ellis (1965).
[2] U.S. Department of Health, Education, and Welfare (1966).

in actuality students attending Catholic colleges are still very much sex segregated.

A very few Catholic colleges enroll a large proportion of the students attending Catholic colleges, but the majority of students attend small sex-segregated colleges which comprise the vast majority of Catholic colleges. At a time when college enrollments nationally are soaring, the number of students enrolled in Catholic colleges increased from approximately 301,000 at the beginning of the 1960's to approximately 390,000 in 1966. The Catholic college enrollments in 1966 represented a 30 per cent increase compared with their 1961 enrollments. The increase nationwide was over 50 per cent, or from roughly 3,861,-000 students in 1961 to 5,924,000 in 1966. At the same time the number of Catholic colleges listed in the *Education Directory* increased by 21 per cent, from 303 in 1961 to 368 in 1966. But apparently the newly accredited colleges enrolled comparatively few students, for the average enrollment in Catholic colleges did not change appreciably during this period; it was approximately 1,000 in 1961, only 43 less than in 1966.

What these data imply is that students who enter Catholic colleges are from the outset a select group, numerically. The data also imply that the trend in Catholic higher education continues toward small men's and women's colleges. As we shall see, this situation is liable to perpetuate problems of student and faculty recruitment, financial support, and provision of adequate facilities as well as questions about the role of Catholic higher education.

Turning to the question of the rate of Catholic attendance at college, there is evidence that Catholics are not yet attending college in the same proportion as their non-Catholic peers. Although Catholics are unquestionably becoming more acculturated and are attaining in greater numbers a socioeconomic level well above that of previous Catholic generations, the most reliable available evidence reveals that this acculturation has not yet extended to equal attendance at college. Of the 9,778 students who were surveyed in 1959 as part of the National Sample, 47 per cent of the non-Catholics, but only 34 per cent of the Catholics, entered college, a difference found to be highly significant statistically (chi square $= 12.7$; $p \leq .01$).[3]

The rate of college attendance of the National Sample showed a

---

[3] It might be argued that the sample included few very large cities, and that Catholics in large cities are more likely to attend college. However, a survey by B. Davis (1946) showed that urban Catholics were much less likely than urban Protestants to apply for college. In urban areas, 43 per cent of the Protestant students, but only 26 per cent of the Catholics, applied for college.

decided increase over that of both Catholics and non-Catholics in the years before 1959. A 1947 study by Helen Davis showed that 36 per cent of Protestants and 25 per cent of Catholics applied for college.[4] Since the number who actually attended in 1947 would be less than those who applied, the increase in attendance for both Catholics and non-Catholics was more than 10 per cent. Despite the increase, however, the proportion of Catholics attending in 1959 was about 12 per cent less than that for non-Catholics. Thus, for students entering college in 1959, the gap between Catholics and non-Catholics had not decreased.

In one recent study the contention is that this discrepancy no longer exists. On the basis of his secondary analysis of J. Davis' study of 1961 college graduates, most of whom presumably entered college in 1957 or before, Greeley asserts that Catholics are now attending college in the same proportion as non-Catholics.[5] He bases this conclusion on the fact that 25 per cent of the college seniors he studied were Catholics, representing the proportion of Catholics in the general population—and also the proportion of Catholics in our National Sample. Greeley failed to consider, however, that the colleges in the National Opinion Research Center study from which his data were drawn are located primarily in the northeastern and north central United States, and that Catholics comprise approximately 45 per cent of the population in the northeastern section of the country.

In the National Sample we found that a majority of high school students attended colleges relatively close to home, and certainly within the same geographic region. Consequently, we would expect to find closer to 45 per cent of the college students in the northeastern National Opinion Research Center sample to be Catholics, if they were indeed represented in proportion to the population.

Another study, *Catholic Schools in Action,* also suggests that the proportion of Catholics attending college may be notably increasing.[6] In this study, which included more than 2,000 Catholic high schools, principals estimated that over 54 per cent of their 1962 graduates went on to some form of post-secondary education. Since this was a study of Catholic schools only, however, and does not include Catholics in public schools, the figures represent only the percentage of Catholic high school graduates who may be attending college and

[4] Davis, H. (1949); see also Herberg (1960*a*).

[5] Greeley (1963) compared his data only to the representation of Catholics nationally rather than to appropriate regional figures such as those reported by Bogue (1959).

[6] Neuwien (1966).

are not representative of all Catholics. Even if the figures are applied specifically to Catholic schools, they present serious limitations, since they are based upon estimates of high school principals and deans. In our National Sample we found that school administrators consistently overestimated the percentage of their students who actually attended college. Moreover, figures based on actual attendance show that proportionately fewer Catholics than non-Catholics in the National Sample attended college. It should be noted also that the "Catholic Schools" figures included students entering seminaries and the religious life. In short, then, the responses of these administrators are encouraging only to the extent that they may indicate increased interest in college attendance by Catholic students, but they cannot be taken as confirmation of an actual increase in attendance. Confirmation will have to await further analysis from research such as that embodied in a large nationwide study known as Project Talent.[7]

Granted that evidence shows that a smaller proportion of Catholics than non-Catholics have been attending college, we must then ask what the characteristics are of the Catholic students who do attend college, and what factors prevent more from attending. In the past, the relative lack of Catholics in college has been attributed primarily to the lower socioeconomic status that has characterized Catholics in this country. It has been argued that, as more Catholics move into

[7] One study that could provide a current and valid estimate of the proportion of Catholics attending college is known as Project Talent, conducted by Flanagan and associates (1964). This national survey of abilities and aptitudes, carried out in 1960, included students in grades nine to twelve in almost a thousand high schools, selected to constitute a stratified random sample of all high schools in the United States.

According to Project Talent data, 42.3 per cent of high school graduates entered college immediately after graduation, a figure comparable to that found in the National Sample. (In the National Sample 40 per cent of students entered full time and another 3 per cent part time immediately after graduation.) The author requested data from Project Talent giving the breakdown of Catholic and non-Catholic students attending college, but such information was refused on the grounds that the Catholic high schools participating in the study had been assured that no information of this kind would be released. Such information would be extremely valuable and should be made available. It has been suggested by Project Talent that this will be the case, after the schools have examined the data and given their permission for its dissemination.

Information about current Catholic college attendance will be forthcoming from a new study being conducted at the Center for Research and Development in Higher Education. This study, "School to College: Opportunities for Post-Secondary Education" (Project SCOPE), traces the careers of 80,000 ninth and twelfth grade students in four states.

higher-level jobs and as their income level gradually increases, Catholics will be more equally represented in college. Accepting this as a tenable hypothesis, we determined to investigate it empirically by examining the pursuits of the high school graduates in the National Sample, classified by their religion and socioeconomic status (Table 1).

TABLE 1. *Percentage of High School Graduates Who Entered College by Socioeconomic Level and Religion, National Sample*

	LEVEL OF SOCIOECONOMIC STATUS AND RELIGIOUS AFFILIATION					
	High		Middle		Low	
PURSUIT GROUP	Catholic	Non-Catholic	Catholic	Non-Catholic	Catholic	Non-Catholic
(Number) [a]	(256)	(969)	(1,398)	(3,800)	(574)	(1,278)
College	59	78	36	48	25	30
Other	41	22	64	52	75	70
Total	100	100	100	100	100	100
(Chi square)	(38.2**)		(59.7**)		(4.6*)	

[a] Numbers do not total 9,778 because some subjects did not report father's occupation.

* $p \leq .05$
** $p \leq .01$

It was found that when Catholics and non-Catholics were compared by socioeconomic status, a smaller percentage of Catholics, even at the high socioeconomic level, attended college. Socioeconomic status was determined by father's occupation, as reported by the students. Professional and managerial occupations comprise the high socioeconomic level; small business, semi-professional, sales, clerical, and skilled occupations comprise the middle level; and semi- and unskilled occupations comprise the low level.[8]

As shown in Table 1, at the high socioeconomic level only 59 per cent of the Catholics, compared with 78 per cent of the non-Catholics,

[8] We originally combined both father's education and occupation to arrive at an index of the subject's socioeconomic status. But this made no appreciable difference compared with our more convenient index based upon occupation alone. This corroborates other research which has found that occupation is one of the best single indicators of the values, opportunities, and circumstances that make up this important variable of socioeconomic status (see, *e.g.*, Berelson and Steiner, 1964; Warner, Meeker, and Eells, 1957).

attended college. At the middle level, 36 per cent of the Catholics attended, compared with 48 per cent of the non-Catholics; and at the low socioeconomic level, 25 per cent of the Catholics attended, compared with 30 per cent of the non-Catholics. For both groups a much higher percentage at the high socioeconomic level attended; but surprisingly, the percentage gap between the two groups was greatest at this level. Differences at the high and middle socioeconomic level were significant at the 1 per cent level; at the low socioeconomic level they were significant at the 5 per cent level. Thus it would seem that socioeconomic status as defined in this study cannot be considered the major deterrent to college attendance among Catholics compared to non-Catholics, and that occupational advancement cannot be considered the complete solution to the problem of low college attendance by Catholics.

One clue to the disparate proportions of students attending college at the high socioeconomic level may be provided by a further differentiation of that level. In looking at the fathers' occupations of students who were actually enrolled in Catholic colleges, we found—as did Weiss and Greeley—that approximately 45 per cent of the students' fathers were employed at professional and managerial levels.[9] This figure was comparable to that for non-Catholic students. When we separated the professional and managerial levels, however, we found that a higher proportion of Catholic fathers had business management occupations. For example, in the West Coast Sample, 26 per cent of the non-Catholic fathers, and 18 per cent of the Catholic fathers were employed at the professional level, with the percentages reversed at the managerial level. Thus, although more Catholics are attaining a high socioeconomic status, they are evidently not yet equally represented at the top professional levels, or at least not in the less business-oriented professions. And it may be that circumstances and values of the business families somehow lead to differences in regard for higher education compared with professional families.

Socioeconomic status, as examined to this point, cannot account for the comparative lack of college attendance among the Catholic high school graduates in the National Sample, and neither can attendance at parochial schools. Of about 2,500 Catholics in the sample, approximately 37 per cent graduated from Catholic high schools and 63 per cent from public schools. Although differences between the two groups of Catholics did not reach statistical significance, 41 per cent of students from Catholic high schools, compared with 33 per

[9] Greeley (1963); Trent (1964); Weiss (1963).

cent of the Catholics from public high schools, attended college. For neither group did the figure approach that for non-Catholic high school graduates, 49 per cent of whom attended college; and it was only at the low socioeconomic level that there was a difference in the rate of college attendance between the two groups of Catholics.

When socioeconomic status and type of high school attended were observed together, the same proportions of Catholics at the high socioeconomic level were found to enter college regardless of type of high school attended, and a smaller proportion of both groups of Catholics entered college compared with their non-Catholic peers. Sixty per cent of the Catholic school students and 58 per cent of public school Catholics at the high socioeconomic level attended college, compared with 78 per cent of non-Catholics at this level. At the middle level, 48 per cent of the non-Catholics attended, compared with 38 per cent of the Catholic school students and 34 per cent of the public school Catholics. Only at the low socioeconomic level did the graduates from Catholic high schools attend college at the rate of their non-Catholic peers. Thirty-three per cent of the Catholic school graduates, 30 per cent of the non-Catholics, and 22 per cent of the public school Catholics at the low socioeconomic level attended college.

The graduates of the Catholic high schools were, overall, at a higher socioeconomic level than were the public school Catholics. Thus, 16 per cent of the Catholic school students, compared with 9 per cent of the public school Catholics, were at the high socioeconomic level; 20 per cent of the Catholic school students and nearly 30 per cent of the public school Catholics were at the low socioeconomic level. There is also a greater emphasis upon college preparatory programs in Catholic schools than in public high schools. Therefore, we might have expected the difference in rate of college attendance between the two groups of Catholics to be greater than it was.

In their survey, *Catholic Schools in Action,* Neuwien and his associates found that in the high schools studied, "a strong guidance program was in effect to direct graduates toward Catholic colleges [and] that very strong guidance was given the academically superior graduates toward Catholic colleges."[10] Almost half the students in these schools who expected to continue their education planned to attend Catholic colleges. Our research indicates that once there they will comprise more than three-fourths of the student body. In the West Coast Sample we found that 78 per cent of students at Catholic col-

[10] Neuwien (1966), p. 63.

leges had attended Catholic high schools, and in the National Sample we found that 87 per cent of these students had attended Catholic schools.

This does not mean that the percentage is similar for all schools. Weiss found at St. Louis that 78 per cent of the students had attended Catholic schools, but at Marquette, three years earlier, only 51 per cent of the students were from Catholic schools.[11] The number and quality of Catholic high schools and colleges in a particular area will certainly affect the percentage of Catholic high school students entering their own church colleges. Since only 32 per cent of high school age Catholics are enrolled in Catholic high schools,[12] the fact that they comprise such a large proportion of the Catholic college population may be evidence of the strong emphasis placed by family and schools on staying within the church school system. It indicates also that students who are not part of the system in high school are not very likely to become part of it in college, whether because of lack of interest, lack of financial resources, or something else altogether.

In other words, Catholic colleges recruit a very select, homogeneous student body on a very important variable: prior attendance at Catholic schools. This may be particularly important in view of evidence to be reported in chapter 5, which indicates that the lack of intellectual disposition found among Catholic college students is conditioned more by their previous family and parochial school experiences than by their experience in a Catholic college. Although the great majority of students at Catholic colleges attended Catholic schools, only 31 per cent of Catholic students at secular colleges and universities in the National Sample did so. This difference in educational background may be highly related to the differences in the intellectual disposition between the two groups of Catholics that we will observe in subsequent chapters.

As has been indicated, the higher their socioeconomic level, the more likely students were to attend college, regardless of the type of college attended. Males were also more likely to attend, a fact particularly true among Catholics. In the National Sample of high school graduates, 41 per cent of the Catholic men and 27 per cent of the Catholic women entered college. Among the non-Catholics, 51 per cent of the men and 40 per cent of the women attended.

By 1963, among the Catholic youths who persisted in college for four years, 63 per cent were men and 37 per cent women, compared

[11] *Educational Reviewer* (1963); Weiss (1963).
[12] Neuwien (1966).

with 57 per cent of the non-Catholic men and 43 per cent of the women. Looking at the National Opinion Research Center's sample of college seniors in 1961, Greeley found that 43 per cent of the Protestant students and 36 per cent of the Catholic students were women.[13] The same pattern of differences existed in the rate of college attendance reported for the parents of the 1961 seniors; and although for both Catholics and Protestants the mothers were reported to have attended college in less proportion than the students' fathers, the percentage of the Catholic mothers who entered college was 12 per cent below that of the Protestant mothers. According to *Catholic Schools in Action,* principals estimated in 1963 that 64 per cent of high school boys, but only 47 per cent of high school girls, planned to continue their education. These figures are only estimates, and presumably high estimates, for both sexes, but they indicate the disparity in college plans that still exists between Catholic men and women.

Education has traditionally been valued more for men than for women. A family with limited resources might manage to send their sons to college, believing it essential for them to advance economically. But in a large family with many boys there would be even less chance than usual for girls to attend college, even if they had the desire, since college has not been considered a prerequisite to a woman's traditional job of raising a family and providing a home-life for her husband. This is especially true in the Catholic church, which has characteristically emphasized the dependent and motherly role of women, and which has in a certain sense limited the freedom of married women by its stand on birth control.

The greater importance attached to a college education for men was demonstrated by one very bright Catholic college woman interviewed in the National Sample. She commented, "A man really needs a college education for a job. A woman does too, but if she gets married, that is usually the end of it. She usually doesn't use her education, and if she doesn't I think it was a waste of money."

The value of college seemed more apparent to another equally bright Catholic woman who had married directly after high school. When interviewed she had been married for three-and-a-half years and had three children. When asked her immediate plans, she said, "Just to go on living. There's not much I can do, except to stay here and take care of the kids." As part of her long-range plans she hoped to go back to school and study Russian, but she seemed to have no confidence that she would ever return to school, and she said that no one

[13] Greeley (1963).

had ever really emphasized to her the importance of college.

A pre-law student attending a Catholic college gave his favorable but limited view of women's education, which was typical of that of many men interviewed. He felt that college was valuable for both men and women, but all women "should be enrolled in arts and letters." He added that a married woman should not try to pursue a profession but should have other interests, such as "charities and social organizations."

The reference to charities and social organizations is typical of the Catholic attitude toward woman's role. Women have been encouraged to care for their families and to help the less fortunate by means of church organizations and charities. They have not been encouraged by their families or their church to pursue a career, and since preparation for a career is one of the primary motives for college attendance, perhaps this has reduced the proportion of Catholic women attending college.

Although indications are that the proportion of both Catholic men and women attending college is low in comparison to non-Catholics, the Catholics who do enter college are at no disadvantage in academic ability. In fact, the average ability level for students attending Catholic colleges exceeds that for non-Catholic comparison groups, making the questions raised in the following chapters about the intellectual disposition of these students especially meaningful. We know that intellectual disposition is, to a degree, related to ability, but the comparative lack of intellectualism and autonomy to be found among Catholic students cannot be attributed to a corresponding lack of ability. Indeed, their greater level of ability makes all the more serious their more limited intellectual disposition.

The ability of Catholic college students becomes evident when the equivalent mean School and College Ability Test scores obtained by Catholic college freshmen in Catholic colleges are compared with those of freshmen in other types of colleges. In Table 2 the mean ability scores obtained by the Catholics and non-Catholics in the West Coast Sample are seen to compare favorably with those obtained by all freshmen in a national random sample of 200 colleges as reported by Darley.[14] The random sampling included 11 per cent of the institutions of higher education in the United States in 1955 and is representative of the geographical region, type of administrative control (public, private, nonsectarian, Protestant, and Catholic), and level of degree and training offered at these institutions. Since Catholic

[14] Darley (1962).

colleges are underrepresented at the top degree level (those granting a Ph.D.), inclusion of a greater number of these schools would presumably only have raised the Catholic ability level in comparison with others, since doctorate-granting institutions generally enroll students who are especially high in ability.

TABLE 2. *Comparison of Freshman Equivalent Mean SCAT Scores Obtained by the West Coast and Random Samples*[a]

College Group	Number	Mean
Catholic, West Coast	1,107	300
Nonsectarian, random	12,689	300
Catholic, random	3,359	299
Public (non-Catholic), West Coast	175	297
Public (Catholic), West Coast	175	296
Protestant, random	10,496	296
Public, random	33,995	295

[a] Source of random sample, Darley (1962).

The distribution of means shows immense overlap among the scores of the different samples. With numbers of this size the means are significantly different, however, indicating that the mental potential of Catholic college students is higher than that of comparable Protestant and public college students, and essentially on a par with private, nonsectarian college students. Darley points out that the average entrant to public institutions is superior in academic aptitude to 71 per cent of high school graduates. Entrants to private Protestant schools are superior to 73 per cent; those entering Catholic colleges are superior to 84 per cent of high school graduates.

This superior ability was verified in Weiss' study of St. Louis University. He found that the median American College Testing Program score of 22.8 placed the 1963 freshmen at St. Louis well above the national average.[15] The superior academic aptitude of students in Catholic colleges might be anticipated, since they come primarily from Catholic high schools, in which, again, the aptitude is higher than in schools in general. *Catholic Schools in Action* points out that admission to Catholic high schools is almost always based upon academic potential, and that there is a high rate of failure, with students

[15] Weiss (1963).

being transferred to public schools. Public schools, of course, cannot be so selective.

Despite all the evidence of academic ability among Catholic college students, it appears that many of the brightest Catholic students have not been attending college. Curtin cited statistics at the National Catholic Educational Association's annual meeting in the spring of 1959 to indicate that the majority of bright Catholic high school students were not going to college. Such a failure to develop potential ability is a matter of national concern affecting students from diversified backgrounds, not a matter of Catholic concern alone. In 1955 Darley estimated that 40 to 50 per cent of students in the top quarter of their graduating class did not go on to college. But in the National Sample we found that close to 70 per cent of all high school graduates in 1959 who were in the top quarter of the sample's ability distribution entered college. This finding was corroborated in the sweeping survey of high school graduates undertaken by Flanagan and his associates a year later.[16] Curtin's estimate indicates a great difference between even the brighter Catholics and non-Catholics in rate of college entrance. The difference is more remarkable since Catholics are not held back by the low socioeconomic status and prejudices that still restrict the opportunities of many other minority students. Thus it would seem to be partly a lack of interest in education rather than a lack of opportunity that negatively affects college attendance among many Catholic youths.

The fact that fewer than 14 per cent of the National Merit Scholars in the college graduating classes of 1960 to 1964 were Catholics is another indication of Catholic underrepresentation in college.[17] Catholics may not be as aware of this source of financial assistance or as interested in using it; however, their ability scores would lead one to expect that there would be more Catholics among the Merit Scholars, since their ability scores show they are in a good competitive position. No doubt, more current data will show that this is so.

It is likely, too, that Catholics, scholarship winners or not, will be found entering college in increasing proportions. In the meantime, from the many scources of data available to us now, we are left with a number of identifying features of the entering Catholic college student. As with his non-Catholic peers, he is more likely to come from a higher socioeconomic background than students not attending col-

16 Darley (1962); Flanagan et al. (1964); Medsker and Trent (1965); San Francisco Monitor, April 30, 1959, p. 3.

17 Nichols and Astin (1966).

lege. Catholics in Catholic colleges are at a higher socioeconomic level than Catholics in public colleges; they also come more often from business-oriented families than non-Catholic college students. Catholic men are more likely to be found in college than are Catholic women. Most students in Catholic colleges come from Catholic high schools and are likely to be more academically able than other students.

But the existing evidence indicates that comparatively few Catholics and especially few Catholic women attend college, even those at the higher socioeconomic and ability levels. There are signs that this situation is changing, but the signs are much less clear that the current Catholic college student possesses an intellectual disposition commensurate with his level of ability or with the level of intellectualism found among non-Catholic college students.

CHAPTER FOUR

Intellectual Potential

We have seen that students who enter Catholic colleges are alike in many ways. They share predominantly the same religion and are evidently so close to the church system that they choose a Catholic college in preference to the many existing public and private institutions. Their allegiance is such that, without yet having tested the meaning of higher education, they uniformly feel that their colleges are educationally superior to all other types of colleges, public and private. We have already seen that they come from a roughly similar socioeconomic background, that they are, as a group, of above average ability, and that most of them are products of parochial education.

The combination of these factors is bound to create a very select and relatively homogeneous student body. Inevitably, this selectivity will have a bearing on the educational qualities of Catholic colleges and the intellectual values of their students. How much effect a college has on the development of the values and attitudes of its students is a matter of some controversy. But assuming that the Catholic college does have an effect on the development of the intellectual disposition of its students, its output will still be dependent upon the intellectual potential with which these students come. Therefore, we seek answers in this chapter to the following questions: What are the intellectual attitudes of the students who do enter Catholic colleges, how do their attitudes differ from those of other students, and what is the intellectual atmosphere of the colleges they enter?

Students in Catholic colleges are generally at a higher ability level and at a higher socioeconomic level than Catholics in secular colleges. There is some relationship between level of ability and intellectual disposition and presumably between socioeconomic status and intellectuality. Consequently, it might be assumed that students in Catholic colleges would also be more intellectually disposed than other Catholic students. Many non-Catholic students are similar to students in Catholic colleges in socioeconomic level but closer to Catholics in the secular colleges in ability level. Then should we expect students in Catholic colleges and non-Catholic students to be similar in intellectual orientation? In this chapter we will look at the differences between the two groups of Catholics and compare both to non-Catholics.

No doubt factors other than ability and socioeconomic status affect intellectual disposition, factors that foster or hinder the development of an open, inquiring, critical mind. It appears that one of these is the student's religious orientation, and evidence to be presented shows that the student who is more enclosed in his religious system and who, in this case, has elected to attend a church college, is less likely than other students to have developed an open and flexible attitude.

Our conclusions are the same, no matter what sample is being considered, whether it is composed of students in a particular region or students throughout the nation. Contemporary Catholic students, when they enter college, do not demonstrate the same amount of intellectual interest and commitment as other students, and this is especially true for Catholics entering Catholic colleges. These conclusions are based upon evidence of many kinds. In this and the following chapter, we will focus our attention upon intellectuality as measured by reliable and validated attitudinal inventories. We will discuss evidence from interviews and questionnaires in succeeding chapters.

As noted in chapter 2, the primary instrument used for measuring intellectual disposition was the Omnibus Personality Inventory (OPI), which is composed of several scales measuring intellectual, emotional, and dispositional personality traits. Many of the scales are correlated, but each measures a distinct dimension of intellectuality. These scales include Thinking Introversion, Theoretical Orientation, Complexity, Estheticism, and several scales which measure various dimensions of autonomy, including the Autonomy, Nonauthoritarianism, and Social Maturity scales.[1] The scales with which we are concerned in this chapter are defined as follows:

Thinking Introversion (TI): Persons scoring high on this scale are characterized by a liking for reflective thought, particularly of an abstract nature. They express interests in a variety of areas, such as literature, art, and philosophy. Their thinking tends to be less dominated by objective conditions, practical

[1] Descriptive information on the Omnibus Personality Inventory is drawn from the Omnibus Personality Inventory Manual (Center for the Study of Higher Education, 1962) unless otherwise noted. Validity data for the various scales and scale intercorrelations may be found in Appendix A. Forms C and D were available for the research discussed in this volume. The Omnibus Personality Inventory has subsequently been expanded and further refined, and a new inventory and manual are to be published by the Psychological Corporation in 1967.

applications, and generally accepted ideas than that of low scorers. Among the items included in this scale (to be answered True or False) are: "I enjoy reading essays on serious or philosophical subjects"; "I like to discuss the values of life, such as what makes an act good or evil"; and "I study and analyze my own motives and reactions." The scale is composed of 60 items and has an internal consistency reliability of .85.[2]

Theoretical Orientation (TO): Here, interest in science and in scientific activities is measured. High scorers are generally logical, rational, and critical in their approach to problems. Items on this scale include: "I would like to enter a profession which requires much original thinking"; "At an exposition I like to go where I can see scientific apparatus rather than new manufactured products"; and "I like to read about science." The reliability of the scale's 32 items is .74.

Complexity (Co): This scale measures experimental orientation rather than a fixed way of viewing and organizing phenomena. High scorers are tolerant of ambiguities and uncertainties, are fond of novel situations and ideas, and are frequently aware of subtle variations in their environment. Most persons who score high on this dimension prefer to deal with complexity, as opposed to simplicity, and tend to seek out and to enjoy diversity and ambiguity. Items on this scale include: "I dislike assignments requiring original research work"; "It doesn't bother me when things are uncertain and unpredictable"; and "The unfinished and the imperfect often have greater appeal for me than the completed and the polished." The 27 items on the scale have a reliability of .71.

Etheticism (Es): Those who score high on this scale endorse statements that indicate diverse artistic interests. The content of the statements in this scale extends beyond painting, sculpture, and music to literature and dramatics. Some examples are: "As a youngster I acquired a strong interest in intellectual and esthetic matters"; "I enjoy listening to poetry"; and "I have spent a lot of time listening to serious music." There are 24 items in this scale and its reliability is .80.

The syndrome of autonomy—qualities of independence, objectivity, openness of mind, and self-reliance as opposed to opinionation and excessive reliance on the guidance and authority of others—often determines the use the student will make of his intellectual capacity; the freedom and openness he possesses will determine the amount of

---

[2] The reliability of a measure is an indication of the accuracy of the score. Reliabilities quoted in chapter 4 are based upon the Kuder-Richardson (KR 21) formula and refer to the consistency of items within a scale. That is, the KR reliability indicates the extent to which the various items of a scale evoke similar responses from an individual. Perfect reliability is signified by a value of 1. Reliabilities in the .70's and above are considered acceptable. However, in the absence of measures with high reliability, a scale may be considered acceptable and may be found to be highly useful, depending on the nature of the scale and the statistical differentiation of group scores. Test-retest reliabilities for the scales are included in Appendix A.

intellectual exploring that he dares to do or can do. The scales measuring some aspect of autonomy are:

Autonomy (Au): The characteristics measured here are nonauthoritarian thinking and a need for independence. High scorers tend to be independent of authority, as traditionally imposed through social institutions, and they oppose infringements on the rights of individuals. They are objective, realistic, and intellectually liberal. Sample items include: "For most questions there is just one right answer, once a person is able to get all the facts"; "Unquestioning obedience is not a virtue"; and "I am in favor of strict enforcement of all laws, no matter what the consequences." There are 40 items in the scale and its reliability is .80.

Social Maturity (SM): This is a very broad, complex scale measuring different dimensions of autonomy, openness, and flexibility as well as some cultural interests. High scorers tend to be flexible, tolerant, and realistic in their thinking and tend to be independent of authority, rules, or rituals for managing social relationships. In general they are not punitive, although they are capable of expressing aggression directly when it is appropriate. High scorers also frequently tend to be interested in intellectual and esthetic pursuits. Sample items are: "I like to write my reactions to and criticisms of a given philosophy or point of view"; "People ought to pay more attention to new ideas, even if they seem to go against the American way of life"; and "I like assignments which require me to draw my own conclusions from some data or body of facts." The reliability of the 67 items in the form of the scale used in this study is .88.[3]

Nonauthoritarianism (Na): Most items on this scale are included in the Social Maturity Scale. The Nonauthoritarianism Scale, in effect, narrows the broader scope of the Social Maturity Scale to matters dealing more explicitly with authoritarianism. High scorers tend to be free from authoritarian thinking and are more democratic in their beliefs. Low scorers tend generally to be conventional, rigid, prejudiced, and emotionally suppressed. Low scorers (authoritarian persons) endorse statements such as: "Most people don't realize how much our lives are controlled by plots hatched in secret places"; "No weakness or difficulty can hold us back if we have enough will power"; and "Most of our social problems could be solved if we could somehow get rid of the immoral, crooked, and feebleminded people." The 20 items in this scale are heterogeneous enough so that the internal consistency reliability was only .51 for the college persisters in the National Sample. The test-retest reliability of the scale has been found to be .92.[4]

As noted in Appendix A the Nonauthoritarianism scale is essentially indistinguishable in its results from the Social Maturity scale, which,

[3] As discussed in Appendix A, the Social Maturity scale used in this study is a shorter form of the original 144-item Social Maturity scale included in Form C of the Omnibus Personality Inventory.

[4] Test-retest reliabilities are usually based upon administration of the same test to the same individuals within a period of a few weeks. This procedure was followed in this case with an undergraduate psychology class at San Francisco State College

however, focuses more on intellectual autonomy. The Nonauthoritarianism scale correlates just as highly with the more refined Autonomy scale as it does with the Social Maturity scale. Therefore, it is not surprising that the findings on the Nonauthoritarianism scale are without exception consistent with those on the other two autonomy scales. Moreover, just as is true with the other scales, its different items are not weighted in the direction of political liberalism, ethnocentricity, or religious skepticism. The content of the Nonauthoritarianism items deals generally with judgmental, opinionated, suspicious and moralistic thinking. Its highest loading is on the factor of "Autonomy and Tolerance" as determined by the factor analysis of the Omnibus Personality Inventory. It is therefore taken as a measurement of the same type of traits measured by the Social Maturity and Autonomy scales. The Nonauthoritarianism scale is regarded as a quite adequate measurement of open-minded autonomous thinking in contrast to closed-minded, rigid, and authoritarian thinking. It, like the other autonomy scales, is presumed to be applicable to Catholics and non-Catholics alike. There is also evidence presented in the discussion of the Repression—Suppression scale in Appendix A that the responses of both the Catholic and non-Catholic groups may be regarded as valid. Neither group indicated a response bias.

Omnibus Personality Inventory scores are available for various groups of students, including Catholic and non-Catholic students in

in the Spring of 1967. Some critics may consider the Autonomy scale, and especially the Nonauthoritarianism scale, to be biased against Catholics. An item here or there may touch on religious or moral conduct in a way that might cause Catholics to respond in a direction that would somehow be judged unfairly as authoritarian. This has yet to be demonstrated, however. The Nonauthoritarianism scale as well as the related Social Maturity and Autonomy scales represent refinements over the original F scale measurement of authoritarianism devised by Adorno and associates (1950). The refinement of the F scale was begun by Christie, Havel, and Seidenberg (1960) who considered the original scale too confined to measurement of fascistic tendencies and too subject to response set. The items in the scales used in the research reported in this book are not confined to any one form of authoritarianism such as ethnocentrism or political or religious bias. The evidence is that any one of the three scales can substitute as a measurement for the other two, and that singly or together they cut across a wide range of prejudicial and close-minded thinking. The development of the measurement of authoritarianism was referred to in chapter 2, and footnote 20 on page 29. The possibility of bias of the measures of authoritarianism used in this study are discussed in some detail from our point of view beginning on page 66. The nature, construction, and interrelationships of the scales are discussed specifically in Appendix A, especially beginning on page 320.

the West Coast and National samples, National Merit Scholarship winners, and freshmen at the University of Notre Dame. All the scores have been standardized, so that they can be compared easily. A standard mean score of 50 on any of the Omnibus Personality Inventory scales is equal to the average score of the students in the normative group. To the extent that each group's score is lesser or greater than the normative mean, to that extent will it be above or below 50. A score of 40 indicates that the group or individual has scored 10 standard points, or one standard deviation, below the normative group; a score of 60 is one standard deviation above the mean. (Over two-thirds of the normative sample score between 40 and 60.) The normative group for the form of the Omnibus Personality Inventory that was used for the West Coast and National samples was composed of students at a state college and a state university. More recent and comprehensive normative data are based upon the scores of over 7,000 freshmen in 34 colleges and universities of all types located throughout the United States. Although the two sets of data are nearly identical in score distribution, when comparisons are based upon the more recent normative sample, that sample will be specifically identified.

The students to be considered have been divided into three groups: Catholics in Catholic colleges (simply termed "Catholic" in the tables), Catholics in secular colleges (sometimes called "secular Catholics" for brevity), and non-Catholics. The term "college" denotes both colleges and universities, except where a definite distinction is made between the two.

Differences between Catholics and non-Catholics exist on several scales, but in the West Coast Sample, as in other groups to be discussed, the scale that differentiates most clearly between Catholics—particularly those in Catholic colleges—and non-Catholics is the Nonauthoritarianism scale, together with the Social Maturity and Autonomy scales when available.[5] It might have been anticipated that Catholic students would score somewhat lower than other students on the Nonauthoritarianism scale, considering the emphasis upon authority and protective closure within the church and in the church schools that a large proportion of these students have attended. Some possibility of biased measurement, referred to in footnote 4 of this chapter and to be discussed in subsequent pages, may also pertain here. But even an exaggerated respect for church or civil authority need

[5] The Nonauthoritarianism scale was normed on the West Coast Sample rather than on the Omnibus Personality Inventory normative sample because the appropriate data were not available at the time the analyses were conducted.

not imply the degree of close-mindedness and opinionation suggested by the score obtained by the Catholic college students in the West Coast Sample. As shown in Table 3, the difference in Nonauthoritarianism between Catholic college students and non-Catholics is over ten standard points, or more than one standard deviation, and clearly identifies students in Catholic colleges as the most authoritarian of the college groups.

TABLE 3. *Standard Mean OPI Intellective Scores, West Coast Sample*

College Group (No. in Parentheses)	Thinking Introversion	Theoretical Orientation	Complexity	Estheticism	Nonauthoritarianism
Catholic (1,053)	45.1	42.6	46.3	48.2	41.8
Secular Catholic (433)	47.7	46.5	47.5	49.3	44.1
Non-Catholic (2,169)	50.5	50.1	50.5	50.0	52.0
Lutheran (593)	48.8	47.1	49.4	50.5	45.3

The Catholics at secular colleges, whose standard mean is 44.1, scored higher on the Nonauthoritarianism scale; but their scores are closer to those of their fellow Catholics at Catholic colleges than to those of their fellow students at the secular colleges, who obtained a mean score of 52. Despite this, however, there is a significant difference (beyond the 1 per cent level) between the two groups of Catholics (Table 4).

The groups show differences almost as great in Theoretical Orientation. On this scale, which measures interest in science and inclination toward rational, critical thinking, Catholic college freshmen obtained a mean score of 42.6, compared to 50.1 for non-Catholics. Catholics at secular colleges again obtained scores between those of the other two groups, but significantly different from both. Here, however, secular Catholics fell halfway between the other two groups, whereas they were much closer to the Catholic college student than to the non-Catholics on Nonauthoritarianism.

The Nonauthoritarianism and Theoretical Orientation scales distinguish those who are given to rational, critical thinking and who are independent and open to other people and ideas from those who are rigid, conventional, opinionated, and intolerant. It would appear that the Catholic college student is given to thinking in terms of sure, absolute answers and, in Weigel's words, that he feels that he "already has all the important answers."[6] This interpretation raises the question of the relative ability and desire of Catholic college students to participate in scholarly inquiry, since such inquiry calls for critical thinking and adaptability to changing situations when necessary—traits which appear, from the present data, to be comparatively alien to them.

The results on the Thinking Introversion and Complexity scales were similar to those on the Nonauthoritarianism and Theoretical

TABLE 4. *Critical Ratios of OPI Intellective Scores, Freshmen, West Coast Sample*

College Group	Thinking Introversion	Theoretical Orientation	Complexity	Estheticism	Nonauthoritarianism
Catholic vs.					
secular Catholic	4.51**	6.81**	2.18*	1.88+	4.11**
Catholic vs.					
non-Catholic	14.74**	22.54**	11.50**	4.81**	30.74**
Secular Catholic vs.					
non-Catholic	5.17**	6.56**	5.76**	1.40+	15.14**
Lutheran vs.					
Catholic	7.49**	9.03**	5.76**	4.42**	6.37**
Lutheran vs.					
secular Catholic	1.71+	.85+	2.87**	1.98*	1.86+
Lutheran vs.					
non-Catholic	3.84**	6.58**	2.22*	1.13+	12.77**

+ p = not significant
* $p \leq .05$
** $p \leq .01$

Orientation scales, with the Catholic college students again scoring the lowest. Catholics at Catholic colleges scored nearly one-half a standard deviation below the mean, and non-Catholics scored slightly above the mean. Catholics at non-Catholic colleges scored between the two groups and were significantly different from both the Catholic college students and non-Catholics. The low scores obtained by Catholic college students on these measures corroborate the earlier picture of a lack of interest in critical thinking, since the Complexity scale

[6] Weigel (1957), p. 305.

reflects a spirit of intellectual inquiry and tolerance for ambiguous situations—prerequisites for any prolonged intellectual endeavor. The Catholic college students' low scores on Thinking Introversion also suggest that these students have comparatively little interest in abstract thinking.

On the Estheticism scale, Catholics at Catholic colleges scored significantly lower than non-Catholics; however, the difference in scores on this scale was not as great as on other measures. The Catholics at secular colleges scored between the other two groups, but were not significantly different from either. The difference in artistic and cultural interests was evidently not as great as other differences, a situation we shall see again in later chapters when we ask specific questions about cultural interests. Thus regardless of type of school, Catholics in general appear to be more attuned to their peers culturally, in an esthetic sense, than in other intellectual areas.

The critical ratios showing the significance of the differences among the groups on the scales are reported in Table 4. The pattern of intellective scores for the three groups is traced in Figure 1. On not a single measure do Catholic students, either in or out of Catholic colleges, score at the mean level obtained by the normative sample. Such a negative pattern may raise questions briefly mentioned in chapter 2 and in previous pages of this chapter about whether there is something inherent in these scales that penalizes students who are Catholics. It should be noted, however, that these scales do not focus on matters of religion.

The 67 items of the Social Maturity scale, which will be discussed as part of the autonomy syndrome, include only two that concern religion and that might possibly be construed as penalizing the Catholic who responds out of religious conviction rather than from an authoritarian attitude. These items are: "In religious matters I believe I would have to be called a skeptic or an agnostic"; and "Every person should have complete faith in a supernatural power whose decisions he obeys without question." Only in the first instance is there definite bias. The second item is too inclusive and extreme to be endorsed by a thinking religious person without qualification. But even if both items should penalize the Catholic, in a very long scale of this kind, any resultant bias would be slight, much too slight, certainly, to account for the great differences found between Catholics and non-Catholics on this scale.

Several other items that might be construed as introducing a source of bias have to do with moralistic judgments rather than personal

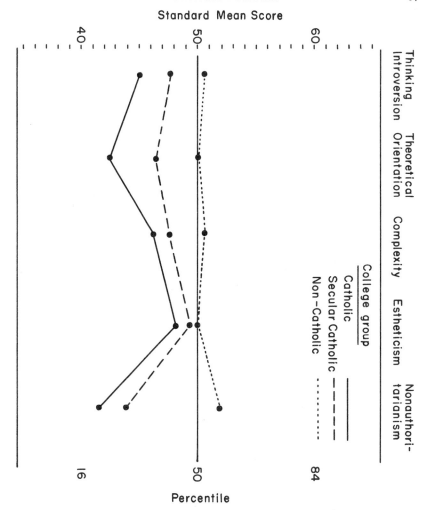

Fig. 1. Profile of standard mean OPI intellective scores, freshmen, West Coast Sample.

moral or religious convictions. Examples are: "There must be something wrong with a person who is lacking in religious feeling"; and "No man of character would ask his fiancée to have sexual intercourse with him before marriage." The Catholic may be more likely than the non-Catholic to reach the unwarranted and authoritarian judgment that a person cannot be normal or of good character because he does not share his religious views or because he indulges in one form of

68   INTELLECTUAL POTENTIAL

sexual behavior that is regarded as sinful by the church (but not necessarily regarded as sinful by the non-Catholic). If a bias such as this exists among Catholics, then it is one that we want to measure.

The other intellective scales have no specific bearing on religion. They deal with a person's ability to think openly, freely, and critically and to say that these scales are biased against Catholics would be to say that there is a Catholic way of thinking that is opposed to such an open, critical approach. Of course, this is precisely what is suggested by the results on these scales; but the results cannot be dismissed on the ground that the scales contain some peculiar anti-Catholic bias.

Table 5 shows the differences between men and women on these scales. Sex differences exist on some, particularly Estheticism and Theoretical Orientation, but the overall pattern remains the same,

TABLE 5. *Standard Mean OPI Intellective Scores, Freshman Men and Women, West Coast Sample*

College Group (No. in Parentheses)	Thinking Introversion	Theoretical Orientation	Complexity	Estheticism	Nonauthoritarianism
Men					
Catholic (492)	43.9	44.6	46.3	45.1	41.8
Secular Catholic (227)	48.1	49.7	48.5	47.6	44.3
Non-Catholic (1,118)	50.1	54.0	50.5	47.2	52.1
Women					
Catholic (561)	46.0	40.8	46.3	51.0	41.8
Secular Catholic (203)	47.3	42.9	46.4	51.1	43.8
Non-Catholic (1,051)	50.8	46.0	50.4	53.0	52.0

with Catholic college women scoring lower than non-Catholic women, and Catholic college men scoring lower than non-Catholic men. Differences between the groups are significant except for those on Thinking Introversion, Complexity, and Estheticism between Catholic women attending Catholic colleges and those attending secular colleges. Also, Catholic and non-Catholic men at secular colleges are not significantly different on Estheticism.

Students at Catholic colleges have thus far been compared with Catholics at public colleges and universities. When they are compared with the state college Catholics separately, the two groups of Catholics

TABLE 6. *Critical Ratios of OPI Intellective Scores, Freshman Men and Women, West Coast Sample*

College Group	Thinking Introversion	Theoretical Orientation	Complexity	Estheticism	Non-authoritarianism
Men					
Catholic vs. secular Catholic	5.1**	7.2**	2.8*	2.5*	4.4**
Catholic vs. non-Catholic	11.9**	20.8**	8.8**	3.6**	21.7**
Secular Catholic vs. non-Catholic	2.8**	5.7**	2.9**	0.6+	11.1**
Women					
Catholic vs. secular Catholic	1.3+	2.3*	0.0+	0.0+	4.1**
Catholic vs. non-Catholic	10.3**	12.2**	8.5**	4.2**	21.7**
Secular Catholic vs. non-Catholic	4.6**	3.8**	5.3**	2.6**	10.0**

+ p = not significant
* $p \leq .05$
** $p \leq .01$

are more alike in intellectual disposition. But the secular college Catholics continue to show a greater degree of intellectualism than the Catholic college students. This is true even though the Catholic college students were at a higher level of ability and socioeconomic status than the state college Catholics, and therefore might have been expected to show a greater degree of intellectualism, to the extent that this trait is related to these factors.

Despite the fact that through years of Catholic schooling, many students have been told that Catholic colleges are superior to the state colleges, it appears that students who enter the state colleges are more intellectually inclined than those who enter Catholic colleges. To the degree that colleges are characterized by their students, and to the degree that the findings here apply generally, there is evidence that the state colleges are at an intellectual level which Catholic colleges have yet to attain.

When we looked specifically at the University of California students, Catholics and non-Catholics were similar on three of the Omnibus Personality Inventory intellective scales, Thinking Introversion, Theoretical Orientation, and Estheticism, averaging scores of 49.7, 52.6, and 47.8, respectively, on these measures. They thus expressed approximately equal interest in reflective thought, scientific endeavor, and artistic appreciation. These students were significantly different on two scales that measure tolerance for uncertainty and openness to new ways of thinking, however. Catholic students had a mean score of 45.8 on the Complexity scale, compared with a mean score of 49 for the non-Catholic students, a difference significant at the 5 per cent level. They differed considerably more on the Nonauthoritarianism scale and on the later and more internally reliable measurement of the authoritarian syndrome, the Autonomy scale. On the Autonomy scale the Catholic students obtained a mean score of 47.2 and the non-Catholics, a score of 52.1, a difference significant well beyond the 1 per cent level.

Even though these were all students who had elected to attend a major public university, the differences between students according to religious background were clear. Since the university has a reputation for high academic standards and presumably would not attract students looking for an "easy" school, it. is interesting to see that even the distinctive group of Catholic students attending such a school were significantly lower than other students in the key areas of autonomy and tolerance for complexity. These Catholics had many Catholic colleges to choose from, as well as many other public institutions of higher learning which do not have reputations as formidable as Berkeley's. They evidently were seeking high academic standards and felt that they could measure up to those at the University of California. On the basis of their ability scores and high school ranks they were in a good competitive position as far as academic achievement was concerned. Nevertheless, they did not match the intellectual level of their non-Catholic classmates in the respects noted above.

At the same time, the secular university Catholics scored significantly higher on all the intellective scales than the Catholics at either the state or Catholic colleges. Most of the differences far exceeded the 1 per cent level of significance, especially on the Theoretical Orientation and the Autonomy scales. Catholics attending the public university were not the intellectual peers of their non-Catholic classmates, but their level of intellectual disposition was higher than that of their fellow Catholics in Catholic or state colleges.

Since, as noted in chapter 2, fundamentalist Protestant groups have been found to manifest a relative lack of intellectual productivity similar to that of Catholics, it is interesting to compare the

Omnibus Personality Inventory scores of the Catholics with those of a group of Protestant college students (Table 3). Here we are dealing with St. Olaf, one of the more select colleges under the control of the presumably conservative Lutheran denomination.

When the students who entered the Lutheran college in 1959 were compared with the other groups of students, they were found to be most similar to the Catholics at secular colleges. The Lutherans scored higher than the Catholic students at the secular colleges on all the scales but differed significantly from them only on the Complexity and Estheticism scales (Table 4). Non-Catholic students scored significantly higher than the St. Olaf students on all but the Estheticism scale. The Lutheran freshmen scored significantly higher than the Catholic college students on all the intellective scales, however, well beyond the 1 per cent level. The difference between the Lutheran and Catholic college students was most marked on the Nonauthoritarianism scale, reinforcing other evidence that differences in autonomy cannot be dismissed as a religious bias, since, as will be seen in chapter 8, the two groups of students resemble each other almost exactly in measured religious orientation in contrast to all other students.

With the exception of the Lutheran college students, we have limited our discussion of the intellectual potential of Catholic college students to our West Coast Sample. Is the picture on the West Coast the same nationwide? To answer this question we replicated the analyses observed above using the personality data obtained from the National Sample described in chapter 2.

In the previous chapter we noted that although Catholics represented over 25 per cent of the original sample of nearly 10,000 high school seniors, disproportionately few of them went to college, with 34 per cent of Catholics and 47 per cent of non-Catholics entering college. In this chapter we will analyze the responses of the high school graduates in the sample who entered college in 1959 and completed at least one year. We will examine the Omnibus Personality Inventory scores obtained by the students in 1959, prior to college entrance. We compare the 1959 and 1963 scores of the four-year persisters in the following chapter.

Because of the limitations of time in a school situation, all the Omnibus Personality Inventory scales were not administered to the National Sample. Therefore, Theoretical Orientation and Estheticism scores do not appear in Table 7. The Social Maturity scale was used in the National Sample but not in the West Coast Sample. The pattern

TABLE 7. *Standard Mean OPI Intellective Scores, Freshmen, National Sample*

College Group (No. in Parentheses)	Thinking Introversion	Complexity	Nonauthoritarianism	Social Maturity
Catholic (135)	47.9	45.2	38.6	48.0
Secular Catholic (372)	46.1	49.1	41.8	50.6
Non-Catholic (2,003)	48.4	50.7	45.7	53.4
Critical ratio				
Catholic *vs.* secular Catholic	2.05*	4.21**	3.54**	2.67**
Catholic *vs.* non-Catholic	.68+	6.58**	9.09**	6.45**
Secular Catholic *vs.*				
non-Catholic	4.80**	2.99**	7.24**	5.04**

+ p = not significant
* $p \leq .05$
** $p \leq .01$

of scores shown in Table 7 is almost the same as that found for the West Coast Sample.

The Catholic college students in the National Sample scored even lower on the Nonauthoritarianism scale than did those in the West Coast Sample, with a score more than one standard deviation below the mean. Approximately 85 per cent of the normative sample obtained a Nonauthoritarianism score higher than the average score obtained by these Catholic college students. Catholics at secular colleges and non-Catholics also scored lower than their counterparts on the West Coast, but the relationship between the groups was the same, with the Catholic college students obtaining the lowest score, the non-Catholics the highest, and the secular college Catholics scoring between the other two groups.

The critical ratios in Table 7 evince the highly significant differences in degree of authoritarianism between each of the groups at the conclusion of their high school years. Expected and comparable differences existed on the correlated Social Maturity scale, which is a complex measurement of autonomy and cultural sophistication related to the Nonauthoritarianism scale.[7] The Complexity scores obtained

---

[7] Since the Social Maturity scale available in 1959 was a briefer scale than that used in Form C of the Omnibus Personality Inventory, the scale was normed on the basis of the total National Sample, including the subjects who did not enter college. This accounts for the inordinately high scores compared with those on the other scales, but it does not affect any of the findings discussed.

by the three groups followed the same pattern as their autonomy scores. The Catholic college students scored half a standard deviation below the normative mean; the Catholics at secular colleges scored higher, but a little below the normative mean; and the non-Catholics scored the highest, somewhat above the normative mean.

There is one deviation from the West Coast Sample in the pattern presented in Table 7. The Catholic college students, although they scored lower, did not differ significantly from the non-Catholics on the Thinking Introversion scale, which measures the students' tendency toward reflective, abstract thinking. This is the only scale on which the secular college Catholics scored lower than the Catholic college students. The difference between the two groups of Catholics is beyond the 5 per cent level of significance, and the difference

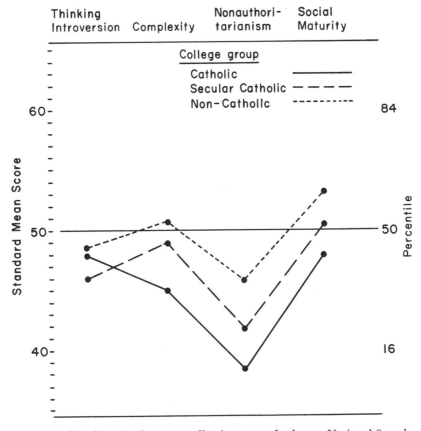

Fig. 2. Profile of standard mean intellective scores, freshmen, National Sample.

TABLE 8. *Standard Mean OPI Intellective Scores, National Merit Scholars, by Religion*

Student Group (No. in Parentheses)	Thinking Introversion	Complexity	Estheticism	Authoritarianism
Catholic (44)	48.4	46.6	49.1	56.5
Non-Catholic (360)	50.0	50.2	50.0	49.2
(Critical ratio)	(0.96+)	(2.65**)	(0.59+)	(4.22**)

+ p = not significant
** $p \le .01$

between the secular college Catholics and non-Catholics is beyond the 1 per cent level of significance on this scale. On all other scales differences in scores exist between each group well beyond the 1 per cent level of significance.

In Figure 2 the standard scores obtained by the three groups on the intellective scales are plotted in relation to one another. The picture has become familiar. Catholic college students are singularly authoritarian in their thinking and lacking in intellectual curiosity and tolerance for ambiguity. Only in preference for abstract thought do these students compare at all favorably with their non-Catholic peers. The secular college Catholics were more autonomous and complex in their thinking than the Catholic college students, but less so than their non-Catholic classmates.

Although Catholic students in all the samples considered so far appear to be less intellectual than their fellow students, we considered the possiblity that Catholics who are especially able academically would be more likely to be on an intellectual level with their non-Catholic peers. With this possibility in mind, we examined the 1956 National Merit Scholars, most of whom graduated from college in 1960. Scores were available for all of the scholarship winners for that year, including 44 students who were identified as Catholics and 360 identified as non-Catholics on the basis of the religion of their parents. Students of mixed religious backgrounds were not included in our analyses. The scholarship winners, whose scores are shown in Table 8, were tested with an earlier version of the Omnibus Personality Inventory. One scale, Theoretical Orientation, which was considered for the West Coast Sample, was not part of the inventory at that time.

There was little difference between the Catholics and non-Catholics in Thinking Introversion and Estheticism, although Catholics scored lower than other students on both scales. Differences between Catholics and non-Catholics were significant at the 1 per cent level, however, on the Complexity and the Authoritarian scales. The non-Catholics had a mean score of 50.2 in Complexity, compared with 46.6 for Catholics. The Authoritarian scale on the form of the Omnibus Personality Inventory that was used at that time scored in the opposite direction from the later Nonauthoritarianism scale. Thus high scores indicate a more authoritarian, dogmatic attitude, an attitude which appears to exist even for these very bright Catholic students. Catholics had a score of 56.5, compared with 49.2 for non-Catholics. Evidently even these students did not manage to incorporate into their lives a very open and flexible mode of thought compared with their peers.

We also investigated the possibility that the more renowned Catholic colleges enroll students who are as high in intellectual disposition as are non-Catholic students. But this is not evident in the CUES data to be considered subsequently nor in the Omnibus Personality Inventory data obtained from a sample considered representative of students who entered the University of Notre Dame in 1965.[8] If we wanted to find Catholic students of high intellectual potential, we thought that the University of Notre Dame would be a likely place to look. Many Catholics consider Notre Dame "the Catholic Harvard." It selects students from many parts of the country, and it is an institution currently attempting many academic innovations. On the basis of Omnibus Personality Inventory scores, however, it is questionable that its entering students have caught up with either the reputation or the innovations, at least in the intellectual attitudes they bring with them to college.

When these students are compared to the current Omnibus Personality Inventory normative group, the Notre Dame freshmen score significantly below the mean on all of the intellective scales. The normative sample represents contemporary freshmen in colleges and universities across the country, including both little-known and well-known schools, some of which are sound academically and others which are not at all distinctive for their scholarly orientation.

The Notre Dame men were compared with freshmen men at a well-known secular university. As shown in Table 9, the Notre Dame

[8] The Omnibus Personality Inventory was administered to a group of 1965 freshmen at the University of Notre Dame by Robert Hassenger, assistant professor of sociology at Notre Dame. Students were enrolled in a variety of major fields and were considered by Hassenger to be representative of entering freshmen at Notre Dame. We are grateful to Dr. Hassenger for permission to use the data.

Table 9. *Standard Mean OPI Intellective Scores, Freshman Men, 1965*

College Group (No. in Parentheses)	Thinking Introversion	Theoretical Orientation	Complexity	Estheticism	Autonomy
Notre Dame (76)	44.8	46.1	45.7	44.8	49.1
West Coast Catholic (278)	45.8	45.4	47.3	47.5	48.2
UCLA (245)	50.5	53.4	51.7	48.3	54.8
Critical ratio					
Notre Dame *vs.* West Coast Catholic	0.83+	0.49+	1.49+	2.38*	1.01+
Notre Dame *vs.* UCLA	4.58**	6.07**	4.89**	2.95**	5.79**
West Coast Catholic *vs.* UCLA	4.97**	9.24**	4.99**	0.98+	9.53**

+ p = not significant
* $p \leq .05$
** $p \leq .01$

freshmen scored more than one-half standard deviation lower on all the intellective scales except Estheticism than did 1965 freshman men at the University of California at Los Angeles. Even on Estheticism the Notre Dame men were significantly lower than the UCLA men, beyond the 1 per cent level. The greatest difference between the Notre Dame and UCLA men was in Autonomy, with Notre Dame students obtaining a mean score of 49.1 and UCLA men scoring 54.8.

The University of Notre Dame men were also compared with 1965 male freshmen at a West Coast Catholic college. Despite the differences in the academic reputation of the two schools, scores for students at the two institutions were almost exactly the same. The West Coast men scored within one point of the Notre Dame men on Thinking Introversion, Theoretical Orientation, and Autonomy, and almost two points higher on Estheticism and Complexity.

Although the Notre Dame Autonomy score compares unfavorably with the UCLA score, it should be noted that the score almost reaches the mean for the 34 colleges in the normative group and is the highest score achieved by the Notre Dame group on the intellective scales. It is much higher than the Nonauthoritarianism score received by the 1959 Catholic freshmen in the West Coast Sample or in the National Sample. These Notre Dame students are entering college six years later and a different scale is being considered, but both measure the general syndrome of open, autonomous thought and action, and the Notre Dame students are approaching the mean for students in general on this particularly critical scale, even if they do not yet nearly reach the level of major secular university students.

Mean scores mask individual differences. Therefore, we examined individual profiles of these Notre Dame students so that we could study the differences among them. Patterns of scores for some individuals manifested great commitment to intellectual concerns, and at the other extreme were profiles that reflected great anti-intellectualism. Unfortunately, the latter were found much more frequently. Only about 8 per cent of the Notre Dame students had Omnibus Personality Inventory profiles that could be called generally high in intellectual disposition, whereas 45 per cent of them had profiles that reflected anti-intellectual attitudes. Profiles were considered high if students averaged five standard points above the normative mean on Thinking Introversion, Theoretical Orientation, Complexity, Estheticism, and Autonomy, and low if they averaged five points below.

It is also possible to compare scores obtained on several scales by these 1965 Notre Dame freshmen with those of a group of 28 freshmen in the National Sample who entered Notre Dame in 1959. The number of Notre Dame students in the National Sample is small and cannot be taken as representative of the entire Notre Dame freshman class for that year. But these students came from many communities and were enrolled in a variety of majors, so that their scores give some indication of the intellectual disposition of 1959 students at Notre Dame. Scores are available for both the 1959 and 1965 groups on three of the intellective measures, those measuring complexity, autonomy, and liking for abstract thinking.

The two groups of Notre Dame freshmen were similar in their attitude toward uncertainty and ambiguity, with both groups scoring below the normative mean on Complexity, but the mean score for the 1959 students was higher, 46.5 compared to 45.7 for the current group. The 1959 group scored considerably higher than the 1965 freshmen on the Thinking Introversion scale, which indicates a liking for reflective, abstract thought. The respective scores were 49.2 and 44.8. The situation was reversed for autonomy. The 1959 students scored only 43.4 on the Nonauthoritarianism scale, compared to 49.1 for current students on the Autonomy scale. In the third instance two different scales were involved and therefore cannot be directly compared. But in any event, these data do not indicate any overall increase in intellectual disposition of incoming Notre Dame freshmen between 1959 and 1965.

The generalizations about the intellectual potential of Catholic college students have been based upon measures of the students' attitudes. We are also able to learn something about how they view the intellectual characteristics of their colleges from corroborating College and University Environment Scales (CUES) data. These scales are based upon students' perceptions of the intellectual, social, and educational atmosphere of their colleges, or the "educationally and psychologically functional environment of a college."[9]

As part of his continuing research based upon his College and University Environment Scales (CUES), Pace has collected data that assess the environments of a large number and variety of Catholic colleges and universities. Scores for these Catholic colleges were made available to us by Pace for our own secondary analyses of the materials.

CUES scores were obtained from students enrolled in 31 Catholic colleges and universities (listed in Appendix B) located primarily in the eastern and central United States.[10] Most of the students were sophomores and juniors enrolled in college between 1964 and 1966; the students in the sample are regarded as representative of the entire student body in the institutions they attended. Seven men's colleges, 14 women's, and 10 coeducational colleges are represented in the sample, with an average enrollment in 1965 of 2,800. There are 6 large institutions with enrollments of over 5,000; 16 with enrollments between 1,000 and 5,000; and 9 schools with enrollments under 1,000.

The average enrollment in these schools is twice that for all Catholic colleges in the United States, although it is very close to the size of colleges which enroll the majority of Catholic college students. Even if these schools are not representative, however, they include an important segment of Catholic higher education. As such, the data from these schools can be compared to normative data based upon 48 colleges and universities in various parts of the country. The normative sample includes public and private colleges with both large and small enrollments; many of the colleges are also represented in Davis' National Opinion Research Center research from which Greeley drew his secondary analyses.[11]

CUES is a 150-item inventory; students respond with "true" or

[9] Pace (1963), p. 3.

[10] Scores from the College and University Environment Scales were available for three additional Catholic colleges. However, these were not included in the present analyses because the numbers of students included in these samples were very small.

[11] J. Davis (1964); Greeley (1963).

"false" to each item, depending on whether they feel the item is typical of their school. The inventory is scored to yield 5 scales with each scale composed of 30 items. The scales are described in the CUES manual as follows:[12]

Scholarship: "The items in this scale describe an academic scholarly environment. The emphasis is on competitively high academic achievement and a serious interest in scholarship. The pursuit of knowledge and theories, scientific or philosophical, is carried on rigorously and vigorously. Intellectual speculation, an interest in ideas as ideas, knowledge for its own sake, and intellectual discipline—all these are characteristic of the environment." Sample items are: "Students set high standards of achievement for themselves"; and "Most of the professors are very thorough teachers and really probe into the fundamentals of their subjects." The reliability of the scale is .92.[13]

Awareness: "The items in this scale seem to reflect a concern and emphasis upon three sorts of meaning—personal, poetic, and political. . . . What seems to be evident in this sort of environment is a stress on awareness, an awareness of self, of society, and of esthetic stimuli. Perhaps . . . these features of a college atmosphere can be seen as a push toward expansion and enrichment." Sample items measuring Awareness are: "Students are actively concerned about national and international affairs"; and "The school offers many opportunities for students to understand and criticize important works in art, music, and drama." The reliability is .87.

Practicality: "This combination of items suggests a practical, instrumental emphasis in the college environment. Procedures, personal status, and practical benefits are important. . . . Order and supervision are characteristic of the administration and of the classwork. Good fun, school spirit, and student leadership in campus social activities are evident. The college atmosphere described by this scale appears to have an interesting mixture of entrepreneurial and bureaucratic features." Sample items are: "Education here tends to make students more practical and realistic"; and "Student organizations are closely supervised to guard against mistakes." The reliability is .83.

Community: "The combination of items in this scale describes a friendly, cohesive, group-oriented campus. The environment is supportive and sympathetic. There is a feeling of group welfare and group loyalty which encompasses the college as a whole. The campus is a community. It has a congenial atmosphere. . . . If the organizational counterpart of 'practicality'

[12] Pace (1963), pp. 24–25; Pace (1962).
[13] Items in the College and University Environment Scales are scored as characteristic of an institution only if they are selected by at least 66 per cent of the students responding at that institution. Since a high degree of consensus is being sought rather than a wide dispersion of scores, Pace points out, "Thus, all correlational and variance methods . . . are incompatible with the assumptions underlying CUES when applied to the responses from a single institution. However, when the data are the scores obtained from different institutions, it is appropriate to use variance methods of estimating CUES reliability" (Pace [1963], p. 48). Reliabilities quoted in the text are Kuder-Richardson (21) reliabilities.

was the bureaucracy, perhaps the counterpart of 'community' is the family." Sample items are: "This school has a reputation for being friendly"; and "Students' mid-term and final grades are reported to parents." The scale reliability is .85.

Propriety: "The items in this scale suggest an environment that is polite and considerate. Caution and thoughtfulness are evident. Group standards of decorum are important. On the negative side, one can describe propriety as the absence of demonstrative, assertive, rebellious, risk-taking, inconsiderate, convention-flouting behavior. Conventionality, in the sense of generally accepting and abiding by group standards, is in some respects a good term for the items in this scale. . . . In any event, the atmosphere on some campuses is more mannerly, considerate, and proper than it is on others." Examples are: "Most students show a good deal of caution and self-control in their behavior"; and "Student publications never lampoon dignified people or institutions." The scale reliability is .81.

For comparative purposes Pace presented his data in percentiles, with the fiftieth percentile designating the median of the distribution of the schools' scores. We have converted the CUES scores for the Catholic colleges to standard scores, with 50 representing the average score of the normative group and 10 representing the standard deviation. As with the Omnibus Personality Inventory scores, this procedure allows us to make direct comparisons among the scales while taking into account the schools' variance on them.

The scores in the normative sample were not weighted according to the number of students in each institution. Thus we left our data unweighted because we wanted to compare the Catholic college and normative samples on an equal basis. This means that as much weight is given to a very small woman's college as to a large university such as St. Louis. The result is an undue inflation of the Scholarship and Awareness scores and a deflation of the Practicality scores for the Catholic college sample as a whole, because the smaller colleges were highest in the more intellectually oriented scales, and the larger colleges enrolling the most students were highest on the practically oriented scale. Therefore numbers of institutions were considered in the averages; numbers of students in the institutions were not taken into consideration.

Table 10 shows the standard mean scores for the 31 Catholic colleges as a group, as well as comparisons within the Catholic college group. The Catholic colleges are significantly lower than the normative group on the two scales most associated with intellectuality. The Awareness score of 45.7 and Scholarship score of 45.5 place the Catholic colleges nearly one-half a standard deviation below the mean on both. But Catholic colleges do not score low on all scales. Their score

TABLE 10. *Standard Mean CUES Scores, 31 Catholic Colleges, by Type of College*

College Group	(Number of Institutions)	Scholarship	Awareness	Practicality	Community	Propriety
Men's colleges	(7)	40.9	43.5	49.7	47.1	49.5
Women's colleges	(14)	51.7	50.6	46.9	67.6	74.4
Coeducational colleges	(10)	40.1	40.3	50.3	49.4	45.6
Critical ratio						
Men *vs.* women		(5.81**)	(3.06**)	(1.19+)	(8.45**)	(7.82**)
Men *vs.* coeducational		(0.76+)	(2.62**)	(0.27+)	(0.85+)	(1.04+)
Women *vs.* coeducational		(7.38**)	(5.18**)	(1.79+)	(9.44**)	(10.21**)
Jesuit colleges	(8)	40.5	42.9	50.5	47.8	46.2
Other Catholic colleges	(23)	47.2	46.7	52.0	60.3	64.2
Critical ratio						
Jesuit *vs.* other Catholic		(2.24**)	(1.49+)	(0.76+)	(3.25**)	(3.30**)
Total Catholic colleges	(31)	45.5	45.7	48.7	57.1	59.5
Critical ratio						
Total Catholic *vs.* normative group		(2.39*)	(2.37*)	(0.76+)	(2.82**)	(2.96**)

+ p = not significant
* $p \leq .05$
** $p \leq .01$

of 59.5 on Propriety is almost one standard deviation above the mean, and their score of 57.1 on the Community scale is also high. Their standard mean Practicality score is 48.7.

These scores may also be expressed as percentile equivalents, according to the CUES normative data. The Catholic colleges have median scores on both the Scholarship and Awareness scales that would place them just about at the thirty-fourth percentile in comparison with the normative group. Sixty-six per cent of the normative group score higher than the Catholic college group. Conversely, on the Propriety and Community scales together, the total Catholic college group scores near the eightieth percentile, so that just over 20 per cent of the national normative sample scored above them on these scales. Obviously, the Catholics are closer to the median on the Practicality scale. Thus the picture that emerges is one of decorum, obedience, friendliness, and emphasis upon the practical aspects of life. Academic, intellectual, and cultural concerns appear to be minimal compared with the normative sample.

There is some diversity among the Catholic colleges on the CUES, as noted in Table 10. Almost half of the colleges are women's colleges, which score especially high in Community and Propriety. But it is these schools that also score the highest on the Scholarship and Awareness scales. On these scales they reach the normative mean, although this might not be true if they were compared with women's colleges separately in the normative sample; that is, the women's colleges in the normative sample might be correspondingly higher than the other colleges. The Catholic coeducational schools score the lowest on these intellectual meaures, with the men's colleges not much above them. The coeducational schools are also generally the largest, and, although relatively few in number, enrolled 65 per cent of the students in the sample. Together with the men's colleges, they account for 80 per cent of the students. Although not shown in table form, the 6 large institutions in the sample, and the 8 schools which identify themselves as universities all fall below the twentieth percentile on the Scholarship and Awareness scales. Over 80 per cent of the normative sample scored above these Catholic institutions on these two scales. This means that at major Catholic institutions, which enroll a large percentage of the Catholic college students, and at schools which are identified as universities, students perceive the intellectual atmosphere to be the most limited.

The standard mean CUES scores of these various groups, together with those of the Jesuit institutions in the sample to be discussed subsequently, are shown graphically in Figure 3. Ideally, these figures should also be shown with such variables as ability and college major held constant. But it is doubtful that the general finding would be much affected by this procedure, especially considering the large differences between the Catholic college and the normative sample, and the fact that the normative sample is also shown without additional categorization or cross-tabulation of other important variables.

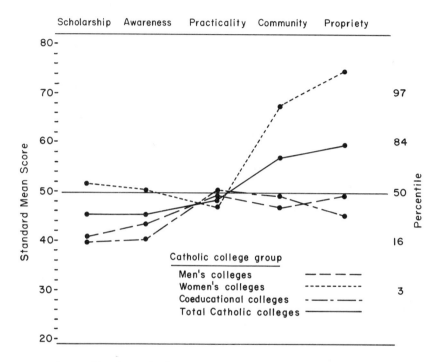

FIG. 3. Profile of standard mean CUES scores for 31 Catholic colleges.

Despite the intellectual picture perceived by most Catholic college students of their colleges, there are some Catholic institutions that students perceive as being above average in Scholarship and Awareness. Two of the 31 Catholic colleges, both women's colleges, have scores on these two scales that approach one-half a standard deviation above the mean, and four other women's colleges are at least above average on the two scales. It is interesting that the two schools which rate highest on Awareness and Scholarship are also the highest in Community and Propriety; decorum and warmth are evidently not sacrificed to the cause of scholarship. But both these schools score very low on Practicality, far below the average for the women's colleges, and farther still below the average for the other Catholic colleges, indicating a negative relationship between practical, applied interests and scholarship.

Both these more intellectually oriented colleges are operated by the same religious order, an order which has a strong cultural tradition in Europe. Both enroll women students high in academic ability, inasmuch as more than two-thirds of the women ranked in the upper 25 per cent of their high school graduating class and over 90 per cent were in the top half. Both schools are almost exclusively residential, and the one rated the highest provides opportunity for study abroad during the junior year, attracted five National Merit Scholars in one year, enrolls a number of foreign students, and also has an active program for bringing outside cultural activities to the campus. Perhaps a religious order with unusual intellectual commitment, emphasis upon academic achievement and cultural enrichment, and an able female student body are factors that, combined, have caused the intellectual climate at their schools to stand out from that generally perceived by Catholic college students.

The 8 Jesuit institutions in the CUES sample enroll 40 per cent of the total student body included in the 31 colleges and universities. Nationally, Jesuit colleges enroll one-third of all students attending Catholic colleges. Jesuit institutions are important numerically, and they are important for their particularly high reputation in the field of Catholic education. Therefore, we singled out the Jesuit colleges for comparison with the other 23 colleges in the sample on the more academically and intellectually oriented Scholarship and Awareness scales (Table 10).

The Jesuit colleges obtained a standard mean score of 40.5 on the Scholarship scale, a score almost one full standard deviation below the normative mean. By contrast, the 23 other Catholic colleges have a mean Scholarship score of 47.2, a score still below that for colleges in the normative group but significantly higher than that of the Jesuits, to the 1 per cent level. And it is not that a few colleges lowered the Jesuit average; all eight Jesuit colleges scored below the average for the non-Jesuit Catholic colleges. The raw mean on the scale obtained by the other Catholic colleges was 9.3; the highest mean obtained by a Jesuit college was 7. This means that at least 85 per cent of the colleges in the normative sample and a majority of the other Catholic colleges scored higher on a scale that indicates a college environment emphasizing academic achievement and serious interest in scholarship.

Comparable results were found on the Awareness scale. The standard mean score for the Jesuit schools was 42.9, compared to 46.7 for the non-Jesuit Catholic schools. The differences on the Awareness scale are less marked than those on the Scholarship scale, but compared with other Catholic college students Jesuit students tend to perceive their campus environments as less attuned to the political, cultural, and artistic world.[14]

We have looked at Jesuit schools as a group on the basis of CUES, and it is possible to look also at two case studies carried out in recent years at particular Jesuit universities. One study was conducted on the West Coast, at the University of Santa Clara, and the other in the midwest, at St. Louis University.[15] For his survey of St. Louis University Weiss used the College Characteristics Index, a 300-item questionnaire from which CUES was developed. The St. Louis data were compared with data from a group of universities and from a group of liberal arts colleges which formed a major part of what was available as normative data.

St. Louis students rated their university higher than the comparison universities in three areas, Student Dignity, Academic Achievement, and Nonvocational Climate. The factor which most distinguished St. Louis from other universities was their rating in Academic Achievement. High scores in Academic Achievement indicate that the schools "set demanding standards of achievement for their students, employing for this purpose course work, examinations, honors, and similar devices."

St. Louis students also responded more favorably than other university students to the Student Dignity scale, indicating that the school "attempts to preserve student freedom and maximize personal respon-

---

[14] The Awareness and Scholarship scales have been emphasized since they measure the intellectual atmosphere of a college and are the most closely related to the Omnibus Personality Inventory intellective scales. The correlations between the CUES and OPI scales are not high, however, which may indicate that the two inventories are measuring different aspects of intellectuality. It is also possible that students who are themselves the most intellectually disposed may be the most critical of their colleges and may be more likely to rate them lower in intellectual atmosphere than would students who are themselves lower in measured intellectuality. Indeed, it is important to keep in mind that the CUES scales reflect college environments only as they are perceived by the colleges' students. The Omnibus Personality Inventory scales, of course, measure the student's own interests, attitudes, and modes of behavior. Considering these possible and actual sources of difference, it would be of particular interest to compare the Omnibus Personality Inventory and CUES scores obtained by the same groups of students.

[15] Foster, Stanek, and Krassowski (1961); Weiss (1963).

sibility." Although St. Louis scored above the other universities, Weiss points out that the total university score was lower on this than on any of the other intellectual factors, "showing that the students thought, with a fair amount of consistency, that many practices which reflect respect for individual students and encourage personal responsibility were lacking."[16] The third area in which St. Louis scored above other universities was in Nonvocational Climate. This factor reflects opportunities to engage in theoretical, artistic, and other "impractical activities" and "implies the absence of demands for student conformity to conventional values."

St. Louis is thus rated by its students as higher than the other universities in this comparison sample in student freedom and responsibility, opportunity for theoretical and artistic activities, and in demands for academic achievement. The St. Louis students rated their university lower, however, in Intellectual Climate, a factor which "reflects qualities of the staff and plant specifically devoted to scholarly activities in the humanities, art, and social sciences." They also rated their university lower in Academic Climate, which stresses "academic excellence in the areas of the natural sciences, social sciences, and the humanities." In addition, they rated their university lower on all five of the scales than students at the liberal arts colleges in the comparison group.

Neither the normative institutions nor the grade levels or fields of the students providing the data from these institutions were identified by Weiss. Also this information was not easily or clearly obtainable from the references he cited on the subject. Therefore, it is difficult to assess the standing of St. Louis University compared with the normative data as given. A valid assessment would necessitate comparing Weiss' data with data obtained from comparable students enrolled in a representative sample of major universities.

Without additional information of this kind, however, the total effect would seem to be that the St. Louis students feel a demand for achievement, combined with considerable individual freedom, compared with other universities in the survey, although not compared with the liberal arts students. But, particularly as rated on the Intellectual and Academic Climate scales, the school does not seem to be offering the genuinely scholarly atmosphere which is to be desired and—on the basis of reputation—to be expected in a Jesuit university.

The study of University of Santa Clara students referred to in chapter 2 is important to mention here in the special context of Jesuit

[16] Weiss (1963), p. 181.

education. Foster and his associates studied students enrolled as freshmen and sophomores at the University of Santa Clara between 1960 and 1961. They used a wide variety of psychometric instruments and two different designs: a cross-sectional and a two-year longitudinal study. The Catholic university students were more authoritarian, more dogmatic, more ethnocentric, and less prone to critical thinking than were contemporary students compared on the same instrument at Michigan State University and at neighboring San Jose State College by Rokeach and Plant.[17] They also changed less than the other students on these scales, and they were the only ones who, as a group, actually became more ethnocentric after entering college. These results are not entirely satisfactory or conclusive, since the authors did not account for ability or socioeconomic differences, which might have had some effect on the results. But as far as these data do go, they provide one more instance of a comparative lack of intellectuality among Catholic and, specifically, Jesuit college students.

Such results may indicate a need to reexamine the preeminent place accorded to the Jesuit schools in the Catholic educational world. Jesuit higher education is generally regarded as representing the best of the Catholic college system. It is widely assumed that a disproportionately large number of the better scholars, deeper thinkers, and more inspiring academicians in the church are Jesuits. That Jesuit institutions draw upon this image is exemplified in a recent advertisement for a Jesuit university in *Commonweal*. The advertisement begins provocatively by asking: "How is Jesuit education like a Volkswagen?" The answers are that Jesuit graduates are dependable; that Jesuit education keeps good things and basic design for basic human needs; that, as Volkswagen puts the car around the engine, the Jesuit colleges put the extras around a basic core of learning; and that, like the Volkswagen, Jesuit graduates are recognizable anywhere for their common devotion to truth wherever it is found.

The Jesuits themselves have recognized the need to examine critically the substance behind their image, however. As a result they have established a center for research in Jesuit higher education in the United States. The Jesuit higher education system compares in size with such systems as the University of California and the New York State University complexes; Jesuits operate more than fifty secondary schools, as well as 28 colleges and universities, and as noted previously, they enroll over one-third of all Catholic college students. Size alone would warrant an examination of these schools to consider why they

17 Plant (1959, 1962); Rokeach (1960).

are necessary and what they are doing. Ideally, the Jesuit's center might attempt to answer such basic questions as: Does a Jesuit education actually do anything that another cannot do? How do students change as they move through the Jesuit school system? What sorts of values, attitudes, and backgrounds do the students have when they enter a Jesuit institution and when they leave? What intellectual contributions do the alumni of these colleges make as a group in the years following their college education that are not made by other Catholic and non-Catholic college graduates?

The data observed in this chapter make it urgent that these questions be asked not only of Jesuit colleges but of all types of Catholic colleges. The questions should not be confined to those raised in this or any other volume on the subject of American Catholic intellectualism. And the questions, to be answered with any surety, must be based on precise research design and instrumentation. The record that has led us to this conclusion is reviewed here.

We compared Catholic and non-Catholic students in the West Coast Sample on a variety of scales from the Omnibus Personality Inventory and found that Catholics in Catholic colleges were markedly lower in intellectual disposition despite their scholastic and economic advantages. Catholics at secular colleges were more intellectually oriented generally than were students attending Catholic colleges but they did not measure up to the level of intellectual disposition of their non-Catholic classmates.

When we looked at the National Sample, again using the Omnibus Personality Inventory, the same pattern emerged: Catholics at Catholic colleges were the least intellectual, with Catholics at secular colleges higher and non-Catholics showing the highest measured intellectuality of the three groups.

When we considered another measure, the College and University Environment Scales (CUES) developed by Pace, the same pattern again emerged. Students at Catholic colleges identified their colleges as less intellectually oriented compared with the perceptions non-Catholic students had of their secular colleges. Among Catholic institutions, a few women's colleges were rated highest in intellectually oriented characteristics and large, coeducational and Jesuit institutions the lowest.

We looked at the current freshmen at one of the most renowned Catholic universities in the country and found them markedly less intellectual than freshman men (Catholics and non-Catholics) at a major state university and those in a broad normative sample of college freshmen. When Catholic and non-Catholic students at a public university were examined, Catholics were found to be significantly less intellectual. When Catholic and non-Catholic National Merit Scholars were compared, Catholics were again found to be less intellectual in attitude, as determined by autonomy and complexity of thinking. And, finally, when we examined case studies of individual Catholic schools, we found once again that the intellectual climate did not compare favorably with other schools.

The final comment of chapter 2 is even more appropriate here. The samples we have observed have been too extensive and current; and the variables and instruments used in studying these samples have been too carefully constructed and probing for us to conclude anything other than that Catholic college students on the whole, today, are highly selective and singular for their comparative lack of intellectual disposition. But as we shall see in the following chapter, in some ways the story does not end quite so negatively.

CHAPTER FIVE

Intellectual Development after
Four Years of College

In discussing the change in intellectual values among the students who have attended college for four years, we come to an area of great concern to social scientists working in the social psychology of higher education. That is the problem of whether college does, or even can, change the values of its students. Or more specifically, does a liberal education bring about intellectual and social commitment in students, as it purports to do?

Jacob, in his survey of the research on change in college students' values up to 1958, concluded that college changes the values of students very little.[1] He found that although students become somewhat more similar to their fellow students in their values, they leave college with basically the same views on life that they had upon entrance. He noted, too, that there was no research of this kind on Catholic college students up to the date of his survey.

Subsequent research has not been consistent in its findings about change in college students' attitudes and values. In general, however, it does lead to a greater expectation of such change in students than would have been anticipated from Jacob's survey. In our own research, we have found that considerable change takes place in the intellectual attitudes of students who attend college for four years, particularly in autonomy. This is very apparent when students are compared with their peers who have not entered college.[2] But does this hold for Catholic college students, who tend to be more intellectually restricted than non-Catholics as they enter college?

Data in chapter 4 have made it clear that at the time they enter college, contemporary Catholic college students are less intellectual and autonomous in their attitudes and values than other students. Even the Catholics who attend secular colleges, and who appear to be more intellectually oriented than their peers at Catholic colleges,

[1] Jacob (1957, 1958).
[2] Trent and Medsker (1967).

score lower than non-Catholics on measures of intellectuality. Assuming that students in general do increase in level of intellectual disposition during college, do these Catholic students, both those attending Catholic colleges and those at secular colleges, increase in this respect as much as do non-Catholics?

In this chapter we will look at the changes in intellectual disposition that occur among college students in the different samples. The groups to be considered are those for whom Omnibus Personality Inventory scores are available both as freshmen and seniors. Such longitudinal information is available for students in the West Coast, National, and National Merit Scholarship samples. In chapter 4 entering freshmen in the West Coast and National samples were examined; now we are only concerned with those who remained in college for four years. When we compare the scores of freshmen with those of seniors, we are considering the same subjects, so that we may see directly what personality changes occurred among these students during their college years.

When we compare the scores for the total group of freshmen in chapter 4 with the freshman scores of those who persisted in college, we find that the scores of the persisters are not appreciably different from those of the total freshman group. For example, the standard mean Thinking Introversion score for the total group of freshman Catholic college men examined in chapter 4 was 43.9, and the freshman score for those who remained in college was 43.6. The mean Thinking Introversion score for the total group of non-Catholic freshman men was 50.1; the freshman score for those who persisted was 50.7. In intellectual disposition, therefore, the students who remained in college appeared essentially no more or no less select as freshmen than their classmates who withdrew from college.

The persisters are more select in numbers, however. The numbers of students considered in this chapter are relatively small compared to those in the previous chapter because of the heavy rate of attrition among the students originally observed as freshmen. Approximately half of the students in the National Sample withdrew from college by 1963, and the dropout rate was much higher in some institutions. However, the responding students are highly representative of the subjects in the original samples who persisted in college for four years. More than 70 per cent of the persisters in the National Sample are included, and an even greater proportion of persisters in the West Coast and National Merit Scholarship samples are included.

We will be particularly concerned with the way Catholic college

TABLE 11. *Standard Mean OPI Intellective Scores, Seniors, West Coast Sample*

College Group (No. in Parentheses)	Thinking Introversion	Theoretical Orientation	Complexity	Estheticism	Nonauthoritarianism
Catholic (243)	50.2	45.3	48.5	52.3	46.5
Secular Catholic (54)	53.7	50.3	50.0	54.0	55.1
Non-Catholic (324)	54.4	52.4	53.4	53.4	58.3
Critical ratio					
Catholic *vs.* secular Catholic	2.18*	3.15**	.93+	1.23+	4.50**
Catholic *vs.* non-Catholic	4.99**	9.15**	5.53**	1.34+	14.60**
Secular Catholic *vs.* non-Catholic	.45+	1.28+	2.23*	.48+	1.80+

$^+ p =$ not significant
$^* p \leq .05$
$^{**} p \leq .01$

students, secular college Catholics, and non-Catholic students compare intellectually as seniors; and with what is most important, the amount that each group changed from their freshman to their senior year. In our comparison of the differences in amount of change exhibited by the three groups, we will provide answers to the key questions: Did any particular group change significantly more than others? Are students in some colleges more likely to change than students in other colleges? After observing students as groups, we will look at several examples of individuals who have changed in either a very positive or a negative way on the highly important dimension of autonomy, as measured by the Social Maturity scale.

The significantly lower intellectual level observed among the Catholic college freshmen in the West Coast Sample compared with Catholic and non-Catholic students in secular colleges in 1959 remained when the persisters among these students were compared four years later in 1963. Table 11 shows that as seniors, the Catholic college students obtained the lowest mean scores of all students on each of the Omnibus Personality Inventory intellective scales. Only on the Estheticism scale did the Catholic and non-Catholic seniors fail to differ significantly. The Catholic college seniors scored significantly lower than the secular college Catholics on all scales but Estheticism and Complexity.

Not only did the Catholic college students score significantly lower than the others on most scales, but on three scales their scores, even as seniors, fell below the normative mean obtained several years previously by a large group of public college and university freshmen. The Catholic college students' scores of 45.3 on Theoretical Orientation, 48.5 on Complexity, and 46.5 on Nonauthoritarianism fall between approximately 5 and 12 standard points below the mean scores of the non-Catholics. The difference exceeds a whole standard deviation on the Nonauthoritarianism scale. Their mean Thinking Introversion score (indicating preference for reflective, abstract thought) barely reaches that obtained by the freshman normative group. It is, therefore, disconcerting that as seniors these students did not display a greater openness in their approach to life and were not more disposed to engage in critical and reflective thinking as measured by the various personality scales. At the same time, however, the Catholic college students did nearly reach the degree of esthetic concern that is manifested by the non-Catholics.

The difference between the two groups of Catholic seniors, those at Catholic colleges and those at secular colleges, on Nonauthoritarianism is almost as great as the difference found between the Catholic college students and non-Catholics on this scale. Catholics at Catholic colleges had a score of 46.5, compared with 55.1 for Catholics at secular colleges, and 58.3 for non-Catholics. Catholics who attended secular colleges were already, as freshmen, less authoritarian than Catholic college students; however, the difference between the two groups was much greater at the senior year. This may be the result of a predisposition among the secular college Catholics to grow in this direction, or it may be the effect of attendance at the secular college.

Data examined separately from the text show that the greatest variation by sex occurs on the Theoretical Orientation and Estheticism scales. The Theoretical Orientation scale measures, to some extent, an interest in applied as well as theoretical science and is a scale on which men usually score higher than women. The Catholic and non-Catholic senior men at the secular colleges in the West Coast Sample scored approximately 6 standard points above the women on Theoretical Orientation. The women's scores are very close to the freshman normative mean, with the men's scores exceeding the mean by over 5 points. In contrast, the Catholic college men scored just 3 points higher than the women on Theoretical Orientation, and scores for both the Catholic college senior men and women fell below the freshman mean.

Women usually score higher on the Estheticism scale than men.

The women in all three groups scored more than 6 points above the men and were all well above the normative mean. Men at the secular colleges also scored above the mean, but the Catholic college men were 2 points below the mean.

There was little difference between the Catholic men and women on the Complexity scale. Non-Catholic men obtained a mean score 3.5 points higher than the women, however. At the secular colleges, men scored somewhat higher than women on Thinking Introversion and Nonauthoritarianism, with both men and women scoring well above the mean. But at the Catholic colleges the situation was reversed. Catholic women were slightly higher than the men on these scales, and the only score above the mean was the women's Thinking Introversion score. Thus, if the Catholic college women cannot be said to be very intellectual at graduation from college, at least they appear to be more intellectually disposed than the men, as indicated by their higher Thinking Introversion and Nonauthoritarianism scores, their almost equal Complexity scores, radically higher Estheticism scores, and the relatively slight difference in their Theoretical Orientation scores.

The more intellectual appearance of Catholic college women may result from the fact that a smaller proportion of Catholic women than men attend college and that those who do attend are therefore a more select group, thus scoring higher. Non-Catholic women also attend in lesser numbers than non-Catholic men (although the proportional difference is not as great as for Catholic men and women) and so these women might also be considered a more select group than the men. The scores of non-Catholic women did not exceed those of non-Catholic men, however.

The finding that Catholic college women appear to be somewhat more intellectually oriented than Catholic college men corroborates the conclusions reached in the last chapter, based on environmental assessment determined by the College and University Environment Scales. Women's colleges were uniformly rated higher in Scholarship and Awareness on the CUES scales. It may be that in their drive toward greater status and affluence, Catholic men have not assimilated intellectual values even to the extent that Catholic women have, or it may be that they are attending colleges—as indicated by the CUES data—that have been characterized by less intellectually stimulating environments.

Since ability has some relationship to intellectuality, students in the West Coast Sample were also divided into high and low ability levels, to see if this would affect the differences in intellectual disposition previously observed among the three groups of seniors. The students were classified at high and low ability levels according to whether they scored in the upper or lower half of the sample's distribution of academic aptitude scores. Catholic college students and Catholics at secular colleges could thereby be contrasted to non-Catholics at the same general ability level (Table 12). We saw in chapter 3 that as freshmen, the Catholic college students' ability scores were above those of non-Catholic college students. Yet these students were lower than other students on almost all the intellectuality scales. How do these

TABLE 12. *Standard Mean OPI Intellective Scores, Seniors, West Coast Sample, by Ability Level*

Ability Level and College Group (No. in Parentheses)	Thinking Introversion	Theoretical Orientation	Complexity	Estheticism	Nonauthoritarianism
High ability					
Catholic (122)	52.2	47.9	50.3	54.0	48.7
Secular Catholic (14)	56.7	52.1	51.3	55.6	59.0
Non-Catholic (164)	56.3	53.7	55.0	54.6	59.6
Low ability					
Catholic (120)	48.1	42.5	46.7	50.4	44.2
Secular Catholic (38)	53.4	50.6	50.2	53.7	53.9
Non-Catholic (148)	52.2	51.2	51.7	52.0	56.8
Critical ratio					
High ability					
Catholic *vs.* secular Catholic	1.63+	1.67+	.34+	.56+	3.79**
Catholic *vs.* non-Catholic	3.52**	5.56**	3.91**	.50+	9.63**
Secular Catholic *vs.* non-Catholic	.12+	.64+	1.24+	.36+	.13+
Low ability					
Catholic *vs.* secular Catholic	2.59**	3.87**	1.88+	1.86+	3.91**
Catholic *vs.* non-Catholic	3.42**	7.40**	3.83**	1.40+	10.57**
Secular Catholic *vs.* non-Catholic	.56+	.28+	.82+	.90+	1.14+

+ p = not significant
** $p \leq .01$

students look as seniors compared with other students of equal ability?

High-ability seniors scored higher than low-ability seniors in the same schools on the various Omnibus Personality Inventory intellectuality scales, with all differences reaching statistical significance except for the Catholics at secular colleges. The largest consistent differences between ability levels were found on the Thinking Introversion and Nonauthoritarianism scales. These differences in intellectual disposition between ability levels were anticipated, but more notable than these were the differences among the Catholic college students, secular Catholics, and non-Catholics at the same ability level. On every scale except Estheticism, the non-Catholic students scored significantly higher than the Catholic college students at the same ability level.

High-ability non-Catholics scored almost 6 points above equally able Catholic college students on the Theoretical Orientation scale, and at the low ability level, non-Catholics scored 9 points above Catholic college students on the scale. Less than 2 points separated the two groups of students at secular colleges, with non-Catholics scoring slightly higher at each ability level.

At both ability levels, non-Catholics scored 4 points higher on Thinking Introversion than did Catholic college students, with Catholics at secular colleges scoring the highest on this scale. Non-Catholics scored approximately 5 points higher than Catholic college students in Complexity, at both ability levels. Complexity was the one measure on which high ability Catholics at secular colleges were more similar to other Catholics than to non-Catholics. Catholic college seniors obtained a mean score of 50.3; the secular Catholics, 51.3; and the non-Catholics, 55.

On the Nonauthoritarianism scale, non-Catholics at the high ability level scored 11 standard points higher than Catholic college students, and non-Catholics at the low ability level scored 12 points higher than Catholic college students. This large difference in Nonauthoritarianism was not found, however, between non-Catholics and Catholics attending secular colleges. At the high ability level, non-Catholics scored less than 1 point higher than Catholics on this scale; and at the low ability level, the non-Catholics scored 3 points higher. The Catholics at secular colleges at the high ability level had a mean score of 59 on Nonauthoritarianism, almost a whole standard deviation above the mean. Even the high-ability Catholic college persisters did not reach the normative freshman mean, and the low-ability seniors were more than half a standard deviation below the mean.

Seniors at the secular colleges scored above the freshman normative mean on all scales regardless of ability level. High-ability Catholic college students were above the normative mean on the Thinking Introversion, Complexity, and Estheticism scales, and the low-ability Catholic college students were above the mean only on the Estheticism scale.

When Catholic college men and women were examined separately by ability level and compared to non-Catholic men and women at the same ability levels, non-Catholic men were significantly higher on every scale except Estheticism, at both the high and low ability levels. The difference between Catholic college and non-Catholic men in Theoretical Orientation was 9 points at both ability levels. Non-Catholic women were higher than Catholic college women on all scales, but the difference for high-ability women did not reach significance on the Complexity or Estheticism scales, and the difference for low-ability women was not significant on Thinking Introversion or Estheticism.

Differences in intellectuality among these seniors cannot be attributed to differences in ability. Regardless of the scale considered, the sex, or the ability level of the students, the Catholic college students scored uniformly lower than the other students. Although there were comparatively fewer Catholics at the high ability level in the secular college group, the Catholics who attended secular colleges compared favorably with the non-Catholics in intellectual orientation nonetheless. When compared by ability level, the secular college Catholics are on a par with non-Catholics in intellectual disposition except in Complexity among high-ability students.

The students were also divided by socioeconomic level on the assumption that in a more affluent environment students have more opportunity, and are more encouraged, to participate in activities that will develop intellectual potential. Three levels of socioeconomic status were distinguished, determined by the occupations of the students' fathers as described in chapter 3. Since few students in the sample came from the low socioeconomic level, middle and low socioeconomic levels have been combined. Thus Catholic college, secular Catholic, and non-Catholic students at the high socioeconomic level can be compared, as can these groups of students at the lower socioeconomic levels (Table 13). As defined in chapter 3, the high socioeconomic level includes all students whose fathers are engaged in professional and managerial occupations.

At the high socioeconomic level, non-Catholics scored significantly higher on all scales than Catholic college seniors. At the low socioeconomic level non-Catholics scored significantly higher on all scales

TABLE 13. *Standard Mean OPI Intellective Scores, Seniors, West Coast Sample, by Socioeconomic Level*

Socioeconomic Level and College Group (No. in Parentheses)	Thinking Introversion	Theoretical Orientation	Complexity	Estheticism	Nonauthoritarianism
High socioeconomic level					
Catholic (76)	49.5	44.7	47.0	51.2	46.8
Secular Catholic (25)	51.6	50.6	49.9	50.7	54.3
Non-Catholic (155)	56.0	52.9	55.1	54.2	58.5
Low socioeconomic level					
Catholic (165)	50.4	45.5	49.1	52.7	46.3
Secular Catholic (28)	55.1	49.9	50.3	57.1	55.9
Non-Catholic (165)	52.8	51.9	51.7	52.6	58.0
Critical ratio					
High socioeconomic level					
Catholic *vs.*					
secular Catholic	0.98+	2.68**	1.21+	0.22+	3.42**
Catholic *vs.*					
non-Catholic	4.74**	6.18**	5.29**	2.23*	9.19**
Secular Catholic *vs.*					
non-Catholic	1.99*	1.24+	2.39*	1.69+	1.93+
Low socioeconomic level					
Catholic *vs.*					
secular Catholic	2.19*	2.11*	0.59+	2.32*	4.31**
Catholic *vs.*					
non-Catholic	2.29*	6.33**	2.28*	0.19+	10.42**
Secular Catholic *vs.*					
non-Catholic	0.98+	0.96+	0.58+	2.24*	8.16**

+ p = not significant
* $p \leq .05$
** $p \leq .01$

except Estheticism, but only on Nonauthoritarianism and Theoretical Orientation are the differences as great as at the high socioeconomic level. Catholics at secular colleges scored between Catholic college students and non-Catholics on all scales except Estheticism at the high socioeconomic level, but their Thinking Introversion and Estheticism scores were higher than those of non-Catholics at the lower socioeconomic level.

Although we saw that students at the high ability level scored consistently higher on the personality scales than those at the lower ability level, the same pattern did not hold for socioeconomic level. The differences between the Catholic college students at the high and low socioeconomic levels was only about 1 point on most scales but it was the lower socioeconomic group which had slightly higher scores on all scales except Nonauthoritarianism. Among secular college Catholics, students at the lower socioeconomic level also scored above their peers, with the greatest differences shown on Thinking Introversion and Estheticism.

Among non-Catholics, however, the higher status students scored higher on all scales. Thus within Catholic colleges, students at the lower socioeconomic level appear to be somewhat more intellectual than those who could be expected to have more access to intellectual and cultural activities. As indicated elsewhere, the increasing affluence of Catholics has apparently not led to an increase in such interests.

To this point, the data show only that the West Coast students who remained in Catholic colleges for four years were intellectually restricted compared with their Catholic and non-Catholic peers who persisted in public colleges. This does not mean, however, that these students did not grow in intellectual disposition during college. All three groups changed in measured attitude between their freshman and senior years, even though they differed from one another in level of intellectual disposition as seniors. To investigate how much they developed, and whether students in one type of college developed more than others, we compared the freshman and senior scores obtained by these groups. We then tested the difference in these scores for statistical significance through the use of a t technique devised for the analysis of correlated means.[3] The results are shown in Table 14, and the t technique employed is described in Appendix C.

Despite the fact that these three groups of students maintained the same relative position intellectually as freshmen and as seniors, each group changed significantly in their mean scores on the various scales, in all but 2 cases beyond the 1 per cent level of confidence. All changes were in the direction of significantly greater intellectual disposition, and for each group the greatest change of all was in Nonauthoritarianism. The average change in standard mean points on the Nonauthoritarianism scale was over 7 points. The groups obtained comparable

---

[3] Since the same individuals were responding to the same scales in 1959 and 1963, their mean scores are considered correlated. Therefore the statistical technique described in Appendix C was used to test the significance of difference between correlated means.

TABLE 14. *Standard Mean OPI Intellective Scores for Students as Freshmen and Seniors, West Coast Sample*

College Group (No. in Parentheses)	Thinking Introversion	Theoretical Orientation	Complexity	Estheticism	Nonauthoritarianism
Catholic (243)					
Freshman	45.7	42.4	44.3	48.3	39.5
Senior	50.2	45.3	48.5	52.3	46.5
Difference	4.5**	2.9**	4.2**	4.0**	7.0**
Secular Catholic (54)					
Freshman	49.5	47.4	46.5	51.3	45.4
Senior	53.7	50.3	50.0	54.0	55.1
Difference	4.2**	2.9*	3.5**	2.7*	9.7**
Non-Catholic (324)					
Freshman	50.2	50.7	49.3	50.5	51.4
Senior	54.4	52.4	53.4	53.4	58.3
Difference	4.2**	1.7**	4.1**	2.9**	6.9**

* $p \leq .05$
** $p \leq .01$

increases of about 4 standard points on the Thinking Introversion and Complexity scales. The least change occurred on the Theoretical Orientation and Estheticism scales.

It might be assumed that students at the higher ability level would be more likely to change than those with less ability. But when students were divided into high and low ability groups (not shown in table form), it was found that non-Catholic students and students at Catholic colleges changed significantly on most scales regardless of ability level. Both the high- and low-ability Catholic college and non-Catholic women changed significantly on all scales. The high-ability Catholic college men also changed significantly on all scales, and the low-ability men in these schools changed significantly on all scales except Theoretical Orientation and Complexity. The non-Catholic men, regardless of ability level, changed significantly on all scales except Theoretical Orientation.

When the Catholics in the sample who were attending secular colleges were divided by ability level, the numbers in some cases were not large enough for changes to reach statistical significance. None of the changes for high-ability women were significant, and high-ability men showed significant change only on Theoretical Orientation and Nonauthoritarianism. At the low ability level, all changes except Estheticism were significant for the women, and all except Theoretical Orientation were significant for the men.

The intellectual development of the Catholic college and secular college students on the personality scales has been graphed in Figure 4, which shows the standard mean scores obtained by the students in each group as freshmen and seniors. The growth shown on these scales may not be all their colleges might wish, and seniors may not be at a level of development that would seem commensurate with a flourishing of intellectual interests and productivity, but for Catholics and non-Catholics alike, the development is observable and statistically significant.

We have seen that students in all three groups increased significantly on almost all the intellective scales. The next question that may be

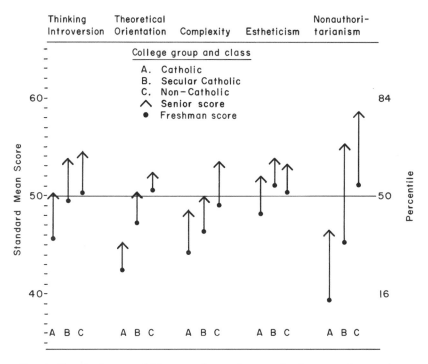

Fig. 4. Standard mean OPI scores for students as freshmen and as seniors, West Coast Sample.

asked is whether any one group changed significantly more than the others. The answer for the West Coast Sample is no. The complex statistical treatment which led to this simple answer may be found in Appendix C. In the manner of the T^2 analysis, this treatment tested the significance of the difference of the variation of the difference or change in scores obtained by the several groups. Although there was variation among groups in the amount of change that occurred, differences were generally small and none of the difference between groups in the amount of change reached statistical significance.

Thus, although Catholic college students as seniors scored lower than students at secular colleges on most of the intellective scales, they showed about as much intellectual growth as non-Catholic students. Perhaps, therefore, Catholic colleges are doing as much as could be expected of them; the colleges simply never overcome the intellectual deficit with which these students enter college.

Much the same situation prevails for students in the more broadly based National Sample, but with some exceptions. The 1963 intellective scores of the Catholic college students, secular college Catholics, and non-Catholic students in the National Sample are shown in Table 15. Again it is to be noted that the subjects represented in the table comprise over 70 per cent of the students in the original sample of nearly 10,000 high school graduates who entered and then persisted in college for four years.

As noted in the previous chapter, all Omnibus Personality Inventory scales are not available for all samples. The Theoretical Orientation scale was not administered to the National Sample, and Estheticism and Autonomy were administered to students in the National Sample as seniors only. The Social Maturity scale, a complex expansion of the Nonauthoritarianism scale, was normed on the National Sample itself, including the subjects who did not enter college. Consequently, the standard scores obtained by the college students on this scale appear inordinately high.

The Catholic college students obtained the lowest mean score on each scale included in Table 15. They did not differ significantly from the secular college Catholics and non-Catholics in measured attraction to reflective, abstract thinking and interest in literature, art, and music, however, as is manifest by the critical ratios of their scores on Thinking Introversion and Estheticism.

When we go beyond a basic interest in abstract thought and artistic matters, we find significant differences among the groups of students

TABLE 15. *Standard Mean OPI Intellective Scores, Seniors, National Sample*

College Group (No. in Parentheses)	Thinking Introversion	Complexity	Estheticism	Nonauthoritarianism	Autonomy	Social Maturity
Catholic (99)	51.8	46.4	49.9	46.7	45.5	54.5
Secular Catholic (183)	52.6	51.6	51.8	51.1	52.0	61.2
Non-Catholic (1,124)	52.7	51.3	51.4	53.2	53.9	63.9
Critical ratio Catholic vs.						
secular Catholic	.58+	4.10**	1.27+	3.52**	6.01**	4.85**
Catholic vs.						
non-Catholic	.79+	4.90**	1.30+	6.40**	9.60**	8.60**
Secular Catholic vs.						
non-Catholic	.13+	.25+	.45+	2.50*	2.60**	2.70**

+ p = not significant
* $p \leq .05$
** $p \leq .01$

with respect to all other measured dimensions of intellectuality. The Catholic and non-Catholic students at secular colleges were significantly higher in Complexity than Catholic college students as freshmen and remained higher as seniors. The Catholic college seniors obtained a standard mean score of 46.4 on the Complexity scale, and both the Catholic and non-Catholic persisters at secular colleges obtained mean scores over a point above the normative mean of 50. Comparable differences exist on the Nonauthoritarianism scale. The Catholic college senior mean score of 46.7 is below the freshman normative mean, and is significantly different from that of the secular Catholics, who scored over 51, and that of the non-Catholics, who scored over 53. Although the secular Catholics are less authoritarian than Catholics at Catholic colleges, they are still significantly more authoritarian than non-Catholics.

The twenty-item Nonauthoritarianism scale measures one aspect of autonomy. Seniors in 1963 were also tested with the Autonomy scale, which is a more comprehensive measure of autonomous thought and action. The forty-item Autonomy scale does not duplicate any of the Nonauthoritarianism items. But the students responded in such a similar manner to the two scales that their standard mean scores were within a point of each other. The mean Autonomy score of 45.5

placed the Catholic college seniors nearly one-half a standard deviation below the normative freshman mean. The Catholics at secular colleges scored significantly above the normative mean on the Autonomy scale, but significantly below the non-Catholics, whose score of 53.9 placed them close to one-half a standard deviation above the normative mean.

As indicated earlier, the standard scores for all students were higher on Social Maturity than on the other scales because they were normed on the original National Sample. Nevertheless, the mean scores of the three groups have almost the same relation to one another as their scores on the Autonomy scale. On both scales the mean scores of the Catholic college and non-Catholic seniors differ by well over 8 standard points, and the mean scores of the two groups of Catholics differ by over 6.5 points. On both scales, too, each group scored differently from the others beyond the 1 per cent level of significance.

Students in the National Sample who persisted in Catholic colleges compared favorably with their Catholic and non-Catholic peers in attraction to the contemplative and esthetic in life as measured by the Thinking Introversion and Estheticism scales. But on the West Coast and even nationally, the Catholic college seniors showed much less interest in intellectual inquiry and in the tolerance for ambiguity demanded by intellectual inquiry as measured by the Complexity scale. Above all, students who persisted in Catholic colleges were far less autonomous, open minded, and flexible in their thinking. The markedly greater degree of authoritarianism among the Catholic college students is evident on the three scales measuring dimensions of autonomy. Therefore any possible—but questionable—anti-Catholic bias contained in the data discussed in chapter 4 and Appendix C would appear to pertain to all three scales. Although persisting secular college Catholics manifested less autonomy than their non-Catholic classmates, they showed considerably more autonomy and complexity of outlook than their fellow Catholics attending Catholic colleges. As with the West Coast Sample, these differences persist when we hold constant levels of ability and socioeconomic status.

In the National Sample the students were categorized at high, middle, and low levels of ability, depending upon whether they fell in the upper 30 per cent, middle 40 per cent, or lower 30 per cent of the sample's distribution of School and College Ability Test scores. At the high ability level non-Catholics and students at Catholic colleges scored significantly higher than students at middle and low ability levels on the Omnibus Personality Inventory scales. High-ability secular Catholics also scored somewhat higher than lower-ability secular Catholics, but differences were less than among other students. When students were compared within ability levels, non-Catholics scored significantly higher than Catholic college students on all scales except Estheticism and Thinking Introversion. Scores of secular Catholics fell between those for Catholic college and non-Catholic students, but were slightly closer to the non-Catholics on the autonomy measures at both high and middle ability levels.

Catholic college students and non-Catholics at the high socioeconomic level scored higher on the scales than their peers at the lower socioeconomic levels. However, among secular Catholics, students at the lower socioeconomic levels scored above those at the high socioeconomic level. In the West Coast Sample the lower-status secular Catholics also scored higher, but in that sample, the same situation prevailed at the Catholic colleges. Thus although among non-Catholics there is a consistently positive relationship between level of intellectuality and socioeconomic status, among Catholics there is not. In fact, there are indications in these two samples of a negative relationship between intellectuality and socioeconomic status among Catholics. This negative relationship is not strong enough to warrant extensive speculation about its causes, but it is an interesting phenomenon and one which warrants further investigation. In the meantime, it is evident that neither ability nor socioeconomic status can account for the difference in intellectual disposition observed among the students.

The persisters in the National Sample were also compared on four of the scales by sex, according to the type of college they attended. In this way, possible sex differences in intellectual disposition could be noted, and, more importantly, the intellectual disposition of Catholic college students could be compared with the disposition of students who persisted in other church-related and private, nonsectarian colleges and universities, apart from public institutions. The results are shown in Table 16.

In general, the men scored higher than the women on the Complexity and Autonomy scales, and the women scored higher on the Thinking Introversion and Estheticism scales. The Catholic college men obtained the lowest scores of all groups of men on each scale, but did not differ much in raw points and not at all statistically when compared with the public college men on the Thinking Introversion and Estheticism scales. All other groups of men scored significantly higher on all four scales than the Catholic college men, with the exception of the sectarian college men on Thinking Introversion. The

Catholic college women did not differ significantly from any of the other groups of women on the Thinking Introversion and Estheticism scales, but the women in all other types of colleges obtained mean scores on the Complexity and Autonomy scales that were significantly higher than the scores of the Catholic college women.

TABLE 16. *Standard Mean OPI Intellective Scores by Type of College Attended, Seniors, National Sample*[a]

Sex and College (No. in Parentheses)	Thinking Introversion	Complexity	Estheticism	Autonomy
Men				
Catholic (85)	50.2	47.4	46.6	45.8
Public (793)	50.6+	51.4**	46.8+	52.2**
Nonsectarian (93)	53.7*	53.5**	50.0*	55.0**
Sectarian (142)	53.0+	51.7**	50.0*	51.5**
Women				
Catholic (69)	52.7	44.4	53.6	44.0
Public (738)	52.2+	49.7**	53.5+	52.0**
Nonsectarian (75)	56.1+	52.9**	56.5+	53.9**
Sectarian (140)	51.0+	48.3*	54.0+	49.6**

[a] Men and women in Catholic colleges total 154, and students in other colleges total 1,981. Other analyses have included only students for whom complete longitudinal data were available, whereas Table 16 includes all students for whom senior OPI scores were available. Catholics in secular colleges are included with non-Catholics, according to type of school attended. The suprascribed symbols with the mean scores in the table indicate the significance level of the critical ratio of the difference in scores obtained by each group on each scale, in all cases compared with the score of the Catholic college students.
+ $p =$ not significant
* $p \leq .05$
** $p \leq .01$

The striking differences observed between students in Catholic and non-Catholic colleges in complexity of outlook and autonomous attitudes held true even when Catholic college students were compared with other church-college students. Although the results are not shown in table form, it was just as true when students in Catholic universities (which grant doctoral degrees) were considered separately from Catholics who attended four- and five-year Catholic colleges. Unlike the non-Catholic students, the Catholic university students tended to be at a lower level of intellectual disposition than the Catholic college students.

The Catholic college and university students in the National Sample were considerably more limited in intellectual disposition in many ways than other students, and they did not excel the others intellectually in any way. But as with the students in the West Coast Sample, both the Catholic and non-Catholic college students showed signs of intellectual development on the basis of their scores obtained in 1963 compared with their freshman scores in 1959 (Table 17).

TABLE 17. *Standard Mean OPI Intellective Scores for Students as Freshmen and Seniors, National Sample*

College Group (No. in Parentheses)	Thinking Introversion	Complexity	Nonauthori- tarianism	Social Maturity
Catholic (99)				
Freshman	48.5	45.9	39.7	47.6
Senior	51.8	46.4	46.7	54.5
Difference	3.3**	0.5+	7.0**	6.9**
Secular Catholic (183)				
Freshman	47.1	48.6	42.8	50.8
Senior	52.6	51.6	51.1	61.2
Difference	5.5**	3.0**	8.3**	10.4**
Non-Catholic (1,124)				
Freshman	49.9	50.7	46.4	54.2
Senior	52.7	51.3	53.2	63.9
Difference	2.8**	0.6*	6.8**	9.7**

+ $p =$ not significant
* $p \leq .05$
** $p \leq .01$

Four of the Omnibus Personality Inventory intellectuality scales were administered to the National Sample in 1959 and 1963. The secular college Catholics and non-Catholics obtained significantly higher mean scores on all four of the scales between 1959 and 1963. The Catholic college students changed significantly on all scales but Complexity, which measures tendency toward intellectual inquiry and tolerance for ambiguity. The change was greatest for all three groups on the two scales measuring autonomy and openness of thinking, but the secular college Catholics and non-Catholics changed an average of 3 standard points more in their mean Social Maturity scores than did the Catholic college students.

The students in the West Coast Sample changed significantly and manifestly on the Complexity scale; however, the students in the National Sample showed the least change on this scale. Only the secular college Catholics varied to any appreciable extent in their mean Complexity scores between 1959 and 1963. The non-Catholics changed significantly in their mean Complexity score in 1963, but the change was less than 1 point. The fact that this change was statistically significant when the change exhibited by the Catholic college students was not may likely be attributed to the much larger number of non-Catholics. Complexity of outlook has been found to be a particularly stable trait among college populations and relatively unrelated to duration in college. We do not know why the West Coast Sample exhibited so much more change in Complexity than did the National Sample.

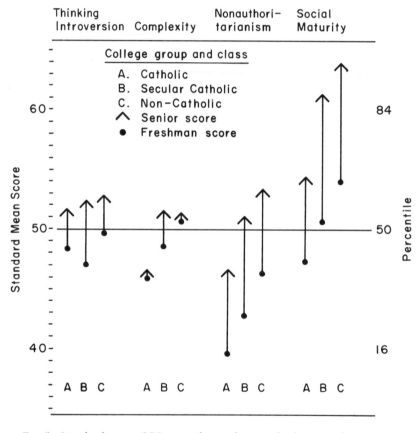

FIG. 5. Standard mean OPI scores for students as freshmen and as seniors, National Sample.

The differences in standard mean scores obtained by the three groups in the National Sample between 1959 and 1963 are shown in Figure 5. With the exception of the Social Maturity scale, all standard scores are based on the freshman scores established by the original normative sample of the Omnibus Personality Inventory. Again, the normative mean is 50, and the standard deviation is 10.

The Catholic college students changed significantly between the two time periods on all scales except Complexity and showed essentially the same amount of change as the non-Catholics on all but the Social Maturity scale. The secular college Catholics showed the most change. The statistical tests of the significance of the differences in mean differences obtained by the three groups in the National Sample may be found in Appendix C. The secular college Catholics changed significantly more than the Catholic college students on all but the Nonauthoritarianism scale. They also changed more than their non-Catholic classsmates on all but the Social Maturity Scale. Non-Catholics in turn changed significantly more on the Social Maturity scale than the Catholic college students.

The secular college Catholics and non-Catholics were at a higher level of intellectual disposition, and particularly at a higher level of autonomy, than were the Catholic college students both as freshmen and four years later. The secular college students also changed more on these dimensions between 1959 and 1963. The West Coast Catholic college students, too, were lowest in intellectual and autonomous disposition both in 1959 and 1963. But they changed proportionately as much as the secular college students between the two time periods.

Since the two samples differ in amount of manifest intellectual development, conclusions about the implications of the different data must be made cautiously and tentatively. It seems noteworthy, however, that in the National Sample, the Catholics in secular colleges, who were more removed from their church system than the Catholic college students, showed the most change in attitude and values.

Although Catholic college students scored uniformly lower than secular college students, it seemed likely that there would be some Catholic colleges in which students would be more on an intellectual level with students in non-Catholic colleges. Certainly this was true of intellectual environment perceived by students through CUES data in the previous chapter. Scores on three of the Omnibus Personality Inventory intellective scales, Thinking Introversion, Complexity, and Nonauthoritarianism, were available for students in both the West Coast and National samples as freshmen and seniors. Since Catholic students in the National Sample attended 74 Catholic colleges, the number in any one school was very small. However, enough students attended three colleges so that their scores and those of students in the five West Coast Catholic colleges could be compared. The eight colleges include two men's colleges, four women's colleges, and two coeducational colleges. Three of these institutions are universities. Figure 6 depicts the pattern of scores obtained by the students as freshmen and seniors in these eight colleges on the three scales.

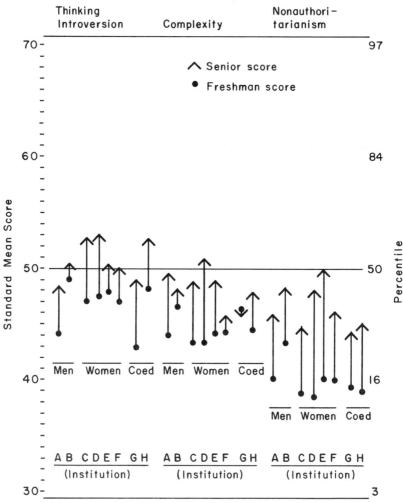

FIG. 6. Comparison of standard mean OPI intellective scores for students as freshmen and as seniors in 8 Catholic colleges.

Students in all the schools increased in Nonauthoritarianism, but in no school did the senior Nonauthoritarianism mean exceed that obtained by the normative freshmen; seniors at all eight Catholic colleges had a standard mean score below 50. Every school was below average, and in three of these schools, students as seniors were still half a standard deviation below the normative mean. Two of the three universities, one on the West Coast and one in the Midwest, were among the lowest three schools in scores. The three schools whose students obtained the highest mean Nonauthoritarianism scores in 1963 included two women's colleges and the third university. It is worth noting that at the two women's colleges the students increased 10 standard points in Nonauthoritarianism, one whole standard deviation, whereas the university men, who obtained a higher mean score as freshmen, increased only 5 points. At three of the schools students began with standard scores so low—below 40—that even with considerable growth in Nonauthoritarianism they increased only to a standard score of about 45.

West Coast Catholic college students changed significantly in Complexity as a group, but this was not true for the National Sample. Figure 6 shows that definite change occurred in individual schools, however. At six of the eight schools scores started below 45; the students in two of these colleges obtained mean Complexity scores at or slightly above the normative mean four years later. The two schools whose students scored the highest in Complexity as freshmen showed the least growth on this dimension as seniors. In fact, the students in one of these schools actually decreased in Complexity.

Having the highest scores at the outset evidently does not insure continued intellectual growth; and it cannot be argued that these students had already reached an optimum level of development, since their scores were high only in relation to those of other Catholic college students. The group of students who showed the least growth in Complexity also showed the least growth in Thinking Introversion. Here again the students started higher than those in the other schools but increased less, so that their freshman scores were slightly below the mean and their senior scores barely above it, with three other schools rating higher. The group of students that showed the greatest growth in Thinking Introversion was the one that decreased in Complexity.

Perhaps these students have little tolerance for living with the questions but enjoy reading the answers; and this possibility may apply to Catholic college students on the whole, considering all the data reviewed in this volume. The increase in Thinking Introversion, although the largest for any school, still left that school below the mean, with only one school lower. These students were also lowest in Nonauthoritarianism. While Thinking Introversion increases somewhat, it may do so within categorical ways of thinking introvertedly. Both the Complexity and Nonauthoritarianism scores are indicative of the limits set: closed-system thinking within defined and accepted areas. Thus many Catholic college students probably enjoy reading *the* answers to important questions rather than seeking their own solutions.

The overall picture of the three intellective scales shows that only in three Catholic schools were the seniors found significantly above the normative mean, and then only on the Thinking Introversion scale. And it must be remembered that these are students who have completed four years of Catholic college being compared to a normative group of freshmen just entering public colleges and universities. Nevertheless, it is evident that definite variation in intellectual development exists among Catholic colleges. Students changed significantly, at the 1 per cent level, at five schools in Thinking Introversion and at four schools in Complexity. In only one school did students fail to change significantly on Nonauthoritarianism. In three schools—two women's colleges and one men's college—students changed significantly on all scales.

This is the picture for the individual Catholic schools. When individuals within the schools are considered, many deviations are found which would place some well above the mean, while leaving many far below it. For example, at a major midwestern Catholic university about 60 per cent of the students increased in Thinking Introversion, but almost 40 per cent decreased. Only half as many students at this university decreased in Nonauthoritarianism as in Thinking Introversion, but this still means that a fifth of the students became more authoritarian after four years of college. More than a third of the students decreased in Complexity, and several of those who decreased the most had the highest Complexity scores as freshmen.

Evidently their college experience was not an enriching one for many of these students, even those who entered with the most intellectual potential as indicated by higher freshman intellective scores. The intellectual attitudes of the university students correspond with the intellectual climate perceived in the universities through the CUES data in the previous chapter. Several times, now, and in several ways, the intellectual qualities of the larger and even more renowned

Catholic universities have not been found to be on a par with the intellectual qualities of the smaller Catholic colleges.

When students in the West Coast Sample were compared according to ability level, the high-ability men and women in Catholic colleges were significantly lower than equally able non-Catholics on most of the intellective measures. When seniors of especially high ability and proven academic achievement, the National Merit Scholars, were compared, Catholics were again found to score below non-Catholics on several scales. (Catholics included those attending Catholic and secular colleges.) As freshmen the Catholics scored significantly lower than non-Catholic National Merit Scholars on Complexity and significantly higher on Authoritarianism.[4] As shown in Table 18, the Catholics were also significantly different on these two scales as seniors in 1960. Scores in Thinking Introversion are the same for Catholics and non-Catholics. Catholics are two points lower in Estheticism, but the difference does not reach statistical significance. Differences in Authoritarianism are significant beyond the 1 per cent level, and the Complexity score difference is significant at the 5 per cent level.

TABLE 18. *Standard Mean OPI Intellective Scores, National Merit Scholars as College Seniors*

Student Group (No. in Parentheses)	Thinking Introversion	Complexity	Estheticism	Authoritarianism[a]
Catholic (44)	52.2	53.0	52.0	48.7
Non-Catholic (360)	52.2	56.7	54.1	43.9
(Critical ratio)	(.05+)	(2.37*)	(1.15+)	(2.99**)

[a] Higher scores on the Authoritarianism scale indicate greater authoritarianism. On the Nonauthoritarianism scale used in later forms of the OPI, higher scores indicate less authoritarianism.

$+ p =$ not significant
$* p \leq .05$
$** p \leq .01$

Although the scores of National Merit Catholics do not equal those of the non-Catholics, differences between the groups are generally less than in other samples, and, in contrast to other samples, all the

[4] Omnibus Personality Inventory scores for the National Merit Scholars were standardized on the basis of scores for the total group of Catholic and non-Catholic Merit Scholars, since other normative data were not available for this early form of the Inventory.

scores of the Catholics except one are above the mean. The exception is Authoritarianism, where all students scored below the mean, indicating less authoritarianism. (Again, the Nonauthoritarianism scale used for the West Coast and National samples measures in the opposite direction; higher scores on the Authoritarianism scale indicate greater authoritarianism.)

When the scores of the National Merit men and women are looked at separately, the greatest difference between the Catholic and non-Catholic men is in Complexity. The Catholic men scored 52.7 and non-Catholic men 56.7. The greatest difference between the women, more than 8 points, is on the Authoritarianism scale; Catholic women scored 50.8 and non-Catholic women 42.2, with low scores again indicating less authoritarianism.

When the non-Catholic group is divided by religion, Jewish men average three points higher than Protestants on Complexity and three points lower on Authoritarianism. Protestant men scored 2.5 points higher than Jewish men on Estheticism and were 1 point below the Jewish men on Thinking Introversion. Jewish women scored 3 to 5 points higher than Protestant women on every scale except Authoritarianism, where they scored 6 points lower. Thus the Catholics scored the lowest in intellectual disposition when Catholics and others were compared; and when non-Catholics were compared, Jewish men and women consistently scored in a more intellectual direction.

Although the intellective scores of the select Catholic National Merit Scholars as seniors were low in comparison to those of non-Catholics, these students had changed significantly on the personality scales between their freshman and senior years, as shown in Table 19. Both the Catholic and non-Catholic scholarship winners increased over 6 points in Complexity and decreased more than 5 points in Authoritarianism. Catholic Authoritarianism scores changed the most, decreasing from 56.5 in the freshman year to 48.7 in the senior year. The Catholics changed significantly on three scales—at the 1 per cent level on the Complexity and Authoritarianism scales, and at the 5 per cent level on the Thinking Introversion scale. The non-Catholics changed significantly on all scales, beyond the 1 per cent level of significance.

The differences in the amount of change exhibited by the Catholic and non-Catholic scholarship winners in Thinking Introversion, Estheticism, and Complexity were not significant (see Appendix C). There was a significant difference between Catholics and non-Catholics in the amount they changed on Authoritarianism, however. In contrast to the West Coast and National samples, the National Merit Catholics changed significantly more than non-Catholics on this dimension. Although their scores as seniors were still half a standard deviation above the non-Catholic scores, they did exhibit significantly more change.

These Catholic scholarship winners were superior in ability and academic achievement and were attending some of the nation's most elite schools; the potential for change was certainly there and was to some extent realized. When these students are compared to non-Catholics of similar ability attending many of the same schools, however, one is reminded how far even these students have to go before they reach the intellectual level of their peers.

TABLE 19. *Standard Mean OPI Intellective Scores, National Merit Scholars as Freshmen and Seniors*

Student Group (No. in Parentheses)	Thinking Introversion	Complexity	Estheticism	Authori- tarianism[a]
Catholic (44)				
Freshman	48.4	46.6	49.1	56.5
Senior	52.2	53.0	52.0	48.7
Difference	3.8*	6.4**	2.9+	7.8**
Non-Catholic (360)				
Freshman	50.0	50.2	50.0	49.2
Senior	52.1	56.7	54.1	43.9
Difference	2.1**	6.5**	4.1**	5.3**

[a] Higher scores on the Authoritarianism scale indicate greater authoritarianism. On the Nonauthoritarianism scale used in later forms of the OPI, higher scores indicate less authoritarianism.

+ p = not significant
* $p \leq .05$
** $p \leq .01$

It is particularly in the area of autonomy, or rather authoritarianism, that Catholic college students differ most from non-Catholics. This was found to be true among both freshmen and seniors in the West Coast and National samples, and even among the highly select National Merit Scholarship sample. At the same time, the Catholic Merit Scholars, including those who attended non-Catholic colleges, did at least show a greater change in mean autonomy scores after four years of college than the other scholarship winners. This is extremely important, since autonomy is constituted of the openness, objectivity, independence, and flexibility of thinking that must underlie intellectual endeavor. Because of the importance of autonomy, we decided to explore the manifest development of this trait in the National Sample more definitively than could be done through the data previously presented.

As indicated earlier, an important measure of autonomy is the Social Maturity scale. Persons scoring high in Social Maturity tend to be more mature, realistic, and less authoritarian in their modes of thinking and in their relations with other people. Social Maturity scores were not available for students in the West Coast Sample, but we have looked at them previously for students in the National Sample. As freshmen and as seniors, the mean for Catholic college students was significantly below that for other students. The Catholic college students increased in Social Maturity between 1959 and 1963, but not as much as the secular Catholics and non-Catholics. The Catholic college students obtained a mean Social Maturity score of 47.6 as freshmen and a score of 54.5 four years later, while the Catholics in secular colleges increased from 50.8 to 61.2, and the non-Catholics increased from 54.2 to 63.9. Although the Catholic college students increased their mean Social Maturity score by nearly 7 standard points, the increase of the secular college Catholics and non-Catholics of approximately 10 standard points was significantly greater than that of the Catholic college students.

But these figures give us information only about the mean differences obtained by the groups; they do not tell us about individual differences within the groups in autonomy. To get a more comprehensive picture of the changes that occurred on the Social Maturity scale among the students in the National Sample, the students were categorized according to the amount and direction of change they manifested. This analysis was originally carried out as part of the total study of high school graduates who did and did not enter college, reported in *Beyond High School: A Study of 10,000 High School Graduates*.[5] The Social Maturity scale was chosen for this analysis because it is a comprehensive measure of the autonomy syndrome, and because it has a high internal consistency reliability. Moreover, as was discussed in the previous chapter, there is only one item out of the 67 in the Social Maturity scale that could be construed as biased against Catholics (or any Christian believers).

In the four years from 1959 to 1963 the young adults in the study increased in Social Maturity an average of 4 raw points, which equals

[5] Trent and Medsker (1967).

an increase of approximately 6 standard points. The amount of individual change spanned 65 raw points, ranging from an increase of 30 points to a decrease of 35 points. On the basis of the amount of change, computed in raw points, individuals were divided into three groups: average changers, exceptional changers, and negative changers. The average changers are those who increased their scores on the Social Maturity scale up to 8 points. Students who increased up to 4 points more than the average amount of 4 points, or who increased, but less than the 4-point average, are thus considered average changers. Students who increased at least 9 points, or at least 5 points more than the average 4-point change, have been designated as exceptional changers. These students changed more than three-quarters of a standard deviation above the average change score of 4 points. Men and women who decreased in Social Maturity are considered negative changers; they changed more than three-quarters of a standard devia-

TABLE 20. *Percentage of Students Exhibiting Negative, Average, and Exceptional Change in Social Maturity Scores, by Type of College Attended*

College (No.)	SOCIAL MATURITY CHANGE		
	Negative	Average	Exceptional
Public (499)	15	44	41
Private (70)	12	51	37
Protestant (98)	11	56	33
Catholic (99)	20	59	21

X^2, college *vs.* Social Maturity change, $= 13.00$; $p \leq .05$

tion below the average change score for the total sample.

Individuals were divided on the basis of the amount of change they showed on the Social Maturity scale and not on their specific scores. Thus a student whose score increased from 45 to 54 would be considered an exceptional changer, as would one whose score increased from 54 to 63. Both individuals have shown exceptional growth, although one may only have reached the point at which the other started. The results of this analysis may be found in Table 20.[6]

[6] It would have been valuable to divide students according to the level of their 1959 Social Maturity scores so that the amount of change could have been analyzed according to the degree of Social Maturity which students evidenced when they entered college. However, the time and expense which would have been involved precluded this possibility.

The exceptional- and negative-change groups each contain about 25 per cent of the total college and non-college sample that responded in 1959 and 1963, with the remaining 50 per cent in the average-change group. When college students were looked at separately, the percentage in the exceptional-change group was found to be much higher, except in the case of Catholic college students. The average change for college persisters was 7 points. Of the students who attended public college, 41 per cent had increased at least 9 points in Social Maturity. Thirty-seven per cent of the students in private colleges and 33 per cent of the students in Protestant colleges exhibited enough growth to be considered exceptional changers. Only 21 per cent of the Catholic college students could be classified as exceptional changers, however, a percentage not only below that for other college students but below that for the total sample of high school graduates who attended college and who became employed.

These results are not simply a reflection of lack of change on the part of the Catholic college students. They had a singularly high representation in the negative-change group. Compared with other college students, they became more authoritarian rather than more autonomous after four years of college. These differences were not significant when Catholic students who attended both Catholic and secular colleges were examined as a whole so that evidently this disproportionate increase of authoritarianism is a development found uniquely among students who attended Catholic colleges for four years.

With Protestants, the distinction between the more conservative fundamentalists and the more liberal Protestant groups made elsewhere in this book applies here in regard to the the interview sample. Since a majority of the approximately 500 interviewed subjects also participated in the 1963 survey, we consider them as more reflective of the original sample than the much larger number of youths who responded to our paper-and-pencil instruments in 1963.[7] This is because the interview sample was carefully selected to be representative of the approximately 10,000 high school seniors originally surveyed, rather than the longitudinal sample surveyed in 1963.

We examined the religious background of students in the interview sample, as we did in the total longitudinal sample, to see whether a relationship existed between a person's religion and measured increase or decrease in Social Maturity. Since it was earlier posited that Catholics and fundamentalist Protestants have in common a more authori-

[7] Catholics represented 27 per cent of the individuals in the interview sample for whom complete test and questionnaire information was available.

tarian approach to life and appear less responsive to intellectual stimulus, two groups of Protestants were considered along with Catholics. Protestants were divided into fundamentalist and non-fundamentalist Protestant groups, with denominations considered fundamentalist by nature of their evangelistic and conservative orientation.[8] Young adults in the interview sample who did and did not attend college are considered in the analysis.

The results met expectations. Fourteen per cent of the Catholics, 16 per cent of the Protestant fundamentalists, and 32 per cent of the other Protestants in the interview sample changed exceptionally in a more autonomous direction on the Social Maturity scale. At the opposite extreme, 30 per cent of the Catholics, compared with 51 per cent of the fundamentalists, and only 19 per cent of the other Protestants changed in a more authoritarian direction. The Protestant fundamentalists, if anything, regressed to a greater degree of authoritarianism than did the Catholics. (The overall differences were significant well beyond the 1 per cent level.)

Of the 80 Catholics in the longitudinal interview sample, only 11 were exceptional changers, that is, increased in Social Maturity more than the 8 points that was within the average range of change. Eight of these 11 who had changed exceptionally in Social Maturity between 1959 and 1963 had attended college, indicating the greater likelihood of positive change among college students. Two of the students had converted to Catholicism prior to marrying Catholics and so were not representative of students raised in Catholic homes. One was in the process of converting from Catholicism to Lutheranism and so could no longer be considered representative of Catholics. Thus in the interview sample there were only 5 students from Catholic families who increased an exceptional amount in Social Maturity and remained Catholic, but there were many who decreased.

What are the students like who change in a negative direction on this personality dimension? When most college students show a considerable increase in Social Maturity, why do some students actually decrease on this scale? We searched through the interview protocols to get a notion of what some of the individuals were like who became more authoritarian after four years of college. Excerpts from the interviews of two of these follow, together with material from the interview

---

[8] It is difficult to establish a clear distinction between fundamentalist and other Protestant groups that is acceptable to all concerned with this subject. Members of such denominations as the Nazarenes, Christian Reformed, Pentecostal and Evangelical United Brethren have been included in the fundamentalist group in this study.

of a student who changed exceptionally toward greater autonomy. The materials are not presented as a scientific analysis of the dynamics of personality change, but they do illustrate features found among the other students who exhibited varying degrees of change on the Social Maturity scale.

Robert, a very serious, polite, and cooperative young man, took a great deal of interest in the interview. Robert came from a large family; he had five brothers and sisters, three other children having died at birth. The family was very religious, and at the time he was in high school, one brother was a priest and one sister was a nun. His mother was widowed and lived in a simple but comfortable home in Pennsylvania. Her main source of support was an older brother of Robert, who had made great sacrifices to take care of his mother, and who was consequently a cause of concern and guilt for Robert.

Robert graduated from high school in one of the two communities where we also interviewed the parents of the sample subjects. Consequently, it was possible to relate Robert's values directly to those of his mother and thereby get some notion of the family climate he came from. Robert's mother had attended grade school and his father had attended high school. The father was a skilled workman who died when Robert was young. The mother described him by saying, "He provided for the family; he never thought of anything but the family. He just thought of work and home."

Robert's mother was very devout but inarticulate about her religion. When asked about her religion, she said, "I am a Catholic. I believe what the church teaches, how to lead a good moral life." She had little more than this to say about the meaning of education and vocational satisfaction. She felt that the purpose of education was "to better oneself in life"; the most important job factor was "that things be nice and smooth with no arguments." When asked how education could be improved she replied, "I didn't like taking the Lord's Prayer away." This was the sum total of her appraisal of the country's educational needs. She felt that the primary problems in the world were "the bomb and too much credit," and that there was too much concern about problems in foreign countries and not enough concern about this country.

Robert attended Pennsylvania State College for three years and then transferred to the University of Maryland so that he could take classes part-time while working for the Defense Department. Robert had wanted to attend a Catholic university, Villanova, but had been financially unable to do so. He was a very able student and had a scholarship while a student at Pennsylvania State. At the time of the interview, Robert was majoring in electrical technology. Although he had considered engineering and teaching, Robert decided he preferred to work with electrical equipment. He felt that engineering and mathematics were "too theoretical," and he was impatient with theoretical classes.

When Robert was asked to describe his religious beliefs, he said, "I am a Catholic. I believe in God." He added that religion was very important in his life. He said that he was not too familiar with other faiths, and that he didn't "like to stretch out things that are simple." His moral beliefs were closely linked to his religion, and he talked to others about his moral beliefs. "If I can't convince them, at least I let them know my ideas," he commented. A crisis had occurred in his life when he had almost suffered "a moral breakdown." Robert commented that he knew little about the opposite sex and was in danger of finding out too much too fast. (His mother mentioned that Robert's father had felt that children "should not be told too much about the facts of life until they're real old.")

Robert said he had some difficulties in college and mentioned one instructor "who deviated." "He got over my head and lost me," Robert said. As a result of some emotional problems in college Robert received "important and necessary help" from a psychologist.

The most important factors in a job for Robert were that it be in the electrical field and that he have opportunities to advance technologically and financially. When asked about the opportunities in his present job, he answered only in terms of financial benefits.

Considering the superficial responses of his mother it is not too surprising that Robert had not grown more intellectually. He shared many of his mother's values, which provided little by way of an intellectual model. Still, it is unusual for a student to lose this much ground intellectually while in college. Robert obtained a standard Social Maturity score of 41 in 1959 and a score of 37 in 1963.

Another example of a college student who changed negatively in Social Maturity is Linda, who attended a Catholic women's college in the East. In Linda's interview it was evident that she was very close to her family and to her church, very rigid in her attitudes toward other people, and primarily was seeking a secure place in life. Her Social Maturity score of 50 in 1959 was at the mean; however, by 1963 her score had declined 9 standard points.

Linda described her religious beliefs as "the center, the nucleus of my life," and added, "I believe the things that the Catholic church teaches." She said her moral beliefs "go right along with the religious beliefs; drinking and gambling are immoral if carried to excess, and premarital sexual relations are out of the question." Her values she listed as her faith first, and her family second. Her interests were bowling, dancing, television, and relaxing; she commented that "I do not do as much reading as I should; there is not much time."

She felt that her first year of teaching was a crisis in her life. Linda had not wanted to teach, but at the suggestion of the sisters in her high school, she received a scholarship to the college she attended, and the scholarship required a year of teaching. Although she did not want to teach and felt very inadequate, at the end of her first year of college she was assigned to a school and given a double grade to teach. When she found that she could not afford to complete college she continued teaching because "afterward, it was the only thing I knew." At the time of the interview she was teaching home economics seven periods a day.

Linda viewed the major issue facing mankind as "brotherly love, especially in our country." She commented, "Segregation is a silly problem, I think uncalled for," and thought there should be more acceptance of people and their ways. Evidently she was opposed to segregation and meant by her response that racial problems should not exist. But the problem of segregation does exist, and to call something so widespread and tragic a "silly problem" implies that she did not feel very deeply involved in the issue personally.

Linda had an extremely rigid attitude toward the roles that people should play in life, as indicated by her comment, "I can't stand people who play the wrong sex role, a feminine man or a masculine woman." She liked people who "are real, who don't put on any kind of appearance that isn't them." Evidently to her, therefore, a woman who acts more masculine than the average woman is playing a role; she did not accept the fact that people can honestly depart from the role which society has assigned to them.

Linda had seven brothers and sisters; of the four who were older than she, one was a college graduate. Her parents both had some high school education. In describing her father she said, "He's the boss, authoritative, silent." Her mother was "very quiet; she's always there." The greatest problem in the family was that her father "doesn't go to church. Everybody is upset about it. They all ask 'Why doesn't he go?' He did before the war, and when he came back from overseas he didn't go any more."

She said she's "very independent of her parents, completely independent," but then she added, "I don't know if anybody is." Later she said that they take a "detailed interest in where I'm going, with whom, what I'm doing, and why." She added that if it weren't for her parents she would probably have been married long before this: "They didn't interfere directly, but they certainly didn't encourage me to marry." Her greatest difficulty in college was "getting adjusted to the fact that I was away from home." The ideal husband Linda described as "thoughtful, understanding, and patient; a family man" and the most important thing in life for her was "peace of mind, and reasonable security in a job."

Linda's lack of growth may be linked to her rather dependent relationship with her family (although she maintained that she was completely independent), her uncritical and moralistic attitude toward her religion, and her particular college experience, which provided limited opportunity for growth.

There was one exceptional changer in the interview sample who had dropped out of college but had returned and had maintained her religious ties while growing in Social Maturity. Ann's standard score in 1959 was 43; in 1963 it was 65. Her responses to the interview give some indication of what a college student who has changed in a positive direction on the Social Maturity scale is like.

Ann majored in English and planned to attend graduate school in psychology. In contrast to the negative and average changers who were interviewed, Ann was deeply concerned about finding herself and her place in life. Her concern extended far beyond attaining a secure job or finding a good husband.

When asked what she considered the most important things in life, she replied, "The opportunity to be myself, whatever I am. I want to see what I am. I want freedom to be myself and make my own decisions. I don't mean anti-social behavior, but the right to follow my own beliefs." Ann considered a successful person to be one who "has the ability to stand on his own two feet, make his own decisions, and not follow the crowd."

In high school Ann said she was afraid to be different; she just wanted to get through. "It's hard to be different," she commented, but she was no longer afraid to try. Ann said she was influenced particularly by a nun in the sixth grade, who was the first person "who ever made me realize I had my own ideas." She attended Catholic elementary school but public high school. In high school she was influenced by an English teacher and a social studies teacher who "didn't have to go by the book, who helped us to think on our own, and allowed us to develop our own ideas." Students read books like *The Catcher in the Rye,* which stimulated their thinking. There was a tremendous difference in her thinking between ages 18 and 22, she said.

Ann represents a fascinating paradox. She was so attracted by the religious life and had such a strong desire "to save my soul and save the whole world" that she at one time dropped out of college to join a religious order. Yet at the same time she was so little a part of the Catholic subculture that she said she had no friends who were Catholic.

Ann left the novitiate where she was preparing to become a professed sister because she felt she had no real vocation and that she was running away. She felt that she should go back into the world and live the best life she could. Yet she commented on how much good the nuns were doing and said that she missed the "good idealistic people" and felt too many people at the college were greedy.

Although she said that she was "strongly Catholic," Ann knew no Catholics outside her family and liked having non-Catholic friends. She had very strong ethical beliefs and emphasized honesty and integrity in particular. She didn't like to smoke, but did drink. Premarital sex was wrong for her, Ann said, but for others, "it's up to them." She added, "I wonder if any group has the right to pass judgment on another."

Speaking of her family Ann said "We've never been closed in; we are all free. I don't want my children to be closed in." However, she said her family "sticks together. We've always been a family unit." Ann said her father, who died while she was in high school, was "very open, very friendly; he wasn't a locked-in person." He was also very idealistic and had a lot of influence on others. Ann said she feels independent of her family in opinions but tied to them emotionally.

Ann felt that education was very important for a woman, since she can then "encourage children to stand up and be individuals and make decisions of their own," and she will not "depend on her husband for her thinking." Her mother was "dead set against" Ann's going to college, however, since she had not attended college herself. Her mother had always felt that "if a woman wasn't married by 20, she was a failure." Yet Ann said that she and her mother were alike in many ways, and that she had always discussed things with her and "never kept anything to herself." She felt she had convinced her mother of the importance of college for herself. Ann had had a difficult time financially and sometimes worked full time while attending Indiana University. She had also dropped out of school at times to work.

Her ideal husband would be "Sure of himself, not swayed by all, but thinking things through for himself." Love and consideration would also be important as well as "gentleness and kindness." He would be "so sure of himself that he can kiss and be kind to his kids without apologies," and he would be interested in the world outside of himself. Ann felt that the ideal size of a family depends on "how many you yourself can educate, handle, and help to develop as individuals."

When asked about the major issues facing mankind, she replied "I wonder if man himself and the way he handles himself, his inability to accept other men and get along with them isn't the major problem. I wonder if we don't have so much trouble because we're afraid of ourselves and others."

What caused Ann to differ from Linda and Robert so much in outlook? All three of these young adults felt close to their families, yet Ann's relationship was in many ways quite different from that of Linda or Robert. Her emphasis was upon openness and freedom within the family and upon sharing her ideas and interests with, rather than being dependent upon, her family. But the differences go beyond family relationships. Ann had definite moral standards for herself but would not impose them on others, and did not in any sense appear judgmental toward others. She had strong ties to her religion but was not closed in by it, any more than she was closed in by her family. She was open and sensitive to the world around her, introspective, and free to grow intellectually. She was fortunate to have had parents and some teachers who evidently encouraged this.

Beyond this sketch we have little to say about the individual dynamics behind the development of intellectual autonomy. Characteristics of the relatively few Catholic college students who show exceptional intellectual potential are discussed in chapter 9. But much has yet to be learned about the factors underlying intellectual growth within and without a religious subculture. Even though much is to be learned about the development of intellectual disposition, however, the findings of this chapter seem to have an important bearing on the problem of intellectual endeavor among educated Catholics.

Students who attended Catholic colleges for four years were found as freshmen to be significantly lower in measured intellectual and autonomous disposition than Catholics and non-Catholics who attended secular colleges. The secular college Catholics were not completely on a par with the non-Catholics, but they shared the intellectual attitudes of their non-Catholic classmates more than they did those of the Catholic college students.

When the same students were again tested four years later, the situation had not changed. All groups of students had increased their mean intellective scores, but the Catholic college students, with few exceptions, remained as far below the measured intellectual level of the other students in their senior year as they did in their freshman year. With the exception of the Theoretical Orientation scale administered only to the West Coast Sample, the greatest discrepancy between the Catholic college and secular college students at both times was on the Complexity and various autonomy scales. This held true for all samples surveyed—the West Coast, the National, and the National Merit Scholarship samples.

Individual differences in change in autonomy were examined more closely in the National Sample. On the basis of the Social Maturity scale, the subjects were distinguished according to whether they changed exceptionally toward greater autonomy between 1959 and 1963, manifested an average amount of change, or changed in a negative, more closed-minded direction toward greater authoritarianism. Considering the sample as a whole, including college students and young adults who did not go to college, Catholics, and conservative, fundamentalist Protestants were overrepresented among the negative changers and underrepresented among the exceptional changers. When the college students were considered separately according to the type of college they attended, it was found that the Catholic college students were the most highly overrepresented in the negative-change group, followed by the students who attended Protestant colleges.

It is regrettable that so many Catholic college students are found to be more authoritarian after their college experiences. Perhaps if we distinguished different directions of change on all scales, as we did on the Social Maturity scale, the Catholic college students would have continued to have the highest proportion of regression toward anti-intellectualism. But, as far as the data have been analyzed to this point, Catholic college students do show significant intellectual development, even though they do not nearly reach the intellectual level of the other students after four years of college.

We may ask, however, whether this is enough. When students start out with such an intellectual deficit as that found among Catholic college students, is it enough that they grow in intellectual disposition nearly as much as other students? Is there not a need for a concerted, all-out effort to raise further the intellectual level of these students? Certainly values are well established before students enter college, and exceptional change is no doubt difficult to effect. Yet, in view of the intellectual restrictions of the students Catholic colleges recruit, they cannot hope to produce graduates at the intellectual level of those from secular colleges unless they do more than the secular colleges to foster intellectual growth among their students.

But this may be asking too much of both the student and the college. Once again, much of the situation may revolve around that problem we raised in chapters 3 and 4. Perhaps the Catholic colleges cannot do more now to encourage intellectual development among their students until the parochial schools provide a much more enriching intellectual stimulus in the students' lives in their earliest years at school and families provide more intellectual models for their children.

CHAPTER SIX

Students' Concepts of Culture, Career, and Society

The extent of Catholic acculturation is a perennial issue in discussions of American Catholics.[1] Have they become acculturated, or are they living in their own world of Catholic schools, periodicals, friends —and values? Is it possible that Catholic students have adapted sufficiently to the larger culture so that their expressed values are very similar to those of other students? That is, is it possible that Catholic students today have become very much acculturated on the surface, although corresponding changes in attitude may not have taken place?

We will be concerned in this chapter first with cultural, educational, and occupational values in an attempt to see to what extent Catholic students share these values with their non-Catholic fellows. We will be concerned secondly with students' values on a variety of subjects that center upon conformity and docility, as opposed to individual awareness, particularly as these traits relate to social issues. The students' religious attitudes and values are discussed in a separate chapter because of the central importance of such values in a study set in a religious context. Information is drawn primarily from questionnaires administered to the National and West Coast samples, with some data included from other relevant studies.

A walk through any major museum or library or a review of the history of music is enough to testify to the church's great contribution to Western culture. But in this respect the church of the past must be distinguished from that of the present; the church of Europe must be distinguished from that of America; and the contributions of individuals or groups within the church must be distinguished from the cultural values of the general Catholic population.

We may look back to the church art of the Renaissance and say that Catholics have traditionally revered art. Or we may look at what has passed for art in some American Catholic churches or at materials such

[1] See, for example, Glazer and Moynihan (1963); McAvoy (1960, 1963); Neuwien (1966).

128

as the *Catholic Art Calendar* and conclude that the church has failed to value art or even understand its meaning. We may look at Catholic learning in the past, or at the Index, or at the expurgated textbooks used in Catholic schools. We may look at the murals, morality plays, and sculpture of the late Middle Ages, or at the picket lines protesting "immoral" movies or plays, or at the lack of noteworthy dramatic and fine arts departments in American Catholic schools and colleges. This is not to say that American Catholics have not attended art galleries and concerts in the past; nor is it to say that they do not now appreciate cultural activities and artistic creations. But we do know that the Catholic church has not been a strong patron of the arts in America, and that, until recently, to look at cultural concerns was to look back into the European past.

The lack of the American Catholic church's emphasis on the esthetic, cultural part of man is evidenced to some extent among contemporary Catholic college students compared with secular college non-Catholics (Tables 21 and 22). For example, in the West

TABLE 21. *Intellectual Interests of Students, West Coast Sample, in Per Cent*

College Group (No. in Parentheses)	Little or No Serious Reading	Own Less than 10 Books	Little Interest in Music
Catholic (1,107)	49	47	20
Secular Catholic (191)	42	46	23
Non-Catholic (194)	37	32	13
Z ratio			
Catholic vs. secular Catholic	1.79+	.26+	1.00+
Catholic vs. non-Catholic	3.08**	3.85**	2.33*
Secular Catholic vs. non-Catholic	1.04+	2.92**	2.58**

+ p = not significant
* $p \leq .05$
** $p \leq .01$

Coast Sample the Catholic students evinced less interest in reading and ownership of books than other students. Although few students reported doing a great deal of serious leisure reading, a higher percentage of Catholic college students than non-Catholics reported doing little or no serious leisure reading, with the difference significant at the 1 per cent level. Almost half the Catholic college students reported little serious reading, compared with 37 per cent of non-Catholics and 42 per cent of the Catholics at the state college. When the Catholic college seniors were considered separately, again almost half (48 per cent) reported little or no serious reading. (Comparable University of California data were not available for most of the analyses in this chapter.)

Catholic college students likewise reported owning fewer books than non-Catholics. About one-third of the non-Catholics but almost half of the Catholics reported owning fewer than ten books. The lack

Table 22. *Intellectual Interests of Seniors, National Sample, in Per Cent*

College Group (No. in Parentheses)	Visit Bookstores	Visit Art Galleries	Attend Concerts	Attend Plays
Catholic (99)	89	70	62	92
Secular Catholic (183)	95	81	65	80
Non-Catholic (1,124)	95	81	75	86
Z ratio				
Catholic vs.				
secular Catholic	1.81+	2.08*	0.50+	2.68**
Catholic vs.				
non-Catholic	2.68**	2.67**	2.84**	1.73+
Secular Catholic vs.				
non-Catholic	0.00+	0.00+	2.89**	2.12*

+ p = not significant
* $p \leq .05$
** $p \leq .01$

of interest in books among the Catholic college students was paralleled by their attitude toward classical music, which here is taken as another index of interest in cultural, esthetic, or intellectual aspects of life. Only 30 per cent of the Catholic freshmen in Catholic and secular colleges reported enjoyment of classical music, compared with 52 per cent of the non-Catholics. As might be expected, the enjoyment of classical music was greater for seniors, with 48 per cent of the Catholic seniors indicating such enjoyment, a percentage similar to that of the non-Catholics as freshmen.

When seniors in the National Sample were asked how often in the last year they had browsed in a bookstore, attended a play, attended a concert, or visited an art gallery, a large majority of both the Catholic and the non-Catholic students said they had done these things at least once during the year previous to the time they were surveyed. But as determined by these items, noted in Table 22, the non-Catholic students reported the greatest interest in books, classical music, and art. For example, 62 per cent of the Catholic college students, compared with 75 per cent of the non-Catholics, reported having attended a concert during the last year, and 70 per cent of the Catholic college students, compared with 81 per cent of the non-Catholics, had visited an art gallery at least once. The non-Catholic students reported a statistically greater interest in cultural events except plays, with the significance level in each case beyond the 1 per cent level of confidence. The secular college Catholics reported browsing in bookstores and visiting art galleries exactly as often as the non-Catholics, but this was not true for attendance at plays or concerts.

In spite of the statistical differences between the groups, they were more nearly alike in their reported cultural interests than were the groups in the West Coast Sample. This finding could be anticipated from the similarity of the mean Thinking Introversion and Estheticism scores obtained by the Catholics and non-Catholics in the National Sample, similarities which were greater than those found in the West Coast Sample. It is not immediately apparent why Catholic students in the National Sample expressed cultural values more similar to their non-Catholic peers than those on the West Coast. Whether this is a regional difference or indicates a changing condition we do not know. The fact remains that although differences in expressed cultural interests existed among the groups in the National Sample, they were more marked among the groups on the West Coast.

The same difference that existed between the West Coast and National samples in cultural values is apparent in educational values. Catholic students in the West Coast Sample placed less emphasis upon the intellectual goals of education than did other students, but this did not hold for the National Sample.

When freshman students in various types of colleges in the West Coast Sample were asked what they considered to be the first or second most important purpose of a college education, a minority of students selected the intellectual aspect, "basic general knowledge and appreciation of ideas." Students in Catholic colleges were even less likely than others to select this purpose, with 19 per cent of the Catholic

132   CONCEPTS OF CULTURE, CAREER, AND SOCIETY

college freshmen selecting this goal and 30 per cent of the freshmen at other schools, a difference significant beyond the 1 per cent level.

The goal considered of first or second importance by the largest proportion of the freshmen was practical training (vocational and social skills), reported by approximately 50 per cent of each group. The Catholic college students placed more stress upon character formation (moral development and marriage preparation) than did either of the state college groups (27 versus 9 per cent). Character formation, however, may be considered a practical goal of education as opposed to a more liberal, general goal of education (knowledge and appreciation of ideas).

If the total responses to these practical goals of education are summarized for each group, the Catholic college freshmen show the greatest practical orientation toward higher education, followed by the Catholics at secular colleges. Seventy-five per cent of the Catholic college students reported the most important purpose of college to be some form of practical training, compared with 64 per cent of the secular college Catholics and 59 per cent of the non-Catholics. The difference between Catholics in church and secular colleges is significant at the 1 per cent level, as is the difference between Catholic college students and non-Catholic students.

Less emphasis was placed on the vocational goals of college education among the West Coast students who remained in college. A majority of the 1963 seniors stressed most the intellectual goals of college education. Fifty-three per cent of the Catholic college seniors and 64 per cent of the non-Catholics considered the most important purpose of college to be the attainment of knowledge and the appreciation of ideas. The difference in proportions was significant at the 1 per cent level.

The persisting students in the National Sample placed less emphasis upon the intellectual goals of a college education than did students in the West Coast Sample, as may be seen in Table 23. Forty-two per cent of both the Catholic college and non-Catholic seniors in the National Sample cited the intellectual goals as most important, compared with 36 per cent of the secular college Catholics.

Although the Catholic college students were more concerned with character formation than the other students in the National Sample, they registered less concern over this as an objective of college education than did either the freshmen or seniors in the West Coast Sample. About half of the Catholic college students in the National Sample were attending Catholic colleges much larger than those in the West

Coast study, and it is possible that in these colleges there is less emphasis on character formation than in the smaller schools.

A majority of persisting students in both samples majored in the more academically oriented subjects in the arts and sciences rather than in the more vocationally oriented subjects such as business, engineering, and education. This was more noticeable among the West Coast students. A reduction in education majors may have occurred because by 1963 West Coast students were encouraged to major in the liberal arts and seek a teaching credential separately, whereas many of the states in the National Sample continued to offer majors in education as a distinct field. And we know that in the National Sample more women majored in education than in the liberal arts, and more secular college Catholics than Catholic college students majored in

TABLE 23. *Percentage of Seniors Reporting Various Goals for a College Education, National Sample*

College Group (No. in Parentheses)	Practical Training	Character Formation	Knowledge, Ideas	Other, None
Catholic (99)	27	12	42	19
Secular Catholic (183)	32	5	36	27
Non-Catholic (1,124)	31	6	42	21
Z ratio				
Catholic vs. secular Catholic	0.87+	2.11*	0.99+	1.51+
Catholic vs. non-Catholic	0.83+	2.26*	0.00+	0.46+
Secular Catholic vs. non-Catholic	0.28+	0.50+	1.55+	1.81+

+ p = not significant
* $p \leq .05$

education. Nearly all the West Coast Catholic college women majored in the liberal arts, a significantly greater proportion than the Catholic college men. It appears that more West Coast non-Catholic than Catholic college senior men majored in academic subjects. Seventy-three per cent of the non-Catholic and 65 per cent of the Catholic college seniors majored in academic subjects, but the difference is not statistically significant.

In the National Sample, a higher percentage of persisting students in Catholic colleges than in others selected academic majors, 55 per cent of the Catholic college students compared with 41 per cent of the other Catholics and 51 per cent of the non-Catholics. The difference in proportion of Catholic college and non-Catholic students who elected academic rather than applied majors was not statistically significant. But the differences between both these groups and the secular college Catholics were significant beyond the 1 per cent level of confidence.

The non-Catholics in larger proportion than the Catholic college students elected majors in the social sciences and education. Proportionately more Catholic college students chose humanities and business majors. The secular college Catholics majored in education in the largest proportion of all. Since most Catholic colleges are liberal arts colleges, it is not surprising that they have a high percentage of students majoring in the liberal arts. And Catholics who elect to attend a public college may do so partly because their interests are in programs not always offered at Catholic colleges. The same may be said of students who choose a large Catholic university over a Catholic college, a distinction not made in the present analysis. The reason for the greater vocational orientation of the secular college Catholics compared with the Catholic college students is not clear, unless it is the heavy emphasis the secular college Catholics placed on majors in education per se rather than on the liberal arts. But why that would be we still do not know.

Nor is it altogether clear why the students chose to attend the particular college they did. They gave similar reasons for their choice of a college regardless of whether it was Catholic or non-Catholic, and they appeared to seek and value similar attributes in these colleges. In both the West Coast and National samples about 30 per cent of all freshmen said they chose their schools primarily for academic reasons, with about 15 per cent of them citing academic reputation as the primary reason and another 15 per cent citing a particular program that was offered. The remaining students gave a variety of reasons for their choice of college, with about a fourth of the students indicating that their choice was based upon the fact that the school was inexpensive or close to home. The latter was less likely to be the reason given by students at Catholic colleges, with only about 14 per cent of the freshmen in the West Coast Sample listing this. We assume that the Catholic college students who listed economy as the reason for their choice of college saw this as a factor only among Catholic colleges but not in comparison to the public colleges they could have attended. Only about one-fifth of these students said they chose to attend a Catholic college because of its church relationship; women reported this reason more than men. It is likely, however, that the church relationship is the primary reason for selection for many more of these students. But they may always have expected to attend a Catholic college and so the immediate reason for selection may have been something else; that is, the question may have been which Catholic college to attend rather than whether to attend a Catholic college.

No matter what school was selected, many students knew little about the college of their choice before they arrived there. Almost all the students in the National Sample were vague about their expectations of college.[2] This held for Catholic as well as non-Catholic students. An example of this was the comment of one student in the National Sample who was enrolled in one of the most renowned Catholic colleges in the country. He said he knew little about the college ahead of time and had never been on campus, but simply "knew it was good academically." When asked if the school had lived up to his expectations, he said there had been "enough intellectual stimulus to satisfy my needs." He expressed dissatisfaction with his major in pre-law, however, saying that the emphasis was on "rote memory rather than on concepts."

When we discuss Catholic participation in student protest activities later we will see that Catholic colleges are the most likely to report student protests about the quality of instruction. The students in the West Coast and National samples expressed considerable satisfaction with their schools in general, however. In fact, the West Coast Catholic college students who were asked separately about the comparative academic standards of their colleges saw them for the most part as superior to all other types of schools.

Whether comparing the standards with those of other Catholic colleges, other private colleges, or public colleges or universities, Catholic college students in the West Coast Sample perceived their schools' standards to be higher than those of other schools. The only exception to this was among the freshman men, 40 per cent of whom considered their own college superior to all other types of colleges. The great majority of both senior men and women reported their college to be at least on a par with, and generally superior to, all other types of

[2] The vague perceptions and expectations students held toward their colleges at the time they entered them were especially evident in interviews with students in the National Sample. See Trent (1965–1966); Trent and Medsker (1967).

colleges. Collectively, 53 per cent of the Catholic college seniors considered their college to be superior to the state colleges in academic standards, and nearly 30 per cent of them felt their college to be superior to the public university.

It is interesting that so many of the students rated the academic standards of their schools as equal or superior to those of the state university when, despite the generally high ability level of these Catholic students, many of them would not have been eligible to enter the state university. Women were especially likely to rate their institutions high in comparison to others. Neither the patterns for the men nor the women were altered when the students were considered by ability and socioeconomic level, although the brighter students appeared to have an especially positive image of their college, as did students at the lowest socioeconomic level.

Of course one may wonder upon what the students based their comparisons, especially since we know that they had little knowledge about their own or other colleges upon entrance. Moreover, in the National Sample it was found that 70 per cent of the students had applied to only one college and often had evidently not even considered others. Students appeared to be attending the colleges of their choice, often dictated by convenience, and Catholic college students appeared to be quite satisfied with their choice. Only 15 per cent of the Catholic college freshmen in the National Sample said they would have preferred to attend a public institution.

The freshmen in the West Coast Sample were also asked whether their college had some special quality, other than religious affiliation, that distinguished it from others. Over two-thirds of the Catholic college students said that it did. Twenty-six per cent of the freshman men who felt that there was a special quality specified some academic feature of the college such as good teaching or the excellence of a particular department. Although 18 per cent of the freshman women also cited academic characteristics, a higher percentage of women, 23 per cent, referred to the warm, personal atmosphere of the campus as being the distinguishing characteristic. This was the feature cited second most often by the men, 17 per cent of whom referred to the friendly atmosphere. About 14 per cent of both men and women specified student-teacher relations.

Thus for men the primary feature was academic and for women it was the personal atmosphere, with both groups also emphasizing student-teacher relations. Since students wrote specific responses instead of selecting among alternatives, the descriptions of schools covered a wide range of possibilities. Some typical responses were: "Theology and philosophy are required, giving a broader background"; "It is small and you have a better chance to excel"; and "The college instills appreciation for the dignity of womanhood." Included among the reponses citing academics were intellectual atmosphere, honors programs, special courses, academic standards, and good teaching.

Catholic students evidently consider their schools to be superior to others. Are they also more likely than other students to think of themselves as intellectuals and of their faculty as intellectually stimulating? When students in various types of colleges were asked which descriptive terms applied to them, usually less than a third called themselves intellectual. Exceptions occurred at colleges such as Reed and Swarthmore, where up to 60 per cent of the students described themselves as intellectual.[3] In the National Sample there was little difference in the way Catholics and non-Catholics described themselves in regard to intellectuality. Twenty-nine per cent of the seniors at Catholic colleges and 32 per cent of the secular college Catholics and non-Catholics described themselves as intellectual; the differences were too small to reach a level of statistical significance. West Coast seniors were less inclined to consider themselves intellectual: 15 per cent of the Catholics and 22 per cent of the non-Catholics called themselves intellectual, a difference significant at the 5 per cent level.

When the 1963 West Coast Catholic college seniors were asked to respond to the statement, "If a student has enough intelligence, good hard work is what makes him intellectual," they were almost evenly divided between agreeing and disagreeing with this statement. The acceptance by so many students of a concept such as "good hard work" as the source of intellectuality makes their responses to questions on this subject difficult to interpret, since such a concept implies a narrow and practical approach, which is the opposite of the open, far-ranging, questioning approach we have associated with intellectuality.

Perhaps this explains the fact that Catholic college seniors at a low level of measured intellectual disposition considered themselves to have developed intellectually at the rate of their relatively few classmates who were at a high level of intellectuality. It may also explain the widespread notion that intelligence and achievement in terms of a good grade-point average are synonymous with intellectuality. At the same time, only 11 per cent of the West Coast Catholic college

[3] Information about students at Reed and Swarthmore is drawn from the Study of Select Institutions (in progress) at the Center for Research and Development in Higher Education, Berkeley.

seniors agreed that intellectuals tend to be radical, immoral, and irreligious, indicating that only a relatively small proportion of these students saw intellectuals in a totally negative light.

We did not ask the subjects what they meant by "intellectual," and it is likely that many of them did not perceive the term as we intend it. In fact, in view of the data just observed, we wonder if these students really recognized intellectuality or the lack of it. But whatever they meant by the term, most of them when freshmen applied it to their faculty. Seventy-seven per cent of them said that most of their faculty were intellectually stimulating. The only other school surveyed at which such a high percentage of students saw the faculty as intellectually stimulating was Swarthmore, where 77 per cent of the students said that more than half the faculty was intellectually stimulating. Thus, students at a school renowned for its stimulating and innovative spirit, and students at schools with no particular record of innovation were more inclined to see their faculty as intellectually stimulating. By contrast, at a public institution known for its high academic standards and its Nobel Prize winners, only 51 per cent of the students considered more than half the faculty to be intellectually stimulating. As seniors the Catholic college students were somewhat less inclined to consider their faculty as intellectually stimulating as they did when they were freshmen. Approximately 62 per cent of both Catholic college and secular college Catholic and non-Catholic seniors considered their faculty intellectually stimulating, whereas 77 per cent of the Catholic college students felt this way four years earlier.

Intellectual stimulation is usually seen as a prime characteristic of superior teachers, but fewer students saw their teachers as superior than as stimulating. This was especially true of the public college students. Forty-six per cent of the Catholic college seniors and 35 per cent of the public college students regarded their faculty as superior teachers, a difference significant at the 1 per cent level. Why the public college seniors regarded the teaching qualities of their faculty more critically and found them less stimulating than did the Catholic college students is a matter for speculation. Perhaps public college students demand more from their teachers than do Catholic students; perhaps they receive less attention from their teachers, who are more involved in research than Catholic faculty; or perhaps the teachers are inferior. We suspect that the real reason is a matter of the generally very positive and uncritical image the Catholic college students have of their colleges, whereas there is less of this kind of indiscriminate loyalty among public college students.

Fewer Catholic college seniors regarded their faculty as superior researchers (31 per cent) than as superior teachers (46 per cent). If one sees teaching and research as opposing and competing activities, such a dichotomy can be expected. If one accepts the view that teaching and research supplement and enrich each other, however, then superior teachers and researchers should be found together. As the Select Committee on Education at the University of California reported in the spring of 1966: "Teaching and research in a University setting do not conflict but support each other. . . . The intellectual qualities that find expression in good research will also contribute to good teaching and vice versa."[4]

Although this wedding of teaching and research may not be within the financial grasp of all institutions, a climate that encourages this could be expected to exist at institutions having a faculty that is truly intellectually stimulating. This is problematical, however. The good researcher is not ipso facto a good teacher; nor is the good teacher by virtue of his teaching ability a good researcher. But in the ideal situation we would hope to find both good researchers and teachers. This would assure the development and also the dissemination of ideas, and to provide one without the other is not to provide the highest quality or even a complete higher education. Of course, the situation is much worse in the college which provides neither good teaching nor research.

Apart from interest in the discovery of ideas and knowledge, one of the characteristics of an intellectual person is that he is aware of the complexities and shadings of issues and does not expect and would not wish to be given a simple answer to a complicated issue. Thus he would value the opportunity to assimilate conflicting opinion and reach his own decisions. The Complexity scale discussed previously measures this trait. We had this kind of disposition in mind also when we asked the West Coast Catholic college students to agree or disagree with the statement: "It is a good learning experience for the student to be left with ambiguous or conflicting opinion so that he must arrive at the solution to a given problem on his own."

It is frankly heartening that a majority of the Catholic seniors (72 per cent) expressed a desire to approach learning through independent problem-solving rather than through rote memorization of given fact. Their Complexity scores indicate this is not a character-

[4] Academic Senate (1966), p. 42.

istic of most of the students, but it is at least their conscious avowal, and perhaps the characteristic will develop more in time.

In the area of occupational values, again there are both similarities and differences to be found among Catholic and non-Catholic students. There appears to be little difference among students as groups in the factors they consider most important in a job. Regardless of religion or type of college, students in both the National and West Coast samples rated job security, salary, and working with or helping people as most important, with a smaller percentage rating use of abilities as most important.

The one factor which would appear directly related to intellectual productivity—the opportunity for creativity—is the factor least subscribed to by all groups, and it is cited significantly less often by Catholic students than others. About 20 per cent of the non-Catholics in the West Coast Sample reported creativity as a major factor in job satisfaction; this figure is twice that for Catholics at either Catholic colleges or secular colleges. The differences are significant beyond the 1 per cent level.

When McNamara asked students at two major Catholic and two non-Catholic universities to cite the most important factor in a job, a similar pattern prevailed.[5] Eighteen per cent of the nonsectarian university seniors gave the highest priority to the job which would "permit me to be creative," and 12 per cent of the Catholic university seniors specified this. The job factor which most distinguished Catholics from non-Catholics was their attitude toward supervision. When the factor, "leaves me free of supervision by others" was considered, 51 per cent of the non-Catholics, compared with 34 per cent of the Catholics, rated this as highly important.

There are indications that Catholics place less value than non-Catholics upon intellectual factors in job satisfaction, and also that they are somewhat more likely than other students to choose occupational fields, such as business, which are more practically oriented. The majority of freshman men in the West Coast Sample indicated plans to enter some type of business venture. A business venture in this sense included not only business management and sales but also business detail such as accounting and administration and business operations such as maintaining one's own store or office.

Seventy-two per cent of the Catholic college freshman men planned to enter a business venture, compared with 51 per cent of the secular Catholics and 60 per cent of the non-Catholics. The difference in proportion between the two groups of Catholics was significant at the

---

[5] McNamara (1964).

1 per cent level, but this was not true when comparing the Catholic college and non-Catholic freshman men.

More Catholic college freshman women than secular Catholic and non-Catholic women also planned to enter a business venture after college. Less than 20 per cent of the women preferred business careers, however, and differences between the three groups in this respect were not significant. About the same per cent of seniors as freshmen planned to work in a business setting.

When business is defined in a much more narrow sense, and limited to only those students who state specifically that they plan to enter a business, the percentages drop greatly. This was done in the National Opinion Research Center's study of 1961 seniors with results consistent with our finding in the West Coast Sample.[6] More Catholics (23 per cent) than Protestants (15 per cent) specified business as their occupational goal. The percentage of Catholics planning business careers was similar regardless of whether students were enrolled in Catholic or secular colleges, and the goals of Catholics were significantly different at the 1 per cent level from the goals stated by Protestants. When the students were asked the type of employer they preferred, 33 per cent of the Catholics and 25 per cent of the Protestants specified a large company. Educational institutions were preferred by 27 per cent of the Catholics and 36 per cent of the non-Catholics.

McNamara looked at the data obtained specifically from six Jesuit colleges that participated in Davis' survey of the 1961 college seniors; again results were consistent with those we have already observed.[7] On the average, 30 per cent of the students expressed a preference for a business career, 7 per cent more than all Catholic seniors and approximately 15 per cent more than the non-Catholics surveyed by Davis. The percentage of students choosing business varied among the schools from a low of 20 per cent at Marquette University to a high of 44 per cent at Xavier University.

Despite the fact that Jesuit schools are known for their liberal arts colleges, the careers these students planned to enter were not especially related to the liberal arts. Among the six schools, in only two cases did any single occupational field outdraw business. Engineering at the University of Detroit attracted as many students as business, 27 per cent for each field; and at Marquette University the proportion of students planning careers in education (21 per cent) rivaled the proportion planning careers in business (20 per cent). Since neither engineering nor education can be considered fields directly based

[6] J. Davis (1964); Greeley (1963).
[7] McNamara (1965).

upon the liberal arts, there is evidently more emphasis upon these practical, applied fields, in contrast to more scholarly and intellectual fields, than one would anticipate at Jesuit schools with their reputation for classical education.

Catholic college students in many ways appear different from other students in their cultural, educational, and occupational values. They report cultural interests and activities in smaller proportion, and they place more value on the practical goals of education and on occupations related to business or to other applied areas. But considering both the National and West Coast samples together with others, the differences in values expressed by Catholic and non-Catholic students, although apparent, do not strike us as either exceptionally pronounced or consistent.

When we turn to social and political concerns, again the picture is not totally consistent, but a distinctive pattern is formed from the responses of Catholic college and non-Catholic students to a series of pertinent questions. To what extent are Catholic students open to the larger culture? To what extent do they form friendships with non-Catholics and participate actively with non-Catholics in the social issues of the larger culture? Do they dissent from traditional policies of church and college? How great is their awareness and concern about social issues of national and international concern?

The opposite of openness would be restricted relationships, conformity to tradition, uncritical acceptance of church and college policies, and lack of concern with broader social issues. What are the values of Catholic college students in these areas? Granted, these students as a whole conform more than we might wish, are more willing to accept easy answers, and are ready to follow what others are doing or have done in the past. Still, do Catholic college students value dissent, even to the extent that other students do? Or are Catholics more likely than others to value docility; or, if they do not actively value it, do they fail to act in a way which would indicate anything but docility?

It is to be expected that students who attend Catholic schools exclusively will make friendships primarily among Catholics, if for no other reason than that the majority of their social contacts are among Catholics. At the same time, the exclusiveness of these friendships must limit the interaction of many Catholics with the larger society. And, as a matter of fact, this was one of the original reasons for the establishment of the Catholic school system.[8]

[8] Ward (1958).

To see to what extent contemporary Catholic college students do in fact confine their friendships to fellow Catholics, we asked about the religious background of the close friends of the 1963 Catholic college seniors surveyed in the West Coast Sample. Although the West Coast Catholic college students reported close friendships with non-Catholics, the great majority of their friendships were with other Catholics (Table 24). Only one individual out of the entire sample of Catholic college seniors reported more non-Catholics than Catholics as close friends. Nearly 33 per cent of the seniors reported 2 or fewer non-Catholic friends although less than 8 per cent reported 2 or fewer close Catholic friends. Over half of the students stated they had more than 10 close friends. Fifty-four per cent of the seniors reported having over 10 close Catholic friends and 20 per cent of the students reported having that many non-Catholic friends.

TABLE 24. *Percentage of Catholic College Seniors Reporting Various Numbers of Close Catholic and Non-Catholic Friends, West Coast Sample*

Friends	0–2	3–4	5–6	7–9	10 or more
Catholic	7	11	20	8	54
Non-Catholic	33	24	18	5	20

$X^2 = 66.02$; $p \leq .01$; no. = 172.

That the Catholic college seniors in 1963 reported that most of their friends were also Catholic met our expectations. But we were not prepared to find that they had as many close friends as they reported. Perhaps the students do not share our sense of semantics, and any relatively good friend meant a "close" friend to them. We may define the term "close friend" too narrowly; or then again, what the students mean by friendship may deserve exploration. But whatever they perceive close friends to be, we note that most of these educated Catholics do not confine their friendships exclusively to fellow Catholics, even though most of their friends do share their religion.

There was no opportunity to inquire into the peer relationships of the West Coast secular Catholics. Greeley and Rossi, however, did take this question up in their recent survey of Catholic adolescents and adults.[9] Eighty per cent of the adolescents in their sample who had all their education in Catholic schools reported that more than

[9] Greeley and Rossi (1966).

half of their friends were Catholic, compared with 37 per cent of those who had had some Catholic education and 28 per cent of those who had had no Catholic education. The differences in reported Catholic friendships between the youths who had all their education in Catholic schools and each of the other two groups were significant.

Fifty-two per cent of a comparative group of Protestant adolescents reported that over half of their friends were also Protestant. This is a low figure in our estimation, considering the preponderance of Protestants in American society. No information was given on the statistical significance of the difference in exclusive friendships reported by the Protestant youths and those who had all their education in Catholic schools. According to our own chi square calculation, however, this difference is well beyond the 1 per cent level of significance.

In the Greeley-Rossi sample, over two-thirds of the Catholic adults who had recieved all their education in Catholic schools and half of those who had received either some or no formal Catholic education reported (by recall) that at age 17 more than half their friends had been Catholic. A Protestant comparison was not given. But because half of the Catholic adults who attended public schools reported a majority of Catholic friends, Greeley and Rossi argued that, apparently, being Catholic rather than attending Catholic schools caused friendships to be restricted. This is part of Greeley and Rossi's rationale for concluding that Catholic schools are not "divisive," that is, do not separate Catholics from the rest of society.

On the basis of these data alone we arrive at quite a different interpretation of the situation from Greeley and Rossi's. The differences are extensive enough that there seems to be no question that exclusive attendance at Catholic schools is highly associated with friendship formation. Not just one of these factors, but both educational background and religion are related to friendships.

But Greeley and Rossi's thesis is contradicted more decidedly by other data of their own. As noted previously, 80 per cent of the contemporary Catholic adolescents in their sample reported a majority of their friends were Catholic, compared with 28 per cent of the Catholic youths who had no Catholic education. Greeley and Rossi also asked the adults in their sample if all three of their best friends today are Catholic. Just over half the adults whose education was exclusively Catholic responded yes to this, compared with 43 per cent of the Catholics who had some Catholic education and 47 per cent of those who had no Catholic education. The differences in response among the three groups were slight in any event and statistically significant only between the "all Catholic education" and "some Catholic education" groups. This finding led Greeley and Rossi to conclude that the differences in friendships formed by youths who do and do not obtain their education in Catholic schools does not persist into adult life, that the type of school a person attends has only a "marginal effect" on the choice of his adult friends.

Quite apart from the problem of determining the "effect" of a school on its students, a valid assessment of change in friendships of the various groups between two time periods requires that it be based on the same source of information at both times. The data are not comparable otherwise. The subjects in the present case were asked to recall whether the majority of their friends were Catholic when they were 17 years old. They were then asked if, as adults, *all* their three best friends were Catholic. In the latter instance the individual could not respond affirmatively to the question if even one of his best friends was a non-Catholic.

Since the two sources of information cannot be compared, there appear to be no grounds for Greeley and Rossi's conclusion. It is yet to be learned what proportion of the adults in their sample had a majority of Catholic friends. Moreover, we do not learn from these data the association of attendance at Catholic colleges and the formation of adult friendships, since Greeley and Rossi considered all Catholic education together, regardless of whether their subjects attended college. Nevertheless it is noteworthy that, all told, a little over half their adult sample do number at least one non-Catholic among their best friends. This is to be expected as a result of the day-by-day association of Catholics and non-Catholics at work and at home.

As friendships proliferate and deepen between Catholics and non-Catholics, their differences in background and value systems are liable to be mutually scrutinized, discussed, and perhaps better understood. In college, at any rate, the difference between Catholic and non-Catholic students goes beyond religion and includes politics as well. A large proportion of college students in the National Sample expressed no choice of political party, but the majority were either Republican or Democrat by preference in 1963 (Table 25).

The Catholic students in the National Sample leaned heavily toward the Democratic Party and the non-Catholics leaned just as heavily toward the Republican Party. Forty-five per cent of the Catholic college students and 24 per cent of the non-Catholics considered themselves Democrats. These percentages were exactly reversed among the students who identified themselves as Republicans. The difference in political choice was even greater between the secular college Catholics and non-Catholics than between the Catholic college students and the non-Catholics. Fifty-four per cent of the secular college Catholics considered themselves Democrats and 17 per cent considered themselves Republicans.

TABLE 25. *Political Party Preference and Political Orientation, Seniors, National Sample, 1963, in Per Cent*

College Group (No. in Parentheses)	PARTY PREFERENCE		POLITICAL ORIENTATION	
	Republican	Democratic	Liberal	Conservative
Catholic (99)	25	45	43	29
Secular Catholic (183)	17	54	51	22
Non-Catholic (1,124)	45	24	44	29
(Chi square)	(92.75**)		(4.58+)	

+ p = not significant
** $p \le .01$

These marked differences in reported political party preferences between the Catholic and non-Catholic students do not necessarily signify comparable differences in political beliefs. As reported in another volume students were for the most part very inarticulate about their political beliefs, and most of them stated that they chose the party they did because it was their parents' party.[10] We also know that both political and religious affiliation are related to socioeconomic background, and therefore without further analysis we cannot tell to what extent political differences between the Catholics and non-Catholics are associated with religious or socioeconomic background, or other unknown factors.

Moreover, in some ways the Catholic college students in the National Sample share the political values of their non-Catholic peers. The Catholic college students identified themselves as liberal or conservative in the same proportion as the non-Catholic students and accepted about the same definitions for these terms as did the other students. About 50 per cent of the students agreed that a liberal favors progress and reform, and another 25 per cent saw a liberal as being primarily tolerant and broad minded. A conservative was seen by 50 per cent of students as being cautious and moderate, with another 25 per cent

[10] Trent and Craise (1967); Trent and Medsker (1967).

identifying him as primarily preserving tradition; the latter response was favored more by students in Catholic colleges than by the other students. Close to 45 per cent of the Catholic college and non-Catholic students considered themselves as liberal, and close to 30 per cent considered themselves conservative. Over 50 per cent of the secular college Catholics considered themselves liberal and 22 per cent described themselves as conservative.

In the poll of 12 colleges conducted by the *Educational Reviewer*, students were asked if their political views had changed since entering college.[11] Marquette and Howard University had the highest percentage of students (41 per cent) who said that their political views had not changed at all since coming to college. At only two other schools did more than a third of the students indicate that their political views had not changed. Marquette was the only school in which a higher percentage of students became more conservative than more liberal.

We cannot generalize from the Marquette sample to say that Catholic college students are less likely to experience change in their political views during college than are other students, or that there is a greater tendency for Catholic students to become more conservative, but we have reservations about how conducive to change the atmosphere is in some Catholic colleges. The reasons for these reservations were documented in the previous chapter. For example, the Catholic colleges in the National Sample, compared with other private and public colleges, had disproportionately large numbers of students who became more authoritarian rather than more autonomous after four years. Whatever the Catholic college students consider themselves to be in name, they are more conservative and authoritarian in measured disposition than other students.

This trait is reflected in their attitudes toward Communism. Catholic students consistently display the greatest opposition to Communism and the least willingness to allow Communists either to speak publicly or to teach. This was shown in the *Educational Reviewer* poll when students were asked, "Do you feel that religious beliefs are among the central issues in the conflict between the Soviet sphere and the West?" Over half the students at Marquette answered "yes," whereas less than a third of the students at other schools agreed. Sixty-nine per cent of the Marquette students were definitely opposed to the recognition of Communist China, again manifesting the highest percentage of opposition in any of the schools polled.

[11] *Educational Reviewer* (1963).

Eighty-three per cent of the Marquette students agreed that "members of the Communist party should not be permitted to hold a teaching position in any American college or university." By way of contrast, only 11 per cent of the Reed College students and 34 per cent of the Stanford University students agreed with this statement. There was considerable variation among schools on this issue, with Marquette having the highest proportion of students opposing such a teacher. To this question, as to many others, the University of South Carolina students responded very similarly to the Marquette students.

In the West Coast Sample 51 per cent of the Catholic college seniors in 1963 but only 27 per cent of the public college seniors would deny a teaching position to someone not informing on former Communist associates. Catholic college students were also more likely to deny a passport to a Socialist, but only half as many students would restrict the right of a Socialist to travel as would restrict the right of a former Communist to teach. The difference between the proportions of Catholic college and non-Catholic students taking these positions was significant well beyond the 1 per cent level of confidence.

When the persisting students in the National Sample were asked a question on a related issue in 1963, the responses of the Catholic and non-Catholic students were much more alike. Only a little more than one-third of the students, Catholic or non-Catholic, agreed that Communist party members should be allowed to speak on the radio. A significantly greater proportion of the non-Catholic college students (36 per cent) than Catholic college students (26 per cent) endorsed the more liberal position on this issue. In the West Coast Sample 50 per cent of the non-Catholic seniors in 1963 agreed that a Communist should be allowed to speak on the radio, however, compared with 27 per cent of the Catholic college seniors, a difference again significant well beyond the 1 per cent level of confidence.

Since the Catholic response was so similar in the different geographic areas, but the non-Catholic response was different by 14 percentage points, one may wonder what factors caused the difference. Presumably the church's militant stand against Communism would be a factor in explaining the similarity of the Catholics' responses; Catholics were well schooled in the negative aspects of "atheistic Communism." Perhaps non-Catholics are not exposed to such a consistent, strong message and are more open to and affected by the general cultural milieu in which they live than are Catholics.

But regardless of the differences found between the two samples of non-Catholics on this issue, whenever a question concerning Communism is asked, one can almost count upon the great majority of Catholic students lining up on whichever side of the issue indicates opposition to Communism. It does not matter whether the real issue in a specific instance is freedom of speech, freedom of employment, or equitable representation in the United Nations, the issue for Catholics seems to boil down to one of "Communism versus the Free World," as one student in the National Sample put it.

Adolfs, in his recent book, *The Church Is Different,* emphasizes the need for a dialogue with Communism. He states, "the Catholic Church has already had a good deal to say about and against Communism; but it has not done nearly the same amount of listening."[12] He maintains that the church has denounced the whole of Communism without examining the parts to see what there may be that is of value. Catholic college students appear to have picked up the label "Communism" and oppose anything with that word in it.

It is probably because of the prevailing church attitude concerning Communism that Catholic students engage in so much less protest about the war in Vietnam than do other students. In Peterson's survey of 849 colleges and universities, including 147 Catholic institutions, active protest about Vietnam was reported in 21 per cent of the colleges as a whole, but in only 8 per cent of the Catholic colleges in the sample.[13] Five possible areas of protest were considered in this study: off-campus issues, such as civil rights and the war in Vietnam; student-administration relations regarding dress, dormitory, and general campus policies; quality of instruction; specific faculty issues; and freedom of expression. The type and amount of protest in all cases was that reported by deans of students or comparable officials (see Table 26).

It should be pointed out that despite all the publicity given to student protest movements, only a minority of the 849 schools surveyed reported organized student protest on their campuses. And no more than 9 per cent of the student body were ever reported to be involved in the protest. Only in regard to civil rights, dormitory regulations, and food service did more than 25 per cent of the schools of any type report organized protest, with the hightest percentage, 40 per cent, reporting protest over civil rights. Catholic college students were generally less likely than those at independent liberal arts colleges and universities and those at public universities to engage in such protest,

[12] Adolfs (1966), p. 133.
[13] Peterson (1966).

but somewhat more likely than students at public colleges and at Protestant institutions to protest over civil rights.

One of the major differences between students at Catholic and non-Catholic schools in Peterson's survey was the Catholics' minimal con-

TABLE 26. *Percentage of Colleges Reporting Organized Student Protest, 1964*[a]

Colleges (No.)	Poor Quality of Instruction	Censor- ship	Civil Rights	Dis- armament	Vietnam
Catholic (147)	16	22	45	5	8
All colleges (849)	12	14	38	12	21
Z ratio Catholic vs. all colleges	1.76+	6.24*	1.61+	6.64**	13.24**

[a] Source: Peterson (1965).
+ p = not significant
* $p \leq .05$
** $p \leq .01$

cern with international issues. Only 5 per cent of the Catholic schools reported protests over disarmament and peace, compared with 12 per cent for schools in general, a difference significant at the 1 per cent level. The 8 per cent of Catholic schools reporting protests about Vietnam, compared with 21 per cent for all schools, was previously noted. This difference is also significant at the 1 per cent level.

Definite differences among types of colleges were evident in regard to Vietnam protest, with 61 per cent of the independent universities and only 6 per cent of the teachers' colleges reporting such protest. The proportion of Catholic colleges reporting student protest over the war in Vietnam was nearly the same as the proportion of the teachers' colleges reporting it; and the teachers' colleges reported almost no protest about anything. (The apathy is perhaps shared by the administration, since only 56 per cent of these institutions returned questionnaires, compared to an overall rate of return of 85 per cent.)

The lack of protest over the war in Vietnam is interesting in another way. Peterson found that the institutions which reported the greatest amount of protest over the war in Vietnam also tended to be the institutions of the highest quality, as defined by the proportion of faculty holding doctorates.

The war in Vietnam is a complex issue. But news accounts indicate that to many Americans it is simply a necessary war against Communist aggression. Presumably the Catholic college students reported in Peterson's survey take this position, or at least do not question it. Rather they manifest apparent conformity with the church's traditional opposition to Communism in whatever form.[14] Other results of the study indicate that Catholic college students conform more than other students to certain school policies and are more conservative in their views on certain social issues. But it is not all one-sided. The Catholic college students have also been found to manifest a disproportionate amount of dissent on some issues. They followed the general pattern of protest reported in all colleges by manifesting the greatest concern over civil rights, dormitory regulations, and the quality of their food. Catholic colleges also reported more protest than others over censorship, the quality of instruction, and the inflexibility of the curriculum.

Catholic participation in protests over civil rights was comparatively extensive. Forty-five per cent of the Catholic campuses reported civil rights protest activities in areas around the college, 23 per cent reported that their students had engaged in work or protest in the South, and 30 per cent reported other types of civil rights protest. When church-associated colleges were compared, the percentage participating in local civil rights efforts was significantly higher for Catholic than for Protestant colleges, although an equal percentage reported activity in the South.

The students in the West Coast Sample were asked if they would object to Negroes living next door to them. A majority said they would not, and there were no significant differences between the Catholic college and non-Catholic students on this issue. Greeley and Rossi considered Catholics to be similarly tolerant of racial minorities on the basis of their survey.[15] Glock and Stark's recent national survey also pertains here.[16] They found only a minority of Catholics to be anti-Semitic, and proportionately more Protestants than Catholics were anti-Semites, according to self-report. Catholics continue to show an unusual degree of intolerance and close-mindedness in respect to other social issues, people, and ideas, as shown by their highly authori-

[14] It is to be noted, however, that there has been increased communication between the Vatican and Communist governments, including the U.S.S.R., in recent years. Areas of mutual concern and agreement have been explored, and there have been visits by Soviet officials to the Vatican.

[15] Greeley and Rossi (1966).

[16] Glock and Stark (1966).

tarian scores on various autonomy scales and their responses to a variety of civil rights and social issues. But they do at least report a tolerance for and interest in certain minorities.

Apparently in this particular area Catholics are very cognizant of the problems in the larger society and are as ready as other students to work toward their solution. This may be a result of the church's recent concern and pronouncements about the rights of Negroes in America and about the injustice that has historically been meted the Jews by the church and the rest of society. We will see in chapter 8 on religious values that this concern may not only be very recent, but also somewhat limited. The same can be said for the society as a whole, however, which has been slow to awaken to the many problems in the area of civil rights.

Peterson's data give evidence that Catholic college students have also openly disagreed with some policies and procedures on their own campuses, principally with censorship of student publications. Protests about censorship are not surprising, since there have been many news stories about it on Catholic campuses, and the student who is attracted to student publications may be expected to protest infringements upon his freedom of expression. Twenty-two per cent of Catholic schools reported protest about censorship, compared to 14 per cent of all the schools, a difference significant at the 5 per cent level. Ten per cent of the Catholic schools reported protests about campus rules regarding speeches and appearances of controversial persons; this was higher than at most other types of schools but not as high as the 17 per cent reporting such protest at public universities.

Students at Catholic colleges and technical institutions reported the most dissatisfaction with the quality of their instruction. Sixteen per cent of the Catholic schools and 12 per cent of the schools in general reported such protest. This difference is not statistically significant, but it does indicate that dissatisfaction with the quality of education in Catholic colleges is now being voiced on some campuses. Catholic colleges also report more protest about inflexibility of curriculum (12 per cent) than other schools (8 per cent). Peterson attributes this protest primarily to the required theology and philosophy courses.

Catholic colleges were among those reporting the greatest incidence of protest (18 per cent) about communication with the administration and inability to voice grievances. In addition, 21 per cent protested insufficient student participation in establishing campus policies, a percentage comparable to that of public and private universities and all Protestant institutions.

The chances are that censorship of publications and speakers is exercised more on Catholic than on non-Catholic campuses. It is known that the administration of Catholic colleges has traditionally and characteristically been relatively autocratic and dominated by the clergy.[17] Rogoff and Donovan have demonstrated the relatively poor quality of large proportions of Catholic college faculty members in their educational background, motivation to teach, and scholarly productivity.[18] Astin has demonstrated the relative inflexibility of curricula in Catholic colleges compared with others, and Neel has shown that this pertains to teaching methods as well.[19] On these issues, therefore, Catholic college students may have more to protest about than most other students. But it does seem significant that some of the Catholic students are registering dissent over these matters rather than accepting the status quo silently, as they might have once done.

In the area of student-administration relationships, Catholic schools reported less protest than did other types of schools. Although more Catholic schools reported protests about dormitory and dress regulations than about any other issue except civil rights, the amount of protest was less than that in other types of schools, despite the fact that regulations at Catholic schools are usually more restrictive.

The disruptions and dissent voiced by faculty and students at St. John's University that received such wide public attention in 1965 and 1966 and the equally great disruption at Catholic University of America in 1967 no doubt have far-reaching implications for all Catholic higher education. But the controversy at St. John's evidently did not leave as its legacy an aroused and active student body. In 1965 students at St. John's were involved in a fight to have political clubs on campus, but during the 1966 election, the student newspaper commented harshly upon the fact that nothing seemed to arouse the student body; that students failed to evince any interest in the election, failed to turn out for political meetings, and seemed uncaring about what was happening in the world. The paper editorialized, "We're not saying St. John's doesn't have its share of activists, but how much longer can they keep playing to an empty house?" They concluded, "Maybe we're starting to swallow what the world outside thinks of St. John's, and if we keep it up, maybe they'll be right."[20]

In Peterson's survey Catholic college students were reported to be

[17] Cf. Coffey (1963); Keating (1963); Lawler (1959); Maguire (1961); O'Dea (1958).
[18] Rogoff (1957); Donovan (1964).
[19] Astin and Holland (1961); Neel (1962); Thistlethwaite (1959b).
[20] *Downtowner* (1966), p. 4.

more concerned over having a voice in policy-making than over the rules and regulations established through the policies of the administration. Catholic college students in general have been found to be more receptive to rules and regulations than have other students. But in spite of their more authoritarian attitudes, Catholic college students were as likely as non-Catholics to express the opinion that college regulations should be more permissive. In the West Coast Sample 42 per cent of the 1963 public college seniors and 46 per cent of the Catholic college seniors agreed that campus rules should be more permissive. The difference in percentages was not statistically significant.

Familiarity with the schools confirms that regulations of conduct in the Catholic colleges are more extreme than those in the public colleges. For example, in one of these colleges, women had a ten o'clock curfew; in another they were limited in the number of times they could stay out late on a weekend date. In several institutions attendance at spiritual exercises such as retreats was compulsory. Characteristically, the resident women were limited in the number of times they could visit friends overnight off campus; and whether or not their parents were concerned, they had to have written permission for these visits, stating the name and address of their hosts. In short, the Catholic college students had more rigid rules to contend with than did their non-Catholic peers. By 1963 many of the students felt that the rules should be relaxed. One might wonder why many more Catholic college students did not express a desire for more permissiveness and self-responsibility, other than the fact that more recently a number of Catholic colleges have relaxed many of their rules of conduct.

In spite of the acquiescence to authority and dictum observed among the Catholic college students on various attitudinal scales and questionnaire items, proportionately as many of them see themselves as nonconformists as do secular college students. A little less than one-fourth of the seniors in the National Sample described themselves in this way, and there were no differences among the Catholic college students, secular college Catholics, and non-Catholics. Fewer West Coast seniors in 1963 considered themselves nonconformists, even though they were higher in measured autonomy than the persisting students in the National Sample. Approximately 12 per cent of the Catholics and non-Catholics so described themselves.

A considerable majority of students did not view themselves as nonconformists, and in the National Sample a majority of students did not even consider student conformity a problem. In the National Sample, 29 per cent of the Catholic college students and 36 per cent of the non-Catholic students felt that there was too much conformity among students. The West Coast seniors in general registered more concern over this issue, with a simple majority of students at public and Catholic institutions agreeing that there was too much conformity among college students. But in neither instance did significant differences exist between the Catholic and non-Catholic college students. Virtually none of the students showed activistic concern over student conformity.

Intellectual ferment is to be found in segments of the Catholic press, and it is shown by the recent strikes against the administration at St. John's and at Catholic University, by a few "Catholic intellectuals," and by a dissident priest, layman, or groups of students here and there. But extensive data show that Catholic college students are not a generation of rebels. This was indicated by a survey of students at Boston College in 1962.[21] Students were asked 32 questions about their attitude toward authority, covering attitudes toward regulations in general and toward rules in particular areas such as dress, liquor, and control of student publications. Less than 20 per cent of the students consistently favored easing restrictions, and only a handful of students favored the elimination of restrictions in any particular area. (For example, less than 3 per cent favored eliminating dress restrictions.)

One of the key questions asked was, "Do you think that, since students are responsible for understanding themselves, for developing self-discipline and control over their own conduct, they therefore should not be subject to regulations regarding their conduct or behavior?" Only 17 per cent responded yes to this. Of course, the question is stated in extreme terms; the student must answer yes, no, or uncertain, regulation or no regulation, and there is no opportunity to express attitudes toward limited use of regulations. But given this choice, the students chose regulations. Only 9 per cent chose the option of being uncertain. In summarizing the results, the dean of women at Boston College commented:

My own conclusion is that the Boston College students responded maturely and responsibly to a questionnaire that gave full scope for expressions of extreme anti-authority attitudes. . . . The result, it seems to me, is a rather heartening affirmation of the role of authority in the operation of colleges in general and of their own college in particular. . . . perhaps this report will keep some of my colleagues in sister institutions from saying too glibly that we have on our hands a generation of rebels.[22]

[21] Kinnane (1963). This is also evident from the description of contemporary students at Fordham University and the University of Notre Dame found in two recent commentaries by Cass (1967) and Schrag (1967).

[22] *Ibid.,* p. 301.

Although Catholic students do not seem extremely different from other students in their own reports about themselves, on the basis of several samples it appears that American Catholics have not become completely acculturated or open even on the comparatively superficial level of the variables forming the substance of this chapter. This is even more evident when it comes to the more ingrained, less changeable, and deeper psychological dynamics such as the attitudinal and dispositional traits considered in the previous chapters. Yet we emphasize again that the many differences in personal values and opinions between Catholic and non-Catholic college students recorded in this chapter, although usually significant statistically, are not impressive in a number of cases. And it is certain that the Catholic is no longer confined exclusively or even primarily to his own world of Catholic ideas, interests, and influences.

Of course, such an isolated existence is not possible today. However, it has not been uncommon in the past, as indicated by the materials in chapter 1 and by the recollections of such Catholics as those represented in the *Generation of the Third Eye*.[23] And the effects of such an enclosed existence are long lasting. They may linger on long after the ghetto is left behind, and parents whose interaction with the larger culture was limited may instill attitudes in their children that inhibit full interaction with the larger culture even when greater opportunities for such interaction exist. And although the student is involved with non-Catholic friends, social causes, and activities, the basic attitudes fostered by the parents may not be greatly affected, so that although he is participating in the general social and intellectual scene, he has yet to become fully a part of it. This will continue to be apparent when we take up the subject of postgraduate education in the next chapter.

[23] Callahan (1965b).

CHAPTER SEVEN

The Surge to Graduate School

One sign that Catholics may be approaching the mainstream of American intellectual life is the growing percentage of Catholic students planning to attend graduate and professional schools. This may be the result of increasing interest in the intellectual life; it may also be the result of the growing affluence of Catholics, coupled with the need for advanced training in many occupational fields. Obviously, a student may attend graduate or professional school for a variety of reasons, only some of them intellectual, and although it is an encouraging sign of awakened intellectual interest, attendance alone cannot be taken as proof of deep scholarly interest and intellectual commitment.

Since in preceding chapters Catholic students on the whole were observed to be relatively lacking in the intellectual attitudes that lead to scholarly endeavor, two questions are in order: First, are the Catholic students who plan to pursue advanced studies more open-minded, creative, and critical in their thinking than their undergraduate Catholic contemporaries; and second, are they as intellectually oriented as current non-Catholic graduate students? To initiate answers to these questions we will be concerned in this chapter with three aspects of the present "surge to graduate school": the percentage of students, Catholic and non-Catholic, who are planning to attend graduate school; what degrees they hope to attain; and their intellectual disposition or attitude as they undertake graduate and professional study.

A number of studies have included information about students' plans for advanced education. Although these studies vary in their scope and method, they furnish information about students in different types of institutions of varying sizes located in many parts of the country. Taken together, they should provide an indication of the plans for graduate study of American Catholic students.

This research shows that the percentage of students who are planning to attend graduate or professional school has been increasing in recent years, so that now a considerable majority of students express

157

158 THE SURGE TO GRADUATE SCHOOL

their intention to undertake graduate work at some time. Enrollments in graduate school more than doubled between 1954 and 1964, and this increase was proportionately much greater than the increase in the number of undergraduate students who obtained baccalaureate degrees during the same period.[1] Although it appears that the percentage of Catholics planning to attend graduate and professional school may not yet be the same as for non-Catholics, there is an indication that Catholic college graduates, too, plan to go to graduate and professional schools in greater proportion than ever before.

Gropper and Fitzpatrick were among the first to indicate that Catholics were showing an interest in graduate and professional education comparable to that of non-Catholics.[2] In fact, they concluded that Catholics were planning to attend graduate and professional schools in proportions similar to non-Catholics. Only two Catholic colleges, Boston College and Fordham University, were included in their sample of 35 colleges, however. Since these colleges are both relatively outstanding East Coast Jesuit institutions they cannot be presumed to be representative of Catholic colleges as a whole. The total sample included primarily the large universities, such as the University of California and Harvard, and the select liberal arts colleges, such as Reed and Radcliffe, which Berelson found produce the vast bulk of graduate students.[3] Consequently, the extent to which this study included a "broad national representation" of college students is questionable. Moreover, more recent research indicates that a lesser proportion of students at Fordham than at other universities studied intend to obtain a doctoral degree.[4]

Following the work of Gropper and Fitzpatrick, Davis, in his more comprehensive survey of the "Great Aspirations" of 1961 college graduates, found that 76 per cent of the Catholics and 77 per cent of the total sample were planning to attend graduate or professional school.[5] In the total sample, 80 per cent of the men and 73 per cent of the

[1] Walters (1965); Cartter (1966), p. 227.
[2] Gropper and Fitzpatrick (1959).
[3] Berelson (1960).
[4] McNamara (1963). This was not true of the University of Notre Dame. As previously noted, however, questions may be raised about the goals of the Notre Dame students, as reported by McNamara, since the Notre Dame sample is based upon students who volunteered for the study and is not, therefore, a random sample or necessarily a representative sample. Although a majority of the pregraduate school students who volunteered evidently intended to seek a Ph.D., generalizations cannot be made about the students as a whole on the basis of their responses.
[5] J. Davis (1964).

women planned on some postgraduate education. It was, of course, on the basis of these data that Greeley concluded that Catholics were planning to attend graduate or professional school at the same rate as non-Catholics, a finding that helped lead him to contend that Catholics had reached a level of scholarship comparable to that of non-Catholics.[6]

Our findings do not entirely parallel those of Davis and Greeley, however, either in regard to scholarly disposition or to attendance at graduate school. This applies to both the National and West Coast samples. In the National Sample we investigated the graduate school plans and subsequent attendance of the graduating seniors. Nearly half the students who persisted in college for four years failed to obtain their bachelor's degree within that time. Of all the students who persisted in college, whether or not they obtained their degree in four years, 44 per cent of the Catholic college students, 55 per cent of the secular Catholics, and 67 per cent of the non-Catholics reported plans to attend graduate or professional school. The plans of the graduating seniors were obviously different from those of their classmates. For the following analysis, we examined only those students who received their degree four years after entering college (Table 27).

The Catholic seniors were somewhat less likely than non-Catholics to enter graduate school, although the difference is not striking. Seventy-one per cent of the Catholics and 80 per cent of the non-Catholics who graduated in June, 1963, said they planned to attend graduate or professional school. Seventy-two per cent of Catholic college seniors and 70 per cent of the Catholics at secular colleges planned to continue their education. Non-Catholics were significantly more likely than Catholics at secular colleges to attend graduate school, although the difference between non-Catholics and Catholic college students did not quite reach a level of statistical significance. For non-Catholics, the results in the National Sample more closely parallel the findings of Davis in one way: essentially the same proportion of non-Catholics in both samples planned on postgraduate education. In fact, 87 per cent of the non-Catholic senior men in 1963 were planning to attend graduate or professional school at some time, 7 per cent more than the figure for the men in the National Opinion Research Center sample.

In all the college groups proportionately more men than women planned to attend graduate or professional school. Approximately 12 per cent more of the Catholic and non-Catholic men than women at secular colleges planned to continue their education. Within the

[6] Greeley (1962a, b; 1963).

TABLE 27. *1963 Graduating Seniors Planning to Attend Graduate or Professional School, National and West Coast Samples*

College Group	MEN		WOMEN		TOTAL	
	(Base no.)	Per cent	(Base no.)	Per cent	(Base no.)	Per cent
National Sample						
Catholic	(35)	80	(26)	62	(61)	72
Secular Catholic	(42)	76	(55)	65	(97)	70
Non-Catholic	(285)	87	(380)	75	(665)	80
West Coast Sample						
Catholic	(139)	64	(272)	62	(411)	63
Secular Catholic	(19)	89	(40)	80	(59)	83
Non-Catholic	(194)	85	(212)	68	(406)	76

Z ratio (sexes combined)	
National Sample	
Catholic *vs.* secular Catholic	0.27+
Catholic *vs.* non-Catholic	1.46+
Secular Catholic *vs.* non-Catholic	2.22*
West Coast Sample	
Catholic *vs.* secular Catholic	3.02**
Catholic *vs.* non-Catholic	4.11**
Secular Catholic *vs.* non-Catholic	1.18+

$^+ p =$ not significant
$^* p \le .05$
$^{**} p \le .01$

Catholic colleges, 18 per cent more men than women planned further education.

When seniors in the West Coast Sample were surveyed in 1963, 63 per cent of the students in Catholic colleges planned to enter graduate or professional school, compared with 83 per cent of the Catholics and 76 per cent of the non-Catholics at secular colleges. A higher percentage of secular Catholic women in the West Coast Sample than in the National Sample planned to continue.

Five per cent more West Coast Catholic college seniors planned to enter graduate school in 1963 than in 1960. But the increase was not statistically significant and was occasioned only by the women. As may be seen in Table 28, there was a decline in the percentage of men planning to continue their education: 70 per cent of the senior men in 1960 and 62 per cent of the senior men in 1963 planned to continue. Conversely, the percentage for women increased from 50 per cent in 1960 to 63 per cent in 1963, thus raising the total percentage for Catholic college students in 1963.

Although the overall difference between the 1960 and the 1963 seniors was not great, there was considerable difference in the plans of the class of 1963 as freshmen and seniors, particularly for women.

TABLE 28. *Percentage of 1960 and 1963 Catholic College Seniors Planning to Attend Graduate or Professional School, West Coast Sample*

Class (No. in Parentheses)	Graduate School	Professional School	Total Postgraduate[a]	Z ratio,[a] Graduate vs. Professional School
Men				
1960 (90)	29	41	70	1.68+
1963 (139)	24	38	62	2.55*
Women				
1960 (132)	30	20	50	1.86+
1963 (172)	26	37	63	2.75**

[a] Z ratio, total postgraduate plans, 1960 versus 1963, men: 1.23+; women: 2.50*.
+ $p =$ not significant
* $p \le .05$
** $p \le .01$

Only 35 per cent of the women had expected as freshmen to continue their education after graduation; but 62 per cent of the senior women expected to, their primary goal being to obtain a teaching credential. As freshmen, 57 per cent of the men had expected to continue their education; but as seniors, 64 per cent of them did. The increase may be attributed to the departure of less scholarly students before graduation, to increased interest in advanced education among the remainder as graduation neared, and to a desire to satisfy professional requirements, such as obtaining teaching credentials.

When Weiss surveyed students at St. Louis University in the fall of 1963, he found that only 53 per cent planned to continue their education, including those who were "definitely" and those who were "probably" going to continue.[7] When only seniors in the arts and science school were considered, however, it was found that 64 per cent planned to continue. This total included 77 per cent of the arts

[7] Weiss (1963).

and science men but only 44 per cent of the women. All told, 37 per cent of the St. Louis students "definitely" planned to attend graduate school. The figure for the arts and science seniors at St. Louis is comparable to that for students in the West Coast Sample, who attended institutions emphasizing the liberal arts. However, the percentage of women planning to attend graduate or professional school was much smaller at St. Louis University than in the West Coast Sample.

When McNamara looked at six other Jesuit institutions individually, using Davis' 1961 National Opinion Research Center data, he found that the percentage of seniors planning graduate study ranged from 89 per cent at Detroit University to 64 per cent at Marquette.[8] Since St. Louis is one of the major Jesuit universities, it is surprising that only 64 per cent of its arts and science seniors and only 53 per cent of all students said that they planned to continue their education.

It cannot be established conclusively whether the percentage of Catholics planning to continue their education is closer to the 50 per cent found at St. Louis University and among all four-year college persisters in the National Sample, or to the approximately 64 per cent found in the West Coast Sample, or to the 71 per cent of the National Sample graduating seniors, or to the 77 per cent found in Davis' National Opinion Research Center study. Differences in results among the samples may be attributable to several factors. Despite the great numbers of students included in the National Opinion Research Center sample, it is difficult to generalize from the data because of the highly complicated and unusual sampling and weighting procedures used. For his purposes, Davis wanted to survey students in institutions likely to have an unusually high rate of seniors who would enter graduate school. He weighted his sample accordingly, using "differential sampling rates . . . because among the chief objectives of the survey was the estimation of parameters pertaining to graduating seniors who were planning to go on for graduate study in particular academic fields."[9]

Within these limits, Davis states that in his study an attempt was made to sample a representative group of students, not representative institutions. But since different types of students attend different types of schools, it seems difficult to get representative students without also getting a representation of different types of schools, not just the institutions more likely to produce graduate students. Moreover, his system of weighting responses from institutions where returns were incomplete

---

[8] McNamara (1965).
[9] J. Davis (1964), pp. 285–86.

seems to us only to weight biased responses, since it is assumed that the respondents in any given class or selection strata represent those who did not respond.

As a result of his sampling design, there is also a disproportionate number of large schools in Davis' sample, a situation indicated by Greeley's analysis of a 10 per cent representative sample. The average enrollment of Catholic schools in Greeley's sample was 4,093 in 1961, well above the average enrollment of Catholic colleges across the nation.[10] On a larger scale, therefore, the problem affecting Davis' data resembles the one already noted in Gropper and Fitzpatrick's.

Students in the West Coast Sample were attending Catholic colleges which had average enrollments equaling the nation-wide average for Catholic colleges. The average 1961 enrollment in the colleges represented in the West Coast Sample was 1,000. Students in the National Sample attended 74 Catholic colleges, but entire classes enrolled in these colleges were not surveyed. It can be argued that the National Opinion Research Center data include proportionately too many large institutions likely to produce graduate students in comparison to the situation nationally, and that the West Coast Sample includes schools not sufficiently likely to produce such students. The National Sample, of course, began with whole high school graduating classes rather than with students who happened to end up as college seniors. But it cannot be considered a random sampling of the nation's college youths any more than can the West Coast or National Opinion Research Center Sample. Perhaps the actual percentage of students planning to attend graduate school may fall close to the average of these conflicting figures.

At the same time, the difference in the postgraduate educational plans of the Catholic and non-Catholic college students in the National and West Coast samples leaves some doubt about the validity of the findings of Davis and Greeley until the matter can be clarified by subsequent, more definitive research. Nevertheless, we may surmise that at least among the men a large percentage of Catholic graduates plan to continue their education, even if it is not conclusive that their proportions equal those of non-Catholics. We may also surmise that the proportion will continue to increase for all male students, as long as graduate school is an alternative to military service and as long as industry considers it a prerequisite for much of its personnel. This leads us to inquire further into the meaning behind these statistics.

A major problem in assessing the meaning of any statistics about

[10] Greeley (1963).

graduate school plans is that they usually include students who plan to attend both immediately and later; or else, if the question is phrased in another way, those who are "definitely" planning to attend, those who are "probably" going to attend, and those who "may" attend. As a result, the percentage of students planning to seek advanced education is amazingly high; in fact, one wonders if the graduate and professional schools of the country can possibly have room for all the students.

Of course, not all these students actually enter graduate school, and those who do enter from a particular graduating class do not enter at the same time. The National Opinion Research Center data reported by Davis indicate that about three-fourths of the students who planned to enter immediately after graduation actually did.[11] Men were more likely to carry out their plans; 81 per cent of the men and 63 per cent of the women who planned to enroll immediately after graduation were actually in attendance the next semester. In 1964 we followed up and received responses from over 90 per cent of the seniors in the National Sample. Subsequently we attempted verification of the attendance at graduate school of all the students who reported they

TABLE 29. *Percentage of Seniors Planning to Attend Graduate or Professional School Who Actually Enrolled within One Year after Graduation, National Sample*

College Group (No.)	Per cent
Catholic (44)	32
Secular Catholic (68)	18
Non-Catholic (532)	37
Z ratio	
Catholic *vs.* secular Catholic	1.67+
Catholic *vs.* non-Catholic	0.69+
Secular Catholic *vs.* non-Catholic	3.80**

+ p = not significant
** $p \leq .01$

were undertaking postgraduate education.

There was no record of attendance for many students who reported that they were in graduate school. We assume many students considered that a summer or an evening course, or attendance at a school of

[11] Davis (1964).

education for a teaching credential constituted graduate student status whereas this may not be deemed so by at least some of the graduate schools. Of those who planned to enter graduate or professional school immediately after college approximately 68 per cent did so. Of all the 1963 graduating seniors, 19 per cent of the Catholic college students, 13 per cent of the secular Catholics, and 28 per cent of the non-Catholics attended graduate or professional school by June, 1964. Differences were significant (chi square = 16.42; $p \leq .01$).

On the basis of combined figures in Table 29, 35 per cent of the seniors who planned to undertake postgraduate education at some time had realized these plans within a year after their graduation, including 37 per cent of the non-Catholics and less than 24 per cent of all the Catholics. Thirty-two per cent of the graduates from Catholic colleges who planned to attend graduate school enrolled. This proportion compares favorably with that of the non-Catholics, but is significantly higher than the proportion of secular Catholics who entered graduate school. There were great differences between sexes not shown in the table as well as between religious groups in rate of attendance. Far more men than women entered graduate school, regardless of religious grouping. Among the men, 52 per cent of the non-Catholics who had planned to enter graduate school did so within a year, 27 per cent more than the secular Catholics, and 16 per cent more than the Catholic college graduates. Unlike the significant differences among the men, the differences among the three groups of women were relatively small, and not statistically significant.

A large percentage of students say they plan to enroll at some later time. Of those 1963 seniors planning to enter graduate school, slightly over one-fourth in the National Sample and one-third in the West Coast Sample planned to enter at a later time. Over half the students planning to attend graduate school in the National Opinion Research Center sample planned to attend later.

It is difficult to estimate what percentage of students, who say they will, actually enter graduate school at a later time. We do not know how many students will return after a period of employment or of military service to pursue their earlier academic goals, or how realistic their goals are, or what their motivations to realize them may be. As a professor at a leading university commented recently, "It's getting harder and harder to convince men to come back to school full time. They have that house in the suburbs with monthly payments to be made." And women have that house in the suburbs to take care of, often along with several children.

Of course, plans to attend graduate or professional school, whether they are immediate or long range, are still only an indication of possible intellectual interest. What advanced education means for any group of students cannot be assessed without considering the educational goals they seek. And, as with plans to attend graduate school in general, it is difficult to evaluate the possible results of plans for advanced degrees. Berelson reports that 35 to 40 per cent of the students who start work toward a doctoral degree do not complete it, and we do not know how many students will actually even begin their doctoral studies.[12] This problem is compounded by the nature of the research on this subject, which provides very limited information on the goals, characteristics, and progress of graduate students.

And yet knowledge of the goals and characteristics of graduate students is important, since there is a vast difference between the student who expects to continue his studies for one or two semesters and the student who plans to spend an average of four to six years earning a doctoral degree. Often the teaching credential or master's degree may be considered only a necessary tool for desired employment, or a requirement set by the state as a prerequisite for employment. Although in some fields the doctorate may also be viewed primarily as a necessary condition for employment, the amount of sustained scholastic effort required to achieve it should indicate some continuing interest in the world of ideas, or at least tolerance for academic and research requirements.

It is in this respect, especially, that questions must be raised about the meaning of a woman's attendance at graduate school. Indications are that the majority of women are attending to be certified as teachers or to obtain increments in units to raise their salaries as teachers, and that regardless of their ability, their intellectual endeavors and productivity may be quite limited. This is evidenced by the fact that consistently less than 11 per cent of doctorates granted are earned by women.[13] Thus, if the increase in Catholic graduate school attendance were found to be primarily caused by women, the increased attendance might lead to little increase in scholarly productivity.

Of course, the important consideration is not the length of time spent in graduate school, but how that time is spent. A student entering professional school may be interested only in his specific field of study and preparation for a particular job. His study is primarily directed toward achievement of skills and techniques in a specialized

[12] Berelson (1960).
[13] Wright (1964).

field, rather than toward study of a broad range of ideas. We know in the West Coast Sample that the students who planned to attend professional schools were at a level of ability and measured intellectual disposition considerably—and statistically—below that of their classmates who planned to enter graduate school. The decided difference in intellectual disposition between students planning to attend graduate and professional school will be further discussed in chapter 9 when we explore the characteristics of students who are more intellectually oriented.

The attitude with which some students approach professional school is exemplified by one extremely bright pre-law student at a large Catholic university. When asked whether graduate school is important, he responded, "Unfortunately, it's like belonging to a union. Do you really learn that much?" When asked the purpose of education in general, he commented, "You can't beat the system without college. The trade departments suit you for a vocation."

This student was clearly attending college to prepare himself for a specific career, in this case, law. No doubt his response is not typical of all professional school students. But since the purpose of professional school is to prepare an individual for a specific occupation, it may be expected that these students will be more interested in their professional training than in exposure to a variety of interests and ideas.

The differences between graduate school and professional school are sufficiently great so that whenever possible the two areas should be considered separately. In some studies, goals are divided only into these two areas, with some variation in the meaning of the terms "graduate school" and "professional school." As used here, graduate school includes the more academically oriented fields such as the humanities and social and physical sciences, and professional school includes the more applied fields such as business, engineering, education, law, and medicine. Since professional school encompasses such a wide range of occupations, it is not surprising that a much greater percentage of students enroll in professional school than graduate school.

In the 1964 follow-up of the post-college pursuits of subjects in the National Sample, we found that more of the men entered professional school than graduate school, with 60 per cent of those continuing their education to be found in professional school and 40 per cent in graduate school. Women were more equally represented in the two schools, and differences between Catholics and non-Catholics were nominal.

In the West Coast Sample, 39 per cent of the Catholic college senior men in 1963 were planning to enter professional school and 25 per cent graduate school. Correspondingly, of the Catholic college senior men in 1960, 41 per cent planned to enter professional school and 29 per cent planned to enter graduate school. The 1963 state college students were nearly equally divided between those planning to enter graduate or professional school, but nearly twice as many university students planned to enter professional rather than graduate school.

The relationship of level of ability and socioeconomic status to plans to attend graduate or professional school was also observed among the West Coast seniors. Forty-three per cent of the 1960 senior men of high ability planned to attend graduate school, 20 per cent more than those of low ability. Ability seems less related to the senior women's plans, with only a 10 per cent difference in plans between high and low ability levels (34 versus 24 per cent, respectively). Well over 50 per cent of the senior men of the low ability level and 29 per cent of the high ability men planned to attend professional school.

Ability level appears to be related to the senior men's future plans, and socioeconomic level shows a similar relationship among the senior women: 40 per cent of the women from the high socioeconomic level, but only 9 per cent from the low level, planned to attend graduate school. The senior men planning on professional school came predominantly from the high socioeconomic level. Few men planning on professional school came from the low socioeconomic level, whereas this pattern appears exactly reversed for the women.

Dividing students into graduate and professional school provides a rough differentiation between groups, but it is important to go further and see what degrees they seek. The intellectual disposition presumed to be a prerequisite for the doctoral degree (although not always found among such students) makes consideration of the extent to which Catholics are seeking this degree especially important.

Greeley contends that Catholics are now seeking the doctorate in similar proportion to non-Catholics.[14] He states that 21 per cent of the Catholic and 22 per cent of the Protestant graduate and professional students plan to get a doctorate. These data, of course, concern plans rather than actual attainment, and they may be caused partly by the high proportion of large Catholic universities in the sample, whose students might be more likely than other Catholic students to seek a doctorate. But even in the face of our previous discussion of the

[14] Greeley (1963).

unique sampling procedures and the initial lack of Catholic repre-
sentativeness affecting Greeley's data, his finding is still of interest,
although it is not verified by more recent research.

As in Davis' and Greeley's National Opinion Research Center sample, it will be recalled that a majority of seniors in our National
Sample expressed plans to attend graduate or professional school at
some time. But these plans apparently did not include obtaining a
doctoral degree.

When the seniors in the National Sample were asked what further degrees they planned to get, 4 per cent of the students in Catholic colleges specified a Ph.D. degree, compared with 4 per cent of
the Catholics in non-Catholic colleges and 16 per cent of the non-
Catholics. These figures are based upon responses of all seniors, not
only seniors planning to attend graduate or professional school. A year
later we asked only the students in the National Sample who were
enrolled in graduate school what degree they were certain of obtaining.
Nine per cent of the non-Catholic men said they were working toward
a doctorate, but none of the secular Catholics or Catholic college
students said this. Among the professional school students, 41 per cent
of the Catholic college men were working toward a law degree; 27 per
cent of the non-Catholics reported this. Approximately 10 per cent
of both Catholic college and non-Catholic students were working for
an M.D. Most men were seeking a master's degree, and only a negligible number of women were considering anything beyond the master's.
On the West Coast, 7 per cent of the seniors at the Catholic colleges
and 13 per cent of the seniors at secular colleges expressed plans to
obtain a doctoral degree ($Z = 3.00$; $p \leq .01$). Over twice as many men
as women reported these plans.

On the basis of data collected in 1961 and 1962 from the senior
classes at Columbia, Cornell, Fordham, and Notre Dame, McNamara
found that there was no difference in the proportion of Catholic and
nonsectarian college students who planned to enter graduate school.[15]
However, a significantly greater proportion of the Cornell and Columbia seniors reported the intention to obtain a doctoral degree than did
those at Fordham. And just as we found in chapter 3 that there were
differences in rate of college entrance between Catholics and non-
Catholics regardless of socioeconomic status, McNamara found that
differences between them in plans to work for the doctorate were

[15] McNamara (1963).

". . . almost completely unrelated to socioeconomic status."[16] These data seem particularly relevant to the question of the scholarly attainment of Catholic college graduates since, as already mentioned, Fordham University was one of the two Catholic institutions in the sample that Gropper and Fitzpatrick considered to be representative of colleges across the country.

Of course, many students may not make a decision to seek a doctoral degree until later, possibly after they have attained the master's degree. But it is one thing to examine the generally stated plans of widely distributed college seniors and beginning graduate students; it is another to examine what actually happens among students enrolled in specifically identified major institutions.

One additional institutional study, conducted at the Center for Research and Development in Higher Education, goes beyond plans and conjecture and focuses upon actual doctoral candidates who had completed all their doctoral work except the dissertation.[17] In 1963 Heiss surveyed all candidates for the doctorate at the University of California, Berkeley. She found that only 9 per cent of the candidates were Catholic, and although the Catholics were underrepresented in all doctoral programs, they were more so in the social sciences and biological sciences.

Heiss's study was not intended to represent the situation for the country at large. Nevertheless, several factors suggest that her research may be indicative of circumstances far beyond Berkeley. It is especially relevant since it was conducted so recently, during the current discussion of Catholic intellectuality, and not ten or twenty years ago. And it was conducted at an institution which has one of the highest enrollments of graduate students in the country.

In addition, the Berkeley campus is located in a region where there is a high proportion of Catholics but no Catholic university that grants the doctoral degree. The nearest nonsectarian doctorate-granting university is Stanford, another select institution, and one which charges a very high tuition. Therefore, there is no manifest reason to believe the situation would be much different elsewhere in California or on the West Coast, or in other regions of the country, for that matter.

[16] *Ibid.*, p. 883. As noted in previous references to McNamara's study, the proportion of Notre Dame students planning to attend graduate school compared favorably with the proportion of the Columbia and Cornell seniors with these plans. However it is not known how representative the Notre Dame data are since they were drawn from a volunteer sample.

[17] Heiss (1964).

In sum, then, we are left with some conflict in the evidence concerning the extent to which Catholics are seeking the Ph.D. degree in comparison with non-Catholics. Greeley concluded from National Opinion Research Center data that proportionately as many Catholics as non-Catholics plan to obtain a doctorate. But evidence from the West Coast Sample, the National Sample, McNamara's study of Fordham University students, and Heiss's study of University of California doctoral candidates shows that Catholics are less likely than non-Catholics to seek the doctoral degree.

Beyond whether Catholics are proportionately represented in graduate schools, or whether they are seeking the doctorate in proportion to their non-Catholic peers, we are concerned with the level of intellectual disposition of those Catholics who do plan to enter graduate school and with the meaning of the doctorate for the few who seek it. It was possible to pursue this concern to a limited degree in the West Coast Sample.

The Catholic college seniors planning to embark upon a graduate school education in 1960 were singled out so that their intellectual disposition as measured by the Omnibus Personality Inventory could be compared with that of their classmates and with samples of beginning graduate students. In general, compared with their Catholic college classmates, the potential graduate students showed greater liking for reflective thinking, more openness to new ideas, greater appreciation for the arts and sciences, and greater tolerance for complexity than their fellow students. These conclusions are based upon results of the Thinking Introversion, Theoretical Orientation, Complexity, Estheticism, and Nonauthoritarianism scales of the Omnibus Personality Inventory (Table 30). Mean differences between the two groups averaged about 5 standard points on each scale and with one exception were significant beyond the 1 per cent level. This applies to students anticipating graduate school; as suggested earlier, if preprofessional students were included, the picture would change considerably, and much less difference would be apparent between the continuing students and their classmates.

Although the intellectual disposition of these students is greater than that of their fellow students, it did not measure up to that of non-Catholic students who had recently undertaken graduate and professional school studies, as shown in Table 31. When the 1960 Catholic college seniors planning to attend graduate school were compared with beginning graduate students at California's Claremont Graduate School, it was found that they scored lower on all the intel-

TABLE 30. *Standard Mean OPI Intellective Scores for Catholic College Seniors Planning and Not Planning to Attend Graduate School*

Student Group (No.)	Thinking Introversion	Theoretical Orientation	Complexity	Estheticism	Nonauthoritarianism
Catholic college seniors[a] (206)	51.9	45.2	46.3	51.6	43.9
Catholic college seniors planning to attend graduate school (62)	58.6	50.4	50.7	57.0	48.9
(Critical ratio)	(5.19**)	(4.72**)	(3.22**)	(4.13**)	(2.48*)

[a] Catholic college seniors include seniors planning to attend graduate school.
* $p \le .05$
** $p \le .01$

lective scales except the Estheticism scale, where the mean scores were the same. The difference in Nonauthoritarianism was an almost unbelievable 14 standard points, compared with 4- and 6-point differences on the other scales.

Compared to graduate students in the education department of the University of California at Berkeley, the Catholic students also fell short, despite the fact that education students score consistently lower on the Omnibus Personality Inventory scales than do graduate students in most other fields. The Catholic students scored significantly lower on Theoretical Orientation, Complexity and Nonauthoritarianism, although the scores were similar to those of the education majors on the Thinking Introversion and Estheticism scales. Again the differences between Catholic students and other students were greatest on the authoritarian syndrome, indicating a much greater tendency toward opinionation and intellectual dependency and less independence of thought and openness to others and their ideas.

These were scores of Catholic college seniors in one region of the country planning on graduate school compared with scores of students actually in graduate school. Some of the Catholic students who planned to enter graduate school of course did not, and perhaps they lowered the average scores of the group. Also, there may be an

TABLE 31. *Standard Mean OPI Intellective Scores, Catholics Planning to Attend Graduate School and Students Attending Graduate School*[a]

Student Group (No.)	Thinking Introversion	Theoretical Orientation	Complexity	Estheticism	Nonauthoritarianism
Catholic college seniors planning graduate school (62)	58.6	50.4	50.7	57.0	48.9
Claremont Graduate School (63)	62.8	56.2	55.0	57.0	63.2
University of California Education Department (38)	59.7	56.2	55.0	55.0	63.2
Critical ratio[b]					
Catholic *vs.* Claremont	3.23**	4.24**	2.51**	0.00+	8.03**
Catholic *vs.* Education	0.55+	2.85**	1.91*	0.95+	11.08**
Claremont *vs.* Education	1.70*	0.00+	0.00+	1.00+	0.00+

[a] Source of comparative data: Whiting (1962); Study of Selected Institutions, Center for Research and Development in Higher Education, University of California, Berkeley (in preparation).

[b] One-tailed test

+ p = not significant

* $p \leq .05$

** $p \leq .01$

increase in intellectual disposition during just one semester of graduate school. Therefore, these data must be regarded as suggestive only.

It must be remembered, however, that these were seniors on the brink of graduate school, and the fact that the differences between Catholic students and graduate students were so significant statistically indicates that Catholic graduate students are not likely to measure up to the intellectual level of their contemporaries. It is especially disconcerting that the potential graduate students exhibited such a high degree of authoritarianism and such a low degree of complexity compared to other beginning graduate students. Above all, these scales measure that openness and flexibility of mind, intellectual curiosity, and tolerance for uncertainty and ambiguity that are essential characteristics for the person engaged in scholarly research and creative thinking. Without these qualities, an individual may settle for predetermined answers or reduce highly complex issues to superficial answers. And the research covered in this volume indicates that this is just what may be behind the lack of intellectualism (as defined in these pages) found among many Catholics, even those with doctoral degrees. Considering the implications behind the data just reviewed, it seems essential that what to this point is only a tentative pilot analysis be extended to a full-fledged representative study of contemporary graduate students and recipients of doctoral degrees.

In this light, it is regrettable that most discussion and research on Catholic intellectualism has been reduced to a question of what proportion of Catholic college graduates go to graduate school. This is an oversimplification for Catholics and non-Catholics alike. It should not be assumed that graduate education represents the one and only road to intellectuality: intellectual productivity should not be equated with the attainment of a Ph.D., nor with the amount of words, graphs, and tables one gets into print. The policy of "publish or perish" may well be a misguided one; in some instances it may generate a great deal of printed material with very little thoughtful, intellectual content. As stated previously, intellectualism, as perceived in this study, is rather a matter of the quality of one's critical thinking, the breadth and depth of one's interests and knowledge, one's openness to life, and the creative insight he brings to all around him.

These appear to be the essentials of intellectual disposition. Without these prior qualities there can be no tangible, material intellectual "product," and the attainment of a doctorate will have little intellectual meaning. Of course, if a subculture fosters a large number of creative, intellectual individuals, some of these people may very well be inclined to impress their creative insight onto a tangible product. Thus, contributions to scholarship may to some degree signify the extent to which intellectuality may be found in the subculture from which the tangible scholarly and creative contributions emanated.

Consequently, graduate education may be viewed as *one potential* criterion of intellectuality inasmuch as it may be viewed as preparation for scholarly endeavor. This being the case, the relative authoritarian and uninquiring mentality of the potential Catholic graduate students remains cause for concern. No matter how many students go to graduate school, if they are not scholarly in attitude and intent, they will not be scholars in fact. It would be tragic if Catholics are attending graduate school only to conclude ultimately that they still have all the answers, but in more technical terms.

In this context, the questions persist: What is the overall picture of Catholics in graduate school? Is there an increase in the proportion of Catholics attending, which would indicate increased intellectual commitment on the part of Catholics? Simply attending graduate school is not in itself a verification of intellectualism. Even if Catholics were attending graduate school in equal proportion to non-Catholics, and the data leave this issue in doubt, this would still not be a proof of intellectualism. Goals and dispositions must also be considered, and data from the National and West Coast samples, and from Weiss, McNamara, and Heiss all indicate that the goals and disposition of Catholics are less intellectual than those of non-Catholics.

CHAPTER EIGHT

Religious Disposition and Problems

In the preceding chapters we have examined the intellectual life of Catholic college students, as reflected in their attitudes, interests, and plans for the future. We must now consider the religious life of these students, since we are concerned not simply with intellectuality but intellectuality in a religious context. This chapter examines the religious life of Catholic college students, and the next chapter will explore the relationship between intellectualism and religiosity.

Of primary interest will be the differences in religious orientation between Catholics at Catholic colleges and at secular colleges. We have seen that there are distinct differences in intellectual disposition between these two groups of Catholics. Are there differences also in their religious disposition—that is, not only in the way they practice their religion, but in their approach and attitude toward religion? Common sense tells us that there are; that there must be some differences between students who have been more fully a part of the church system, not only at the college level but during the years preceding. As reported in chapter 3, more than three-fourths of the Catholic college students attended Catholic high schools, compared to about one-third of the Catholics at secular colleges.

It has been argued more than once that it is not only attendance at Catholic schools, but attendance reinforced by family religiosity, that produces "better" Catholics.[1] Regardless of the cause, however, we would expect these students to be, if not "better," at least different Catholics from those who have been and continue to be less a part of the total Catholic system.

But if the secular college Catholic differs from the Catholic college student, does he also differ from the non-Catholic? Does he manifest more of the religious orientation of his non-Catholic classmates or is he more like his fellow Catholics who have remained closer to the church system? If the Catholic who is more exposed to a pluralistic

[1] Greeley and Rossi (1966); Kelly (1946); Thomas (1956); Trent (1964).

176

environment is found to reflect the religious values of that environment more than the values of his church, what has this to say about the existing church system, when more Catholics are being educated in secular than in Catholic colleges? With questions such as these in mind, we shall also examine the differences in religious orientation between Catholics and non-Catholics.

Questions of this kind have also prompted us to examine the comparative change in religious orientation that occurs among Catholics and non-Catholics attending Catholic and secular colleges over a period of four years. Much has been made of the effect of church-related education on religious values. Until recently Protestant denominations as well as Catholics have operated expensive school systems under the assumption that they would provide a religious education unobtainable otherwise and simultaneously provide a liberal education that would be as good as, if not better than, that offered by secular school systems. Both these premises are now being questioned, verbally and empirically. But to date, almost all research on the subject of religiosity, at least, has examined religious behavior after the fact. That is, the values and behavior of the research subjects have been surveyed after their different educational experiences, not before and after. This is a shortcoming, if it may be assumed that college influences students' values, since whatever differences are found between Catholics who have attended Catholic and secular colleges cannot be directly related to the different college experiences. They might only be reflecting differences that existed before they entered college. This problem, encountered in respect to intellectual development in chapter 5, is a crucial one when evaluating the impact of a church-related college on the religious values of its students.

Therefore, it is particularly important to review the longitudinal data available for the West Coast Sample. Again, as in chapter 5, we will be examining the scores obtained by the students who responded to the same religious measurements upon entrance to college and four years later, in 1963. Although we still will not be able to argue that different college experiences caused whatever differences in religious orientation we find, we can determine if there is an association between difference in college experience and difference in amount of change in religious orientation between Catholics in Catholic and secular colleges.

Information about the religious life of these students has been drawn from many sources and types of measures. Central to our discussion are the religious scales and indexes developed at the Center for Research and Development in Higher Education at the University of California, supplemented by a variety of questionnaire responses and protocols of the National and West Coast samples. In addition, we include relevant data from several other national and institutional studies concerned with many aspects of religious orientation.

The complexity of the religious factor is suggested by Glock's identification of five interrelated but distinct dimensions of religiosity.[2] These are (1) the ideological (religious belief); (2) the ritualistic (religious practice); (3) the experiential (religious feeling); (4) the intellectual (religious knowledge); and (5) the consequential (religious effects).

Since the primary concern of this book is intellectuality rather than religiosity, we will not attempt to explore all these dimensions in detail, but will emphasize religious attitudes, beliefs, and practices. We will be concerned primarily with the attitude with which students approach their own and other religions, the beliefs they hold, and how they practice these beliefs, both within the church and in the community. Just as in discussing intellectuality we were concerned not so much with how much a man knows but with his attitude toward knowledge, so here we are concerned more with his attitude toward the church than with his knowledge of its dogma. Although an open, questioning attitude is worth little if it is not based upon and does not lead to greater knowledge, we will discuss the extent of this knowledge only briefly here.[3]

Among the primary instruments developed for the measurement of religious attitudes is the Religious Liberalism scale of the Omnibus Personality Inventory. On this scale, students are asked to respond "True" or "False" to such statements as: "My church, faith, or denomination has the only true approach to God"; "I believe in a life hereafter"; and "It doesn't matter to me what church a man belongs to, or whether or not he belongs to a church at all." The scale is composed of 29 items and has an internal consistency reliability of .84. The higher the score, the more skeptical the person is likely to be toward religion. High scorers tend to reject religious beliefs and practices; low scorers are fundamentalistic and orthodox in their religious beliefs.

The Religious Concepts Inventory, which was developed by the author and Farwell, provides a method for gauging religious beliefs and attitudes conjointly. The scale's highest possible score is 42, and it has an internal consistency reliability of .89. High scores indicate reli-

---

[2] Glock (1959, 1962); Glock and Stark (1966).

[3] The Danforth Foundation has published a 75-item, multiple choice "Test of Religious Knowledge" and has conducted pertinent research in this area (Pattillo and Mackenzie, 1965).

gious fundamentalism, thus measuring in the opposite direction of that of the Religious Liberalism scale. Through the combined measurement of six subscales, the Religious Concepts Inventory indicates the person's position along a continuum from fundamentalist religious beliefs (highest), through liberalism, to fundamentalist disbelief (lowest). The subscales measure an individual's attitude toward the Bible, prayer, man, God, sin, and eternity in such a way that it is possible to categorize a person in one of five groups.

The fundamentalist person is thought to be more constricted in outlook, to have implicit faith in dogma, to hold his faith generally without reason or inquiry, and to show comparatively little toleration for any outlook other than his own. The orthodox person may be expected to subscribe to definite dogma, but with more show of reasoning, inquiry, and toleration than the fundamentalist. The neoorthodox person, described as a religious freethinker, is considered religiously liberal; he may be expected to subscribe to certain positive religious beliefs, such as the existence of a supreme being, but also to manifest a liberal deviation from many conventional beliefs. The agnostic may be expected to manifest liberal disbelief by showing doubt or confusion or both toward any religious doctrinal convictions without categorically denying validity of all doctrine. The nonreligious fundamentalist, atheistic in conviction, may be expected to register categorical denial of and even animosity toward any positive religious conviction.

A third measure, also devised by the author, is the Religious Practices Index. This is a summary measure of the extent of various religious practices and provides a better index of overall religious engagement than does reliance upon a single item, such as frequency of church attendance. A measure of this kind is especially appropriate when church attendance is considered obligatory, as it is for Catholics. Items on the Religious Practices Index assess (1) frequency of church attendance; (2) the person's faith compared to his parents' faith; (3) frequency of church attendance if under no obligation to attend; (4) frequency with which the person commits serious breaches against the tenets of his faith; (5) practice of the person's religious tenets compared to that of his friends; and (6) the extent of the person's disagreement with the dogmas of his religion. The Spearman-Brown corrected reliability coefficient is .73. The index correlates highly with the Religious Liberalism scale of the Omnibus Personality Inventory and with the Religious Concepts Inventory while maintaining independent variance. Further details of these scales may be found in

Appendix D and in the Omnibus Personality Inventory Manual.[4]

When we look at the specific dimensions of religiosity as measured by these scales, the differences between Catholics in Catholic colleges and Catholics in secular colleges are dramatically evident, as are the differences between both groups of Catholics and non-Catholics. On every measurement the Catholic college freshmen upon entering manifested a great deal more religious commitment than the other students. As shown in Table 32, the 1959 freshmen in the West Coast Sample obtained a standard mean score of 36.2 on the Religious Liberalism scale, placing them almost one and one-half standard deviations below the mean; that is, over 90 per cent of the normative sample obtained a more liberal score than the average score obtained by the Catholic college freshmen. Catholics at secular colleges were much higher than

TABLE 32. *Standard Mean Religious Liberalism Scores, Freshmen, West Coast Sample*

COLLEGE GROUP	MEN		WOMEN		TOTAL		CRITICAL RATIO, MEN vs. WOMEN
	(No.)	Mean	(No.)	Mean	(No.)	Mean	
Catholic	(444)	37.9	(508)	34.7	(952)	36.2	5.00**
Lutheran	(249)	41.1	(344)	39.5	(593)	40.2	1.92+
Secular Catholic	(226)	44.3	(203)	41.1	(429)	42.8	3.33**
Non-Catholic	(1,118)	52.3	(1,050)	49.1	(2,168)	50.7	7.80**

Critical ratio (men and women)	
Catholic *vs.* Lutheran	7.84**
Catholic *vs.* secular Catholic	11.57**
Catholic *vs.* non-Catholic	39.18**
Lutheran *vs.* secular Catholic	4.19**
Lutheran *vs.* non-Catholic	23.33**
Secular Catholic *vs.* non-Catholic	15.19**

+ p = not significant
** $p \leq .01$

the Catholic college students in Religious Liberalism, with the difference significant well beyond the 1 per cent level. Their standard mean score of 42.8 placed them nearly 7 standard points, or well over one-half a standard deviation, above their Catholic college peers. In other words, the two groups of Catholics are much different in their

4 Center for the Study of Higher Education (1962).

approach and attitude toward religion. By the same token, the Catholics at secular colleges are much different in religious attitude from their non-Catholic classmates, again by more than one-half standard deviation. The non-Catholics obtained a mean score of 50.7 on the Religious Liberalism scale, a score significantly different from both groups of Catholics (beyond the 1 per cent level). In view of these differences, there is reason to believe that the Catholic college students are hardly in the same religious world as their non-Catholic contemporaries and are quite removed from the religious world of secular college Catholics.

Table 32 also includes the mean scores obtained by the incoming freshmen in a major Lutheran college and demonstrates the similarities in attitude between Catholicism and Protestant fundamentalism that have been referred to earlier. The differences between the scores obtained by the Lutheran college students and both groups of Catholics are significant. However, it is notable that the Lutheran students' measured religious orientation is closer to that of the Catholic college students than is that of the secular college Catholics. Thus, the Catholic college students and Lutheran college students appear to be the most orthodox, with the Catholics at secular colleges maintaining a relatively orthodox position, but one significantly less so than their Catholic college peers. The fact that Catholic and Lutheran students are the least liberal in attitude was anticipated, since the Lutheran church is one of the more conservative Protestant churches and may be expected to instill attitudes toward church authority and doctrine similar to those instilled by the Catholic church, especially among students committed enough to their religion to attend their own church colleges.

As with all groups of students, a greater measured religiosity was found among the women than the men. The standard mean Religious Liberalism scores for women were 3 points lower than the mean for men within all groups except the Lutheran college students, where the difference between men and women was only 2 points. Scores for Catholics at state colleges and universities are combined in Table 32. However, when these students were observed separately, state university Catholic men were found to be more liberal than state college Catholic men, although there was no difference among the women. Similarly, university non-Catholics, both men and women, were found to be somewhat more religiously liberal than state college non-Catholics.

Since high scores on the Religious Liberalism scale indicate a skeptical attitude toward religion, a Catholic who believes in the basic doctrines of the church and follows church practices could not be expected to receive a high score. A raw score as high as 8, however, corresponding to a standard score of 39, could be achieved by an individual who is very orthodox religiously yet who would not subscribe to items that are strictly authoritarian. This would mean rejecting such statements as: "One needs to be wary of those persons who claim not to believe in God," and "My church, faith, or denomination has the only true approach to God." But the raw mean score of 6 obtained by the Catholic college freshmen (translated to a standard score of 36 in Table 32) means that they endorse out-and-out authoritarian statements. Many of these students evidently accept all the tenets of their faith without question and mistrust those who do not share their religious beliefs.

Even the most devout Christian may be expected to have some doubts about his religion and may even subscribe to the statement "We cannot know for sure whether or not there is a God." Such an individual may feel quite certain himself that there is a God, but not be able to say that we can know this with certainty. Such a person may also agree that "Each person should interpret the Bible for himself." Agreement with such statements as these would lead to a higher score on Religious Liberalism, without placing an individual in the realm of the agnostic or atheist. But entering Catholic college students, intensely religious in orientation as a group, express no religious doubts and reflect no critical insight into their religion.

The differences between the attitudes expressed by Catholic students and by other students were equally evident when scores on the Religious Concepts Inventory were compared. The patterns of difference found among the various freshman groups on the Religious Liberalism scale remained the same on the Religious Concepts Inventory, and with the same statistical significance (Table 33).

The differences in both attitude and belief between Catholics at Catholic and at secular colleges may be illustrated by examples from the Religious Concepts Inventory. The secular college Catholics more often saw God in the more general aspect of "a supernatural power beyond man's comprehension" and the Bible as "an account of man's experiences with God." The Catholic college students, on the other hand, more often saw God as "a Divine Being" and the Bible as "God's revelation written by inspired men." The concepts of "God" and "Bible" were accepted by both groups, but the Catholic college students appeared to choose a more specific, doctrinal approach than did the secular college Catholics. The two approaches are not contradic-

TABLE 33. *Standard Mean Religious Concepts Inventory Scores,*
West Coast Sample[a]

College Group (No.)	Mean
Catholic (952)	56.6
Secular Catholic (429)	52.4
Non-Catholic (2,168)	45.1
Lutheran (593)	55.1
Critical ratio	
Catholic vs. secular Catholic	10.3**
Catholic vs. non-Catholic	50.0**
Catholic vs. Lutheran	4.8**
Secular Catholic vs. non-Catholic	16.6**
Secular Catholic vs. Lutheran	7.2**
Non-Catholic vs. Lutheran	36.8**

[a] The Religious Concepts Inventory norms are based on the total West Coast Sample. Approximately 100 students out of the sample did not complete the inventory.
** $p \leq .01$

tory, and the same person could accept both ideas, but the question is which one he will select when given a choice. The Catholic college students consistently chose the more orthodox approach.

It should be remembered that the Religious Liberalism scale and the Religious Concepts Inventory were administered to these students as freshmen, and the results therefore demonstrate the difference among students as they enter college rather than measuring the effect of college. The fact that Catholics at secular colleges are less orthodox in their beliefs and practices cannot therefore be considered the consequence of attendance at secular colleges. This is not to say, of course, that the students will not change in varying degrees once having entered college, nor is it to say that what has been observed here is independent of prior educational and familial experiences.

Most of the Catholic college students attended Catholic high schools, whereas only a minority of the secular college Catholics did so. Therefore, the differences in religious orientation found between the two groups probably are in part a result of religious education and attitudes fostered by different family and educational environments. And no doubt differences in environment and associated value systems are to be found between parents who are so aligned with their church that they prefer to have their children attend its schools and those who

TABLE 34. *Standard Mean Religious Liberalism Scores for University Freshmen Whose Parents Are of Different Religions*

Religion of Parents (No.)	Mean
Catholic college freshmen[a] (952)	36.2
Catholic (272)	43.5
Catholic-Protestant (181)	48.4
Protestant (1,580)	50.5
Catholic-Jewish (12)	54.2
Jewish (296)	56.9
Jewish-Protestant (23)	57.4
Critical ratio	
Catholic *vs.* Catholic-Protestant	5.00**
Catholic *vs.* Protestant	11.05**
Catholic *vs.* Catholic-Jewish	5.94**
Catholic *vs.* Jewish	18.42**
Catholic *vs.* Jewish-Protestant	6.69**
Catholic-Protestant *vs.* Protestant	2.88**
Catholic-Jewish *vs.* Jewish	1.23+
Protestant *vs.* Jewish	13.10**
Protestant-Jewish *vs.* Jewish	.34+
Protestant-Jewish *vs.* Protestant	3.45**

[a] Included for comparative purposes only; tests of statistical significance include university data exclusively.

+ p = not significant

** $p \leq .01$

do not care about church education. No doubt, too, the environments in church-related and public schools differ.

We have seen that students entering Catholic colleges are the most religiously oriented of all students observed and non-Catholic students are the least religious, on the basis of the Religious Liberalism and Religious Concepts scales. Catholics attending secular colleges fall between these two extremes. These Catholics, who form a majority of the Catholics who enter college, already are less committed to their faith. In their non-Catholic environment, the chances are that they will form close social relationships with non-Catholics in greater proportion than Catholic college students. In the end, this no doubt means that a growing number of Catholics attending secular colleges will marry non-Catholics. Therefore, it is interesting to speculate upon

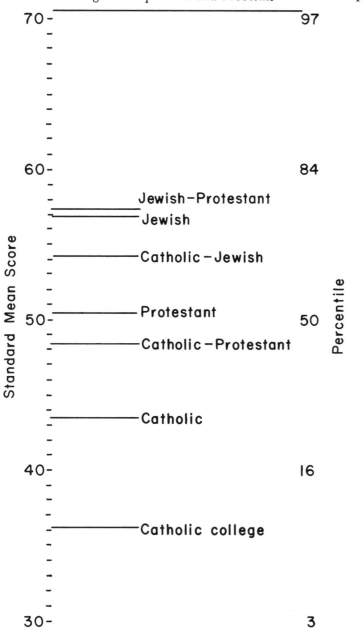

FIG. 7. Standard mean Religious Liberalism scores for university freshmen whose parents are of different religions.

the religious orientation of the children whose parents are from different religions.

The sample of freshmen entering the University of California was varied enough so that we were able to compare the mean Religious Liberalism and Religious Concepts Inventory scores for groups of students who reported their parents were of different religious affiliations: those who reported both their parents were Catholic, or both Protestant, or both Jewish; one Catholic and one Protestant, one Catholic and one Jewish, and one Protestant and one Jewish. In this analysis the scores of these two scales so paralleled each other that only the standard mean Religious Liberalism scores are shown in Table 34 for the student groups by their religious background. As a point of reference, the mean Religious Liberalism score is also shown for the Catholic college freshmen. The university students who reported no religious background have been omitted from the analysis. A comparatively large number of students reported a mixed Catholic and non-Catholic background. Of all students who reported at least one Catholic parent, 272 or nearly 60 per cent reported both their parents were Catholic, and 193 or over 40 per cent reported one of their parents was Catholic.

The results shown in Table 34 are more graphically presented in Figure 7. At the lower extreme falls the very religiously oriented score obtained by the Catholic college students. This is followed, but at a considerably higher level, by the mean score obtained by the university freshmen who reported both their parents to be Catholic. At the upper extreme fall the mean scores of the students who reported both their parents to be Jewish, or one Jewish and one Protestant. In between fall the mean scores of the students who reported their parents to be Catholic and Protestant, both Protestant, or Catholic and Jewish.

Note that the university freshmen who reported one parent Catholic and one Protestant obtained a mean score within approximately 2 standard points of the score of the students whose parents were both Protestant, but nearly 5 points (or the equivalent of one-half standard deviation) above the score of their classmates whose parents were both Catholic. The students who reported one of their parents to be Catholic and one Protestant differed significantly in religious orientation from their classmates whose parents were both Protestant, but they differed much more from their classmates whose parents were both Catholic. Again, the few students who reported one parent Catholic and one parent Jewish obtained a religious orientation score much more like that of the students with two Jewish parents than that of the students with two Catholic parents. In fact, the students coming from a mixed Catholic-Jewish parentage are much more liberal in religious orientation than students with Protestant parentage.

The implications of these findings are quite clear. If these data are at all representative of the situation elsewhere, then youths who have one Catholic and one non-Catholic parent are much more likely to adopt a religious orientation more characteristic of non-Catholics. This is remarkable considering that the Catholic church has traditionally required the children of mixed marriages to be brought up in the faith of the Catholic parent. Of course, we do not know what religious training these students have received, or what the religious beliefs and practices of the parents are like. Individuals who marry outside of the religious tradition in which they were raised may hold an attitude toward religion different from the common one; a Catholic who marries outside his religion may well be one who holds more liberal views than most of his fellow Catholics, and these views might have been transmitted to his children even if they were members of the Catholic church and instructed in its doctrine.

But regardless of the reason for the more liberal views, children of mixed marriages do display mixed religious values, a matter that may be of some concern for the Catholic church. The church is liable to witness a greatly increased proportion of mixed marriages among its constituency in the years to come, even more so now with the eased restrictions on Protestant-Catholic relationships resulting from the Ecumenical and Vatican councils of the 1960's. And, assuming that this constituency remains at all allied with the church, the church will also probably witness greatly different intellectual perspectives among its members. This possibility is demonstrated in the following chapter, which considers the relationship between intellectual and religious disposition.

When we examine behavior in addition to attitude and belief, the comparatively high degree of religiosity found among Catholic college students compared to secular college Catholics and freshmen of a mixed Catholic and non-Catholic background remains apparent. Religious behavior may be distinguished in various ways, including practices and morals. Religious activity involves personal spiritual concerns and church-centered activities; moral activity involves personal moral behavior and behavior related to relevant social issues.

The Religious Practices Index does not measure social attitudes or activities, but it does measure moral and religious practices and the extent of conformity to church teachings. The index takes a comprehensive view of the individual's religious behavior, including (1) his self-report of how well he follows his creed and conscience compared to others; (2) how much he agrees with the proscriptions and policies of his faith as he sees them; and (3) his frequency of voluntary as well as duty-bound church attendance.

As shown in Table 35, freshmen in Catholic colleges in the West Coast Sample achieved a standard mean score of 50.8 on the index. A comparison group representative of Catholic freshmen at a California junior college obtained a mean score of 43.7, compared with a score of 39.9 obtained by their non-Catholic classmates.[5] Differences between the Catholics at Catholic colleges and at the junior college were highly significant statistically, as were differences between Catholics and non-Catholics. The Religious Practices Index was designed primarily to differentiate religious practices among Catholics and its items might

TABLE 35. *Standard Mean Religious Practices Index Scores, Catholic College and Junior College Freshmen, West Coast Sample*[a]

College Group (No.)	Mean
Catholic (1,173)	50.8
Junior college Catholic (24)	43.7
Junior college non-Catholic (74)	39.9
Critical ratio	
Catholic *vs.* junior college Catholic	18.14**
Catholic *vs.* junior college non-Catholic	35.64**
Junior college Catholic *vs.* non-Catholic	6.36**

a The junior college students include a few sophomores.
** $p \leq .01$

have a different meaning for non-Catholics. Presumably, however, the two groups of Catholics responded to the index from roughly the same frame of reference, and their responses indicate that Catholic students entering Catholic and public colleges differ considerably, not only in religious attitude but also in the practice of their faith.

One question on the Religious Practices Index inquires into fre-

[5] Normative data for the Religious Practices Index are based upon the 1,271 Catholic college and junior college students who responded to the index in 1959. Because of the preponderance of Catholic college students in the sample, the mean score is higher than would be likely in a more diversified sample.

quency of church attendance, and the high rate of attendance among Catholic students is notable in all studies. But here again, differences are evident between Catholics attending Catholic colleges and those attending secular colleges. For example, 99 per cent of the Catholics at Catholic colleges in the National Sample reported attending church at least once a week, while 75 per cent of the Catholics at other colleges did so. Only 43 per cent of Protestant students in the National Sample reported weekly church attendance. Over 50 per cent of the students at Catholic colleges and less than 20 per cent of the secular Catholics reported attending Mass more than once a week.

In several ways, therefore, evidence of religious practice is consistent among Catholics and consistently greater among those who enter Catholic colleges. But as we have noted, these differences in measured religious orientation for the most part were found just as the students were entering college. They did not show what the religious orientations of the students were after they attended college. How, then, did the students' religious values change during college? Jacob's summary of available research led us to believe that although students in general did not necessarily lose their religion while in college, they became more liberal in their religious views.

Granting this possibility among students in general, we theorized that it would be least apparent among Catholic college students for a variety of reasons. We knew Catholic college students to be comparatively homogeneous in family and educational background and religious commitment. We knew this commitment to be high, so high that most of the students after having attended Catholic elementary and secondary schools preferred to attend a Catholic college as well. We also knew that an avowed purpose of their colleges was to maintain the faith. Finally, when comparing the 1959–60 Catholic college freshmen in the West Coast Sample with the seniors in that same academic year in a previous report, we found essentially no difference—statistical or otherwise—in the religious orientation of the two groups as measured by the various scales previously discussed.[6]

Of course, lack of change in religious attitude could occur if the Catholics obtained such extreme scores on the religious attitude scales that they would be unable to score higher when responding to the scales a second time. However, this is not evident upon investigation. The Catholic college freshmen did not score so high that it would not have been possible for seniors to score higher. The highest score on the Religious Concepts Inventory was achieved by freshman and

[6] Trent (1964).

senior Catholic college women, with a raw mean score of 36 out of a possible score of 42. By contrast, 80 novices in several religious orders obtained a mean score of 39.

It is also possible that the factors of ability and socioeconomic background would affect the differences in religious disposition. But, here again, the lack of differences found between these freshmen and seniors in the previous research were not markedly altered when scores were analyzed by socioeconomic and ability level. However, both freshmen and seniors at the high ability level obtained a somewhat higher measured degree of religiosity than students at the lower ability level—which is also evidence that there was no negative correlation between intelligence and religion for these students. Assuming, then, that the freshmen represented the same segment of the population and would be subject to similar educational experiences, we expected that the 1959 freshmen would change little in religious orientation by 1963 and would therefore reflect the religious outlook of the seniors four years before them.

TABLE 36. *Standard Mean Religious Liberalism Scores for Students as Freshmen and Seniors, West Coast Sample*

	COLLEGE GROUP		
CLASS	Catholic (No. = 243)	Secular Catholic (No. = 54)	Non-Catholic (No. = 324)
Freshman	35.5	41.0	51.2
Senior	37.8	48.0	56.2
Difference	2.3**	7.0**	5.0**

** $p \leq .01$

Our expectations were realized. The scores of the Catholic college students on the Religious Liberalism scale were the lowest of all the students as freshmen, and despite an overall increase in liberalism, the difference in religiosity between the Catholic college students and the others as seniors was even greater. As shown in Table 36, when the Catholic college freshmen in the West Coast Sample were retested as seniors, their standard mean Religious Liberalism score had increased approximately 2 points, from 35.5 to 37.8. The increase was statistically significant, but it was the smallest increase recorded for any group of students and the senior score was well below that obtained by the non-Catholic students as freshmen. There was no opportunity to administer the Religious Concepts Inventory for comparison in 1963.

Catholic students at secular colleges, who started out with considerably higher Religious Liberalism scores than those of the Catholic college students, also changed in measured religious orientation much more than did their peers at Catholic colleges. In fact, this group showed the greatest change of all, going from a standard mean of 41 as freshmen to a mean of 48 as seniors. The non-Catholics began with the highest mean Religious Liberalism score as freshmen and increased 5 standard points, from 51.2 to 56.2.

For all groups, the rate of increase was approximately the same for men and women, although women started out lower and thus as seniors obtained a lower mean score than men. In all these analyses the same students are compared, just as in the longitudinal analyses of intellectual development in chapter 5; scores of those students who were originally surveyed as freshmen but who were unavailable as seniors have been excluded from the freshman computations. Since we are talking about the same students at both times, and since there are marked differences in change scores obtained by the three groups, it is evident that the secular college Catholics and non-Catholics changed more in measured religious attitude than Catholic college students after four years of college.

This is confirmed by the analysis of the statistical differences in the amount of change recorded among the three groups through the statistical technique, which was described in chapter 5 and which may be found in Appendix C. We are, of course, speaking here of the significance of the differences among the change scores obtained by the three groups. These differences in change in Religious Liberalism among the three groups are shown in Figure 8, which presents graphically the mean standard scores obtained by the same students as freshmen and as seniors (noted in Table 36).

Although all the groups of students became somewhat more liberal in religious attitude, the attitudes of students in Catholic colleges changed significantly less than did those of the other students. There was a significant difference in the degree of change between students in Catholic colleges and Catholics in secular colleges, as well as a significant difference in the amount of change between the Catholic college students and the non-Catholic students. The difference was significant at the 5 per cent level when the two Catholic groups were compared and significant at the 1 per cent level when Catholic college students and non-Catholics were compared. The Catholics at secular

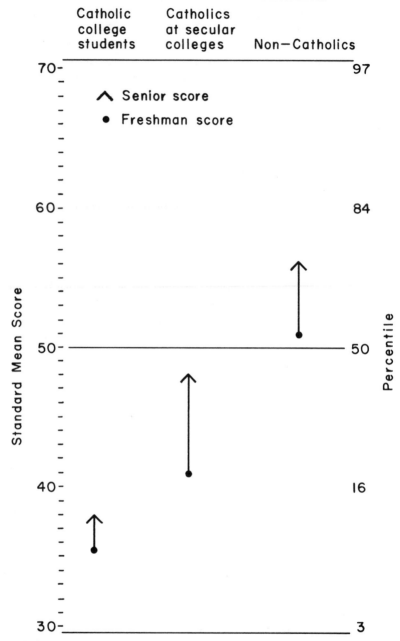

FIG. 8. Comparison of standard mean Religious Liberalism scores for students
as freshmen and as seniors, West Coast Sample.

colleges changed more than the non-Catholics at these schools, but not significantly. Differences between the sexes are not significant.

That the West Coast Catholic college students changed as much in intellectual disposition as other students was determined by data in chapter 5, but this is not true for religious orientation. We have also seen that there is little difference to be found in the religious attitudes of students at Catholic colleges in the West Coast Sample, whether we are talking about the students in the class of 1960 or in the class of 1963, tested as freshmen or as seniors. The scores are all well over one standard deviation below the normative mean and are below those for both Catholics and non-Catholics at secular institutions.

When we turn from the West Coast Sample and look at 1963 seniors in the National Sample, we find that the standard mean for Catholic college students is very close to the West Coast mean (Table 37). The National Sample mean is 35.5, which does not differ significantly from the West Coast mean of 37.8. The Catholics at secular colleges in the National Sample scored 46.4, compared with 48.0 in the West Coast Sample, and non-Catholics in the National Sample scored 50, which differs considerably from the score of 56.2 obtained by the non-Catholics in the West Coast Sample. As expected, the mean for the men was higher than for women, regardless of the type of college the student attended. The men averaged 2 points higher in Religious Liberalism.

There was no opportunity to administer either the Religious Lib-

TABLE 37. *Standard Mean Religious Liberalism Scores, 1963 Seniors, West Coast and National Samples*

| | WEST COAST SAMPLE | | NATIONAL SAMPLE | |
COLLEGE GROUP	(No.)	Mean	(No.)	Mean
Catholic	(243)	37.8	(99)	35.5
Secular Catholic	(54)	48.0	(183)	46.4
Non-Catholic	(324)	56.2	(1124)	50.0
Critical ratio				
Catholic *vs.* secular Catholic	4.53**		12.63**	
Catholic *vs.* non-Catholic	21.90**		23.76**	
Secular Catholic *vs.* non-Catholic	5.57**		5.03**	

** $p \leq .01$

eralism or Religious Concepts Inventory to the National Sample in 1959. Therefore, we have no direct knowledge of how much these students changed in religious orientation during four years of college. But we do know that the patterns of differences among these students as seniors is the same as that for the West Coast seniors in both 1960 and 1963. That is, the Catholic college seniors in the National Sample were considerably more committed and less liberal in their responses to the Religious Liberalism scale than the Catholics at secular colleges; the non-Catholics were the most liberal.

We know, too, from the data in Table 38 that these differences continued to exist with level of ability held constant. With the exception of the low ability non-Catholics, the mean Religious Liberalism scores obtained by the three student groups at each of three levels of ability roughly varied by only 1 standard point. However, the differences among the three groups of students are as evident at each level of ability as they are for the total groups (Table 37). Further analysis is needed to delineate the exact sources and correlates of variation in religious orientation, and the small numbers of low ability Catholics must be taken into account. But as the data stand, measured religious orientation varied a great deal by the three student groups, and very little by differences in level of ability. We noted this same situation earlier when referring to the original West Coast Sample.

TABLE 38. *Standard Mean Religious Liberalism Scores, Seniors, National Sample, by Ability Level*

	COLLEGE GROUP					
	Catholic		Secular Catholic		Non-Catholic	
ABILITY LEVEL	(No.)	Mean	(No.)	Mean	(No.)	Mean
High	(66)	35.2	(114)	46.8	(712)	50.2
Middle	(29)	35.9	(51)	45.6	(321)	49.7
Low	(4)	36.3	(11)	45.6	(65)	47.3

We can also learn something of the change of religious values of the students in the National Sample from their self-assessment (Table 39). In 1963 we asked the students in both the West Coast and National samples how they felt their value for religion had changed since they entered college four years previously. Specifically, we asked if their value for religion had increased, remained the same, or lessened after a four-year exposure to college. The differences among the Catholic college students and secular college Catholics and non-Catholics are highly significant.

TABLE 39. *Percentage of Students Reporting Change in Religious Values, National Sample*

COLLEGE GROUP (No.)	Value Religion More	No Change in Value	Value Religion Less	No Response
Catholic (99)	82	15	3	0
Secular Catholic (183)	42	27	29	2
Non-Catholic (1,124)	47	25	27	1
Z ratio				
Catholic *vs.*				
secular Catholic	6.36**	2.19*	5.18**	
Catholic *vs.*				
non-Catholic	6.79**	2.08*	5.17**	
Secular Catholic *vs.*				
non-Catholic	1.10+	0.66+	0.64+	

+ p = not significant
* $p \leq .05$
** $p \leq .01$

In the National Sample, 82 per cent of the Catholic college seniors said they valued religion more since their freshman year, and only 3 per cent said they valued it less. This is quite different from the other students, Catholic and non-Catholic alike. The Catholics and non-Catholics in public colleges and universities were remarkably similar to each other in their reported change in religious attitudes. Forty-two per cent of the Catholics and 47 per cent of the non-Catholics at these colleges said they valued religion more. Twenty-nine per cent of the Catholics and 27 per cent of the non-Catholics said they valued it less.

Although little difference in religiosity between freshmen and seniors is indicated by test scores, when seniors in West Coast Catholic colleges were asked how their attitude toward religion had changed since coming to college, 72 per cent said they valued it more, and 23 per cent said their attitude had not changed. When asked what contributed to the change, the highest proportion, almost one-third, specified personal contact with instructors. Contacts with students, friends, and courses in such areas as theology and philosophy also reportedly contributed in a major way to change. The two main reasons listed for change of religious values by students in the National Sample were, first, contacts with students and friends and, second, contacts with instructors.

The singularly increased value for religion, rather than any great liberation of religious attitudes, among students who persist in Catholic colleges is suggested in yet another way. In 1959 and 1960, when the students in the West Coast Sample were asked whether or not they felt a personal need for religion, 58 per cent of the freshman men and nearly 75 per cent of the freshman women replied that they did; but among the seniors, almost 100 per cent of both men and women gave affirmative answers. A large majority of the seniors also stated that colleges should stress religion more (79 per cent of the men and 89 per cent of the women). The overall significance of the corresponding chi squares of these differences holds regardless of ability and socioeconomic level.[7] Apparently the seniors' increased endorsement of the importance of religion on both a personal and institutional level exists without any great shift in basic attitudinal or doctrinal position, such as that measured by the Religious Concepts Inventory. Thus, these students may feel a greater need for religion as they progress through a Catholic college without becoming essentially any more or less liberal in their religious orientation.

Since only 3 per cent of the Catholics at Catholic colleges and 29 per cent of the Catholics at public institutions said they valued religion less as seniors, it might be concluded that public institutions have a negative effect upon religious belief, and this might very well be true. However, since evidence indicates that Catholics at non-Catholic colleges were less religious to begin with, this may simply be a continuation of an already existing tendency. The change in measured religious attitude may indicate the same thing. There is no definite evidence that the decline resulted from attendance at a particular type of school. Regardless of their religious affiliation, better than two-thirds of the students at public institutions indicated increased value or no change in the value they placed upon religion. Thus there appears to be no mass devaluation of religion by students attending public institutions. This is also evident from an extensive sample of students surveyed recently who were attending a variety of private, Catholic and public colleges in Rhode Island.[8]

Many students, when asked in interviews to describe the change in

7 *Ibid.*
8 Riggs (1967).

their religious views, said that their views had "not really changed but have deepened." Others said they had come to understand what they had always believed. As one National Merit Scholar at Marquette expressed it, "You believe something, and once you study things you realize that you aren't really accepting all this on faith. There is a reasoning process involved, so that you aren't changing your views, you're just understanding them." This particular girl felt that for her the increased understanding came primarily from contact with other students and only secondarily from courses in religion. In her opinion, "some of the courses [on religion] were a little time-wasting and some were very good."

Whatever the quality of the particular course or institution, attendance at a Catholic college is to all appearances related to a greatly increased emphasis upon the importance of religion and leads to considerably less change in religious attitude than for Catholics and non-Catholics attending secular colleges. The very strong religious commitment observed among Catholic college students is manifested in a variety of other ways both in our research and in that of others. But their commitment does not appear to lead to exceptional insight into Christian principles or to the extensive translation of these principles into constructive intellectual or social action.

The students in the 12 colleges who were polled in the 1963 *Educational Reviewer* survey were asked to subscribe to one of several descriptions of the church.[9] A majority of students at all but two of the schools adopted the description: "On the whole, the Church stands for the best in human life, although certain minor errors and shortcomings are necessarily apparent in it as in all human institutions." In contrast, a majority (61 per cent) of the Catholic contingent, represented by the University of Marquette students, agreed that: "The Church is the one sure and infallible foundation of civilized life. Every member of society ought to be educated in it and [be] required to support it." This description not only establishes that society is founded upon the church but demands that all members of society must support the church. It implies an unquestioning acceptance of the church as the one sure foundation of society, a position taken by no more than 10 per cent of the students in any of the other colleges.

In light of the current ecumenical spirit, it is interesting to see what the attitude of Catholic college students is toward their religion in relation to other religions. When the 1963 Catholic college seniors in the West Coast Sample were asked to indicate a statement which best

[9] *Educational Reviewer* (1963).

typified their present thinking the responses were almost evenly divided between "My faith has the only true approach to God and eternity," and "My faith has the only approach to God and eternity acceptable to me; however, I recognize the possibility that God may be revealed differently in other faiths." A slight majority favored the second, more liberal response. The narrowness of the margin, however, indicates that there is still a long way to go in eliminating the idea that Catholics possess the only way to heaven. Less than 4 per cent of these students were willing to accept the statement, "Many faiths are corrrect in their views toward God and eternity."

Catholic students have been taught that theirs is the one true faith; in addition, they readily identify themselves as more religious than other students. This was evident in data from the Religious Practices Index provided by the West Coast Sample and from junior college students previously discussed and from other research as well.[10] As a matter of fact, there is every indication that the Catholic college students are right in perceiving themselves the most religious of the students, at least as far as strict adherence to doctrine and related issues is concerned.

Catholic students inside and outside Catholic colleges present a very different picture in their attitudes on these issues. Catholic college students express general agreement with the right of the church to advocate moral positions and with the moral positions the church takes. When asked whether they disapprove of certain practices because of their religious beliefs, from 85 to 89 per cent of students at Marquette expressed disapproval of birth control, divorce, premarital intercourse, extramarital intercourse, homosexuality, and legalized abortion. Only homosexuality and extramarital relations were disapproved of on religious grounds by a majority of students at any of the other 11 schools polled, and the evidence indicates that secular college Catholics share the views of their non-Catholic classmates in great part.

In the National Sample less than 20 per cent of the students who entered Catholic colleges condoned premarital sexual relations for engaged couples, while more than 50 per cent of the Catholics at secular colleges approved of it. Similarly, less than 25 per cent of the students at Catholic colleges approved of divorce for themselves or

---

[10] According to National Opinion Research Center data, 92 per cent of seniors in Catholic colleges, compared with 76 per cent of Catholic seniors in other colleges and 70 per cent of Protestants identified themselves as very or fairly religious (Greeley, 1963).

others, but more than 50 per cent of the Catholic students at non-Catholic colleges approved. It is interesting to note, too, that in the National Sample 37 per cent of the seniors at Catholic colleges considered "lack of morality" and "lack of religious convictions" as society's most important issue, but only about 12 per cent of the Catholics at secular colleges did so.

Thus, whether the subject is religious disposition as measured by an attitudinal scale or their stand on church doctrine, the two groups of Catholics are distinctly different in religious orientation. But the firm beliefs and conformity to doctrine or ritual observed among the Catholic college students do not constitute critical insight into their religion, an intelligent understanding of it, or even its application to everyday behavior and relations with others.

Generally, when students are asked to describe their religious beliefs, responses are usually extremely superficial. Interview responses of students in the National Sample typically focused upon acceptance of the church's teachings, without indication that students had thought about them in connection with their own personal feelings or about the ways they could be applied to their own lives and to society.[11]

It is probable that in a two-hour interview devoted to many topics, few persons are likely to plunge into an exploration of their deepest religious feelings and beliefs. But it seems clear that the student has given little thought to his own personal beliefs when he responds, as a bright one in the National Sample did, "I believe there's a God and Heaven and Hell. Of course I'm a Catholic and believe everything Catholics believe." This type of unthinking, uncritical ingestion of religious beliefs was expressed by a majority of the students interviewed. It was not limited to Catholics alone, but it was particularly apparent among Catholics and members of Protestant fundamentalist sects.

Perhaps it is this type of acquiescence to faith rather than intellectual involvement with it that has led to the finding of the recent Greeley-Rossi report that only 53 per cent of the Catholics who had received a Catholic education agreed that love of neighbor is more important than abstinence from meat on Friday.[12] The situation is compounded when we find that a higher percentage of Catholics who had received no Catholic education (60 per cent) adopted this position. It may be that this finding would have been different had only Catholic college students been studied. It may be that the respondents to the question considered both the breach of church precept about

[11] Trent and Medsker (1967).
[12] Greeley and Rossi (1966). This study was carried out prior to the 1966 easing of restrictions regarding the eating of meat on Friday.

Friday abstinence and the breach of the fundamental spirit of Christian brotherly love as serious offenses against the tenets of their faith, and, therefore, that both were equally important. It may also be that specific rules are stressed more or are easier to teach than essential principles of Christianity. Regardless of the explanation, it is evident that the years of Catholic teaching do not necessarily result in increased regard for Christian charity over church precept.

There are other ways to gain a notion of the understanding and application of Christian principles among Catholic college students. In the National Sample, justice and understanding among humans was seen as the most important issue by the greatest number of students in all colleges, by about 25 per cent of the Catholic college and secular Catholic students, and 31 per cent of the non-Catholics. More than 13 per cent of the students specified race relations as the major issue.

The Catholic church has become increasingly involved in problems of race relations in recent years. Members are often reminded that brotherly love and concern for one's fellow man are essential parts of church doctrine. The extent to which this doctrine is incorporated into the actions of individuals is debatable, however, as indicated by the response of St. Louis students to the statement: "Most students could be depended upon to protest if a minority group met with unfair discrimination on the campus."[13] Only a bare majority, 52 per cent, agreed that most students would protest; 22 per cent disagreed, and the rest were uncertain. Of course, the question does not ask whether students are opposed to discrimination; it asks whether most would protest discrimination. Since only a certain percentage of people anywhere will fight for what they believe, it would be unrealistic to expect all students to protest such discrimination. But it is discouraging that only a bare majority feel sure that most students would be ready to act on the Christian principles upon which the school is founded.

Of course, the transfer of Christian principles from church to daily life is a matter of concern for all churches, and seldom does the extent of transfer live up to the hopes of the church. When students at St. Louis were asked to respond to the statement, "Christian principles are applied by most students in their daily campus relationships," only 61 per cent of the students agreed. Even less application of Christian principles was seen in relationships off campus. Only 45 per cent agreed with the statement, "Christian principles are applied by most students of this university in off-campus relationships."

The term "Christian principles" is an extremely general one, which

[13] Weiss (1963).

may be given many interpretations by the person responding. A person might be said to be applying Christian principles if he is simply a good person who follows the rules of his faith and does not hurt others. Or it might be said that only the person who is really Christlike in his attitudes and behavior is truly applying Christian principles. In any case, it is evidently harder to apply the general principles than to adhere to specific regulations.

The problem becomes more acute when Christian principles and consequent social involvement lead to controversy, as they often must. Catholic college students, who see themselves as exceptionally religious, are willing to accept church teachings about moral practices, but they are less willing to accept clerical direction or discussion in other areas of social concern, even though it may be difficult to see how the two can be separated. To illustrate, less than 30 per cent of the Marquette students and from 38 to 60 per cent of the other students in the *Educational Reviewer* poll felt that the clergy should speak on such issues as foreign aid and recognition of Communist China. Slightly more of the Marquette students, but a correspondingly higher percentage of other students approved of the clergy's speaking on local issues.

Although our chief concern is with religious attitudes, beliefs, and practices, these should be backed by religious knowledge. Apart from lacking insight into the spirit of Christianity, many students evidently complete a Catholic education without ever being really exposed to the thoughts of eminent Catholic thinkers. For example, out of the entire class of over 1,100 Catholic college freshmen in the West Coast Sample, only one student correctly identified priest-paleontologist Teilhard de Chardin. When queried again as seniors in 1963, only 8 out of over 300 students adequately identified Chardin or were able to name one of his writings. Half the students at Catholic women's colleges and only one fifth of the students at a Catholic men's college attempted an identification of this much-publicized and highly controversial figure. Less than one-third of the women and one-tenth of the men gave an identification which could be considered even partially correct. For example, many students identified Chardin only as a scientist, theologian, or philosopher.

Although both men and women indicated a lack of familiarity with such a major Catholic scholar, it is again the students in women's colleges who, as noted in chapter 4, manifested the greatest intellectual awareness of all the Catholic college students surveyed. The works of Chardin are relatively recent, but how much attention even older works receive is questionable. Marquette students reported that they read early theologians, such as Augustine, only slightly more often than do students at secular schools, and they read the works of contemporary theologians and philosophers, such as Maritain, less often than did their fellow students at secular colleges.

With little knowledge and with little understanding and questioning of one's religion, little intellectual appreciation and critical evaluation of it is to be expected. Of course, critical evaluation of one's religion often involves some type of either temporary or permanent reaction against it. However, this type of evaluation apparently is not common, even now, among Catholics. Catholic college students indicate great acceptance of the religious tradition in which they were raised and little insightful reaction toward it.

In the *Educational Reviewer*'s poll of 12 colleges, 70 per cent of the Marquette students but not over 40 per cent of students at other schools said there had never been a time when they reacted either partially or wholly against the religious tradition in which they were raised. When the 1963 Catholic college seniors polled in the West Coast Sample were asked to what extent they disagreed with the principal dogmas of their religion, 75 per cent said they disagreed in no respects whatsoever. Twenty per cent said they disagreed in a few respects. (This question was not asked of the National Sample.)

It is possible to question aspects of a religion and arrive at satisfactory answers so that there is no reaction against the religion itself. It is also possible to maintain a questioning attitude toward certain aspects without feeling that one is reacting against his religion. In our judgment this is a healthy, positive approach to religion. Without this kind of involvement and dissent religion becomes a sterile, irrelevant rubric, a creed docilely accepted. The prevalence of this very situation no doubt constitutes much of what is behind Vatican II. The signs are that there are increasing numbers in the church who are approaching their faith with a great deal of zealous and intelligent, critical evaluation. But there are also signs that for many others in the church, Vatican II provided much too little change in the more intellectually valued directions. Finally, there are signs that there remain a great many unquestioning Catholics who are relatively unconcerned about the whole issue.

We are left to conclude with a summary of findings that many Catholic educators may find problematic, if not a source of disturbing dilemmas. In general, Catholic college students are much more religious, orthodox, and conservative in their religious attitudes than are Catholics in secular colleges. Although their attitudes become somewhat more liberal, they do not change nearly as much as do those of Catholics or non-Catholics in secular colleges.

Perhaps the faith of Catholic college students has been protected in Catholic schools and continues to be protected in Catholic colleges. Perhaps too, the environment does not invite a critical challenging of one's faith. This was indicated by the CUES data in chapter 4, as well as by the lack of critical evaluation of religion shown by the students through data presented in this chapter. The students spend their time with other students, and in many cases with faculty members, who share their faith. The students have entered a Catholic college with much the same background, intellectual disposition, and religious orientation. They have lived in an atmosphere that protects and defends, not one that tests and tries a person's religious convictions. Under the circumstances there is little reason to suppose that students' religious attitudes would change very much at most Catholic colleges.

And so these students are more religious than their fellow secular college students in attitude, belief, and practice; and so they change less in religious attitude during their college years than do their secular college peers. They arrive more religious and leave more religious, and we wonder what has happened in the years between. But this leads us immediately to ask, what should Catholic colleges do for a student's religion? The answers do not come easily, and the implications of some of the answers are perplexing.

Three commonly accepted criteria for good Catholics are that the individuals be practicing Catholics, that they be orthodox in their beliefs, and that they be willing to accept the role of the church as teacher. But in many ways we would urge that the opposite approach be taken. One of the purposes of a Catholic college should be to deepen a student's intellectual understanding and appreciation of his religion. If there is little or no change in religious attitudes after four years at a Catholic college, it may indicate that the college has failed to stimulate the student's thinking about his religion. If a student has failed to gain depth and breadth in his religious life, one may wonder what the religious courses and atmosphere of the college have accomplished.

After four years of college, students may be expected to take a more critical approach to their religion, to seek greater understanding of their own religion and that of others. Students who show no change in their religious attitudes may be accepting religion blindly, without personal thought or evaluation. At the same time, we shall see in the next chapter that students within Catholic colleges who develop most intellectually continue to have a high regard for their religion, but they question their church much more and are much more critical of its policies than are their classmates who conform without question. And among the more intellectually oriented Catholics at secular colleges there are a large number of students who sever themselves from the church altogether.

The consequent problems, therefore, become more apparent. Diversity is traditional in American higher education and has much to commend it. And if this diversity is to continue there is no reason why Catholic colleges should not continue to exist. But from the church's point of view there should be a better reason for the existence of its colleges. If it is simply to increase somewhat the religious knowledge of their students, however, or to assure among them a more regular attendance at Mass and adherence to other church regulations, is that enough? Certainly, it is not enough to provide the education offered by other colleges, which are, by and large, doing a better job of educating.

The raison d'etre of the Catholic college presumably, even logically, revolves around religious factors. And assuming that these factors now go beyond the presence of a chapel and the teaching of standard catechetical doctrine, what then? Surely Catholic college students should know more about their religion, understand it better, and perceive its role in the social order beyond the new liturgy, ecumenical dialogue, and the incessant argument over birth control. They should know more about other religions; they should be introduced to all aspects of their own religion, good and bad. With open, liberalized attitudes they should learn to examine their faith critically and become involved with it intellectually. They should be open to the values of other religions while maintaining their own. They should openly have doubts and disagreements about their faith—and yet believe! But is this too much to expect? If educated Catholics approach their faith with critical insight and an inquiring rather than acquiescent attitude, this may mean a gradual loss of devoutness and even disengagement among a number of them. This leaves us to wonder if the church can withstand such a critical examination among large numbers of its members, and if its colleges will permit it. It leaves us to wonder even more what alternatives exist.

CHAPTER NINE

What It Means to Be a Catholic Intellectual

Catholic college students are more deeply committed religiously in a number of ways than are their fellow students. They are also less committed intellectually. This is enough to provoke yet again the age-old question of whether there is an inevitable antithesis between religion and scholarship—between religious faith and the questioning mind. Of course there have been, and are now, many great scholars, artists, and scientists in the church. They are too numerous for it to be said categorically that the same individual cannot be both religious and scholarly.

The distributions of personality measurements observed in this volume have been such that we also know that there are some contemporary Catholic college students who manifest considerable intellectual interests. But their numbers remain proportionately low compared with their non-Catholic peers, just as American Catholic scholarly productivity is meager in comparison with that of non-Catholics. Therefore, it is of concern to know more about the comparatively few Catholics who do register a high level of intellectual disposition. Do they display a commensurate degree of religiosity, or does intellectualism exist at the expense of religious faith and practice?

In the present chapter the relationship between religiosity and intellectualism is explored. Attention is given as well to the factors that characterize the highly intellectual Catholics, particularly their related attitudes, cultural interests, and family backgrounds. We will be concerned with the extent, the characteristics, and the effects of intellectualism on Catholic students and on the church. What percentage of Catholic students can be considered intellectually committed, and how intellectual are these students compared with non-Catholic students? How are these students different from other Catholic students in their background, behavior, and attitudes? And what can be expected from these intellectual students in their future relations with the church?

We reiterate a theme recurrent in this study: the more intellectual

205

students in question here are not merely intelligent; that is, they have more than just the capacity and aptitude for retention and learning. As described earlier, intellectuality is a complex of intense interests in scholarly and cultural pursuits, an appreciation of all forms of the arts and sciences, an openness to a wide range of ideas and experiences in life. To examine the characteristics and backgrounds of the students who are more intellectually oriented and committed in the manner we have described, we divided the students in the West Coast and National samples into high and lower intellectuality levels on the basis of their scores on three of the Omnibus Personality Inventory scales.

The scales selected to distinguish the more intellectual person as we have defined him were the Thinking Introversion scale, which measures an interest in abstract thought; the Complexity scale, which measures avidity for inquiry and tolerance for ambiguities; and the Estheticism scale, which measures interest in the beautiful and artistic. These three scales have been singled out as a basis for identifying these students because operationally they pertain to many of the dimensions that form our theoretical definition of intellectual disposition. But we will also be concerned with the way the highly intellectual students compare with their less intellectual peers on the Nonauthoritarianism scale, as well as on two scales not previously discussed, Impulse Expression and Lack of Anxiety.

The three scales used to distinguish the more intellectual students comprise a summary measure of an intellectuality syndrome. The students' standard scores on Thinking Introversion, Complexity, and Estheticism were added and then divided by the constant 3, to provide a single intellectuality score for each student. To illustrate, if a person had a standard score of 60 on Thinking Introversion, 40 on Complexity, and 50 on Estheticism, his total intellectuality score would be 150 divided by 3, or 50—the freshman normative mean presented in the Omnibus Personality Inventory Manual for each scale.

A student has been designated as high in intellectualism if his intellectuality score was within the range of scores for the uppermost 30 per cent of the original Omnibus Personality Inventory normative group. In previous research, the West Coast students were also classified at a middle and low level of intellectual disposition according to whether they fell in the middle 40 per cent of the distribution of comprehensive intellectuality scores or in the lowest 30 per cent, respectively.[1] Large and significant differences existed between the middle and low intellectuality level students on the variables to be examined

[1] Trent (1964), pp. 162–64.

in the subsequent pages. Comparable differences existed between the middle and high level students. The differences between the high and low intellectuality students were much more extreme than will be observable in this chapter. But our main concern was with students highly disposed to intellectualism. For this reason, and for the sake of simplicity, we determined to combine the students at the middle and low intellectual levels into a single group to be compared to the students at the high level of intellectual disposition.

The West Coast Sample was comprised of 1960 seniors and 1959 freshmen. Responses of the two groups have been combined, since we were concerned with differences between intellectuality levels and not differences between class groups. Omnibus Personality Inventory scores for the 1959 freshmen have earlier been reported for both their senior and freshman years, but only their 1959 OPI scores and questionnaire responses have been considered here. The West Coast public university students were not included in the present analyses because of the expense of the extra computer analyses that would have been required. In the National Sample, all students who entered college full-time and who responded to the 1963 survey were included, even if they did not persist in college for four years.

Since the study from which the National Sample was drawn did not originally deal primarily with Catholics, there are many more non-Catholics than Catholics in the sample, inasmuch as there are more non-Catholics than Catholics in the population. As a result, the number of highly intellectual students in the Catholic college group is small. As we observed earlier, however, it is a sample which should be very representative of students entering Catholic colleges, since it evolved from an original group that included all or almost all of the 1959 Catholic high school graduates in the 16 communities surveyed, and since it included a great majority of those who persisted in college for four years. These students chose to attend many different Catholic colleges throughout the country, so they are also representative of students in a variety of schools.

The distribution of students in intellectuality level is shown in Table 40. In the West Coast Sample, Catholics were found to be grossly underrepresented in the high intellectuality group. Whereas 30 per cent of the original normative group and 29 per cent of the non-Catholics in the West Coast Sample fell in this category, only 17 per cent of the Catholics in Catholic colleges and 18 per cent of the Catholics at secular colleges were found at the high intellectuality level. Although Catholic students were underrepresented at the high

TABLE 40. *Percentage of Students by Intellectuality Level,*
West Coast and National Samples

COLLEGE GROUP	INTELLECTUALITY LEVEL				TOTAL	
	High		Low			
	(No.)	Per cent	(No.)	Per cent	(No.)	Per cent
West Coast Sample						
Catholic	(212)	17	(1,050)	83	(1,262)	100
Secular Catholic	(33)	18	(155)	82	(188)	100
Non-Catholic	(62)	29	(155)	71	(217)	100
$(X^2 = 17.19;$						
$p \leq .01)$						
National Sample						
Catholic	(20)	15	(115)	85	(135)	100
Secular Catholic	(62)	17	(310)	83	(372)	100
Non-Catholic	(333)	17	(1,670)	83	(2,003)	100
$(X^2 = 0.30;$						
p, not significant)						

intellectuality level overall, in some schools students approximated
the normative group. At one Catholic college 29 per cent of the students scored at the high intellectuality level. But this was offset by
scores at other Catholic colleges, with only 13 per cent at one college
scoring at the high intellectuality level.

In addition to being underrepresented at the upper intellectuality
level, Catholics who were at this level still did not obtain intellective scores as high as those of the non-Catholics. This was particularly true of students at Catholic colleges, so that the intellectually
superior non-Catholic students in the West Coast Sample were higher
on the distribution of the upper 30 per cent of the normative scores
than were the intellectually superior Catholic college students.

In the National Sample, all groups were underrepresented at the
high intellectuality level. Roughly, only 17 per cent of the students
were found at that level, indicating that the entire sample was skewed
toward the lower level. The Catholic college students were only
slightly less represented at the high level than were the secular college
Catholics and non-Catholics. This was anticipated, since we saw in
chapters 4 and 5 that the two Omnibus Personality Inventory scales
on which the Catholic college students compared favorably with the
non-Catholics were Thinking Introversion and Estheticism, and these

were two of the three scales used in the comprehensive intellectuality measurement assembled for the purposes of this chapter.

A slightly higher percentage of women than men was found at the high intellectuality level in both samples except among Catholics at secular colleges in the West Coast Sample. Women represented 55 per cent of the high intellectuality students in the National Sample, although only half the total sample were women. In the West Coast Sample, in which 56 per cent of the total were women, 62 per cent of the high intellectuality students were women. This slight over-representation of women among the more intellectually oriented students may be attributed partly to the fact that women consistently score higher on the Estheticism scale. Had Theoretical Orientation been included in the comprehensive intellectuality measurement, men might have scored higher, since this scale is concerned with scientific interests and men usually score higher on it than women.

For all students, level of ability was related to level of intellectual disposition. But this was much more true for Catholic college students than for either secular college Catholics or non-Catholics. We have seen that ability alone is not a guarantee of intellectuality; but ability appears to be an important precondition for intellectuality, as evidenced by the fact that the majority of students high in intellectuality are found also to be high in ability. The relationship between ability and intellectuality was especially evident in the National Sample, in which students were divided into three ability levels on the basis of their equivalent SCAT scores. As previously noted, the students in the top three deciles of the distribution of scores were identified at the high level of ability, those in the next four deciles at the middle level, and those who scored in the bottom three deciles, at the low level.

At the Catholic colleges in the National Sample, 90 per cent of freshmen at the high intellectuality level were also at the high ability level. The relationship was not as great for other groups of freshmen, but 66 per cent of the highly intellectual Catholics at non-Catholic colleges and 71 per cent of the non-Catholics at these schools were also found at the high ability level. None of the high intellectuality students at Catholic colleges were found at the low ability level, and only 8 per cent of the Catholics and 4 per cent of the non-Catholics at other schools were found there. For each group the relationship between level of ability and intellectuality was significant at the 1 per cent level on the basis of overall chi squares, with the relationship being greatest for the Catholic college student.

In the West Coast Sample, students were divided into high and low ability groups only, with the high group composed of students who scored in the upper 50 per cent of the ability distribution of the total sample (Table 41). With this more gross division, ability differences between intellectuality levels were not as apparent as they were for the National Sample, but the pattern of differences between the Catholic college students and the others was the same. Among the students at the high intellectuality level, 71 per cent of the Catholic college students were at the high ability level, compared with 42 per cent of the state college Catholics and 53 per cent of the state college non-Catholics. On the basis of overall chi squares, significant differences existed among the three student groups classified on ability at the high intellectuality level but not at the lower level. The relationship between intellectuality and ability was highly significant for the Catholic college students but not for the secular Catholics or non-Catholics. This was manifested by the chi squares at the bottom of Table 41, which were computed separately for each student group.

TABLE 41. *Percentage of Students at Each Ability Level by College Group and Intellectuality Level, West Coast Sample*

INTELLECTUALITY LEVEL AND COLLEGE GROUP	ABILITY LEVEL					
	High		Low		TOTAL	
	(No.)	Per cent	(No.)	Per cent	(No.)	Per cent
High						
Catholic	(129)	71	(52)	29	(181)	100
Secular Catholic	(11)	42	(15)	58	(26)	100
Non-Catholic	(27)	53	(24)	47	(51)	100
(X^2, college group *vs.* ability $= 12.23^{**}$)						
Low						
Catholic	(405)	47	(464)	53	(869)	100
Secular Catholic	(58)	42	(79)	58	(137)	100
Non-Catholic	(52)	39	(81)	61	(133)	100
(X^2, college group *vs.* ability $= 3.15^{+}$)						

X^2, intellectuality *vs.* ability level	
Catholic	36.47^{**}
Secular Catholic	0.00^{+}
Non-Catholic	2.88^{+}

$^{+}$ $p =$ not significant
** $p \leq .01$

TABLE 42. *Percentage of Students at Each Intellectuality Level by College Group and Ability Level, West Coast Sample*

ABILITY LEVEL AND COLLEGE GROUP	INTELLECTUALITY LEVEL					
	High		Low		TOTAL	
	(No.)	Per cent	(No.)	Per cent	(No.)	Per cent
High						
Catholic	(129)	24	(405)	76	(534)	100
Secular Catholic	(11)	16	(58)	84	(69)	100
Non-Catholic	(27)	34	(52)	66	(79)	100
(X^2, college group *vs.* intellectuality = 6.77*)						
Low						
Catholic	(52)	10	(464)	90	(516)	100
Secular Catholic	(15)	16	(79)	84	(94)	100
Non-Catholic	(24)	23	(81)	77	(105)	100
(X^2, college group *vs.* intellectuality = 13.85**)						

X^2, ability *vs.* intellectuality level	
Catholic	36.47**
Secular Catholic	0.00+
Non-Catholic	2.88+

+ p = not significant
* $p \leq .05$
** $p \leq .01$

It is difficult to account for the stronger relationship between ability and intellectuality among students in the Catholic colleges that is consistent in both samples. We know from a variety of data that the atmosphere is generally less intellectually oriented in these colleges than in many others. And it may be that only students who have the most intelligence or academic aptitude recognize the value and meaning of intellectual activity and take advantage of what opportunities for intellectual development exist for them. The homogeneity of ability scores in Catholic colleges undoubtedly also affects the relationship. Since ability level is generally higher in Catholic colleges than in most others, more students are likely to be classified in the high ability group. Thus students at the high intellectuality level could be drawn from this group but still leave many high ability students who are not intellectual.

This fact is evident in Table 42. Here, instead of the ability levels of the students at each level of intellectual disposition found in the previous table, we observe for each ability level the proportion of students at the two intellectuality levels. For each college group a considerable majority of high-ability students did not obtain a commensurate intellectual level. The non-Catholic students at both ability levels had the greatest representation at the high intellectuality level. The secular college Catholics and the low-ability Catholic college students were least represented among the more intellectually oriented students. Twenty-four per cent of the high-ability and 10 per cent of the low-ability Catholic college students were at the high intellectuality level.

Although intellectuality is related to mental ability, little relationship exists between intellectuality and socioeconomic level. When students in the West Coast Sample were divided into three socioeconomic levels, based upon father's occupation as described in chapter 3, a low nonsignificant correlation between socioeconomic status and intellectuality level was indicated. The overall chi square was computed for all the students matching the original three levels of intellectuality against the three levels of socioeconomic status. The chi square value of 3.22 for the 3 by 3 table was not significant. This low correlation was especially evident among Catholic college students.

Few students, regardless of their intellectual disposition, were at the low socioeconomic level, and less than one-third of the students at the high intellectuality level in both the West Coast and National samples were found at the high socioeconomic level. The implication of these data is that socioeconomic level has little bearing on intellectuality as measured in the present context. However, it may be that if more differentiation were made of the middle socioeconomic level, or if we had a more refined index of this variable, a greater relationship would be found between it and intellectuality.

With or without such refinements of socioeconomic indexes we still expected to find that family and cultural background would have more bearing on the students' intellectual disposition than the data we have reviewed would imply. What, then, has caused some students to be concerned with and committed to intellectual pursuits, when the vast majority of students are not similarly involved? In particular, what has caused some Catholic students to be more intellectually oriented when most of their peers have developed so little intellectually?

We suspected that the answers to these questions could be found in the background of the students and that the answers would be especially related to the personal characteristics and values of the parents. In seeking clues to the sources of intellectuality, we examined the responses to a series of questions put to the students in the National

Sample inquiring about their parents' education and temperaments and their home environment. We looked especially for factors in the students' environment which would encourage the more open and critical approach to life that characterizes the intellectual individual.

Our hypothesis was that the homes of the more intellectual students would be more permissive and democratic and that the parents of these students would probably have more education and would themselves be more intellectually oriented than the parents of the less intellectual students. We based our hypothesis on the assumption that it is in early childhood that individuals develop their primary attitudes and values and that intellectual attitudes and cultural enrichment displayed in the home might be expected to be the primary contributors to intellectual development.

On the basis of this assumption, we first examined the educational level of the parents. A college education is in no way a guarantee of intellectuality any more than is intelligence or academic aptitude. Still, some relationship might be expected between the educational level of the family and a student's intellectual disposition.

In actuality, the educational level of the parents of the Catholic college students appeared to have as little relationship to a student's intellectual disposition as did the socioeconomic status of the family as determined by father's occupation. Fathers of the highly intellectual students in Catholic colleges were somewhat less likely to have had some college than were fathers of the less intellectual students. Thirty-five per cent of the fathers of the high intellectuality students had some college, over 10 per cent less than the fathers of the less intellectual students.

But the situation was reversed at the secular colleges. Among the Catholics, 34 per cent of the fathers of students at the high intellectuality level and 28 per cent of the fathers of less intellectual students had some college. Among the non-Catholics, 51 per cent of the fathers of the more intellectual students and 34 per cent of the fathers of the less intellectual students had some college, a difference significant at the 1 per cent level. Thus, only among non-Catholics was fathers' education significantly related to the students' intellectual disposition, and the trend among the Catholic college students was the opposite of what we expected.

Although women traditionally are less likely than men to attend college, the mothers of the highly intellectual students were as likely as the fathers to have had some college education. Unlike the fathers, proportionately more mothers of the intellectually oriented Catholic college students than the others had some college education. Thirty-five per cent of the more intellectual Catholic college students and 24 per cent of the less intellectual reported their mothers had some college. Regardless of intellectuality level, about 22 per cent of Catholics at non-Catholic colleges reported that their mothers had some college education. But once again, it was only among non-Catholics that a significant relationship existed between the students' intellectual attitudes and their parents' education. Forty-six per cent of the mothers of high intellectuality non-Catholic students and 35 per cent of the other mothers had some college, a difference significant at the 1 per cent level of confidence.

The relationship between intellectuality and mother's education is especially interesting since all the groups of students reported feeling closer to their mothers than to their fathers, and since a slightly higher percentage of women than men were found at the high intellectuality level. We cannot say that the intellectuality of students is dependent upon the amount of formal education the mother has received, but the relationship is worth additional exploration.

Another possibility we explored was that the first or last child in a family and children in small families may have received more individual attention and stimulation from their parents, which may have led to greater development of intellectual interests among them. But few students at either intellectuality level reported that they had no brothers or sisters, and students at the high intellectuality level were as likely as others to report more than three brothers and sisters.

The intellectual development of students cannot be traced to the occupational or educational status of their parents or to the number of children in the family. And thus far we have been able to trace very little intellectual development to any particular constellation of personal parental characteristics. For example, only a few features of parents' temperament and their interaction with others in the family, as described by the students, differentiate the highly intellectual students from the others with any clarity or certainty. This may be seen in Table 43. It should be noted that the small number of highly intellectual Catholics in the sample requires that the difference in proportional responses be very large to reach statistical significance. Differences of 10 to 20 percentage points might be considered as indicative of what would likely be significant were larger numbers of subjects available for examination as categorized in the present instance.

Few personality traits described by the students significantly distinguish the parents of the more intellectual Catholic college students

TABLE 43. *Percentage of Catholic College Students Reporting Various Parental Characteristics, by Intellectuality Level, National Sample*

Intellec-tuality Level (No.)	Father Ener-getic	Father Easy-going	Neither Parent Strict	Neither Parent Orderly	Neither Parent Loving	Decision-making Shared
High (20)	35	45	65	65	30	70
Low (115)	16	24	53	32	16	54
(Z ratio)	(2.03*)	(1.94+)	(0.99+)	(2.84**)	(1.95+)	(1.32+)

+ p = not significant
* $p \leq .05$
** $p \leq .01$

from parents of the less intellectual students. A minority of students described their parents as intellectual, and the low intellectuality level students were as likely as the highly intellectual students to describe their parents this way. Thirty-five per cent of the highly intellectual students and 16 per cent of the others described their fathers as energetic, a difference significant at the 5 per cent level. The fathers of the more intellectual students were also described as easygoing in greater proportion than the others; 45 per cent of high intellectuality students reported this, and 24 per cent of other students, a difference which, although sizeable, was not statistically significant. The more intellectual students were significantly less likely to indicate orderliness as a characteristic of either parent. Sixty-five per cent of the highly intellectual students indicated that this was a characteristic of neither one of their parents, compared with 32 per cent of the less intellectual students, a difference significant at the 1 per cent level of confidence.

At first glance, these may seem strange dimensions on which to differentiate parents whose children vary in intellectual disposition. But there is some logic to the distinguishing traits. Speaking speculatively, it may be that the fathers described as more easygoing, and also as more energetic, have a great deal of drive but are not unduly demanding in their relations with others. Orderliness implies that things must be done in a certain order and kept in a certain order, and if this is an outstanding characteristic of a person it is unlikely that he is extremely flexible and experimental in his approach to life, or that he would encourage this kind of approach to life in his children.

The more intellectual students were less likely to see their parents as strict and more likely to say that decision-making was shared by mother and father. Sixty-five per cent of the highly intellectual students, compared with 53 per cent of the less intellectual, said that neither parent was strict. Seventy per cent of the highly intellectual students, compared with 54 per cent of the less intellectual students, said that decisions were shared in their homes. Although these differences are not statistically significant, they add support to a picture of a less rigid and more open home atmosphere among the more intellectual students.

One somewhat surprising difference was that the highly intellectual students saw their parents as less loving than did other students. Thirty per cent of the high intellectuality students and 16 per cent of the others did not identify either parent as loving. In the same vein, the more intellectual students were less likely to report that their parents were always appreciative or full of praise for their achievements.

Related to this picture of a home life which is perhaps less supportive and sheltering than that of other students are the students' perceptions of the major problems in their home. Lack of communication was cited as the greatest problem in the parents' household by students at the high intellectuality level, whereas finances were rated the most important problem by other students. Whether communication was really a greater problem or whether these students simply had more insight and were more aware of the problem we do not know. Problems of children's behavior and parental incompatibility were also frequently cited by all students, but considerably less often than were communication and finance, and differences between the two intellectuality groups were nominal in these areas.

Highly intellectual Catholics at secular colleges reported a similar pattern of parental characteristics, but differences between intellectuality levels were less pronounced. Highly intellectual secular college Catholics were more likely than their peers at Catholic colleges to report conflict within the family. Relatively few students in Catholic colleges reported conflicts with their parents. The secular college Catholics in general reported more conflict with their parents and more unreasonable demands on the part of their parents than did other students. Twenty-four per cent of these students responded that their parents made unreasonable demands about their general behavior, with somewhat fewer of them reporting conflict over particular decisions, such as about friends, choice of college or employment, or time of marriage. Eighteen per cent of the highly intellectual Catholics at secular colleges reported conflicts about their friends and 16 per cent reported conflict about their choice of college, percentages much higher than those for the other students.

The greatest conflict was reported in regard to choice of a mate, with 26 per cent of the intellectually oriented secular college Catholics reporting conflict on this issue, 16 per cent more than any other group. We shall see that these students reported a greater loss of faith or loss of value for it than either other secular college Catholics or Catholic college students. Some of this lessened regard for religion may result from the increased contacts with non-Catholics and participation in non-Catholic activities. Therefore, we suspect that much of the conflict with parents over choice of mate reported by the intellectual Catholics at secular colleges has revolved around friendships and dating that have led to marriage outside of the church. But this speculation says nothing of the values and attitudes of the parents of the highly intellectual secular college Catholics that might have fostered their intellectual development.

We cannot be certain of the relationship between parental characteristics and the intellectual disposition of the children. Our numbers are small and our data are limited; but this is a provocative area for further research. We assume that because intellectuality is characterized by nonauthoritarianism, openness, and greater flexibility, parents who exhibit these qualities will foster them in their offspring, and many studies have indicated this.[2] But for Catholic families there are complicating factors to be considered. Families who send their children to Catholic schools are likely to be more religious than other Catholic families, a relationship especially apparent when attendance extends not only to Catholic elementary and high schools but also to Catholic colleges. And there are forces of authority within the church that have limited intellectual openness in many ways. We have yet to know how the effect of greater closeness to the church is offset in these families, or in the church system itself, so that some students emerge who are more open than their Catholic peers to the world around them.

We know that the secular college Catholics enter college with a different religious orientation than Catholic college students and, on the whole, are different in socioeconomic background. But there must be many other characteristics which distinguish these students and their parents. Here, too, we have yet to know what leads some Catholic students to a high level of intellectualism in a secular environment when most of their Catholic classmates are at a relatively low level.

The sum of it is that the more intellectual students are likely to be high in ability, but ability, alone, is a poor predictor of a high intellectual disposition. They are also slightly more likely to be women.

---

[2] Becker (1964); Mussen, Conger, and Kagan (1956); Rosen (1961); Rosen and D'Andrade (1959); Strodtbeck (1958).

But there is little relationship between intellectuality and socioeconomic or other aspects of family background as determined by the data at hand. The fact is that we know very little about the background factors that encourage intellectual development, particularly in a religious subculture. We know much more about the current personality attributes and behavior of the highly intellectual students. What, then, are their interests, attitudes, and activities?

Since the scales comprising the measurement of intellectuality level include items that in part reflect an interest in literary and cultural activity and knowledge, it would follow that the highly intellectual students would show the greatest interest in such activities as reading and music. Thus, responses to specific questions dealing with cultural interests may be regarded as illustrative of, and even as a rough assessment of, the validity of the measurement of intellectuality in this study.

As shown in Table 44, the reported enjoyment of poetry and classical music and the reading and owning of books is highly related to intellectuality level. The more intellectual students in all schools attach greater importance to these items than do less intellectual students, with most differences reaching statistical significance. In the National Sample, when questions were asked about attendance at plays and concerts and visits to art galleries and bookstores, again the high intellectuality students expressed significantly greater interest than other students, regardless of religion or type of school attended. For example, about 60 per cent of highly intellectual students had visited an art gallery 3 or more times during the last year, compared with 28 per cent at the lower intellectuality levels. About 70 per cent of the high intellectuality students had attended concerts 3 or more times, compared with less than 50 per cent of the less intellectual students.

Highly intellectual students may be expected to show a greater concern for creative activities as well. When considering occupational values, these students did place significantly more emphasis upon creativity. Roughly 19 per cent of both groups of the highly intellectual and less than 6 per cent of the less intellectual Catholic students felt that the opportunity for creativity was the most important requirement for job satisfaction. Thirty-one per cent of the high intellectual level and 8 per cent of the low intellectual non-Catholics held this view.

A negative relationship was found between business-associated occupational choices and intellectuality. And this relationship would have been much greater had women not been included in the analysis, since so many college women enter the teaching profession and so few enter business. Emphasizing this negative relationship between business and

intellectuality is the fact that by far the largest proportion of students majoring in business and applied fields like engineering are at the low intellectuality level, in contrast to those majoring in an academic field. For example, 50 per cent of the Catholic college students with an academic major were at the high intellectuality level; 6 per cent of the business and engineering students were at this level.

We anticipated that the more intellectual students would be more likely than others to see the goal of college as the attainment of knowledge and appreciation of ideas and less likely to emphasize vocational or other practical goals of college. This proves to be the case, but the difference is statistically significant only for the Catholic college students, and even for these students the percentage difference in responses is less than for other items.

The fact that an item such as this does not clearly differentiate the more intellectual from the less intellectual students indicates the danger of placing too much reliance upon a student's response to any particular item. Not only is it possible for the student in his response to any one item to deviate considerably from his overall attitude and disposition, but it is also possible that his self-knowledge is limited and that his response does not convey an accurate picture of his attitude on a particular issue. Thus very inaccurate conclusions may be reached on the basis of one or a few such items, and it is a pattern of responses to many such items which becomes more meaningful and reliable.

In respect to other educational goals, all three groups of highly intellectual students did clearly respond differently from their less intellectual peers. Students at the high intellectuality level significantly more than others planned to undertake post-baccalaureate work in academic fields. Among the non-Catholics the percentage of high intellectuality students who planned to enter graduate school was five times that for less intellectual students. The percentage was only twice as high among Catholic college students, however.

Since there were more students at the lower intellectuality levels, this means that when the actual numbers of students planning graduate school are considered, only 30 per cent of potential graduate students from Catholic colleges and 38 per cent of the Catholics from secular colleges were found at the high intellectuality level. This compares with a total of 67 per cent of the non-Catholic potential graduate students who were found at the high intellectuality level. Thus more than twice as many non-Catholics as Catholics were approaching graduate school with the intellectual disposition that seems to us an essential prerequisite for scholarly activity.

Although they are not shown in Table 44, of those students at Catholic colleges planning to attend professional school (including majors in medicine, law, technology, and education), only 15 per cent were at the high intellectuality level, compared with 22 per cent of the Catholics at secular colleges and 32 per cent of the non-Catholics. These data raise the same serious questions about the intellectual potential of current Catholic graduate and professional school students that were raised as the result of data presented in chapter 7.

In chapter 7 we saw that Catholic college seniors who were, at graduation, planning to attend graduate school revealed a lower level of intellectual disposition when compared with two groups of beginning graduate students. This was true when we compared Catholic college students with their public college peers, all of whom planned to enter graduate school. From all that we can surmise, the two sets of data do not portend, in the near future, a level of intellectual scholarship among Catholic graduate students commensurate with that of their non-Catholic contemporaries.

When cultural, educational, and occupational interests were looked at by ability and socioeconomic levels, these controls appeared only to increase the differences between the intellectuality levels.[3] The highly intellectual non-Catholics showed the greatest intellectual and cultural interests of all students, regardless of ability or socioeconomic or intellectuality level. The only exception to this was in the enjoyment of poetry, which did not differentiate the highly intellectual Catholic college and non-Catholic students. It is surely noteworthy and, to a degree, baffling that the Catholic college and secular college Catholics at the high intellectuality level showed so much less interest in intellectual activities and values than the highly intellectual non-Catholics.

It is also perplexing that even the more intellectual non-Catholic students did not display greater interest and commitment than was reported. In the West Coast Sample the only cultural interests to which a majority of the high intellectuality students responded in a really positive manner were the enjoyment of poetry and a liking for classical music. Interest in graduate school was expressed by the next highest percentage of the more intellectual students, but all told this involved less than half these students. (This percentage is, of course, much greater among seniors considered separately.)

Nevertheless, the students were differentiated by intellectuality level on the basis of cultural, educational, and vocational interests. They were also very different from others in their attitudes on various social,

[3] Trent (1964), pp. 174–75.

political, and moral issues. We saw in chapter 6 that Catholic college students were less likely than other students to uphold the civil rights of individuals who espouse political philosophies which may be seen as alien to American democracy. We might assume that the more intellectual students are more liberal on such issues, but can we also assume that this is as likely to be true for Catholics as for non-Catholics?

One characteristic that clearly identifies the more intellectual student is his attitude toward freedom of speech. An example of this is the students' reaction to members of the Communist party speaking on the radio. In the National Sample only about a third would grant a Communist the right to speak on the radio; significantly fewer Catholic college students approved of this. Among the more intellectual students, however, regardless of the type of college they attended, approximately half would grant this right, more than twice the proportion of the low intellectuality students. It should be noted, however, that even among the highly intellectual students, only a bare majority favored free speech for Communists.

Students in the West Coast Sample were asked their views on a related issue. The question was whether a person who refused to inform on a former Communist associate should be refused a teaching position. The responses were similarly divided by intellectuality level, but in this case, Catholic college students at the high intellectuality level were significantly different from the other highly intellectual students.

High intellectuality students at Catholic colleges were significantly less likely than their less intellectual classmates to deny a teaching position to a former Communist. Sixty-four per cent of the low intellectuality Catholic college students took this stand, compared with 46 per cent of the students at the high intellectuality level. However, a much greater proportion of the highly intellectual Catholic college students would deny the position compared with the secular college students. Less than 21 per cent of the highly intellectual Catholics and non-Catholics at secular colleges would restrict the teaching privileges of a former Communist. Thus, although they were more liberal than their fellow college students, highly intellectual students in Catholic colleges were less liberal than high intellectuality students in other colleges on this issue.

On another civil liberties issue, the students were asked if they would refuse a passport to a Socialist. More students in general would restrict the teaching of a former Communist than the travel rights of a Socialist. But the pattern by intellectuality level was the same as that already demonstrated. The higher intellectuality students were less likely to sanction this infraction of civil liberties, but at each intellectual level significantly more Catholic college students than others would withdraw freedom of movement from those whom they may consider politically suspicious.

The more liberal attitudes of the more intellectual students were obvious in their responses to other social issues as well. For example, the highly intellectual students in the National Sample were more liberal in their attitudes toward a woman's role in society. A majority of the high intellectuality non-Catholics believed that a woman can successfully combine a career and marriage. Fewer Catholic than non-Catholic students took this position at either intellectuality level. The highly intellectual Catholics were more likely than their fellow Catholics to believe that a woman can maintain a career and a family, however. Thirty-five per cent of high intellectuality Catholics at Catholic colleges and 48 per cent of the more intellectual Catholics at secular colleges agreed with this position, compared with 12 per cent and 31 per cent, respectively, of the less intellectual Catholics at these schools.

The fact that Catholic college students are less liberal than other groups in their attitudes toward a woman's role is further indicated by their responses to the statement, "A man is head of the household and always should have the last word." The highly intellectual Catholics at Catholic colleges were even more likely than the less intellectual students at those colleges to agree with this position, 55 per cent compared with 28 per cent of the less intellectual students. Only 14 per cent of the more intellectual non-Catholics agreed that the man should always have the last word, compared to 23 per cent of the highly intellectual Catholics at secular colleges. A slightly higher percentage of the less intellectual students at secular colleges agreed with this position.

The responses of Catholic college students indicate a much more authoritarian approach to family life than that shown by other students. While few persons would feel that a lack of respect for the father is healthy in a home, it is an extreme view to say that the man must always have the last word. Society has changed considerably since St. Paul admonished women to be subservient to their husbands, but among some Catholics the attitude toward women has not changed greatly. It seems inconsistent that it is the more intellectual and—as we shall see—the more independent, autonomous Catholic college students who in greater proportion uphold the church's traditional stand that the husband is in all respects the head of the household.

This may be an example of a situation discussed earlier—the deviation of a single item from the general pattern.

This exception notwithstanding, the bulk of the data at hand confirms our assumption that intellectual interests, even among Catholic college students, are associated with an openness to others and their ideas. It is the characteristic of the intellectual that he is better able to identify with others outside his position in life, or at least show an objective appraisal or understanding of others. This is evident in the more intellectual students' attitudes toward civil rights.

It is also evident on the basis of data solicited from West Coast Catholic college seniors in 1960. The highly intellectual seniors, more than their less intellectual classmates, reported having gained a considerable understanding of religions and philosophies other than their own, regardless of the ability level of these students.[4] Presumably, with ability level controlled, opportunity for learning would be the same for students at each intellectuality level. Thus, granting that little comparative religion or philosophy has been taught in most Catholic colleges, the more intellectually oriented students still profess an increase in understanding in these areas. Twenty-six per cent of the highly intellectual Catholic college students felt that their colleges contributed considerably to their understanding of other religions, compared with less than 13 per cent of the low intellectuality students. Fifty per cent of the intellectually oriented students and 37 per cent of the others felt the same way about their understanding of philosophies other than the Scholasticism taught almost exclusively in their colleges.

That the most intellectual students would report the most increase in understanding various schools of thought and least often advocate infractions of civil liberty indicates their ability to view people alien to their own ideas with more understanding, objectivity, and fairness. This tendency holds true with few exceptions, regardless of ability and socioeconomic level. It is less true for high intellectuality Catholics than their non-Catholic peers, but not when they are compared with their low intellectuality classmates. Thus, the more intellectual students indicate more openness to others, whether in understanding religions and philosophies different from their own or in treating political issues with tolerance and justice.

The students in both the National and West Coast samples who have been identified as being more intellectually inclined on the basis of their liking for thinking, for complexity, and for beauty and who have been shown to be more objective and open to others may also be

[4] *Ibid.*, p. 272.

expected to display certain related personality characteristics. In particular, they may be expected to be more independent in their actions, less authoritarian in their thinking, and more open to new ideas and new experiences. As might be expected, therefore, students who scored at the upper levels in Thinking Introversion, Complexity, and Estheticism also scored higher than other students in Nonauthoritarianism, Autonomy, and Impulse Expression.[5]

TABLE 45. *Standard Mean OPI Scores by Intellectuality Level,*
West Coast Sample

College Group and Intellectuality Level (No.)	Nonauthoritarianism	Lack of Anxiety	Impulse Expression
Catholic			
High (212)	48.9	47.3	52.0
Low (1,050)	40.0	49.0	44.4
(Critical ratio)	(17.6**)	(2.9**)	(8.1**)
Secular Catholic			
High (33)	52.5	50.0	57.0
Low (155)	40.0	50.0	44.5
(Critical ratio)	(7.4**)	(0.0+)	(5.3**)
Non-Catholic			
High (62)	56.1	50.0	58.0
Low (157)	45.4	50.0	44.5
(Critical ratio)	(4.8**)	(0.0+)	(4.6**)

+ p = not significant
** $p \leq .01$

Data from the West Coast and National samples verified the fact that high intellectuality students were less authoritarian and more autonomous in their thinking and actions (Table 45). In the West Coast Sample, high intellectuality students scored significantly higher than others in Nonauthoritarianism, with differences significant beyond the 1 per cent level of confidence. In the National Sample, the same significant relationship existed in regard to the correlated Autonomy

[5] The Omnibus Personality scales are described in chapter 4, in Appendix A, and in the Omnibus Personality Inventory Manual (Center for the Study of Higher Education, 1962). The Impulse Expression and Lack of Anxiety scales, not included in the analyses in chapter 4, measure readiness to express impulses or overt anxiety. These scales are described in greater detail beginning on pp. 227 and 231 of this chapter, as well as in the Omnibus Personality Inventory Manual and Appendix A.

scale, which is the successor to the Nonauthoritarianism scale. (The Nonauthoritarianism scale measures the absence of authoritarianism; the Autonomy scale measures the presence of objective, autonomous, and independent thinking.)

In the West Coast Sample, the standard mean Nonauthoritarianism score for highly intellectual Catholics at Catholic colleges was 48.9, which placed even these students slightly below the normative freshman mean. Lower intellectuality students at these schools obtained a mean score of 40, placing them 1 standard deviation below the normative mean. Highly intellectual Catholics at secular colleges, with a mean score of 52.2, displayed more autonomy than their Catholic college peers. Perhaps they demonstrated some of this independence by enrolling in a non-Catholic college, and it may be indicated also by the amount of conflict they reported having with their parents. The less intellectual Catholics at secular colleges had a mean score of 40, which was the same as that of the lower intellectuality students at Catholic colleges. Although the highly intellectual Catholics at secular colleges reflected less authoritarianism than their Catholic college

TABLE 46. *Standard Mean OPI Scores by Intellectuality Level, National Sample, 1963*

College Group and Intellectuality Level (No.)	Autonomy	Lack of Anxiety	Impulse Expression
Catholic			
High (20)	51.7	49.0	52.6
Low (115)	44.3	51.2	44.9
(Critical ratio[a])	(3.94**)	(0.09+)	(3.56**)
Secular Catholic			
High (62)	57.3	48.8	59.9
Low (310)	46.4	51.0	49.9
(Critical ratio)	(8.24**)	(1.58+)	(7.02**)
Non-Catholic			
High (333)	60.3	48.0	58.4
Low (1,670)	49.7	52.0	48.4
(Critical ratio)	(21.78**)	(5.90**)	(16.64**)

[a] Because of the small number of high intellectuality students in Catholic colleges a t test used for small sample statistics was computed instead of the usual critical ratio.

+ p = not significant

** $p \leq .01$

peers, they still did not manifest the degree of nonauthoritarianism obtained by the non-Catholics. The non-Catholics in the West Coast Sample obtained a mean score of 56.1 at the high intellectuality level and 45.4 at the low level.

In the National Sample high intellectuality students scored higher than low intellectuality students on the Autonomy scale, with the differences for all groups significant beyond the 1 per cent level, as may be observed in Table 46. (Consistently in this volume when group differences are treated for statistical significance, and when one of the groups compared is composed of less than 30 students, a t test designed for small-sample statistics has been employed in place of the critical ratio, although the latter heading is maintained.) Although more autonomous than their fellow students, characteristically the more intellectual Catholic college students compared unfavorably with the more intellectual secular Catholics and still more unfavorably with the highly intellectual non-Catholics. These differences were significant well beyond the 1 per cent level. The high intellectuality non-Catholics also scored significantly higher in Autonomy than their secular Catholic peers. The same significance in differences existed when comparing the Catholic and non-Catholic students at the lower level of intellectual disposition (Table 47).

The mean Autonomy score for Catholic college students at the high intellectuality level was 7.4 standard points higher than that of their classmates at the lower level. Catholics in non-Catholic colleges again manifested more autonomy, with a mean score nearly 6 points higher than that of the high intellectuality Catholic college students and nearly 11 points higher than the low intellectuality secular Catholics. The more intellectual non-Catholics scored 3 points higher than the secular Catholics at the high intellectuality level and also nearly 11 points higher than their less intellectual non-Catholic classmates. The high intellectuality Catholic college students who scored over 7 standard mean points above their low intellectuality classmates still scored only 2 points higher than the low intellectuality non-Catholics. The discrepancy in Autonomy between the high intellectuality level Catholic college and non-Catholic students corresponds with the difference in attitudes toward civil rights observed between these groups earlier in the chapter.

The greater openness and flexibility of the high intellectuality students implied in their Nonauthoritarianism and Autonomy scores is corroborated on the Impulse Expression scale. This scale measures the general readiness of a person to express his impulses in overt action

TABLE 47. *Critical Ratios of OPI Scores by Intellectuality Level, West Coast and National Samples*

Sample, College Group and Intellectuality Level	Nonauthori-tarianism	Lack of Anxiety	Impulse Expression
West Coast Sample			
High intellectuality			
Catholic *vs.*			
secular Catholic	1.9+	1.7+	3.2**
Catholic *vs.*			
non-Catholic	3.2**	2.2*	2.4*
Secular Catholic *vs.*			
non-Catholic	1.3+	0.0+	0.0+
Low intellectuality			
Catholic *vs.*			
secular Catholic	0.0+	0.0+	2.3*
Catholic *vs.*			
non-Catholic	9.1**	0.0+	0.0+
Secular Catholic *vs.*			
non-Catholic	7.1**	0.0+	1.8+
National Sample[a]	(Autonomy)[b]		
High intellectuality			
Catholic *vs.*			
secular Catholic	2.5*	0.1+	3.0**
Catholic *vs.*			
non-Catholic	4.9**	0.4+	2.6**
Secular Catholic *vs.*			
non-Catholic	2.3*	0.5+	1.0+
Low intellectuality			
Catholic *vs.*			
secular Catholic	2.2*	0.2+	4.6**
Catholic *vs.*			
non-Catholic	7.0**	0.7+	3.9**
Secular Catholic *vs.*			
non-Catholic	5.6**	1.5+	2.1*

[a] Because of the small number of high intellectuality students in Catholic colleges, a t test used for small sample statistics was computed instead of the usual critical ratio.

[b] The Autonomy scale was administered to the National Sample in place of the highly correlated Nonauthoritarianism scale.

+ p = not significant
* $p \leq .05$
** $p \leq .01$

or in conscious feeling and attitude. High scorers are characterized as impulsive, imaginative, irrepressible and sensitive to feeling and fantasy; low scorers tend to be cautious, dutiful, constricted in imagination, and docile. The internal consistency reliability of the 75-item scale is .85. Sample items are: "I find that a well-ordered mode of life with regular hours is not congenial to my temperament"; "I enjoy discarding the old and accepting the new"; and "I often act on the spur of the moment without stopping to think."

Dramatic differences between intellectuality levels are found on this scale, indicating that the more intellectual students avoid intellectual docility, are more imaginative and independent, and tend more to flexible and individualistic thinking than to conforming acquiescence. In the West Coast Sample, the highly intellectual non-Catholics showed the least docility, just as they showed the most nonauthoritarianism and autonomy (Table 45). However, the mean differences were statistically significant between intellectuality levels regardless of sample group, and they remained statistically significant by intellectual level regardless of ability or socioeconomic level.[6]

The highly intellectual students at Catholic colleges scored just above the normative mean, with a mean score of 52; the score of 44.4 obtained by their less intellectual classmates was nearly 6 standard points below the normative mean. The mean scores for the more intellectually oriented West Coast Catholics and non-Catholics at secular colleges were similar, 57 and 58 respectively, compared with a mean of 44.5 for the less intellectual students. Thus students more closely bound to the church, through the church college, were significantly more constricted in their ideas and actions and less able to express themselves freely than were students at the same intellectuality level at secular colleges (Table 47). Even so, this tendency toward docility and rigidity was considerably less prevalent among the more intellectual Catholic college students than among their classmates.

Impulse Expression scores of students in the National Sample were almost a duplicate of those in the West Coast Sample (Table 46). Thus the high intellectuality Catholic college students scored just above the mean, whereas those at secular colleges scored a whole standard deviation above the mean. The low intellectuality students in Catholic colleges were well below the mean, but Catholics in secular colleges almost reached it. Differences between intellectuality levels were significant at the 1 per cent level for all groups, and the highly intellectual non-Catholics scored significantly higher than the Catholic

[6] Trent (1964), p. 275.

college students, again beyond the 1 per cent level (Table 47). Somewhat surprisingly, however, Catholic students at the secular colleges scored even higher than the non-Catholics in Impulse Expression.

The positive relationship between intellectuality and autonomy and the negative relationship between intellectuality and docility were evidenced by responses to a question about student conformity asked of the West Coast students. Fifty-five per cent of the highly intellectual Catholics, regardless of type of school, felt that there was too much conformity, while less than 35 per cent of the less intellectual students did so. Among the non-Catholics, 42 per cent of the highly intellectual students but only 28 per cent of the less intellectual felt that there was too much conformity. Differences in all cases were significant beyond the 1 per cent level of confidence.

Why Catholics were the most likely to see conformity as a problem is somewhat puzzling, unless perhaps they were surrounded by students who were conforming, particularly in the Catholic colleges, and so were more aware of the problem. Non-Catholic high intellectuality students had the highest mean Impulse Expression score; perhaps they associated more with nonconforming friends and consequently saw conformity as less of a problem than did their Catholic counterparts. But in spite of this qualification, both personality measurement and personal opinion testify to a divergence between intellectuality and docility.

The more intellectual students, as we observe them in this study, are more in tune to a wide range of life's experiences. They operate at a higher level of awareness than less intellectual individuals, and they deal with greater complexity, conflict, and ambiguity of ideas. As a consequence, we expected the more intellectual students to pay a price for their intellectualism in greater anxiety. We particularly expected that the Catholic intellectuals would manifest anxiety, since they face not only the discomfort of ambiguity, but also the possibility of religious conflict.

We have theorized that because the highly intellectual students are more open to the world around them, ideas and positions that the less intellectual students may simply accept uncritically are subject to constant challenge. More authoritarian students may shut off open discourse and the exchange of conflicting ideas. But the intellectual Catholic opens himself more to such discourse and thus might be expected to show signs of anxiety in the face of this encounter. These students may find that dogmatic positions of the church and accepted ideas about their role in life may be especially challenged. The hypothesis that the existence of more anxiety might be anticipated as a consequence of increased discourse and encounter with the non-Catholic world was supported statistically in the West Coast Sample to some extent. But the National Sample data indicate that the relationship between anxiety and intellectuality is not unique to Catholics.

Bendig's version of the Taylor Manifest Anxiety Scale was incorporated in the Omnibus Personality Inventory as the Lack of Anxiety scale and was administered to the West Coast and National samples (Tables 45 and 46).[7] The internal consistency reliability of this 20-item scale has ranged from .61 to .82. Sample items are: "I frequently find myself worrying about something"; "I find it hard to keep my mind on a task or a job"; and "I have sometimes felt that difficulties were piling up so high that I could not overcome them." On this scale, low scores indicate great anxiety and high scores indicate freedom from anxiety.

In contrast to the other scales, differences between students at the two intellectuality levels are small, but they are consistent and in two instances they are highly significant. However, the evidence is that the high intellectuality Catholic college students do not always show the most anxiety. The only significant difference in anxiety scores obtained by the three groups of students at the high intellectuality level was between the Catholic college and non-Catholic students in the West Coast Sample (Table 47). Otherwise the results are in the direction of our expectations. The differences found reverse the pattern of the other scales, since it was the less intellectual students who had higher scores, indicating less anxiety. The difference between intellectuality levels was significant well above the 1 per cent level for the West Coast Catholic college students and National Sample non-Catholics. The differences in scores between students at the two intellectuality levels varied from less than 1 standard point for the West Coast secular college students to 4 points for the National Sample non-Catholics.

Catholics at secular colleges may not experience as much anxiety because they are not as close to the church system; since they do not adhere so strictly to church doctrines they neither have to defend nor reconcile their beliefs to the extent that their Catholic college peers must. Too, they may not be experiencing their first extensive contacts with the non-Catholic world, whereas the more intellectual Catholic college students may now be seeking such contacts for the first time and experiencing anxiety as a result. Nevertheless, although the anxiety level is not as great, the more intellectual secular college Catholics, at

---

[7] Bendig (1956). Although he did not have access to data of this kind, Van Kaam (1963) takes up the subject of anxiety in his discussion of the psychology of the Catholic intellectual.

least in the National Sample, also tended toward greater anxiety than their less intellectual peers.

This, together with the fact that the more intellectual National Sample non-Catholics manifested significantly greater anxiety than other students, suggests that it is not just the intellectually oriented person with a strong religious background who experiences increased anxiety. Anxiety may be associated with a high degree of intellectualism whatever one's background. We still suspect that this condition could be expected to exist more for the person whose intellectual activity represents a break from his particular subculture, however defined, be it family, neighborhood, race, or religion. But it is logical that this is also a condition inherent in dealing with the complex and ambiguous, which is part of intellectual activity.

This relationship between anxiety and intellectuality was apparent regardless of sex, although it appears to hold especially for the men. The relationship also existed with ability and socioeconomic levels controlled, with the exception of the low socioeconomic level which was affected by the small numbers.[8] Even so, the relationship warrants replication to see if it is consistent and if it is more apparent among those with strong religious ties or other unique cultural backgrounds. But on the basis of the above data, the less docile and authoritarian college students, who seem to be more intellectual, express greater anxiety.

The psychometric data so far reviewed in table form in this chapter may be seen graphically in Figure 9. Since the midline of 50 represents the Omnibus Personality Inventory normative standard mean score for each scale, a comparison of the intellectuality levels may be made between one another, among the study groups, and between the study groups and the normative data. Major similarities between the West Coast and National samples are depicted in the graphs. They highlight the differences in autonomy and imaginativeness between the high and low intellectuality Catholic students, and, concomitantly, the large differences on these dimensions that existed between Catholic students and non-Catholic students at the high level of intellectual disposition.

Since in opinion and personality the more intellectually oriented Catholics differed so much and in so many ways from the majority of Catholic college students, and since they differed as well from intellectually oriented secular college Catholics and non-Catholics, questions inevitably arise about the religious differences of these students. How

[8] Trent (1964), p. 277.

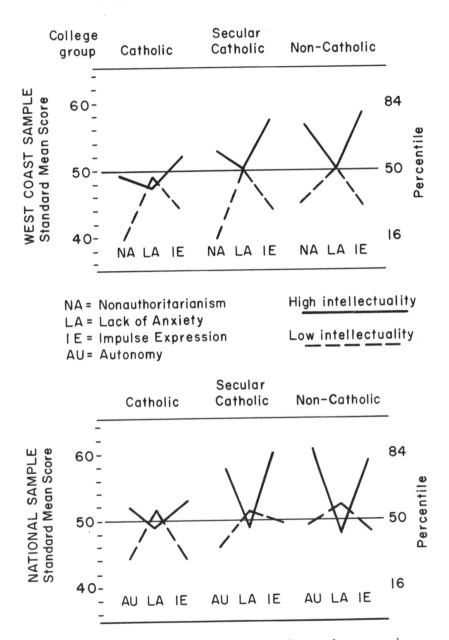

Fig. 9. Profile of standard mean OPI scores by sample group and
intellectuality level.

do the two groups of intellectually oriented Catholics compare in religious orientation? What is their religious orientation like compared with the less intellectual Catholics and with non-Catholics? How is a significant increase of intellectually oriented Catholics liable to affect the church?

TABLE 48. *Standard Mean Religious Liberalism Scores, West Coast and National Samples, by Intellectuality Level*

SAMPLE AND INTELLECTUALITY LEVEL	COLLEGE GROUP AND SCORE					
	Catholic		Secular Catholic		Non-Catholic	
	(No.)	Mean	(No.)	Mean	(No.)	Mean
West Coast						
High	(212)	37.8	(33)	50.6	(62)	52.3
Low	(1,050)	36.9	(155)	40.2	(155)	49.0
(Critical ratio)		(1.39+)		(6.11**)		(3.90**)
National						
High	(20)a	38.5	(62)	49.7	(333)	53.1
Low	(115)	35.5	(310)	44.1	(1,670)	47.9
(Critical ratio)		(2.26*)		(3.92**)		(8.67**)

a Because of the small number of high intellectuality students in Catholic colleges, a *t* test used for small sample statistics was computed instead of the usual critical ratio.
+ *p* = not significant
* *p* ≤ .05
** *p* ≤ .01

Among both Catholic and non-Catholic students at secular schools, the degree of religiosity and intellectuality appeared to be directly—and negatively—related, but for the most part this relationship was not found among Catholic college students (Table 48). Regardless of intellectuality level, students in Catholic colleges were alike in religious attitudes and orientation as measured by the Religious Liberalism scale of the Omnibus Personality Inventory and the Religious Concepts Inventory. Their scores showed considerable religious commitment on the Religious Liberalism scale and reached a very orthodox position on the Religious Concepts Inventory.

By contrast, the high intellectuality Catholics at secular colleges were very liberal and unorthodox in their religious beliefs. The difference in the scores of the two groups were highly significant (Table 49). The non-Catholics at the lower intellectuality level also were more liberal than the Catholics at these levels, but considerably less liberal than the high intellectuality non-Catholics, who displayed the most liberalism in their religious attitudes.

TABLE 49. *Critical Ratios of Religious Liberalism Scores by Intellectuality Level, West Coast and National Samples*

Intellectuality Level and College Group	West Coast Sample	National Sample[a]
High intellectuality		
Catholic *vs.* secular Catholic	7.6**	4.5**
Catholic *vs.* non-Catholic	10.4**	6.5**
Secular Catholic *vs.* non-Catholic	0.8+	2.3+
Low intellectuality		
Catholic *vs.* secular Catholic	4.9**	12.6**
Catholic *vs.* non-Catholic	13.5**	22.3**
Secular Catholic *vs.* non-Catholic	7.0**	7.5**

a Because of the small number of high intellectuality students in Catholic colleges, a *t* test used for small sample statistics was computed instead of the usual critical ratio.

+ p = not significant

** $p \leq .01$

In the West Coast Sample the highly intellectual Catholics at Catholic colleges obtained a standard mean score of 37.8 on the Religious Liberalism scale, and the less intellectual Catholic college students scored 36.9. This difference did not reach a level of statistical significance. The high intellectuality Catholics at the secular colleges scored 50.6, 10 points higher than the score of the less intellectual secular Catholics, a difference significant well beyond the 1 per cent level of confidence. The respective scores for non-Catholics were 52.3 and 49.0, with the more intellectually oriented students manifesting significantly more liberality in religious orientation. The differences in Religious Concepts Inventory scores obtained by the groups were almost identical to the differences in their Religious Liberalism scores.[9]

The same pattern of differences in religious orientation among the three student groups existed also in the National Sample. There was little difference among students in Catholic colleges on the Religious Liberalism scale, regardless of intellectuality level. The high intellectuality students in these colleges obtained a standard mean score of

9 *Ibid.*, p. 189.

38.5, and their less intellectual classmates obtained a score of 35.5. The difference of 3 standard points is statistically significant, but both groups of students were more than 1 standard deviation below the normative freshman mean, as were the Catholic college students on the West Coast.

In the National Sample the high intellectuality Catholics at secular colleges achieved a mean score of 49.7, nearly at the normative mean, and about 6 points higher than that obtained by the less intellectual secular Catholics. The high intellectuality non-Catholics obtained a score of 53.1, and their peers at the low level of intellectual disposition obtained a score of 47.9. Although the scores of the secular Catholics did not indicate that the highly intellectual Catholics at secular colleges were extremely liberal in their religion, they did indicate a great difference between the more intellectual Catholic students at the two types of schools. Eleven points separate the scores of the highly intellectual Catholics in secular and Catholic colleges, a highly significant differential that indicates that the groups held very different beliefs and attitudes concerning their religion (Table 49).

The more intellectually oriented Catholics at secular colleges were much less orthodox and much less committed to their religion than were less intellectual Catholics in the secular colleges. They were also just as unorthodox and uncommitted religiously compared with students at the high intellectuality level who attended Catholic colleges. There was a greater tendency toward religious liberalism among the more intellectually oriented Catholic college students than among the majority of students in Catholic colleges. But this greater liberalism was a nominal tendency compared with that among the secular college Catholics. The more intellectual Catholics at secular colleges, outside the church's school system, were radically different from other Catholics in religious orientation.

These differences in religious attitudes between the more intellectually oriented Catholics in the two types of schools are dramatically evident when their opinions toward specific teachings of the church are considered. That Catholics at Catholic colleges as a group adhere more closely to the teachings of the church than do Catholics at secular colleges was demonstrated in the previous chapter. This is equally apparent when observing the positions on certain moral issues taken by the two groups of Catholics at the same level of intellectual disposition (Table 50).

Regardless of intellectuality level, less than 15 per cent of the students at Catholic colleges in the National Sample approved of premarital sexual relations among engaged couples or approved of abortion. Although it was not statistically significant, there was a greater difference between the Catholic college students at the two intellectual levels in their opinion about divorce than about abortion: 30 per cent of the highly intellectual and 22 per cent of the less intellectual students reported their approval of divorce; 10 per cent of the more intellectual students and 7 per cent of the others approved of abortion.

TABLE 50. *Percentage of Catholics Approving Specific Moral Positions, by Intellectuality Level, National Sample, 1963*

College Group and Intellectuality Level (No.)	Premarital Sex	Divorce	Abortion
Catholic			
High (20)	10	30	10
Low (115)	14	22	7
(Z ratio)	(0.50^+)	(0.78^+)	(0.47^+)
Secular Catholic			
High (62)	70	68	44
Low (310)	53	53	30
(Z ratio)	(2.45^*)	(2.16^*)	(2.16^*)
Z ratio Catholic *vs.* secular Catholic			
High	4.67**	3.01**	2.76**
Low	7.37**	5.66**	5.02**

$^+ p =$ not significant
$^* p \leq .05$
$^{**} p \leq .01$

The situation was much different at secular colleges. A majority of secular Catholic students approved of divorce and premarital relations; averaging figures, over 32 per cent of them approved of abortion. In each case this disagreement with church teachings was intensified at the high intellectuality level, with all differences significant beyond the 5 per cent level. Approximately 70 per cent of the high intellectuality students and 53 per cent of the less intellectual Catholics at secular colleges approved of premarital sexual relations and divorce. Although not as many students favored abortion, 44 per cent of the highly intellectual Catholics and 30 per cent of the other Catholics at the secular colleges approved of it.

238 WHAT IT MEANS TO BE A CATHOLIC INTELLECTUAL

As noted by Z-ratio entries at the bottom of Table 50, at each intellectuality level the secular college Catholics differed significantly from the Catholic college students in their disagreement with the church's traditional teachings on moral issues. The differences were significant well beyond the 1 per cent level of confidence. We have seen that there is a different kind of Catholic at the secular colleges, and this situation is particularly evident among the highly intellectual students.

These data indicate that the high intellectuality Catholic college students, although somewhat more liberal than their fellow students, have essentially the same religious orientation as their less intellectual classmates. In terms of personal endorsement of religion, the high intellectuality Catholics actually appear to exceed their classmates in degree of religiosity (Table 51). In the West Coast Sample, a majority of Catholic college students felt a personal need for religion and thought that colleges should put more stress on it. But it is the Catholic college students at the high intellectuality level who in significantly greater proportion expressed a personal need for religion and the conviction that college should emphasize it more. In addition, the high intellectuality Catholic college students significantly more than the others viewed religion as a prime source of life satisfaction, as observed in data not included in table form.

TABLE 51. *Percentage of Catholic College Students Expressing Opinions about Religion, by Intellectuality Level, West Coast Sample*

Intellectuality Level (No.)	Need Religion	Colleges Should Stress More	Disagree with Church Policy Considerably	No Disagreements with Church
High (212)	73	67	27	19
Low (1,050)	66	53	12	40
(Z ratio)	(2.02*)	(3.74**)	(5.66**)	(5.82**)

* $p \leq .05$
** $p \leq .01$

As noted in chapter 8, in the National Sample the students were asked how they thought their value for religion had changed in the four years following their high school graduation rather than about their need for religion. Just as the high intellectuality West Coast Catholic college students expressed the greatest need for religion, the Catholic college students at the high intellectuality level in the

National Sample were most likely to say that they valued religion more than they did when they entered college (Table 52). Ninety per cent of the Catholic college students at the high intellectuality level, compared with 78 per cent at the low intellectuality level, reported this increase in value. All told, a considerable majority of the Catholic college students valued religion more after four years in college regardless of their intellectual disposition, and less than 5 per cent of them expressed less value for religion. But this was not the case among the secular college Catholics.

TABLE 52. *Percentage of Catholics Reporting Change in Their Value for Religion between 1959 and 1963, National Sample*

College Group and Intellectuality Level (No.)	Value It More	No Change	Value It Less
Catholic			
High (20)	90	5	5
Low (115)	78	20	3
(Z ratio)	(1.24[+])	(1.60[+])	(0.47[+])
Secular Catholic			
High (62)	38	14	48
Low (310)	50	29	21
(Z ratio)	(1.73[+])	(2.40*)	(4.44**)
Z ratio			
Catholic *vs.* secular Catholic			
High	4.05**	1.05[+]	3.41**
Low	5.29**	1.84[+]	4.65**

[+] p = not significant
* $p \leq .05$
** $p \leq .01$

At the high level of intellectuality, less than 40 per cent of the secular college Catholics expressed greater value for religion and nearly half valued religion less. Unlike the Catholic college students, the secular Catholics at the high and low levels of intellectual disposition differed significantly in the value they placed on religion. But at each level of intellectuality the secular Catholics placed significantly less value on religion than the Catholic college students. The evidence is that the more one is removed from the church system, and, at the same time, the more intellectually oriented he is, the less likely he will feel a greater value for religion after four years of college.

The decreased value many of these students placed upon their religion is reflected in their defection from the church (Table 53). Better

TABLE 53. *Percentage of Catholics Reporting Various Religious Affiliations in 1963, National Sample*

College Group and Intellectuality Level (No.)	Catholic	Atheist or Agnostic	Other
Catholic			
High (20)	95	5	0
Low (115)	99	1	0
(Z ratio)	(1.63^+)	(1.63^+)	(0)
Secular Catholic			
High (62)	67	18	15
Low (310)	91	4	5
(Z ratio)	(5.24^{**})	(4.05^{**})	(2.67^{**})
Z ratio Catholic vs. secular Catholic			
High	2.49^*	1.40^+	1.85^+
Low	2.83^{**}	1.50^+	2.23^*

$^+ p =$ not significant
$^* p \leq .05$
$^{**} p \leq .01$

than 95 per cent of the students in the National Sample who entered Catholic colleges in 1959 were still Catholics in 1963, but the percentage who remained Catholic after four years was much lower among students who entered non-Catholic colleges. The greatest rate of apostasy occurred among the highly intellectual secular college Catholics. Only 67 per cent of these students still considered themselves Catholics in 1963, compared with 91 per cent of students at the low intellectuality level. Eighteen per cent of the more intellectual students considered themselves agnostics or atheists, and 15 per cent had affiliated with other religions or specified no religion. Only 4 per cent of the less intellectual secular Catholic students had become atheists or agnostics, and 5 per cent joined other religions.

TABLE 54. *Frequency of Church Attendance Reported by National Sample Catholics in 1963, in Per Cent*

College Group and Intellectuality Level (No.)	More than Once a Week	Once a Week	At Least Once a Year	Never
Catholic				
High (20)	70	25	0	5
Low (115)	50	50	0	0
(Z ratio)	(1.65+)	(2.06*)	(0)	(2.04*)
Secular Catholic				
High (62)	11	50	25	14
Low (310)	13	65	19	3
(Z ratio)	(0.44+)	(2.26*)	(1.08+)	(3.48**)
Z ratio Catholic vs. secular Catholic				
High	5.25**	1.95+	2.43*	1.05+
Low	8.08**	2.84**	5.08**	2.13*

+ p = not significant
* $p \leq .05$
** $p \leq .01$

These data make it apparent that defection from the faith occurred proportionately more among students who entered non-Catholic colleges, and especially among those at the high intellectuality level. They do not indicate, however, that the colleges necessarily caused this phenomenon, a problem we discussed previously.

Under the circumstances, it is not surprising that the Catholics at Catholic colleges reported the greatest rate of church attendance, as noted in Table 54. All Catholic college students reported attending Mass at least once a week; and 70 per cent of the high intellectuality students reported attending services more often than that. Fifty per cent of the less intellectual Catholic college students were attending Mass weekly in 1963 and the others were attending more often than that. Among the low intellectuality Catholics at non-Catholic colleges, 65 per cent attended services weekly, but only 13 per cent said that they attended more than once a week, and 19 per cent said they attended at least once a year. The more intellectual students at Catholic colleges reported the highest rate of Church attendance, but the situation was reversed for high intellectuality Catholics at secular colleges. Nearly 40 per cent of the highly intellectual secular college Catholics failed to attend Mass every Sunday as required by the church. Twenty-two per cent of the less intellectual secular Catholics failed to attend weekly services.

As shown in Table 55, among the West Coast Catholic college seniors queried about their perception of their religious and intellectual development after four years of college, it was again the more intellectual students who reported the greater religious commitment. The high intellectuality students in significantly greater proportion than the others reported having gained "considerable" spiritual development from their college experience. Similarly, it was the high intellectuality students who most committed themselves to intellectual pursuit out of religious motivation, implied by the role of "intellectual apostolate." These significant differences between Catholic college students at the two intellectuality levels were even greater when ability and socioeconomic levels were held constant.[10]

TABLE 55. *Percentage of Catholic College Seniors Reporting "Considerable" Intellectual and Religious Development by Intellectuality Level, West Coast Sample, 1960*

Intellectuality Level (No.)	Spiritual Development	Interest in Intellectual Apostolate	Intellectual Development
High (62)	69	52	85
Low (151)	42	20	87
(Z ratio)	(3.58**)	(4.62**)	(0.38+)

+ p = not significant
** $p \leq .01$

Despite the greater personal religious development perceived by the more intellectual students, almost all of the Catholic college seniors reported having gained "considerable" intellectual development as

[10] *Ibid.*, p. 280. The summation of these data offer additional evidence that the various autonomy or nonauthoritarianism scales do not have an anti-Catholic bias. The highly intellectual Catholic college students were considerably more autonomous and nonauthoritarian than their less intellectual classmates; they were also considerably more religious in orientation. If the autonomy scales were indeed anti-Catholic it is difficult to see how the more intellectual students, who also had more religious commitment than their classmates, could at the same time score so much higher on the autonomy scales.

a result of their college experience. Seniors at the low intellectuality level testified to their intellectual development fully as much as did their classmates at the high intellectuality level. Earlier in the chapter we also saw that the low intellectuality students were just as prone as the high intellectuality students to perceive their parents as intellectual. It is possible that the low intellectuality students developed as much intellectually as their measurably more intellectual classmates, even if they did not reach the level of intellectual disposition of the high intellectuality students. It is also possible that the parents of the two groups were equally intellectual. But it is likely, too, that the meaning the researcher brings to questionnaire items of this kind does not conform to the frame of reference of the respondent. What the students perceived as intellectual may have had little relationship to our definitions and measurements of intellectualism.

Whereas the least intellectual Catholic college seniors felt that they developed intellectually at the rate of their high intellectuality classmates, at the same time they reported less spiritual development. Although the lower level students may have developed intellectually from their own frame of reference, empirical criteria (on the basis of the measurements in the present study) revealed that the students who were lacking in intellectual disposition also appeared to lack objective insight into themselves. We can also conclude, however, that a high degree of intellectuality evidently is not incompatible with religiosity, at least for these Catholic college students, since the self-reports of the more intellectually oriented regarding their intellectual and religious development corresponded with validated personality measurements.

But the more intellectual Catholic college students, who in so many ways showed themselves to be more religious than their classmates, were also more intellectual about their religion. They differed in their religious thinking from the many less intellectual Catholics in what seemed a very important way. For even as they endorsed their religion more, so were they also more critical of it. More than their less intellectual classmates, the highly intellectual Catholics in the West Coast Sample disagreed with their church's customs, policies, and practices (Table 51). Only 19 per cent of the high intellectuality students expressed no disagreements with the church's policies and customs, compared with 40 per cent of their classmates who appeared to be so aligned with the church system. Twenty-seven per cent of the more intellectual students reported "considerable" disagreement with their church's policies, over twice the proportion of their less intellectual classmates who reported such disagreement.

The more intellectual Catholic college students have shown themselves to be more open and critical in their religious orientation than their classmates. They also seemed to appreciate the intellectual aspects of their religion more. But they were practicing Catholics; they remained very devout by self-report and, apparently, valued their religion more than did their less critical and less intellectual classmates. The most intellectual students might therefore be aptly designated as the *critical devout.*

A number of the differential qualities of intellectually oriented Catholics in Catholic and non-Catholic educational environments are illustrated in interviews with two students, one at Marquette University and the other at Harvard University. Both students were National Merit Scholarship winners and both had shown great intellectual development apart from their academic aptitude.

In describing his intellectual awakening, the Marquette student said:

I hadn't ever done very much reading or thinking in high school. I rather thought coming to college would mean having a lot more, bigger, and better parties, and I'd get most of my kicks by running around. However, my friends and I found that we got much bigger kicks out of reading and talking to each other. So, our kicks are, in a sense, intellectual kicks. This I didn't expect, hadn't even thought of, didn't even know that it could happen.

This student felt that much of his interest in intellectual matters stemmed from a seminar, run by a priest "for the brightest students in the school." In describing the seminar he said:

What the priest did was discuss our whole academic problem with us, try to set up programs for us that would set us in new directions—directions that we wouldn't have come across by ourselves. He gathered us together every other week and sat us down and set us talking about things we hadn't thought very much about—intellectual-type questions that he thought would be very good meat for us. I learned to have more fun with them and get big kicks out of reading books and things of that sort. This all happened all at once, from the association with this priest.

His intellectual awakening was accompanied by the discovery of what artistic dedication can mean to a person. This happened through his involvement in the campus theater group. He seemed moved by the talent and dedication this group possessed: "The two forces—the intellectualness from the priest and the dedicated artistic approach from the other kids—have kind of converged to give me a special direction in the work that I'm doing."

This student valued his Catholicism and had even considered the priesthood seriously enough to enter a seminary for a brief period. But

Catholicism seemed to be important to him primarily as a cultural way of life. He spoke of the commonality the students share because they have the same background. "We were all speaking from the same center of reference," he related, and then amplified:

We share the same culture. This cultural background is more important here than our doctrinal position, which we share, too, of course. But we have all been formed by approximately the same influences. We can talk in the same language and know that we mean precisely the same ideas. This is something that you couldn't achieve in a more cosmopolitan university.

But he valued going to a Catholic college for reasons other than the cultural satisfaction he described. He felt that the special advantage of going to a Catholic school was "a spiritual involvement that I didn't have in my home experience."

This person apparently was able to grow intellectually in college and yet also grew closer to his religion. The way that he has grown closer to his religion—by claiming a cultural as well as a religious unity with all Catholics—is perhaps his own unique solution. This may have been a way of enriching the bond with his church and of negating a strictly doctrinal interpretation of Catholicism.

The Harvard student was in a very different position. He was thinking of leaving the church, and thinking about it very seriously. To him, the issue boiled down to this:

The questioning started off with things like arguments about the existence of God. Part of Catholic teaching is that you can arrive at this by reason. Well, I began to think you couldn't. Then moral and ethical issues, and matters of practice—whether I was going to submit to an authoritarian system in respect to these matters of what I ought to do, and what my purpose is, and all that sort of thing. Seems to me that the plain assumption around here is that you have a moral obligation to try to find out the answers for yourself. And the assumption of Catholicism is, I think, just exactly the opposite. Your obligation is not to discover but to believe what is known, what has been discovered, what is thought. And I was reluctant to get involved in that sort of system. The upshot is that I am leaving the Catholic Church.

He went on to say that the decision was not definite yet: "I am now making another careful review of Catholicism and my relation to it. If I find out that my reaction at the present time is that I want to get out of it—I will get out of it; if I want to stay, then I will stay."

Another complication in his life was that he was planning to marry a non-Catholic girl whose parents were strongly anti-Catholic. He felt that the only way he could remain Catholic in this marriage would be if he were *"strongly* Catholic," and this feeling was part of the impetus for his reassessment of his religion.

While it may be argued that only the more committed Catholics go to Catholic colleges anyway, yet in this example, it seems that the Harvard student was exceptionally committed to his religion. The "thinking through" process for him was arduous, and he did not seem content with easy answers. He said that he was talking to many people about his doubts and that he was also taking a course for Catholic doubters to help him decide. All this expenditure of energy does not denote a weak commitment to his religion.

Why, then, were the two students heading in such opposite directions? Both young men appeared to be sensitive, thoughtful, perceptive individuals, and yet one was leaving the church while the other became more closely bound to it. Of course, one student was in a non-Catholic environment while the other was attending a Catholic college, but the reasons for their differences no doubt go deeper.

The Harvard student believed that Catholicism was essentially an anti-intellectual, authoritarian, and anti-rational system. The Marquette student, on the other hand, believed that Catholicism could embrace intellectual endeavor, as evidenced in the seminar conducted by the priest. The priest himself was a strong influence on this youth —an influence, it seems, toward both increased intellectual commitment and commitment to the church. One student felt that he could combine his growing intellectual awareness with his growing religious commitment; the other felt that any intellectual activity and desire on his part would come into conflict with the church.

The conflict of opinion about the fostering of intellectual development within the church as represented by these two young men is of major consideration. Discussion of the source of this conflict, the theoretical accounting for it, its dynamics, its possible resolution, and the repercussions of such a resolution takes up the remainder of this volume. It is immediately evident, however, that even if we know little about the background that leads to a high degree of intellectual disposition, we know a great deal about the relevant characteristics of the more intellectual Catholics and their import to the church.

These characteristics are likely to have an immense impact on the church. They may well go beyond that conceived in 1967, even as recent ecumenical innovations are being implemented. And, obviously, the greater the numbers of Catholic intellectuals that emerge in the church, the greater the impact that can be expected from them.

CHAPTER TEN

The Church-Family-Self System:
Maintenance of Anti-intellectualism

In a number of ways our data indicate that the comparatively few intellectual Catholics are much different from their fellow Catholics. Historical considerations that help account for the intellectual status of American Catholics were presented in chapter 1. But what are the dynamics underlying these obvious historical factors that have led to the development of the American Catholic subculture as it is now characterized? Out of an effort to answer this question we shall propose a theoretical model to help explain the Catholic's lesser involvement in intellectual matters and to indicate what might be expected in the event of increased intellectualism in the Catholic population.

The basis for this model is the position that Catholics' nonintellectualism or anti-intellectualism springs from their self-perception; it is a result of how Catholics see themselves in relation to others. Conceivably, to the extent that Catholics perceive the role of the intellectual as comprising behavioral and attitudinal patterns contrary to those they believe they should emulate, to that extent will they fail to appreciate or understand that role. Indeed, such a role may seem alien, or even menacing.[1]

Intellectual attitudes and behavior do not suddenly emerge in full maturity as an adolescent reaches college age. In his earliest years these attitudes and behaviors (or their opposites) are included in the answers to the most meaningful questions his existence poses: Who am I? Who should I be? Who are others? The disposition we have been calling "intellectual" cannot stand apart from these questions, and the slowly evolving answers will determine the direction and development of the individual's intellectuality.

---

[1] Other authors who directly or by implication theorize variations of a relationship between role theory and belief systems—and religious beliefs specifically—include: Rokeach (1960); Rommetveit (1955); Sarbin (1954); and Stewart and Hoult (1959).

The first answers to these questions are provided by others who are immediately significant in his life. In the terminology of role theory, the Catholic is assigned a "position" which determines the "role" he is to live out in society as well as the roles he is to avoid. Who the Catholic is may be defined behaviorally as his role, and its definition comes primarily from his family and church. The child is told by his parents who he is, who he should be, and who they—and the rest of the world—are. But devout Catholic parents have received many of these answers from the church as well as from their parents, who, in turn, were closely influenced by the church. In essence, the child's role in life is first defined by his superordinates, his family; and through his family by their supernatural authorities embodied in the church.

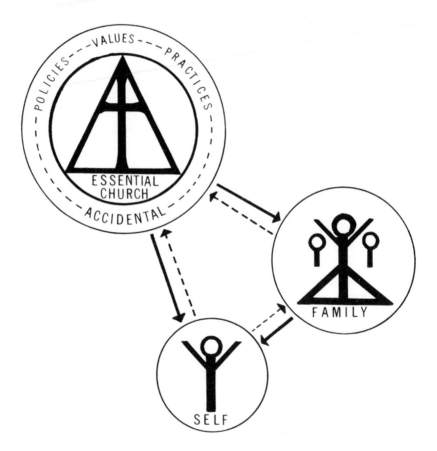

FIG. 10. Relationship between church, family, and self.

The questions then become: In what ways can, and do, the family and church influence the self? What are the interrelationships and interplays among these three entities? How do these interrelationships influence the Catholic's value system, beliefs, behavior, and corresponding roles?

A hypothesized relationship between the church, the family, and the individual is depicted in Figure 10. In this diagram, the American Catholic church, by nature of its religious authority and apostolic character, as well as by its historical role of guiding its immigrant congregation, has traditionally wielded a great influence on its members, as indicated by the heavy arrow leading to the family unit, a smaller circle-unit. The church as a whole is stronger in body than the family; its officials have in the past had more education than its lay members. They have also been the administrators of the church's sacraments and sanctions. Therefore, the church's influence on the basic familial unit of society is much more pervasive than the family's reciprocal influence on the church (indicated by the broken arrow).

Similarly, the family taught by the church then influences its individual members, who are soon jointly influenced and taught directly by the church as well through the parochial schools and more recently by the Confraternity of Christian Doctrine (which provides religious training to Catholics attending public schools). The individual is therefore immediately influenced by two strong authorities (the heavy arrows leading from church and family) upon whom he has much less influence, as indicated by the two broken arrows leading from the self, the smallest circle-unit. Indoctrination in the church thus seems certain and swift.

But the church itself is not a monolith. Here it is shown as consisting of two parts: (1) its essential ministry of propagating its basic faith and dogmas—that is, its inflexible, unchanging part indicated by the solid inner triangle; and (2) the values, habits, policies, and practices upheld by the individuals and groups within the church that are not essentially related to the church's ministry. These secondary characteristics may be values held by a member of a religious community that are a part of his family background, for example, rather than anything inherently religious, or they may be "rules" of an order of the church, or church customs peculiar to a particular country or region.

These peripheral aspects of the church are not all equally related to its core. Those on the outermost perimeter are the least related to the essence of the church; the closer the element is to the inner triangle, the closer is its relationship to the church's essential ministry. Between the peripheral and the core areas is a fringe area, which could be said to contain church precept apart from the core dogma. The prescribed practice of celibacy or the former rule of abstaining from meat on Friday are examples of such precepts, which theoretically are capable of change.

The church is in part the composite of members of the hierarchy, its leaders. Therefore, all that these leaders bring to the church—regardless of whether it is essential to the church—is yet seen as coming from the church itself. Thus, the church may officially endorse intellectual values, but if its ministers are characteristically anti-intellectual in their attitudes or practices, it is the latter which will be fostered by the church and which will characterize its congregation. That is, the congregation will embrace these peripheral, accidental values as if they emanated from the essential church.

Figure 11 illustrates the way the church's influence is maintained. The church, relatively unchanging, remains the central authority.

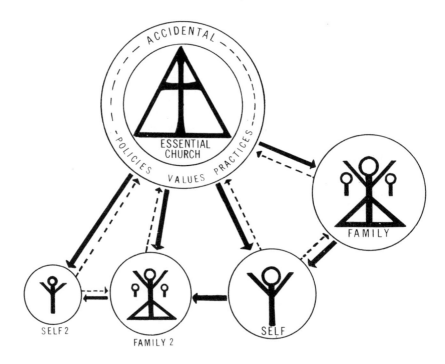

Fig. 11. Maintenance of the closed church-family-self pattern.

As the family's child matures and moves away to start his own family (Family 2) he is fully committed to the church, and the pattern in Figure 10 is repeated, beginning with his first child (Self 2). The cycle is able to go on perpetuating itself; it is maintained through the power of church sanction, buttressed by parental authority and traditional familial and ethnic solidarity. Moreover, a pluralistic society may heighten the impact of the church and the family on the individual's knowledge and standards.

Figure 12 depicts the church, the family, and the self as they exist in the macrocosmic unit of society. In a pluralistic society, various environmental forces impinging on the family and the self may often be contrary to the ideals and ideology of the church. The church has reacted by surrounding its families and their individual members with a shield (the squares surrounding the family and the self in the diagram). This protection has taken many forms, including separate church schools, exclusively Catholic friendships, the agreement that the children of mixed marriages will be raised as Catholics, and the inhibition of dissent within Catholic ranks by imposing censorship through the Imprimatur, the Index of Forbidden Books, the Legion of Decency, and excommunication. Shielding the individual this way also assures his conformance to the church system.

This protection is most effective in a close family, as shown by the solid-lined square and the broken environmental arrows that signify a relatively weak press or influence of society upon the Catholic family. Church protectiveness is least effective when it is applied to the individual alone (as shown by the broken-lined square and the solid societal arrows on the left side of the figure). Clearly, the stronger the protective lines, the more isolated the Catholic becomes from all aspects of the outer society, good and bad. And the more this protection originates from accidental values held by official church members —that is, from values not directly related to the essential church—the more isolated from society will the Catholic be and the more restricted will he be in societal roles that he can understand and act out. If the background and training of the teaching sister and pastor have led them to hold suspect the role of the inquiring intellectual or the creative artist, then they will foster lack of respect for these roles among their students and congregation.

The system has been able to maintain itself not only because the group (church) ideals have been supported by this conformity, but also because the individual's security is rooted in the group. In fact, the more the outside world is seen as threatening and hazardous, the

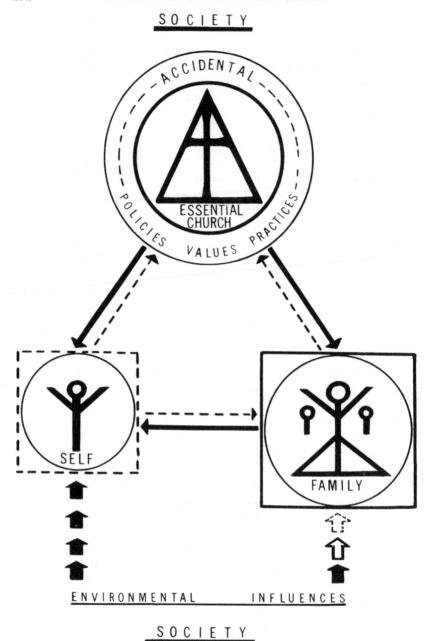

FIG. 12. Exclusion of society's influence from the church-family-self system.

more the individual turns to the group and the more the ministry seeks to fortify and to protect the group—and the bonds between the three thus become increasingly cohesive.

However, in spite of these pressures for conformity, deviation does take place, as illustrated in Figure 13. Family members become exposed to society's multitudinal roles and realities outside the family-church pattern depending on the degree that the family feels threatened, depending on the family's style of authoritarianism (the extent to which it is characterized by objective thinking and democratic relationships) and on each member's responses to internal and external pressures. Conceivably, a Catholic family that feels relatively safe in the world, has a relaxed and democratic style of discipline, and is composed of autonomous, independent members would be more open to a wide range of societal influences than would a family that stresses dependence on authority and views the outside world as a potential danger threatening its security.

In other words, the less protective isolation (the self's broken-lined square) there is, the more societal acculturation may occur. Acculturation, however, does not have the same effect on every individual. One person may become "secularized" and move in the direction of apostasy, signified by the deviating arrow on the left in the diagram. But apostasy may be the result of factors other than secular acculturation; for example, the church may be made a scapegoat as a result of personal emotional problems. Another person may maintain his ties with the church while assuming many of the attitudes, roles, and insights of outer society. In such a case, he may be dissatisfied with many of the more peripheral aspects of the church but remain basically devout. In collaborating with others who feel the same way (the expanded arrow circulating through the sphere of society and terminating at the church), the individual participates in a group aptly termed the *critical devout*. Together, the critical devout can exert a certain amount of influence on the secondary area of the church. Thus, the church itself becomes more acculturated, changes, and shifts its style of interaction with its family units (symbolized by Family 2).

This type of change may be responsible for the current dialogue between the Catholic church and other religious groups; or for the recognition of the existence of "Catholic intellectuals"; or for the current criticism of Catholic education, literature, art, architecture, homilectics, and of the neglected voice of the layman; or countless other emerging aspects of the church to be discussed in the following chapter. Perhaps these critically devout Catholics, at home both in

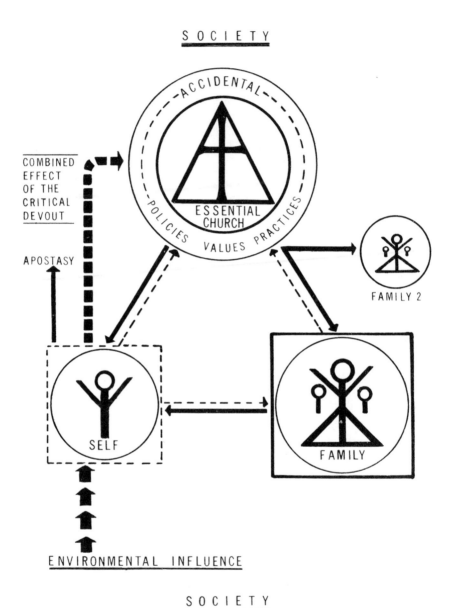

FIG. 13. Influence of society on the church-family-self system.

the church and in pluralistic society, are the ones working for the reconciliation (not identification) of the two.

We have demonstrated these conditions in various ways. The students who maintained a closer relationship with their church system by attending its schools and colleges showed by far the greatest degree of religious conformity, general lack of autonomy, and lack of intellectual disposition compared with all other students. This was true among all the samples considered and by the different measures of religious attitudes and practices, the Omnibus Personality Inventory's intellective and autonomy scales and the CUES data. Catholics who attended college outside the church system were less religiously oriented and generally more intellectually oriented than the Catholic college students. A more liberal religious orientation was particularly marked among students who reported one parent to be Catholic and one to be non-Catholic.

Most Catholic college students stressed the importance of their religion and registered essentially no disagreement with the principles, policies, practices, and dogmas of their faith. However, most of the relatively few Catholic college students at a high level of intellectual disposition decidedly disagreed with certain principles advocated by their church, even though they placed as much importance on their faith as did their less intellectual peers. The intellectually oriented Catholic college students, then, as indicated in chapter 9, form the group theorized as the critical devout.

A large proportion of secular college students who were also at a high level of intellectual disposition and who were Catholics when entering high school reported having given up their faith by the time they were seniors in college. This exodus was unique even compared with the less intellectual Catholics who attended college outside the church system and thus gives evidence of the group of apostates that we theorized as a natural development of the intellectually oriented Catholics who are also removed from the influence of the church system.

Perhaps it is the church's growing awareness of this group of defectors, as much as the activity of the critical devout, that helped to bring about the Ecumenical and Vatican councils. But even the changes being urged by the critical devout, if emerging, are not predominant. The authoritarian isolationism of the Catholic still appears to be the rule rather than the exception. Many of the old patterns continue in the old ways—and the nonintellectual (or anti-intellectual) characteristics of the church's ministers continue to be confused with the essence of the religion. In a few years, after the innovations of Vatican

II have had more chance to be implemented and expanded, this may not be so. Since much of the implementation of current innovation and change in the church will be dependent upon its schools as a major voice of the church, it is important to consider how the Catholic schools fit into the model of the church-family-self system.

The postulated relationships between the church, the family, and the self have provided insulation and protection from the outside "secular" world. The more the family and the individual have operated within this system, the more they have been surrounded by it, the closer has been their adherence to the faith. In such a closed system, the Catholic school has existed as an extremely important element, one which has directly influenced the family's children and therefore the family as well.

From the earliest years in the American Catholic church the bishops ordained that Catholics receive their entire education in the church's schools. Ideally, each parish was to have a school and each diocese enough high schools and colleges to attend to the further education of the church's youth. This dictum has been difficult to carry out at the high school and, especially, at the college level and is becoming much more so at the elementary level.[2] But to date a majority of Catholic children attend parochial elementary schools. When Catholic children attend Catholic schools, they and their families strengthen their bonds with the church. The church indoctrinates the children, who in turn bring their religious lessons home to the members of their families, and who will eventually help indoctrinate their own children.

The school's main objective has been religious indoctrination for the sake of maintaining the faith. In other words, the primary function of the schools has been to reinforce and to mold further the selective roles first assigned to Catholic youths by their church and family. For this objective to be met, it is very likely that both the essential religious and accidental values of the church have become magnified in the school system. Examples of this are the immense stress on docility, the unquestioning obedience to authority, and the infusion of religious elements into purely academic matters that have been found in the Catholic schools, frequently to the detriment of intellectual questioning. Once again, the more limited the understanding and appreciation of intellectual and other societal roles—of a religious nature or not—have been among Catholic educators, the more restricted has been the exposure of students to these varied roles, and therefore the more con-

[2] Cf. Neuwien (1966); Ryan (1964). The forced closing of one parochial school is described in the *San Francisco Sunday Examiner and Chronicle*, June 5, 1966, p. 13; many have since been closed, and many more are likely to follow (see *Time*, 1967).

fined their positions and contributions in society will be.

The church school has been essentially an additional shield from the outside world, covering the family and its individual members with its mantle of doctrine, rubric, and even Catholic-oriented social relationships. For Catholic families who do not send their children to church schools, the shield is necessarily less broad, and such families are potentially more open to outside environmental influences. Thus, Catholics whose children attend Catholic schools are more completely within the church system than are the Catholics whose children go to public schools. Under the circumstances, it is no wonder that Catholic-educated Catholics were found to be so different from secular-educated Catholics in measured religious orientation and practice.

In fact, some Catholic spokesmen contend that students who have attended Catholic high schools should go on to Catholic colleges because they have been sheltered and are not ready, in effect, to face the outside world. They see one of the purposes of the Catholic colleges to be fortifying the student to withstand the pressures of the antagonistic outside world, as if the fortification received in high school is insufficient and must be strengthened in college.

Different authors put it different ways. Catholic schools should exist to deepen intellectual understanding and appreciation of the faith, or to be true to a religious purpose, or to keep Catholics out of other schools, or to provide a shelter from religious cross-currents, or to develop a sense of truth and style of thought—the implication being that these are to be Catholic truths and Catholic styles. In fact, it has often been asserted that the existing mammoth Catholic school system was developed precisely for these purposes—essentially to insulate and to protect the Catholic child from the alien and corrupting influences of the outside world.[3]

In the first chapter we noted that this protection was felt to be necessary because the Catholic immigrants of the 1800's and early 1900's were subjected to the widespread bigotry and prejudice of others, which produced a pervasive Catholic defensiveness, most clearly manifested by the church's separate school system. This defensiveness led to ever widening circles of exclusion, until American Catholics were largely isolated from the secular world of knowledge and ideas. It has even been suggested that this ghetto mentality has not only affected the Catholic's attitude toward intellectual life but that it has also influenced every phase of culture not clearly Catholic.[4] The isolation was

---

[3] Cf. Bland (1959); Fugate (1964); Ong (1956); Ward (1958).

[4] O'Dea (1958, 1959); Ong (1956).

accomplished not only by a separate school system staffed by convent- and seminary-educated teachers who provided few intellectual models for emulation, but also in a number of other ways: restricting students to carefully edited books by Catholic authors, or to special editions of non-Catholic books such as the high school *Prose and Poetry* series; ridiculing non-Catholic thinkers and systems; substituting thorough treatment of church history and theology and their attendant problems and close study of the Bible for memorized and routinized catechism, even at the college level; excluding laymen from the administration and policy formation of the schools and church proper; and, for all of that, maintaining a complacent attitude about the church and its school system.

This complacency, of course, has now been shattered. The critical and not so critical devout have recently been scrutinizing every aspect of what we see as the inevitable products of a closed church-family-self system. There are many Catholic leaders who remain complacent in the face of the scrutiny, however. As indicated earlier, this was evident in the National Catholic Educational Association's annual meeting in 1966[5]; it is evident in any number of Catholic news weeklies. Few leaders or church members show awareness of the pervasive lack of intellectual disposition observed among educated Catholics in the pre- vious pages. But many leaders show concern over the more obvious problems, such as the quality of teacher preparation in the schools, the lack of scholarly productivity, the lack of the relevance of the church to contemporary life and problems, and the lack of communication among factions within the church and between the church and secular society. Their concerns have led to many changes in the church system and suggest more to come.

The whole matter may be summarized in this way: on the basis of a wide variety of contemporary research, Catholic college students, graduates, and even faculty members have been found disproportion- ately lacking in intellectual attitudes and scholarly productivity com- pared to their non-Catholic peers and colleagues. This lack may be in part a matter of historical circumstances; it may be in part a matter of, or even a result of, role restrictions imposed by the educational and belief formation of a relatively closed religious system in which nonintellectual (or anti-intellectual) characteristics of religious min- isters are confused with the essence of the religion itself. And, in the end, this pattern of intellectuality and its correlates may be chang-

[5] *National Catholic Reporter,* April 20, 1966.

ing among some groups of Catholics. We expect these changes to have a radical effect on the intellectual and religious life of the entire church system, in light of the theory presented in this chapter and the data we have examined in the previous chapters. These changes and their repercussions provide the subject matter for the next two chapters.

CHAPTER ELEVEN

Changing Colleges and a Changing Church

That contemporary graduates of Catholic colleges are in general less intellectual than the graduates of other colleges is not necessarily or primarily the fault of the Catholic colleges, for we have seen that Catholic college students are less intellectual than others when they enter college. Catholic colleges do bear some responsibility for the intellectual development of their students, however. Colleges, whether or not they are church related, are created to serve intellectual functions and to attempt to instill and expand a spirit of inquiry and sense of scholarship. And as we have already noted, the less students are concerned with these values upon entering college, the greater is the burden upon the college to foster such values and to maintain an atmosphere conducive to their development.

If the college is itself too much a part of a church system that has molded these students and contributed to anti-intellectual attitudes, it cannot fulfill its functions. Anti-intellectualism, we have argued, is not inherent in the Catholic church system, but it is fostered by the accidental values adopted by its members. Therefore, rather than conforming to what has been too characteristic of the church in the past, the Catholic college should be in the forefront of dispelling such accidental values and restoring the essential values that are at the heart of the church and that are not contrary to intellectual endeavor. There are signs that some Catholic colleges are now attempting to assume this function.

The close of the Vatican Council in the mid-1960's left the church in the midst of a great questioning of these accidental values and of the practices that have contributed to its anti-intellectual image. Its colleges, too, are looking to their image and to what lies behind it. They are beginning to recognize their responsibility to improve radically the quality of Catholic education. They began doing this before Vatican II; they cannot afford to neglect these efforts as the result of the Council.

When the extent of the changes made following Ellis' criticism of Catholic colleges in 1955 was being discussed recently, the provost of a Protestant college commented, "You mean that after ten years of criticism, that is all that has happened?" In all fairness, one might ask how extensive the changes have been in Protestant-controlled education, which shares many of the problems of Catholic education. Still, it is true that large-scale reforms did not come into being at once when Ellis and others first raised the issue of the intellectual quality of Catholic education. Many did not feel that change was needed. But Catholic colleges, a large system in themselves, are also a part of the vast Catholic church system. And systems—particularly large ones—characteristically change slowly.

But changes in the colleges have accelerated since Vatican II, which gave impetus to change in all parts of the Catholic system, including church, family, and school. We believe that these changes are interdependent, and that to be effective they must occur in all areas of the Catholic system. There must be greater emphasis upon openness and critical thinking of the sort now observable throughout the system if Catholics are to increase in intellectuality. This kind of change may be found in the family in personal ways too subtle to be clearly visible as yet.

Changes in the colleges may be seen in their very philosophies as expressed by their presidents. Change is also presaged by the interest in research by many of these institutions and by their concern about improving their faculty, liberalizing course requirements, enlarging student self-responsibility, and increasing cooperation with other schools.

A full appraisal of the philosophy, process, and products of Catholic higher education must take into account the diversity that exists among Catholic colleges. We discussed earlier the fact that there is variation among Catholic colleges in the type of students they attract and the extent to which they encourage intellectual attitudes. Assessment of campuses using the College and University Environment Scales (CUES) showed differences in the way schools were perceived by their students. Assessment using the Omnibus Personality Inventory revealed differences in the intellectual disposition of students attending different Catholic colleges. These findings were explored in chapter 4. In chapter 5, differences in intellectual growth among students in different Catholic colleges were also noted, again based upon the Omnibus Personality Inventory.

There are unquestionably some Catholic colleges that are intellectually alive, stimulating, and searching. There are schools that evince the "atmosphere of intellectual ferment" that has been described in the Danforth report. In the words of the report:

This quality is manifested in the encouragement of independent study and thought, in the involvement of the faculty and students in the intellectual issues of the day, in freedom of discussion, in student interests, in the centrality of the library, in the academic economy, in the educational aspirations of graduates, and in other ways.[1]

The editors of the report note that this quality is difficult to measure, but that it "strikes the visitor dramatically" as he talks with students and faculty members on the campus.

Catholic colleges that display this quality sometimes appear in unexpected places, and the expected sources of excellence, as we have seen, do not always produce it. An indication of this is that the Jesuit schools, which are renowned for their "intellectual independence," as Wakin[2] terms it, evidently do not display to their students the scholarship and awareness associated with such intellectual ferment. Moreover, the Omnibus Personality Inventory scores of entering freshmen at the University of Notre Dame do not indicate that these students arrive with any notable spirit of intellectual inquiry. As a result, there is a question about whether that university itself can instill such a spirit to any great extent, despite its drive for eminent faculty and large-scale government grants.

Women's colleges rated the highest on Scholarship and Awareness on the basis of CUES data, and students at women's colleges also rated highest in intellectual disposition on the Omnibus Personality Inventory scales explored in chapter 4. Apparently, some of the most radical and creative efforts toward intellectual excellence also appear to be coming from some of the women's colleges. Although many colleges are seeking to improve their image, perhaps the most publicity has gone to Webster College and its energetic president, Jacqueline Grennan, who until 1967 was a member of the religious order which controlled the college. The news media delighted in capturing pictures of this intelligent and vivacious woman, while still a nun, as she darted across the previously secluded campus at Webster Groves and across the country at large. She has proved to be as quotable as she is photogenic, and she has not hesitated to speak frankly about the problems of Catholic education as she sees them.

Miss Grennan is a woman not given to easy, conventional answers,

[1] Pattillo and Mackenzie (1965), p. 32.
[2] Wakin (1963), p. 78.

and she expresses a belief in seeking out truth wherever it may be. She allows her students more freedom than even the bishop in her district has thought wise, and in a 1966 national television broadcast of "Open End," her views on religious life made it clear that she was a nun who had thought about and questioned most aspects of her life.

In discussing her philosophy of education she has stated, "Only insecure people require closure. It is a travesty of Christianity to build any sort of blockade against free inquiry. Anything that requires intellectual closure is the most dangerous position in which you can place an intelligent Catholic."[3] She added that if the church member is faced with opposites he cannot explore, he may "simply choose between the opposites and his choice may well not be the Church." But if he is encouraged to explore, "he may find that he can reconcile seemingly opposing ideas, or find that what seemed to be in conflict, on closer examination, isn't."

Much of President Grennan's philosophy is shared in one form or another by the leaders in a number of other women's colleges. For example, on the East Coast, Marymount College in Arlington, Virginia, has for some time now provided special programs in a deliberate attempt to stimulate intellectually their students who otherwise would have little opportunity for intellectual appreciation and challenge.[4] Manhattanville College, which is already rated high intellectually by its students on the CUES scales, is providing what appears to amount to an intellectual shock treatment for a special group of summer students.[5] According to the director of its religious education program, "What we set out to do was to put nuns in touch with the kind of thinking that is shaping twentieth-century man." In the process of this "study of Christian humanism," students are directly exposed to "radical" and "avant garde" Catholic and non-Catholic thinkers along with the rich cultural experiences available in New York City. In reacting to the curriculum one student commented, "Now I'm anxious to learn more about the great thinkers. We always received the impression that men such as Kant, Freud, Darwin, Dewey, and their numerous colleagues were writers to avoid. Now I can see that they did have much to offer, although we don't agree with all their teachings."

Another women's college that has shown signs of unconventional development is Mundelein College in Chicago. In 1962 this school began a self-study program that assessed faculty, students, and alumnae

---

[3] Trombley (1966), p. 1.

[4] Majella (1962).

[5] *National Catholic Reporter,* August 10, 1966, p. 10.

on a wide range of topics, such as the usefulness of their curricula and the college's contribution to their personal lives.[6] The results of the study showed that Mundelein girls, on the whole, were educated carefully to live carefully; they were rather passive and uninvolved with the world around them. Since the study, standards have been raised, the curricula considerably changed, and the physical plant improved.

One of the most innovative, intellectually spirited, and developing of all is Immaculate Heart College, a small women's liberal arts college situated on the outskirts of Hollywood. The tenor of its intellectually active faculty is reflected in its students. At the beginning of the 1966 academic year, the college's newspaper editor admonished her classmates on the front page of the paper that they had to ask why they were really attending their college, that honest intent, and not good grades, made a student, and that the time was approaching that they were going to have to recognize their individuality and "think a personal thought."[7]

On the second page, the assistant editor of the paper reflected on questions raised by 30 Catholic college student leaders who attended the annual convention of the National Student Association the previous summer.

Can I call myself Catholic if I question, challenge, even contradict in thought and action the traditional teachings of Mother Church? If my conscience gives a thoughtful "yes" to artificial contraceptives, premarital sex, therapeutic abortion, meat on Friday, trial marriages, or infrequent Sunday Mass observance, am I a hypocritical Catholic? Can I seriously consider situation ethics? . . . I shudder to think that when I form personal decisions for or against Church-established traditions that I am no longer in the favor of Christ. . . . I abhor the thought that I can be so simplistic as to be absolutely positive of anything except God.

On the same page the freshman spokesman summarized in part the reactions of her classmates to their college with the statement that: "The faculty and student body have swept us into an atmosphere of friendship, a challenge of awareness, a world of intellectualism, and a sense of liberalism."

Although the reactions of the freshmen may be tempered after four years, allowance may be made for their enthusiasm. Immaculate Heart College houses the cramped, cluttered studio where the renowned serigraphs and other fine arts of Sister Mary Corita and her colleagues originate. The library at this college, too, is cramped, but it has assisted with serious commentary on Christian existentialism and humanism.

---

[6] Hruby (1966); Office of the Vice-president, Mundelein College (1966); Sutor (1965).
[7] *Comment,* September 26, 1966, p. 1.

From its small laboratories have come significant (and published) research in the life sciences. Beyond all this there is evident spirited teaching by a committed faculty.

It may be quite natural, then, that Immaculate Heart College is undertaking what is probably the most radical innovation in American Catholic higher education. Upon the completion of its new facilities the college is moving into the Claremont College complex. This goes much further than the many consortia being established between Catholic and non-Catholic colleges. It represents a direct affiliation and interaction with an elite complex of colleges that have a reputation for educational quality.

Of course, the women's colleges are not alone in their concern about the quality of Catholic intellectual life and in their desire to improve their schools. For example, the president of St. Louis University, Father Reinert, is actively involved in efforts to further improve his school, and he, too, has warned against the dangers of closure. In his words:

Catholic students—and that includes seminarians—must study in an atmosphere that is ecumenical and pluralistic. They must learn the give and take of ideas and beliefs because this is the kind of world they are going into. It is ludicrous for a Catholic university to regard itself as a citadel against an unfriendly world in this day and age.[8]

St. Louis is a large, major Jesuit university, and tradition there has not been abandoned as it has at newly experimental Webster College. The messages of Grennan and Reinert are essentially the same, however. Both agree that Catholics must be open to the world around them and that they must not be restricted to Catholic ideas and experiences.

To a great extent the change which occurs in an institution depends upon the philosophy of those administering the institution. Thus the statements of college presidents (and their actions following up the statements) are extremely important in indicating what change may be expected. But if the change is to be coordinated and meaningful it needs to be based upon a thorough knowledge and understanding of the institution involved. Thus it is encouraging that a number of colleges are engaged in some sort of self-study or assessment. These studies seek to answer questions about who really goes to the colleges, what the colleges offer the students, and what happens to students during and after the school years.

Self-studies have been carried out at a number of Catholic colleges, among them the University of Santa Clara, St. Mary's College of Cali-

[8] Trombley (1966), p. 2.

fornia, Mundelein College, College of St. Scholastica, and Arlington's Marymount College. Weiss studied many aspects of St. Louis in his doctoral dissertation. Other schools have participated in environmental assessments, including the 34 Catholic colleges whose students had responded to the College and University Environment Scales or their predecessor, the College Characteristics Index, by the summer of 1966. We have already mentioned the proposed study of Jesuit colleges by a new Center on Research and Development for Jesuit Higher Education.[9]

The need for research beyond the individual institution was emphasized by the president of the American Catholic Psychological Association at its annual meeting in 1964. McCarthy cited several studies concerned with the conformity of Catholic students and urged that there be a searching out of "attitudinal and behavioral effects of Catholic education on every level." He urged, too, that the research be carried out "with fearless integrity." McCarthy continued that all education "is remiss in understanding the people it serves and in assessing the influences on them . . . [and is] in danger of giving succorance to a ticky-tacky culture that pays excessively high compliments to uniformity."[10]

Another way many Catholic colleges are seeking to improve their intellectual impact is to upgrade and diversify their faculties. Catholic colleges are increasing the percentage of non-Catholic and lay faculty members. This is occurring not only because of the difficulty of finding enough qualified priests and professors within the church, but because of a desire to broaden the faculty perspective and course offerings.[11] Indications are that laymen already comprise the majority of the faculty at most major Catholic colleges. As noted in Weiss' study, only 25 per cent of the faculty at St. Louis University in 1963 was composed of priests. At the University of Notre Dame in 1966 only 15 per cent of the full-time professors were priests.[12]

Notre Dame has made a serious effort to attract eminent figures, not only in the areas of law and science, where the university has traditionally been strong, but in the humanities as well. Inducements have been high salaries backed up by guarantees of freedom in research and teaching.

Although Catholic colleges are increasing the percentage of non-

[9] Emmet (1965).

[10] McCarthy (1965).

[11] Reinert (1964) in particular has noted the need for additional lay faculty.

[12] Weiss (1963); Trombley (1966).

Catholic faculty members, it appears that few nonbelievers are being added in many institutions. As indicated at St. Louis, the administration wants to be sure the faculty member is comfortable and feels himself to be a part of the college. The Danforth directors raise the question of the religious qualifications of a person who is to teach in a school that intends to be a "Christian community" and to conduct its work within a Christian context. Naturally, schools seek a person who is sympathetic to the aims of the school and can make a contribution toward those aims. The Danforth directors conclude, however, that "the importance of freedom in academic institutions argues for some diversity of faculty outlook, even at the risk of reducing religious impact." They note that very few church colleges restrict their faculty to persons who belong to that church. "People who think that rigid sectarianism is the principal defect of church-related higher education are 50 years behind the time."[13]

At present, Catholic scholars of the first order are limited in number in Catholic undergraduate and graduate schools. Donovan demonstrated this prior to 1960, and it was evident in 1966 when an assessment of quality in graduate education was published by the American Council on Education.[14] Over 4,000 scholars, including department chairmen and selected junior and senior scholars, rated the graduate departments in their field. Twenty-nine departments were rated in the 100 universities comprising the Council of Graduate Schools and in 6 additional universities which had granted 100 or more doctorates in the preceding decade. None of the departments in the 7 Catholic universities which were included were rated as "distinguished" or "strong," on the basis of the quality of their faculty. Two departments were rated "good," chemistry at Notre Dame and Spanish at Catholic University, and 18 departments were rated "adequate plus."

Of course, to attract scholars eminent in their fields, whatever their religious persuasion, colleges will have to give them a greater voice in the policies of the institution and not just higher salaries. Colleges are now ruled by the religious, and their academic councils are "weighted" toward a religious centered administration.[15] Even at St. Louis and Notre Dame, where the innovating spirit is evident, such a situation

---

[13] Pattillo and Mackenzie (1965), pp. 27–28.

[14] Donovan (1964); Cartter (1966). FitzGerald found the latter assessment to be "very encouraging for Catholic higher education" arguing that "for the first time in a national study of quality graduate education, Catholic universities appear in respectable competition for academic consideration" (FitzGerald, 1966, p. 511).

[15] Trombley (1966).

prevails. However, beginning in 1967 the University of Notre Dame and its sister institution, the University of Portland, were in the process of putting the control of their institutions under a lay board of regents.

What can happen when the faculty is lacking in power and administrative representation was exemplified by the uprising at St. John's University in 1965. The Vincentian board of directors summarily dismissed 31 professors in the middle of the quarter, resulting in a revolt of students and faculty unprecedented in the history of American Catholic higher education. The firing followed a walk-out of over 200 faculty members, reportedly in protest over low pay, paternalism, and lack of academic freedom. Among the aspects of academic freedom at issue were: the absence of contractual tenure for faculty; lack of provision for faculty control over curriculum, text books, and student activities; the denial of the right of a faculty union to function on campus; and the firing of faculty without stated cause. Apart from the discrediting publicity and allegedly misleading advertising of their cause, the administration accused the rebellious faculty of the following:

The deliberate and studied attempt to subvert the responsibility of the officials of the university.
A continuing effort to impugn the credibility of the Vincentian community.
The continual challenging of the responsibility of the trustees to function as the policy-making body of the university.[16]

Included among the faculty members dismissed were the president of the campus teachers' union (a priest), the head of the honors program, and several faculty members who were directing doctoral theses and who therefore were leaving their students without consistent guidance in their advanced research. As an English professor at St. Louis University said, "In recent years we've been climbing out of the intellectual ghetto, really making something out of Catholic higher education. Then along comes this St. John's thing, which is a reversion to a time we all thought had been left far behind."[17]

But it was not just the "St. John's thing." Between 1965 and 1967 a number of disruptions at Catholic colleges received national attention. Siena College students and faculty members clamored for clarification when Bishop William Scully of Albany, New York, suddenly curtailed the civil rights and social work of Father Bonaventure. This Franciscan priest, a faculty member of Siena College, had been an active worker in Albany's inner city and a frequent critic of the

[16] *National Catholic Reporter,* January 5, 1966, p. 1.
[17] Trombley (1966), p. 1.

city's administration. The Siena College administration upheld the bishop's action. We quote the bishop's stand from the *National Catholic Reporter:*

The bishop's statement, published Thursday in *The Evangelist,* the diocesan weekly newspaper, said that the decision to curtail the Franciscan priest's work was "an administrative decision, not one of policy" and added that "such decisions are the responsibility of the bishop alone and the reasons for such decisions must be left to God and the conscience of the bishop."[18]

At San Diego College for Women two faculty members were dismissed without the customary warning needed to find another academic position. They believed that their dismissal resulted from their criticism of the college. One assistant professor had written memos urging changes in curriculum, upgraded academic standards, a salary schedule, and faculty tenure. The only reason given for his dismissal appeared in a letter to him from the administration announcing his termination:

It appears from your letter of January 18, 1966, that your views of how the operations of the San Diego College for Women should be conducted are in irreconcilable conflict with the long-standing policies of the college administration.[19]

Presumably, this was also the reason for the second professor's dismissal. A third professor who had made a motion to retract the suspensions of the other two faculty members was also summarily dismissed. A fourth professor, out of 62 full- and part-time faculty members, quit out of sympathy.

At Duquesne University eight philosophy professors left of their own volition. The exact reasons for this move are not altogether clear, but they apparently had to do with curricular changes and administrative inaction in the face of student and faculty dissent over these changes. The dissident professors objected to their new department chairman's attempt to and method of suddenly deemphasizing the university's specialized program in phenomenological existentialism, which had won for their university international prominence. The chairman has described his move as one toward intellectual honesty, of opening up his department to a variety of points of view.[20]

Similar incidents have taken place at College of St. Thomas and at Catholic University of America.[21] Revisions of the theology curricu-

[18] *National Catholic Reporter,* November 24, 1965, p. 1.
[19] *Ibid.,* February 16, 1966, p. 3.
[20] *Ibid.,* March 23, 1966, p. 5; Pauson (1966).
[21] *Ibid.,* November 16, 1966, p. 1; April 26, 1967, p. 1; May 3, 1967, p. 1.

lum proposed by members of the theology department at St. Thomas included a course on the teachings of the controversial Teilhard de Chardin. The rest of the faculty voted to reject the proposal, or at least to delay it, reportedly so that the theology courses could be coordinated with revised curricula in other departments. Regardless of the reason for the vote, it allegedly led to a rift between liberal and conservative elements of the college. At Catholic University a merger of two departments without adequate prior consultation with the students and faculty precipitated a large-scale protest over the general lack of communication among students, faculty, and administration at the university. The rector tried to merge the Department of Religious Education of the Graduate School of Arts and Sciences with the School of Theology—and he notified the respective head and dean only an hour before the proposal was to be placed before the Academic Senate. This was not the end of Catholic University's troubles. In the spring of 1967 it was affected by a student-faculty protest as severe as that which took place at St. John's University two years previously. The trustees of the university dismissed an assistant professor of moral theology just after his promotion to the rank of associate professor had been approved by the academic senate. No reason for his dismissal was reported, but it was presumed that the trustees disapproved of his liberal teachings and his involvement in the Institute for Freedom in the Church recently established to protect the rights of individuals in the church. Reaction was swift and led to a general strike by students and faculty that shut down the university until the professor was reinstated the next week. Since a great majority of the trustees were cardinals and archbishops, the strike was considered to be a direct confrontation of the hierarchy by the students and faculty over the issue of academic freedom, and as one spokesman put it, specifically "a matter of life and death for the faculty." The event was also regarded by some as a major step toward "reform" in Catholic higher eduction.

A problem of academic freedom of a different sort has arisen in Chicago.[22] Over 200 faculty members from 6 Catholic colleges in the Chicago diocese objected to Archbishop Cody's decree that priests coming from outside the diocese to teach or speak at Catholic institutions must have prior permission from the chancery. The dissenting faculty, including priests and nuns, consider this a restriction of academic freedom, arguing that it constitutes prior censorship over academic activity. The archbishop's rejoinder was that it is simply a matter of traditional ecclesiastical regulation and good order.

[22] Ibid., October 12, 1966, p. 1.

At the University of Dayton restriction of academic freedom was urged not by the administration but by a young lay faculty member.[23] He charged four of his colleagues with teaching or writing ideas contrary to Catholic doctrine. As far as is known, this professor was objecting to their discussing situation ethics with their students. Condoning situation ethics could constitute a sensitive issue in a Catholic school since this would be tantamount to holding that the good or evil of an act is determined by the circumstances and subjective consciences involved in each given situation and not exclusively by predetermined, absolute moral laws, which has been the traditional teaching of the church. Subsequent exoneration of the accused faculty members by the administration led to a charge of "whitewash" from the young protestor and other colleagues.

The recounting of these incidents is not to imply that the colleges involved were necessarily delinquent in their provision of academic freedom. The situations are complex, and no doubt there is a legitimate argument on both sides of the issue in most cases. What is immediately evident is the many problems that can arise in the quest for academic freedom. These cases do not show the official church lined up authoritatively against the layman, since in most instances the religious as well as the laity were included among the dissenters.

Although some institutions are having trouble providing academic freedom, others are not. Increasing numbers of Catholic colleges are now establishing academic senates, whereby the faculty may have a direct channel of communication with the administration and a voice in its policies. In many Catholic colleges high administrative posts such as dean of faculty or academic vice-president are now being assigned to laymen. There is now a lay-operated Catholic college, Sacred Heart University, Connecticut, and it is likely that even colleges maintained by religious orders increasingly will have laymen as presidents, as has now occurred at Webster College. At the same time, the universities of Notre Dame and Portland have taken steps to put their institutions under control of lay trusteees who would have the power to appoint a lay president.

Student freedom and responsibility are also being extended. Thus great liberalization of student regulations is reported at places like the University of Notre Dame, and Georgetown University, where liquor is now allowed in the dormitories and curfew has been greatly relaxed.[24] Emphasis has turned to promoting self-responsibility rather

23 *Ibid.,* November 2, 1966, p. 10.
24 *Time,* 1966, 88 (21), p. 95; *San Francisco Chronicle,* September 26, 1966, p. 6.

than controlling behavior through administrative surveillance. The maturity and academic freedom of the students at Pennsylvania's St. Vincent College were even respected enough that the administration backed their right to have the national Communist leader Dr. Herbert Aptheker speak before them.[25] This support was given to the students in the face of an outburst of community protest.

But perhaps the function of academic freedom in the Catholic college was best expressed by Father Reinert of St. Louis University. He compared a professor who is a Catholic to one who may be a democratic candidate or to one who holds scientific theories that are unpopular, and reasoned that:

All three . . . come to the classroom with certain personal commitments but the test of their right to the podium in their classroom is the ability and knowledge and inspiration and objectivity they display in teaching their subject. . . . The danger of improper academic relationships has not always been adequately guarded against in some church colleges and universities, as the St. John's university case demonstrates. . . . But such unfortunate incidents do not prove the essential incompatibility of the Church and higher education. They do highlight the imperative that church colleges and universities must be wise and bold enough to maintain administrative procedures that will keep the avenues to the world of learning and culture wide open for their faculties and their students.[26]

With improvement in faculty recruitment and academic freedom in Catholic colleges, there must also be improvement in curricula. Much of the dissension reported in Catholic colleges centered on curricular problems. And it is ironical that the weakest programs in Catholic colleges would be those which have been so highly emphasized and which have been required of most students in these colleges: theology and philosophy. Poole notes that most American Catholic universities and colleges "do not have any real schools of theology," and that "religion is often the least important discipline in a Catholic college or university, and it is frequently among the worst taught."[27] He adds that little original work in theology is being done in Catholic universities and seminaries. The Danforth Foundation concluded that philosophy and theology were the departments in Catholic colleges that were the weakest.[28] Surveying schools for his series of articles on Catholic higher education, Trombley notes that theology was the weakest department at St. Louis University, that it was also weak at the Univer-

[25] *National Catholic Reporter,* October 12, 1966, p. 3.
[26] *Ibid.,* February 16, 1966, p. 3.
[27] Poole (1965), p. 87. See also Tavard (1963).
[28] Pattillo and Mackenzie (1965).

sity of Notre Dame, and that students at Mundelein felt classes in religion were "irrelevant."[29] Webster College has abandoned its requirements in this field, but St. Louis University, for example, still requires 15 hours of philosophy and 8 hours of theology.

In commenting upon the value of the religion and philosophy classes required in Catholic colleges, the Danforth directors stated, "Students frequently complain that the courses are artificial and unrelated to contemporary issues."[30] They trace some of the problem to the fact that so many instructors have only the practical knowledge gained through seminary training and not the scholarship to be gained through graduate theological studies in a good university. However, they see considerable hope for change in this area, noting that through the influence of the College Theology Society and under the impact of changes in the church at large, courses in religion and theology are undergoing major revision. These courses are supplemented in some institutions by special programs such as the Center for the Study of Contemporary Values established for the undergraduate students at the University of Santa Clara in the fall of 1967. The purpose is to stimulate intellectual dialogue on important contemporary value issues including the role of theology as an undergraduate subject and the future of the church-related college.

Curricular reform in American Catholic colleges is not, and should not be, limited to theology and philosophy. There is to be found in Catholic colleges a general weakness in the liberal arts, but particularly in the social sciences, and even more particularly in psychology. Here and there a good social science department can be found, or a good social science professor can be found. And, until recently at least, Duquesne University had gained prominence for its contributions to the phenomenological approach to philosophy and psychology. But such a situation is rare. And when we consider that an institution like the University of Notre Dame was only in 1966, establishing a department of psychology, we can see why American Catholic creative and scholarly thought has been slow to develop. The church's antipathy to Freudian psychology is an example of the type of attitude that has limited access to large segments of the world of science, literature, and philosophy. Radical change in curricula, therefore, cannot come too soon.

Changes are to be seen not only in the recruitment and status of the faculty and in the courses being offered, but in other areas as well.

[29] Trombley (1966).
[30] Pattillo and Mackenzie (1965), p. 43.

Many programs have been initiated to combine facilities for their joint use by several Catholic colleges, by a Catholic college and a seminary, or by a Catholic college and public and private colleges. There is good reason for this development.

At the college level, at least, there has been no plan or organization. The more than three hundred Catholic colleges in America today are run mostly by many diverse religious orders, and there is no functional mechanism whereby the orders can get together to avoid duplication of effort. Each college seems to have sprung up by and unto itself. This problem is shared by other religious groups as well, but as pointed out by the Danforth Foundation, "the problem is perhaps most acute in Roman Catholic higher education where the various religious orders and congregations are free to begin new colleges without any central restraint. . . . The result is a dissipation of available resources and the maintenance of many weak institutions."[31] Long before the Danforth report, Ellis argued in the same vein. He was caustic in his criticism, calling this "waste and pretense" among small, closely situated colleges "almost sinful."[32]

As noted in chapter 3, in 1965 there were almost 80 Catholic colleges listed in the *Education Directory* with enrollments under 100. The National Catholic Educational Association listed 165 institutions with enrollments this low. The majority of these have been founded by orders for the education of their own members, but one wonders what kind of education can be offered in them. And additional, new, small colleges are being established even as moves are going ahead to combine, coordinate, or at least initiate some cooperation among older institutions. The National Catholic Educational Association reported that 139 Catholic institutions admitted their first students between 1950 and 1965. There was a net increase of 78 Catholic colleges listed in the *Education Directory* between 1961 and 1966, including those which lacked sufficient accreditation to be listed previously. All but 3 of the colleges which started since 1950 enrolled fewer than 300 students in 1966.[33]

The problems and inadequacies of the extremely small colleges are severe. They cannot provide adequate faculty or curricula, or key facilities such as libraries. But even schools that are considerably

[31] *Ibid.*, p. 56. Power (1958) has described the development of Catholic higher education in the United States.

[32] *San Francisco Chronicle,* June 8, 1962, p. 2.

[33] Ford and Roy (1966); U.S. Department of Health, Education, and Welfare (1961, 1966).

larger have certain inherent limitations. If the school offers a wide range of courses, individual departments are small. The Danforth report highlights the problem of the small department noting that "it is difficult for departments with one or two faculty members to provide the breadth of scholarly competence, the intellectual stimulation, and the diversity of outlook which are essential ingredients of good education."[34] The fact that small, financially limited Catholic colleges also have problems in providing adequate facilities is evident from a 1963 survey of the quality of American liberal arts college libraries.[35] The libraries in 666 colleges were ranked according to their number of books, number of books per student, and salary budgets. The best of the 184 Catholic college libraries included in the rating ranked thirty-first. A majority of the Catholic libraries ranked in the bottom half of the rating distributions.

It is in part to cope with problems of this kind that small Catholic colleges have been joining together in many ways. In some cases one order offers freshman and sophomore classes in a community as a branch campus of a college operated by another order. In other cases several schools run by the same order are considered different campuses of essentially one school. Nuns in some cases may begin their training at the mother house and finish at a center on a university campus.

Although these steps strengthen the position of these schools, they do not necessarily greatly improve the quality. Bringing together several weak schools will not automatically improve them, and having classes on a university campus will not necessarily inject new light into the students' lives, if classes are restricted in caliber of student and content. It is not enough that schools may now be able to hire enough teachers, pay the bills, and offer the basic courses. The changes must represent more than weak institutions clinging together merely to subsist; there must be actual improvement.

In some cases colleges have decided to terminate programs. Whatever the specific reasons behind the closing of St. Mary's College graduate school of theology, and some reasons may have been regrettable, there is a logic behind the statement issued by the college—that it did not seem wise to continue a graduate school of theology there when those needs could be served as well at the University of Notre Dame. Notre Dame is less than a mile from the St. Mary's campus, and to continue a separate program there when Notre Dame was opening a graduate school of theology would seem like duplication of effort, and at an

[34] Pattillo and Mackenzie (1965), p. 25.
[35] *National Catholic Reporter,* September 21, 1966, p. 3.

advanced level where such duplication can be ill afforded. It is perhaps unfortunate that a joint doctoral program could not have been worked out between the two schools, however, especially since a precedent has been set and students are now able to share a number of undergraduate classes on both campuses.

There are several instances around the country in which Catholic colleges and universities have joined with Catholic and non-Catholic schools in their area to increase the range of courses open to students. This has the advantage not only of increasing course offerings but of encouraging understanding and interaction among students in different colleges. One example is the District of Columbia Joint Graduate Consortium in Washington, D.C. Formed for a five-year period, the group is composed of five universities, American University, Catholic University of America, George Washington University, Georgetown, and Howard University. Graduate students at each school are invited to take courses offered by other schools in the consortium. Unnecessary duplication can thus be avoided and greater opportunities for graduate study at the highest level can be offered. Teaching and research can be undertaken in areas that might be too costly or too specialized for the individual university.

Another way in which education can be enriched and the interchange of ideas between religions facilitated is through such efforts as the Graduate Theological Union. Nine Catholic and Protestant theological schools and seminaries in the San Francisco Bay area are participants in this union. In addition to the course work offered by the union's interdenominational faculty, students may take graduate classes at the University of California; these are counted toward doctorates granted by the union. Several of the cooperating institutions are renowned in their own right. They have increased their effectiveness by joining with other institutions to offer, in the words of the director, "a new context for theology work . . . a place in which the scholarly encounter does not obscure issues which divide, but provides new possibilities for dealing with them."[36] And this cooperation is further enriched by ties with an outstanding public institution.

There are examples of cooperation at the undergraduate level also, some of long standing. In St. Paul, since 1953, four Catholic and Protestant colleges have jointly offered a program of area studies which no school could afford to offer alone. These studies integrate all the liberal arts into the study of a particular geographic area.

[36] *Catholic Voice*, June 16, 1966, p. 8.

Another example of undergraduate cooperation involves Mundelein College which has joined with another Catholic college and 10 Protestant institutions so that students and faculty on each campus can take advantage of classes and facilities offered on other campuses.

Under the Winona Plan a diocesan seminary was built in 1948 on the campus of a Catholic men's liberal arts institution. Seminarians take all classes with other college students and participate in activities of the campus. They reside in a special hall on the campus and have their meals, conferences, and spiritual exercises there. This is designed to meet the needs of a small diocese, which would have difficulty providing a full college faculty for its seminarians. In the process it probably offers them a better education than they would receive otherwise.

The variety of these interinstitutional programs show great potential if put to expanded, serious use. Salerno surveyed approximately 300 Catholic colleges and found that at least 95 of them reportedly were engaged in cooperative programs in 1964. However, half of these 95 institutions were cooperating with other colleges only on the loose basis of informal verbal agreements. Only a fourth of them had formalized their cooperative programs through written contracts. Most of the cooperative programs were bilateral, that is, between only two colleges; and most programs involved only a very small part of any college's enterprises.

The amount of student and faculty participation in these programs is yet to be known. Salerno comments: "Although there is general interest in the number of students and faculty members participating in cooperative programs, an effort to determine the number in current programs proved fruitless."[37] It is even more important to determine empirically the effectiveness of this participation. But it is to be hoped that interinstitutional cooperation represents an important way for Catholic colleges to help solve their problems of improvement.

One Catholic college in Canada found a unique way to save itself— the hundred-year-old college has been converted into the University of Windsor, a state-supported secular institution.[38] The Basilian Fathers have remained as faculty and administrators and have been guaranteed a minimum number of seats on the board of directors. Of course, this transition was possible because of the different traditions of the country and because of the ecumenical spirit of the Basilians, who have been described as exponents of "soft-sell Catholicism." A public college in

[37] Salerno (1966), p. 10.
[38] Wakin (1965).

the United States could not keep the religious connections Windsor has maintained.

Our concern has been with changes in the Catholic colleges, in their faculties, curricula, and their cooperation with other schools. Changes are also occurring that affect Catholics on secular campuses. It has been estimated that about 66 per cent of Catholics attending college are attending non-Catholic schools, and by 1985 the percentage is expected to be about 80 per cent.[39] For such students, Newman Club has, in the past, theoretically been the center of Catholic activity. However, all too often Newman Club has been little more than, in Getlein's words, "a social gathering place."[40]

Attempts are now being made to change the Newman image. There is some recognition that the church should go where the students are, and if the Catholic students are at secular colleges, then the church should be expending more of its energies on students at these colleges. Thus the Newman effort is being expanded and has acquired a new name, the Newman Apostolate. Newman Club chaplains are now recognized as "educators" by the National Catholic Educational Association and are no longer considered only chaplains. Although there is general agreement that Newman efforts should be expanded there is disagreement about the nature of the expansion. Nevertheless, physical expansion is already occurring; in 1955 there were 100 priests and 80 centers, and in 1965 there were 250 priests and 203 centers.[41] Obviously these centers have not been overstaffed with priests. It has been proposed that nuns be brought into the Newman movement; this would provide not only the additional staff needed, but would add another dimension to the program. In 1965, 20 nuns were regular staff members at Newman centers.[42]

A question of what should occur at these centers remains. One present aim is to provide the classes in theology and philosophy that are lacking on the secular campus and to make them "so academically respectable" that college credit is given. There are many, however, who feel this academic approach is wrong, that such classes should be given in the colleges' theology or philosophy departments, and that secular colleges should be encouraged to offer more courses of this kind. It is argued that the emphasis of the Newman Apostolate should be upon showing the relevance between faith and the academic world,

[39] Ellis (1965); Kirvan (1964).
[40] Getlein (1964).
[41] Butler (1965).
[42] Evans (1967).

with special attention to social issues and personal spiritual development, rather than concentrating upon a strictly academic approach.[43]

After the 1965 National Newman Federation convention, Ellinger
concluded that "only the name has been changed," and that really it
was the same old Newman Club.[44] He based this conclusion partly on
the fact that there was little discussion of civil rights and other social
issues at the convention, issues which have been of major concern to
other student groups in recent years. Walsh's paper given in the Newman Education Section of the 1966 Annual Meeting of the National
Catholic Educational Association did devote a great deal of attention
to these issues.[45] But his excellent paper on "The Secular and the Sacred
in American Universities" had essentially nothing to say about the role
of the Newman Movement in the contemporary Western university.

Although exactly what direction the Newman Apostolate will take
cannot be predicted as yet, an increase in efforts seems certain. A new
Newman Center near the University of California campus at Berkeley
was dedicated in May, 1967. Many observers do not think that the exte-
rior architecture of the center's massive building reflects the open spirit
of the times, but perhaps its activities will. Indeed, the activities must
if they are to involve the Catholic and other students who elect to
attend the secular college. Cox says of activities of this kind that, "It
is clear . . . that the future witness of the Church will be in the secular
university and not in some reversion to the medieval pattern." Yet he
feels about the role of the church in the "secular City's" university that:

The "organizational church" has no role. It should stay out. The church as a
reconciling community of servants determined to serve the university even
when no one thanks them, praises them, or notices them *does* have a place in
the community of the university. That place will be evident to those who
have eyes to see.[46]

But perhaps the most significant area in which change is needed
and appears to be starting is in the training of the persons who are
going to teach in Catholic colleges and Catholic centers on secular
campuses. A large percentage of these persons are priests who have
been trained in seminaries throughout the country. Even when they
have gone on to advanced study elsewhere, their initial collegiate
training has been in the seminary.

Poole has called seminaries "the Achilles heel of American Catholi-

[43] See Kirvan (1964).
[44] Ellinger (1965).
[45] Walsh (1966).
[46] Cox (1965), p. 236.

cism."[47] An abundance of articles and books attest to recent concern over the quality of education received in seminaries. In their recent books about seminaries, Poole and Lee and Putz have joined others such as Callahan in calling for changes in the total environment of Catholic seminaries.[48]

The criticism mounts at a crucial time. Paradoxically, at a time when the student population and college enrollments are increasing each year, seminary enrollments are dropping radically.[49] Many reasons are given for this, but most of them seem to relate to three major factors. First, there is a disenchantment with the training, with the anachronistic restriction on the individuality of the religious, and with the irrelevance of their way of life to modern living and its problems. Secondly, there is a growing feeling that apostolic and philanthropic endeavors can be undertaken as well if not better through existing opportunities and professions outside the closure of the religious life, be it that of the religious order or that of the diocesan seminarian or priest. Finally, orders of priests and sisters are being more selective in the recruitment of their candidates in terms of ability and of personality.

The need for seminaries to be open to the world is touched upon repeatedly in current writing. Lee and Putz state in their conclusion to *Seminary Education in a Time of Change*: "If aggiornamento is to take place in the church, it must have its starting place in the seminaries. No permanent or effectual reform and renewal within the Church can transpire unless there is first a reform and renewal within the seminaries." They point out that despite the central role of the seminary in the life of the church, ". . . there has been less than negligible research done in this vital educational area."[50]

Poole believes that the problems of seminary education stem not so much from anti-intellectualism as from apathy and indifference. Seminaries are not integrated with Catholic higher education; they are just a continuation of high school, removed from society. Mangan cautions, however, that "we can never expect an atmosphere of sincere intellectual enthusiasm to be created in our seminaries if the educators themselves do not possess it."[51]

Lee criticizes the fact that obedience is usually seen as the key issue

---

[47] Poole (1965), p. 29.
[48] Callahan (1963); Lee and Putz (1965); Poole (1965).
[49] *National Catholic Reporter,* September 21, 1966, p. 1.
[50] Lee and Putz (1965), p. 557.
[51] Mangan (1966), p. 173.

in seminary training. He relates that "The Sacred Congregation of Seminaries and Universities has noted that unquestioning, complete, and single-minded obedience in every matter, enforced by strict disciplinary measures, constitutes the core of seminary formation." Poole observes that seminarians are judged by the quality of their obedience and docility, and Callahan has similarly stated that the virtues of seminarians have been obedience and acceptance of discipline.[52]

Lee would abolish almost all seminaries and would limit training to five or six centers either attached to large Catholic universities or existing as colleges within universities. Seminarians would take almost all their classes with other students. Poole recommends a union between seminaries and universities, centered in one or two major Catholic universities. He refers to other possibilities, such as the German plan, in which seminarians are not removed from the world but live with various families during their training.[53] He also suggests the Winona plan, discussed above, where the seminary program is carried out at a regular college.

Although Lee and Poole are in general agreement on the ills of the seminary, there are some areas in which they do not agree. For example, Poole believes that the priesthood demands individuals of uniformly high ability, whereas Lee, using the apostolic maxim "like to like," suggests that in the priesthood "there is a definite and valuable place in the pastoral ministry for zealous young men with an IQ of 80–110." He notes that there will be "many dull and unintelligent persons in the parish [who] will be most pastorally served by having priests of average or perhaps even of below-average intelligence minister to them." Poole, on the other hand, states that "the work of the priesthood presupposes and demands broad intellectual achievement" and adds that ". . . it cannot be attained by anyone who is not capable of achieving at least a bachelor's degree in an accredited college." He notes the "strong anti-intellectual sentiment among many priests who extol more 'human' qualities at the expense of intellectual excellence, originality, and creativeness."[54]

Poole's position seems more tenable. As indicated in chapter 9, ability alone is not enough to guarantee the sort of open, critical thought that we would wish to see among priests and see them foster in their parishioners; the absence of ability only aggravates the problem of lack of intellectualism. Since ability appears to be a precondi-

[52] Callahan (1963); Lee (1965), p. 135; Poole (1965).
[53] Poole (1965).
[54] Lee (1965), p. 119; Poole (1965), p. 25.

tion for intellectual disposition, its absence can be expected to increase the present obedient and docile approach toward learning and conduct fostered in seminaries. Moreover, we believe that members of the parish are neither spiritually nor intellectually benefited by a priest of limited capacity. A dull priest is likely, if anything, to be less able than his more intelligent colleagues to work with the complex problems of a complex parish, including those of its less intelligent parishioners. In the meantime, he may alienate the intelligent and thoughtful members of his parish in many ways.

Debate of this kind is symptomatic of the dramatic questioning and ferment throughout seminary and religious life. The desire of seminarians for changes was evident in Boston in April, 1966, when protests at St. John's Seminary led to the expulsion of eight students. They were protesting a "lack of personal and academic freedom" and objected particularly to the authoritarian methods of the seminary and the lack of adequate means of communication with those in authority.[55] These eight seminarians and more than a hundred others complained also that the rector was unsympathetic to the changes encompassed in the decrees of the Vatican Council.

Important changes are taking place in the formation of the seminarian. The isolated, monastic life of old is for some seminarians being replaced with practicums. Thus some students are taking up residence in slum areas. Others are becoming involved part time in the "social apostolate" of large cities while residing in their neighboring seminaries and working toward their college degrees. Many seminarians now are given much more autonomy over their lives. They share in the decisions about their subject majors and careers, and in increasing numbers, they undertake their studies with lay students at a regular Catholic college instead of on their own seminary campus. Catholic seminaries are now found on Catholic college campuses and may soon be found on some non-Catholic ones as well. Examples are the Winona plan and the Catholic-Protestant consortium now existing at the Graduate Theological Union adjacent to the University of California. The Catholic Seminary of Indianapolis has initiated similar plans for cooperation and shared facilities with the Christian Theological Seminary (Disciples of Christ). Catholic clerics are also attending non-Catholic divinity schools such as those at the University of Chicago and at Yale University.

Improvement and innovation in the religious life must and does extend beyond changes in the seminaries. In writing about the Sister

[55] *National Catholic Reporter,* April 13, 1966, p. 1.

Formation Movement in 1964, the author noted that there was not yet a "Priest Formation Movement."[56] Since that time, however, there have been efforts to establish something more than a formation movement. The Rev. William DuBay has been the leader of an effort to establish a union for priests. DuBay started out ministering to a predominantly Negro parish in Compton, California, in the archdiocese of Los Angeles. As a result of his subsequent experiences, he cabled a request to the Vatican that Cardinal McIntyre, head of the diocese, be removed from office for his "failure to provide moral leadership" against discrimination. Father DuBay was relocated several times after that and became a frequent subject of the news media. In the process he published his views on the role of religion in his book *The Human Church*.[57]

The avowed purpose of DuBay's union is to work for "professional freedom within the Catholic priesthood." Among the announced goals of the union, called the American Federation of Priests, are the establishment of grievance machinery within the church, a tenure policy to guarantee a hearing before a priest can be suspended, and an end to "arbitrary and oppressive transfers by chancery officials."[58]

Father DuBay's union had yet to prove itself workable up to 1967; it may well stand little chance of success. But in Chicago more than 1,300 priests have now officially formed the Association of Chicago Priests. Leaders of the new organization have expressed fears that it would be regarded as a union. In making it clear that the organization is not a union, they have stated, "We recognize the bishop's word is law," and Archbishop Cody has at least accepted the formation of the group.[59] It appears to be a group that will work for improved training for priests and better communication with church leaders, although it can hardly be expected to seek changes as revolutionary as those DuBay might seek.

The religious sisters in the United States initiated comparable changes long before the Vatican Council. And if many of the religious have a long way to go before they are fully attuned to the modern world, the changes they have been making in their way of life have been consistent, rapid, and remarkable. The emergence of the nun into the world is evident in the new style of activity as well as in the new style of clothing. For example, in Illinois in the summer of 1966, 30

[56] Trent (1964).
[57] Dubay (1966).
[58] *San Francisco Chronicle*, February 23, 1966, p. 3.
[59] *National Catholic Reporter*, August 17, 1966.

nuns participated in a two-week conference preparing them for more collaboration with lay professional women. After the conference they worked briefly in municipal mental health and welfare departments, voluntary service organizations, newspapers, and industry.

In their reactions, phrases were heard such as, "We have to learn how to talk with the professional women in the world. . . .We just don't have the vocabulary," and "It's a revelation—just the mechanics of getting to a job." In talking about the slums in which they worked, one nun commented, "It shows how asleep we are to what is going on ten blocks from our boundary." These women were deeply impressed by their encounter with the world and were eager to continue this encounter; as one nun commented, "We have our foot in it and we can't stop."[60] The reactions indicated not only what might be expected of nuns in the future, but also how cloistered many nuns have been in the past.

Although not all nuns have been so restricted, this has been the pattern. Numerous publications have heralded the new role of the nun. Of special significance are the 1965 and 1967 books, edited by nuns called *The Changing Sister* and *The New Nuns*.[61] They might be called the American successor to Cardinal Suenens' widely acclaimed *The Nun in the World*.[62] Of course, the group that led the way in updating the nun's role in America is the Sister Formation Conference. It was inaugurated in 1953 "to work for improved education for all sisters." The expressed goal was the "integration of the spiritual, intellectual, professional, and social elements in the life of a religious."[63] The roots of the movement could be traced to a plea by Pope Pius XII in 1951 that sisters be masters of their teaching subjects and possess an education at least matching state standards.

During its first ten years the group sponsored yearly regional and national institutes and workshops for superiors and formation directors. It spearheaded statistical studies and curriculum studies and has promoted programs to improve the quality of professional training for the religious. It established Marillac College to provide an adequate undergraduate education for a variety of the country's orders of religious sisters.

In August, 1964, the Sister Formation Movement became a committee of the Conference of Major Superiors of Women. This group

---

60 *Ibid.,* November 2, 1966, p. 3.
61 Borromeo (1967); Muckenhirn (1965).
62 Suenens (1963).
63 *Sister Formation Bulletin* (1964), p. 32.

was formed in 1958 at the instigation of the Holy See and is composed of the leading officers of religious women's groups, representing sisters across the nation. As a committee, the goals and programs of the Sister Formation Movement are to be maintained but carried out under the control of the Conference of Major Superiors.

Some leaders involved in the development of sisters see the effect of this merger as enabling the groups to work in the "closest possible harmony" and as ensuring to sisters all over the United States a "maximum of coordinated service for their growth and development."[64] To others the merger represents an end to their hopes for a broadened and revitalized Sister Formation Movement. They point to the fact that leaders of the movement have been criticized by some church officials for "seeking a dream world" rather than attending to what must be done here and now. Some of the leaders of the movement have been removed from positions of influence and even removed geographically to places where their contacts with other sisters will be reduced. The editor of the *Sister Formation Bulletin* was removed from her position and subjected to unexplained actions by her superiors.

We do not know what the effect of this merger will be, but the goal of the Sister Formation Movement—improved education and personal development for sisters—is a goal too critical to be ignored. If this goal can be attained by working through the Conference of Major Superiors, marshalling their authority and interests on behalf of educational improvements, the realignment may be beneficial. If, instead, the merger is a convenient burial ground for the ideas of some nuns whom others consider too liberal, it will be a tragic ending to a noble and sorely needed cause.

Lee has commented on what he considers to be the major weakness of the Sister Formation Movement—that they have "not reformed the basic structure." Preparation of sisters is still conducted in a "recluse-like setting with no opportunity for daily contact in an everyday setting."[65] It is to be hoped that such reform in the structure will be forthcoming. A number of examples indicate that it will. Increasingly, professed nuns and even novices are undertaking serious undergraduate and graduate studies on secular as well as Catholic college campuses. They are also undergoing special education and in-service training programs, as may be illustrated by the study of Christian humanism at Manhattanville College. Another important example of the broadened educational experience of the sisters is given by

[64] Luke (1965).
[65] Lee (1965), p. 1.

the president of Loretto Heights College who in 1965 completed an administrative internship at the highly select, nonsectarian Antioch College. Sisters are also assuming diocesan leadership roles, once reserved for priests, illustrated by the nuns who are now directing the religious education program of the archdiocese of New Orleans.

The critiques that sisters are directing to their own system are as important as the education and experience they are undertaking outside their system. The bureaucracy of religious communities has been dissected as a medieval, autocratic, feudal system where the master-servant relationship exists instead of democratic respect for the individual, her rights, and her needs. There has been a call for the application of social science to the religious life to stimulate creativity, to permit proper use of individual aptitudes, and to evaluate the sisters' programs and way of life. Sisters have been urged to put aside their secretive and ritualistic way of life and be contemporary American women as well as nuns. There has been open discussion of the psychological consequences of virginity and whether celibacy is a sacrifice any longer needed, whether the sisters themselves are any longer needed as they now operate, and what further improvements are needed among the religious sisters.[66]

Priests and nuns represent a vital link between church and college, and consideration of changes in their status brings us to other changes within the church. These changes are widespread, affecting all areas of church life, and they are certain to affect its intellectual life. As noted in chapter 1, the questioning of traditional beliefs and practices within the church had its beginnings in Europe after World War II. This spirit was conveyed to Americans by European theologians such as Hans Küng. During his lecture tour in 1963 he spoke repeatedly of freedom within the church, of freedom of conscience existing within a framework of order.

Americans have been late in heeding the spirit of innovation, freedom, and reform that has swept Europe. Despite the vastness of the Catholic church in the United States, few American churchmen were involved in the intellectual ferment that culminated in Vatican II. John Courtney Murray, who was the principal architect of the Declaration on Religious Freedom, is one of the exceptional Americans considered to be among the leaders of Vatican II.

Although the initial impetus for reform came primarily from Europe, the effects are beginning to be felt in this country. Since the

[66] These issues have been consistent subjects of discussion in the Sisters' Forum of the *National Catholic Reporter*. See also Novak (1963), Wakin and Scheuer (1965).

approval of the principle of collegiality, the bishops now formally share with the pope ruling power over the church. This power is being dispersed with a greater concern for democracy and respect for personal freedom and responsibility than has existed before in the church. The national collegiality of bishops, with an elected president, is designed to involve more bishops in decision-making and to provide machinery for coping with national problems. Jesuits now locally elect their delegates to the governing body of their order in Rome. Simplification of church externals has been urged, including the titles and dress of the hierarchy. A plea has been made for tolerance and equanimity in the jurisdiction of superiors. Less legalism in the canon law of the church generally and a greater balance among its executive, legislative, and judicial organs is being urged.

As they embark upon a new role in helping to determine church policy, many clerics are making a similar concerted effort to involve the layman in local church policy. In many parts of the country diocesan councils are being organized, in which laymen may participate in the discussion of issues raised by Vatican II and sometimes consult on diocesan policy. Furthermore, it has been suggested that in every diocese a senate be established, similar to the synod of bishops which Pope Paul has proposed to advise him on the governing of the church. By the end of 1966, 30 American dioceses had established a senate of priests and many more were underway.[67] Senates and councils on the parish level were also being initiated so that more communication and counsel could take place between each congregation and its pastor. In a few cases laymen were on diocesan school boards and key policy committees.

This emphasis involving the layman in dialogue and on calling on him for help in the decisions of the church presents a radically different picture from the traditional one in which the clergy led and the laity unquestioningly followed. The new role of the layman has been widely acclaimed in the secular and church press. Keating has urged the layman to end his "scandal of silence" and participate with his head in the affairs of the church and not just with his hands through fund-raising.[68] The hierarchy has been told pointedly that it no longer speaks for all the laity, whether it be in changes in New York's divorce laws or in other matters.[69]

The new freedom has precipitated much frank discussion of major issues in the church that have yet to be resolved. For instance, there is

[67] *National Catholic Reporter,* November 23, 1966, p. 9.
[68] Keating (1965).
[69] *Commonweal,* 1966, 83: 572.

now increasing discussion of whether celibacy is necessary or even desirable for the priesthood. The requirement is not a matter of dogma, but it is a deeply ingrained tradition in the church formalized in canon law. Fichter, in a major survey of "rank-and-file" diocesan priests, found in 1966 that 62 per cent of his respondents believed that diocesan priests should be free to choose between marriage and celibacy, and 31 per cent of the priests said that they "probably" or "unquestionably" would marry if the church permitted.[70] Apart from the arguments in favor of eliminating the requirement of celibacy, such as increased emotional stability and better understanding of lay problems, a basic concern is whether the number of priests needed can continue to be supplied from those persons willing to forego marriage. In the meantime, the church is continuing to concentrate its efforts on orienting seminarians to the meaning and value of the celibate life.[71]

Although discussion of the celibate clergy has only become apparent recently, the many issues regarding birth control have been perennial topics of discussion, albeit never as extensively and publicly as at present.[72] The issue concerns not only what is right for individual couples, but what is appropriate public policy regarding state laws, welfare clinics, and assistance to underdeveloped nations. There is even discussion of what constitutes natural law.

The Vatican Council affirmed that conjugal love is as important a reason as procreation for sexual intercourse. It also affirmed the value of responsible parenthood; that is, the value of couples having only the number of children they can properly care for psychologically and economically. But the council did not explain how there could be the free expression of married love and the simultaneous maintenance of responsible parenthood without the use of artificial birth control. The results of the special commission convened to advise the pope on the issue did not clear up matters. Late in 1966 Pope Paul announced that the commission's findings were not definitive and that they remained a matter for "study and reflection." This left the Catholic population puzzled, aggravated, and in disagreement, especially

[70] *San Francisco Chronicle,* December 12, 1966, p. 2.

[71] *Commonweal,* 1964, 80: 223; Dewart (1966); Kilduff (1966). Van Kaam (1965) has also discussed the problems of celibacy in the context of religious counseling for seminarians.

[72] Perhaps no topic in recent years has been debated more in print by Catholics than the issue of birth control. The *National Catholic Reporter* is one comprehensive source of information on the Church's actions on the subject of artificial contraception. Noonan (1965) has published one of the more recent books on the subject.

when it was learned in the spring of 1967 that the majority of the commission favored some form of artificial birth control.

Renowned theologians like George Tavard expressed their conviction that oral contraceptives are morally legitimate for Catholics. But Francis Connell, Dean Emeritus of Catholic University's School of Theology, argued that the church's traditional teaching on this issue has not changed and saw only a remote possibility that it would.

In the spring and again in November of 1966 the National Catholic Welfare Conference, composed of the nation's bishops, charged federal agencies with coercing the poor into practicing contraception and challenged the government's right to use antipoverty funds for family planning purposes. In contrast, many Catholics praised the court decision striking down the Connecticut law that banned the sale, dispensing, or use of contraceptives. There was widespread recognition among Catholics that regardless of their personal views about contraceptives, this was not an appropriate area for legislation. In fact, the Catholic Council on Civil Liberties entered the case on the side of those opposing the Connecticut law. In the meantime, Westoff and Ryder's nationwide survey sponsored by Princeton's Office of Population Research and the National Institute of Child Health and Human Development revealed that in 1965, 53 per cent of American Catholic wives between the ages of 18 and 39 practiced artificial birth control, compared with 38 per cent in 1960 and 30 per cent in 1955. Twenty-one per cent of the wives up to the age of 45 had used oral contraceptives.[73]

Not only are many Catholics using contraceptives, but they are also involved in the studies of the problems of overpopulation and of new birth control methods. For example, a team of sociologists from the University of Notre Dame is studying family and fertility problems in several Latin American countries, operating under a grant from the federal government. A Catholic physician was a member of the United States committee that reported on the efficacy and safety of oral contraceptives. And when another Catholic physician, Dr. John Rock, wrote a book setting forth views very contrary to Catholic theology, Cardinal Cushing contented himself with simply pointing out what he believed to be the author's inaccuracies.

It may be that the church is now withholding a change in its doctrine on birth control not so much because it is convinced of the truth and universal applicability of the doctrine but because if fears a loss of credibility in the church if it reverses a doctrine it has stressed under the sanction of mortal sin. Whether or not a justification can be found

[73] *San Francisco Chronicle,* December 3, 1966, p. 1.

for allowing some form of artificial contraception that is in some way compatible with former theological pronouncements, it seems likely that many more Catholics will change on this issue.

Another area of change involves mixed marriages. Marriages between Catholics and members of other religions, or persons with no religion, are becoming increasingly common, and the church is more liberal in its attitude toward these marriages. The non-Catholic partner is no longer required to sign an agreement that children will be raised in the Catholic faith, non-Catholics may now participate in the marriage ceremony, and non-Catholic ministers may assist in a limited way at the ceremony. Interfaith Communion has been allowed, but on a very limited basis. Excommunication is no longer a penalty for marriage outside the faith. In New York the church removed its opposition to making the state's divorce laws more lenient, and a priest-psychologist and several theologians are also asking that the church review its stand on the indissolubility of marriage.[74]

Certain practices have especially limited Catholic access to new ideas, but these practices are now being modified, and it is to be hoped that they will eventually be abandoned. The Index and the Imprimatur were discussed in chapter 1, but there are other practices that have limited the Catholic's intellectual horizon. Novelist and critic Thomas Curley has described with particular annoyance the procedure whereby Catholics are requested annually at Mass to pledge, on their honor, to abide by the judgments of the Legion of Decency and to attend only those films that have been duly approved.[75]

The Legion has since changed its name to the National Catholic Office for Motion Pictures, and changes in approach are apparent. Films that might have been totally condemned earlier may now be labeled only "morally objectionable in part for all." One recent film was labeled as objectionable because of certain erotic elements "unduly emphasized and without dramatic necessity."[76] This recognition of dramatic necessity implies a concern for the artistic merits of a production that has not often been evident in the past. As Curley noted, if Catholic schools are going to teach children to read, they ought to teach them to distinguish between art and morality. He emphasized the problem of the artist, who has "no wish to scandalize or offend, but every time he writes honestly, with genuine hilarity, with the spontane-

[74] *Commonweal*, 1966, 84: 44; *National Catholic Reporter*, July 6, 1966, p. 6; *Time*, 1966, 88 (4): 65.

[75] Curley (1965).

[76] *San Francisco Chronicle*, March 8, 1966, p. 45.

ity of scorn or hate, he is almost sure to scandalize or offend someone."[77]

In citing problems of the Catholic writer, author Harry Sylvester maintains that Catholics have judged work according to whether they agreed with it. If they agreed, it was good; if they disagreed, it was bad. The result has been that "we have not only extolled our apostles of mediocrity but have honored them."[78] The United States has many apostles of mediocrity to honor but few first-rate Catholic writers. Catholic writers of distinction in Europe, however, include Mauriac, Bernanos, Peguy, Claudel, Bloy, and Marcel in France; Scheler, Adam, Rahner, and Guardino in Germany; Undset in Norway; and Belloc, Chesterton, Waugh, Edith Sitwell, and Greene in England. Included in this list are several writers who have converted to Catholicism, including Greene, Undset, Sitwell, and Waugh.

In the United States we have a reverse situation, that is, writers of distinction who have left Catholicism. Such a list of former Catholics would include Dreiser, Hemingway, O'Neill, Fitzgerald, O'Hara, Farrell, Barry, and Katherine Anne Porter. In 1948 Sylvester noted that there are "no living American Catholics who are major writers."[79] Fifteen years later Philip Scharper assessed the literary scene and found no major Catholic writers, evidently, either living or dead.[80]

American Catholics, especially compared with their European peers, are also noticeably absent in the realm of art, music, and philosophy.[81] When the dearth of scholarship and artistic endeavor among American Catholics is contrasted to the productivity of European Catholics, one cannot help but wonder when American Catholics will begin to make some contribution to the world's culture. This is not to imply that there are no signs of talent evident among Catholics. There are. And a scanning of Catholic publications reveals many competent Catholic writers and scholars, some of whom no doubt could make contributions of universal appeal if they would go beyond the confines of purely Catholic topics, issues, and publications.

The change within the church is mirrored in the Catholic press, both the part officially sponsored by the church and that under individual Catholic ownership. Of course, it is hardly possible to speak of a "Catholic press" any more, since so many types of newspapers and

[77] Curley (1965), p. 21.

[78] Sylvester (1948), p. 109.

[79] *Ibid.*, p. 108.

[80] Scharper (1960). Of course, there may be exceptions to this trend, as Powell (1967) argues in the case of Paul Horgan.

[81] Dawson, J. (1959, 1961); McNamee (1961); Murphy (1964); Scharper (1960); Weigel (1956*a*, 1956*b*, 1957).

magazines are published under Catholic auspices and they expound so many different views. Such differences have not always been evident, however. In 1959 at the national convention of the Catholic Press Association (which followed a theme of "The Essential Unity of the Catholic Press"), the complaint was made in the keynote address that the Catholic press "has so much unity it is almost literally true that when you have read one paper, you have very nearly read them all." The speaker said this did not mean there was a Catholic position on everything, but "we are agreed on principles and never get down to facts."[82]

Even before the start of Vatican II the picture began to change; the open windows of the council were reflected in the open columns of the Catholic papers. By the beginning of 1965, however, one Catholic editor was moved to state, "The Catholic press is once more its cautious, colorless, docile, predictable self."[83] He labeled it a house organ, controlled by the establishment, and felt that such a press would never attract young intellectuals, who would not even consider it a professional medium.

Such harsh criticism has been well earned through the years by many diocesan papers and by such mass circulation publications as *Our Sunday Visitor* and kindred materials. There are still papers whose columns are filled with trivialities and parochial defensiveness and that omit anything likely to be controversial or critical of the church or any of its institutions. But there are also publications that have headlined the conflict between individual priests and the hierarchy regarding church reform, civil rights, the war in Vietnam, academic freedom, and other vital issues, and that have continued to report these conflicts long after they have dropped from sight in the secular press.

In a number of Catholic weeklies, such as *America, Commonweal,* and the *National Catholic Reporter,* major and controversial issues are discussed and analyzed extensively. There are complaints that the 43-year-old *Commonweal* dwells too much on its "stock-in-trade" subjects of "pluralism, ecumenism, and Catholic education," and that it might contribute some depth reporting of other issues.[84] Although *Commonweal's* subjects and points of view may often be predictable, the magazine can also be thoughtful and provocative. The *National Catholic Reporter,* which began serious publication in 1965, grew in

[82] Lally (1959), p. 424.
[83] Deedy (1965), p. 666.
[84] Herzfeld (1964), p. 295.

circulation from 11,000 to 80,000 within two years. It has been attacked by individuals such as Bishop Shannon of St. Paul for its candid, forthright, and critical reporting of the affairs of the church; it has been widely praised by the secular and religious press for the very same reason.[85]

Catholic publications also include scholarly journals like *Thought* and *Review of Politics,* and monthlies and quarterlies like *The Catholic World, The Catholic Mind, Cross Currents, Jubilee, The Critic,* and *Continuum,* devoted to man's cultural and intellectual life as well as to his religious life. Magazines like *Cross Currents* and *Commonweal* appear to seek out controversy for the sake of stimulating and developing truly intellectual thought in a religious context.

One of the newest entries in the quality Catholic press, *Ramparts,* has been a highly critical review from its beginning. It has ceased to be a Catholic publication, and now as an organ of the New Left it is so far beyond the establishment that it seems willing to tackle any issue. The defensive Catholic news columnist who labeled *Commonweal* a "Pontius Pilate" would be hard-pressed to find a name for a magazine like *Ramparts.* In some quarters the Catholic press is now considered so liberal and so "unethical" that in 1965 a fund-raising drive was started to found a conservative Catholic magazine. An appeal letter stated that liberal Catholics had secured a near-monopoly control over the public voice of the church, especially over the Catholic press, and that the left speaks through magazines written for lay audiences, such as *Commonweal, America, Ave Maria, The Sign, Jubilee, Catholic World,* and *U. S. Catholic.*[86]

The Catholic press has been criticized by some as too docile and by others as too liberal. As mentioned in chapter 2, at the National Catholic Educational Association meeting in 1966, the Catholic press was labeled as irresponsible, primarily for its criticism of Catholic higher education. If the Catholic press is willing to criticize, this is a change all to its credit. Educators may call it irresponsible when it fails to present the picture they wish to portray. Any newspaper which presents only the optimistic picture of Catholic colleges in the age of renewal, without indicating that major difficulties exist and will continue to exist, would be indeed an irresponsible press.

Changes are occurring not only within the church but also in the relationship of the church with other religions. In 1961 Cardinal Bea stressed that the coming Ecumenical Council should be considered as

[85] Kinsolving (1966); *Time,* 1965, 86 (21): 118.
[86] *National Catholic Reporter,* November 17, 1965, p. 10.

preparing the way for future Christian unity and emphasized that in the meantime groups could certainly collaborate in facing common social problems and in working together for world peace.

A step toward Christian unity was taken three years later when leaders of the Roman Catholic and Eastern Orthodox churches met, embraced, and agreed to explore paths of reconciliation. The same spirit was manifest when the Archbishop of Canterbury flew to Rome in 1966 to meet with Pope Paul, as his predecessor had met with Pope John in 1961. The meeting in 1961 had been the first such meeting since the days of Luther. In 1965 representatives of the Holy See and the Lutheran World Federation met for three days of intensive talks on their differences.

This involvement with other faiths has not been limited to the Christian religion. Cooperation with Jews has been facilitated by the Vatican II Declaration on the Attitude of the Church toward Non-Christian Religions. Although some church leaders had hoped the declaration would go further and admit the error of the church's position through the years, the declaration does at least reject collective Jewish responsibility for the Crucifixion and deplores anti-Semitism.

That such a declaration was needed is evidenced by the study reported by Glock and Stark which indicates that millions of Americans still believe that the Jews living today are implicated in the death of Jesus.[87] This religious attitude evidently carries over to secular matters, establishing a "generally hostile reaction to Jews" by many Americans. The study indicates that the more orthodox the person is in his religious beliefs, the more hostile his attitude toward Jews tends to be. This is apparently even a greater problem among Protestants. Glock and Stark found that a greater proportion of Protestants (37 per cent) than Catholics (22 per cent) were anti-Semitic.

The lack of cooperation among the religions in pre-Vatican II days was underscored by O'Gara in a *Commonweal* article in 1961: "If Pope John can meet with the Archbishop of Canterbury and if he can extend a cordial welcome to visiting American Jews, why is it often so hard to get an American priest on the same platform with a minister and a rabbi?"[88] Representatives of the three faiths are getting together now, not only on platforms but in books and magazines. Thus the Protestant and Jewish churchmen like Robert McAfee Brown and Rabbi Hertzberg write in *Commonweal* and *The National Catholic Reporter* on issues such as the attitude toward authority in Catholic

---

[87] Glock and Stark (1966).
[88] O'Gara (1961), p. 306.

and non-Catholic religions. Catholics like Novak and Callahan write on ecumenism in the non-Catholic religious press, and all write in the secular press.

Much of this writing is devoted to an attempt to understand one another, to explore the differences and commonalities in the various religions. There is also an attempt to share scholarly research. Certain biblical studies are a case in point, but more recently there has been cooperation among Lutheran and Catholic scholars in an attempt to come to grips with the conditions that led to Luther's edicts and the emergence of Protestantism. A Jesuit scholar recently appraised Luther as correct in his theological edicts, and Catholics and Protestants now share a commonly approved Bible.[89] Other dialogues have paid respect to the great theologians of other faiths, disagreeing on interpretations but not belittling the conflicting points of view. Still other dialogues have been in the form of a clarification of differing viewpoints on a moral issue.

Cooperation between the faiths is increasing at such a fast pace that the National Council of Churches stated that it is hard to keep track of all the developments. Whether it's a matter of Catholics celebrating Mass at Episcopal churches in Vermont, or Protestants and Catholics building a common church to be shared in Kansas City, or Presbyterians joining forces with Catholics to support a hospital in San Francisco, or Catholic-Protestant dialogues organized in homes, signs of cooperation abound.

Members of the various faiths are not only talking together, however, but are also acting together in many ways. The most striking example of cooperation is in civil rights. The general secretary of the World Council of Churches, Eugene Carson Blake, emphasized this cooperation when he stated, "Never in the life of the nation have churches and synagogues through their best leadership beeen so fully united on any moral issue confronting the American people" as in the present struggle for civil rights. Blake continued,

I like the comment of the mother superior of a Chicago convent who, when asked to give permission for some of her nuns to demonstrate in Chicago's streets, said: "I have seen pictures over these years of nuns playing jazz instruments, running out base hits, coaching basketball teams—I don't see any reason why there shouldn't be some pictures of nuns acting as Christians as well."[90]

There can be no doubt that the church has involved itself in the

[89] *National Catholic Reporter*, July 13, 1966, p. 2.
[90] Blake (1966).

present struggle for racial equality, even if that involvement has not yet reached a level that might be desired, and despite areas such as Los Angeles where the hierarchy has steadfastly sought to avoid involvement. As an advocate of civil rights, however, the church has arrived late on the scene. Certainly there have been individual Catholics like the Jesuit, John LaFarge, whose work in the area has been outstanding. But Callahan points out that historically the church has kept aloof from causes, and lack of concern with civil rights can be traced back to the Civil War when Catholics "passively supported the status quo" and were generally antiabolitionist.[91]

But now the church's involvement in social issues is extensive, and it is not limited to civil rights. In California priests called attention to the plight of farm laborers, exhorting workers to join in the strike that was gaining momentum in the southern San Joaquin Valley. At first the workers' primary allies were priests from northern California; the local diocesan paper limited itself to presenting both sides of the issue. However, shortly before the workers began a march to Sacramento, which culminated there on Easter Sunday, the Catholic bishops of California joined in announcing their support for unionization of farm workers. The labor class has been the main source of the constituency of the American Catholic church; the church, in turn, has traditionally been a champion of the labor movement. In their declaration the bishops announced support for extending to farm laborers all legal rights granted most other workers, including a minimum wage, social security, and unemployment insurance coverage.

Pictures of priests and nuns "acting as Christians" have indeed appeared recently, the best known showing nuns marching for civil rights in Selma. Throughout the country priests and nuns have joined in civil rights and social issues demonstrations, but not always with the blessings of the church. In January, 1965, *Ave Maria* carried an article concerning 13 "silenced priests" who had been transferred to other posts because of their protests.[92] In most cases the protests were concerned with civil rights, but two involved the war in Vietnam and one was protesting liturgical change.

These transfers took place in different parts of the country and under varying circumstances. In some cases they were evidently the result of sermons devoted to racial injustice; in others they resulted from direct action in voter registration and from demonstrations pro-

---

[91] Callahan (1963). The current involvement of the church in the social problems of various countries is discussed by Gremillion (1964).
[92] *Ave Maria* (1966).

testing instances of segregation. The circumstances surrounding these events may have been complex, and there may have been some good reasons for the actions taken by the superiors of the disciplined priests. Nevertheless, the silencing signifies a conservative reaction within the church. This is to be expected during a period of such immense transition and newfound freedom in a tradition-bound institution. And examples of reaction are many.

Hans Küng, one of the heralds of the church's new freedom, has been officially forbidden to speak in such dioceses as Cardinal McIntyre's in Los Angeles and has appeared in such places only surreptitiously. John Leo's Allentown, Pennsylvania, talk on the "Open Church" was cancelled by the local bishop, presumably because of Leo's printed criticism of church officials, criticism which has sometimes extended all the way up to the pope and which centered last year particularly on the actions of the Vincentian governing board at St. John's University.

St. Paul's *Wanderer* stands opposed to such criticism. It was deliberately designed as a conservative national Catholic weekly, and in 1966 sponsored its second annual forum. At this meeting speakers labeled *Ramparts* "theological pornography" and condemned the federally sponsored Project Head Start, along with liberal spokesmen and scholars of the church and state such as Küng, Berrigan, Novak, Cogley, United Nations Ambassador Goldberg, and Teilhard de Chardin. They also attacked the new liturgy, Mass in the vernacular, and the common Protestant-Catholic Bible.[93] In similar fashion Father DePauw has organized the Traditionalist Movement to turn back the tide of liberalism in the Church.[94]

There has been a persistent clash of conservatives and liberals in the Oklahoma City-Tulsa diocese, which has led to the publication of a Yellow Sheet filled with castigation of the new and innovative in the church. Anonymous Yellow Sheets are also circulated out of Boston and Notre Dame, Indiana, containing scathing criticism of the "intellectual mess" in the changing church. Three liberal priests with responsible positions in the St. Louis archdiocese allegedly were ousted because they were disapproved by the diocese's conservative elements. Cardinal Ritter originally expressed approval of the Little Council assembled to provide consultation and communication between the hierarchy and laity. But by the end of 1966 the council was bogged down in misunderstanding and disappointment. There had been no

[93] *National Catholic Reporter*, July 13, 1966, p. 7.
[94] *Ibid.*, January 12, 1966, p. 1; February 9, 1966, p. 7.

direct communication between the cardinal and the laity at all.[95]

The secondary role in the church assigned to laymen is particularly evident in the fact that of all the Catholic high schools polled, over 95 per cent reported in 1965 that they would not allow a layman to be principal.[96] But laymen are not the only second-class citizens in the church. In spite of the new emphasis upon structural reform and personal responsibility, assistant pastors were reported to be generally without status and defined rights in October, 1966. Two months later Fichter's survey of diocesan priests, cited in the discussion of the question of celibacy, corroborated this statement.[97] Opinions were obtained from 3,000 replies in a canvass of 5,963 diocesan priests who were not pastors, monsignors, or members of a religious order. Over 50 per cent of the priests reported feeling there is little or no free communication between them and their bishops, 60 per cent felt that their bishops demonstrated little personal interest in them, and 90 per cent agreed that every diocese should have an elected grievance committee.

But with few exceptions, the most inferior role in the church is assigned to women, be they members of the laity or of the professed religious. Examples are the refusal to allow women at the lectern or to allow them to serve at the altar, an innovation attempted by a priest in Oklahoma. Continuing restrictions on nuns were brought to national attention in 1966 in the case of the Glenmary Sisters.[98] It began when one of their members, a major in communications arts at the University of Detroit, was prohibited from playing the lead role in a campus play two days before it was scheduled to open. She had won the role in open competition and planned to use her theater craft in her missionary work with the poor Negroes and Caucasians from the rural South.

In their attempt to reach and help the poor, the Glenmary Sisters have been reported to adopt unconventional methods of operation, such as the occasional use of secular dress, following Appalachian families to large cities to help them adjust to a new life, and renting a Chicago tenement apartment to be closer to these families. Several nuns allegedly felt they were too liberal in their zeal, despite the fact that their comportment has been of unquestioned repute. Nevertheless, it is believed that because of these complaints, Archbishop Alter

[95] *Ibid.,* April 27, 1966, p. 1; November 30, 1966, p. 3; July 20, 1966, p. 1.

[96] *Ibid.,* October 29, 1965, p. 7.

[97] *San Francisco Chronicle,* December 12, 1966, p. 2.

[98] *National Catholic Reporter,* March 23, 1966, p. 1; September 21, 1966, p. 1; August 2, 1967, p. 1.

imposed heavy restrictions on them. Books they read at meal times must be approved by the chancery office; the sisters may not attend night school outside the convent, and must give the name of any sister taking a course, describe the course, and note the institution offering it; they are to be in bed by 10 P.M.; they are to "keep a proper religious spirit and reserve" in their relations with the laity and are specifically not to have laymen eat with them in the convent; and they were not to resume taking new recruits until September, 1967. By August, 1967, all but 15 of the original 102 members of the order had left. Fifty of these had banded together as laywomen to continue the work they had been doing before, accepting the supervision of the hierarchy in their churchwork but not over their private lives.

Although this may be a more extreme case than usual, nuns in general are under close surveillance by their superiors and the hierarchy. *Commonweal* quoted the Vatican Council decree that religious communities "should resort to suitable techniques, including modern ones, and abandon whatever activities are today less in keeping with the spirit of the community and its authentic character." The editorial then added, "Yet the Glenmary Sisters have been humiliated and placed under severe, even childish, restrictions, for precisely this kind of attempt at updating."[99] O'Gara wrote a week later that:

There is more ferment inside the religious communities of women, I am convinced, than anywhere else in the American Church. This indicates that in the convents, at least, *aggiornamento* and Vatican II are being taken seriously. But Sisters intent on reform and renewal face many obstacles, one of the main ones being men.[100]

Cardinal Suenens finds the epitome of the church's anti-feminist attitude in the thinking of St. Thomas Aquinas, who wrote:

In her particular nature woman is something defective and accidental. . . . If a girl child is born, it is due to weakness of the generative principle or imperfection in the pre-existing matter, or to a change produced by external causes, for example by the humid winds from the south, as Aristotle says.[101]

Another problem the church must continue to deal with is censorship. The Index no longer carries the effect of ecclesiastical law, but the Congregation for the Doctrine of the Faith continues to require for the Imprimatur that the laity and religious submit their writings for official judgment prior to publication. If the work is found to include error in any position dealing with faith and morals, the author

[99] *Commonweal*, 1966, 85: 5.
[100] O'Gara (1966).
[101] Suenens (1963), p. 46.

is asked to amend it. If he refuses, he is subjected to public condemnation. Schall complains that since anything having to do with faith and morals must be submitted to prior censorship by the Congregation for the Doctrine of the Faith, this technically could include subjects like sociology and politics. As a result the writer cannot write as he sees fit, but must write "to pass censorship."[102]

Vatican action removed the Imprimatur from the French priest-psychologist Father Marc Oraison's latest book, *The Human Mystery of Sexuality*. Oraison is also forbidden to speak on moral theology.[103] Whether it be censorship of this sort or that of the Glenmary Sisters, Callahan states that he feels that there have been more observable infractions of personal freedom in the church since the Vatican Council than during it.[104] A serious warning has also been issued by Mannion, the Executive Secretary of the Liturgical Conference, that so far reform in the church has been limited to externals. This situation was highlighted by a publication in 1967 of a popular but controversial book, *A Modern Priest Looks at His Outdated Church*, which dramatically criticized the church for its persisting anachronistic positions regarding such issues as the regulation of the lives of religious sisters, the drainage of so many resources into inferior schools which cater only to a minority of Catholics, sexual morality, birth control, and divorce.[105]

Cardinal Ottaviani has issued a warning of his own—that there exist ten major and widespread abuses in church reform having to do with false interpretation or rejection of traditional dogma such as original sin, the meaning of the Holy Eucharist, and the absolutism of moral law.[106] From his point of view, there is reason for concern, considering the multiplying examples of freedom and experimentation in religious practice and interpretation. They are especially apparent in the Netherlands, but exist throughout the church. They include the questioning of some of the deepest and most absolute dogmas of the church, such as the real presence of God in the Eucharist. They are also reflected in the tendency of many Catholics to subscribe to situation ethics, basing moral judgments and behavior on the evidence and

---

[102] Schall (1966).
[103] *National Catholic Reporter*, August 10, 1966, p. 1.
[104] *Ibid.*, September 21, 1966, p. 6.
[105] Kavanaugh (1967); Mannion (1966).
[106] *National Catholic Reporter*, October 19, 1966, p. 7.

situation of the moment rather than on a reference to a categorical absolute.[107]

As a result, in America and in Europe there is said to be an increasing number not just of defectors from the faith but of "Uncatholics." The Uncatholic in many ways do not accept or live according to the rules of the church, but neither do they fully sever themselves from it. They are selective in their faith and show a questioning, fearless irreverence toward ecclesiastical tradition and authority.[108]

Pope Paul recently stated that "one cannot demolish the Church of yesterday to build a new one today."[109] The Uncatholic is very likely no longer concerned with the church, as such, even that of tomorrow. In any event, the church today is faced with many excesses of restriction and indulgence in religious freedom. This is inevitable for an institution of this kind in a period of great transition. At the 1966 annual meeting of the National Catholic Educational Association, a major Catholic lay spokesman, John Cogley, examined this situation in American Catholic higher education specifically, and concluded: "There will, of course, be excesses of revolutionary zeal just as we have already seen excesses of counter-revolutionary reaction, but we can survive both extremes."[110]

At the same time, Cole indicated in *Generation of the Third Eye* that he was pessimistic about the rapidity with which change would occur and deplored "the accidental practices hallowed into absolutes."[111] The many reactionary elements of the church lend credence to the position that change will not occur quickly. However, during the present period of renewal and reform, many supposed absolutes are being openly questioned, and with questioning, change is not only inevitable but in some cases already apparent. But widely implemented changes will not come easily. The recognition of this fact has led to the newly formed Institute for Freedom in the Church. In its early advertisement the institute asserted that: "Ideally, the Church is a community which brings its members to the fullest realization of their freedom and autonomy; in fact it fails to achieve this ideal, and to the extent that it does fail, needs reform from within."[112]

It noted that the Vatican Council moved the church in the direction

---

[107] Callahan (1966); Fletcher (1966); McCabe (1966).

[108] *Time*, 1966, 87 (3): 55.

[109] *National Catholic Reporter*, November 23, 1966, p. 3.

[110] Cogley (1966).

[111] Cole (1965), p. 55.

[112] *National Catholic Reporter*, September 28, 1966, p. 6.

of freedom, but did not give it the machinery for freedom. The institute hopes to act as a "vehicle for action" toward freedom in the church, coupled with understanding and respect, by serving as a clearinghouse of ideas through the dissemination of social science studies, case studies, and experiences of institute chapters; by mediating in college and diocesan communities split by dissension; and by conducting annual conferences and programs dealing with problems in parishes, schools, seminaries, and religious communities.

The establishment of the Institute for Freedom in the Church highlights the enormous changes potentially or actually taking place in the church and its schools, together with their concomitant problems and possibilities.[113] We have only been able to touch on these issues. But we have reviewed enough material to see that these changes signify a great upheaval in the church-family-self system as depicted in the previous chapter. Troublesome, delaying, and reactionary crosscurrents continue to exist. Still, there is observable loosening of the bonds of the church with its constituents, and the establishment of a much more reciprocal relationship between the self and the church than existed previously. There is apparent a great shift in the accidental values promulgated by the church, and much less influence of these values, whatever they may be, on its congregations.

There is in the church a much greater exposure to ideas and much more freedom to deal with them than existed previously. There is less fear of reprisals resulting from censorship of ideas, and censorship is liable to be increasingly ignored as academic and personal freedom gains momentum. This upheaval is especially significant in the church's colleges, many of which are seeking intellectual development and status, and many of which are facing serious problems in this search. The immense implications these changes and problems have for American Catholic scholarship and faith in the future warrant a separate, concluding discussion in this volume, and further serious study.

[113] Callahan (1965a) has written particularly about the need for free expression within the church and honest communication by the church.

CHAPTER TWELVE

Conclusion

At a time when extreme change is occurring within the church system, when each day seems to bring word of anticipated, proposed, or achieved departures from tradition, any assessment of Catholic intellectual life may be considered valid only for the past and the immediate present. We do not know how extensive or lasting the changes within the church will be, nor how greatly these changes will affect the intellectual lives of individuals within it.

We would speculate, however, that the indicated increased interest of Catholics in intellectual matters will continue only if this interest is encouraged actively and consistently by the church, its schools, and by the families within the church. Intellectual growth will not occur without effort, for Catholic anti-intellectualism has been too deeply rooted and pervasive to be eliminated easily. Its roots are found in the distant past; the results are evident right up to the present.

Religion in general has not been hospitable to intellectualism in America, but Catholicism in particular has not encouraged intellectuality. In our automated age, we are particularly concerned about the disregard for intellectualism because our fast-moving and transitional culture requires creative thinkers concerned with human issues and potentialities to master its technological advances.

The study reported in this volume inquired into the meaning of intellectualism and explored in particular the extent of intellectual development and productivity in a religious subculture which has been identified as lacking in scholarly contributions in this country. Our task was to explore the intellectual life of American Catholics in college, to explore the psychodynamics and related issues involved in intellectual development in a religious context. We are not equipped to predict or to determine what role the Catholic college will play in the future. We would be remiss to explore problems without suggesting something of what these problems portend, however.

When our data are considered within the historical and theoretical

303

framework outlined above we may anticipate a number of events which may deeply affect the church. The openness resulting from the Vatican Council which took place in the mid-1960's likely will lead to expanded dialogue between Catholics and non-Catholics and, subsequently, to a greater sharing of ideas and more mixed marriages. This openness also will lend strength to voices and opinions of individual church members, lead to more autonomy and less dependence upon church authority, and encourage greater individual responsibility based upon the individual conscience. Loosening the bonds and lifting the shield the church has placed around the individual will allow the values of the larger society to permeate the Catholic culture. Catholics will assimilate values once alien to them. Consequently, many Catholics are likely to defect from the church, and many others will undergo reorientation of their religious beliefs. Catholics no longer will be uniformly aligned with the church, and the more intellectual members who continue to remain close to the church will ask more of it, from the quality of its pastors and schools to the quality of its bishops. Many of the more pluralistically oriented Catholics will be less concerned with the church altogether, and, no doubt, it will become increasingly difficult to distinguish the religious orientation of the Catholic from that of the Protestant.

Along with the signs of greater openness in the church noted so far have come change in religious orientation and the trend toward defection we expected. Where the bonds are being tightened we find the anti-intellectualism and lack of scholarship characteristic of the past. Conservative Catholicism and creative scholarship do not flourish together. Instead, a greater degree of scholarship, of intellectualism, is associated with a greater change in religious attitudes and, thus, a different kind of Catholicism.

If there are to be intellectual Catholics, many of them will register dissent which sometimes might appear offensive to the church. Many of these Catholics will hold unorthodox views on theology, too; their concern will be with mankind and not with maintaining a faith they feel is no longer relevant. The intellectual Catholic is going to ask questions about everything, from the need for celibacy to the infallibility of the pope. And the church should encourage this questioning if it wants to cultivate an intellectual life within its sphere.

Perhaps the church has concentrated too much attention on dogma, catechetical formulas, and sexual morality at a time when Catholics and non-Catholics are forced to confront the compelling issues of war, poverty, civil rights, automation, the role of women, human dignity, and the whole movement and understanding of society in this tumultuous century. From the viewpoint of many intellectuals, these latter issues warrant more of the church's concern than the argument over the aspect of sexual morality in the issue of contraception.

Underlying the specific issue of birth control appears to be an issue which may be critical to the intellectual life of the church, if not to the church itself. That is the question of the infallibility of the church. It seems to us that the church is reluctant to change its position on the matter of birth control for fear that its teaching authority will be questioned in the future. If the church reverses the judgment it once considered correct, its members might well question the church's infallibility on all issues from that time on. This would have very serious ramifications considering how central, the doctrine of infallibility is to the church, and considering that its entire teaching authority is based on this doctrine. As a result the questioning of the church's infallibility by its members probably would create difficulties going to the core of the church. Nevertheless, we submit that this need not mean that the church will lose all value. Obviously non-Catholic church bodies hold value without subscribing to the doctrine of infallibility.

Indeed it is evident from the data that if the intellectual Catholic is not given freedom to dissent, whether it be over birth control or other matters, he will withdraw from the system either by complete severance or by becoming an unorthodox, uninvolved "Uncatholic." This may be expected even of the heretofore critical devout. By 1967 examples of defection were plentiful, even among members of the clergy and the religious. If the church is to preserve and enhance its intellectual life, it must look more closely at the reasons behind these defections and institute additional changes to prevent wider defection.

In the changing church are many crosscurrents. There are signs of change and signs of cultural lag and of a tenacious clinging to tradition—signs of comparatively liberal innovations and evidence of harsh, reactionary conservatism. It is to be expected that a large, cautious, conservative element will continue to exist in the church, and major changes cannot be expected overnight. But we do see opening doors and loosening bonds, a more reciprocal relationship between the individual and the church.

Signs of openness are evident not only in the church itself but in the church's colleges, presumably the prime movers in its intellectual life. Most Catholic colleges as yet show few signs of academic quality and creative scholarship, however. They have a long way to go before they can provide an education of consistently high quality, but many

Catholic educators share an awareness of the need to initiate improvements. Certainly the climate appears to be conducive to significant developments within Catholic colleges.

Two writers in particular have taken note of the innovations, of the upgrading of faculties, facilities, and curricula, and of the general educational development underway at Fordham University and the University of Notre Dame.[1] These universities were observed to be making great strides toward educational excellence, although they had yet to attain the quality of major non-Catholic universities. But either directly or tacitly two questions were posed in the articles: Can these universities indeed become great universities? If they become great centers for intellectual inquiry, can they remain Catholic? Both questions were left unanswered.

Before the church can develop topflight colleges, it must give careful attention to at least five major problems: (1) the need to clarify the role of the Catholic college; (2) the need for innovation; (3) the improvement and redistribution of the colleges' educational resources; (4) selective student and faculty recruitment; and (5) the continued need for the appraisal of the worth and effect of the institutions.

One of the acknowledged major objectives of colleges in general is to prepare youth to understand, live in, and contribute to society. We live in a radically changing society, and yet we are relying upon a tradition-bound college system to accomplish the preparation of our youth. Therefore, educators might well reconsider what should constitute the role and nature of the contemporary college. The Catholic college, in particular, which claims to have a special reason for existence, should be very clear about what that reason is.

In the past the reason for the existence of Catholic colleges admittedly and avowedly has been to maintain the faith. However, Catholic educators today appear to have only vague ideas of what the special role of their colleges should be. The National Catholic Educational Association listed "the formulation of definition" as "one of the most critical needs" in Catholic higher education.[2] The statements of purpose issued by Catholic colleges rarely go beyond the loosely stated goals of development of the whole man, Christian character, and the Christian thinker. At the close of 1966 the president of the University of Portland wrote of the unique value of "a truly Catholic higher edu-

[1] Cass (1967); Schrag (1967).
[2] Ford and Roy (1966).

cational experience," but it is not clear from his article what this experience is.[3] Catholic women's colleges typically claim to foster some unique development or formation of their students, but this special formation seldom is defined or demonstrated.

Hazo and his associates state that there is something unique about Christian, and specifically, Catholic intellectuality.[4] These professors consider that the Catholic scholar's special function is to synthesize the intellectual and spiritual traditions and to liberate the mind through intellectual study in the humanities while exploring the problems of belief occasioned by such study.

But intellectual activity in whatever form or in whatever religious or philosophical context it is undertaken would still appear to have its own, constant exigencies or not be intellectuality at all. Therefore, the notion of the Christian intellectual or Catholic scholar must be qualified. One cannot be a Catholic historian or sociologist, for instance, unless he has become intellectually. and, therefore, inquisitively involved in historical or sociological scholarship in addition to professing his Christian faith.

This is not to say there is no special role for Catholic colleges; there are at least three open to them. They could be centers for theological studies; they could be centers for studies in the liberal arts, including the physical and social sciences; and, as an arm of private higher education in general, they could initiate educational experimentation and development not feasible for public colleges.

There is a striking deficiency noted in Catholic colleges' current performance of the special role they have embraced in the past—presentation of theology and philosophy. Although the primary purpose of these colleges historically has been to maintain the faith, the colleges have not carried out this purpose in a scholarly, intellectual manner, or even in a way very relevant to contemporary living. The Catholic college could move to the forefront of theological thinking by providing unexcelled theological schools that need not be exclusively Catholic—perhaps modeled after the one at the University of Chicago.

Catholic colleges have been and continue to be very weak in that in which they profess to be the best—the liberal arts. No Catholic liberal arts colleges can match the educational quality of first-class nonsectarian colleges such as Swarthmore, Bennington, Radcliffe, Antioch, Reed, or the Claremont Colleges. This weakness is also apparent in the fact that the church (by its nature concerned with

[3] Waldschmidt (1966), p. 9.
[4] Hazo (1963).

the welfare of mankind) has colleges that neglect the social sciences.

The church is a traditional stronghold of liberal arts colleges in American higher education, even if the education in these colleges is not of the highest quality. Since liberal arts, along with the creative arts, bring to society that which is most human, Catholic colleges would be fulfilling a role apostolic to them and essential to the nation if they would make their institutions excellent liberal arts colleges, attractive to good students of all religions.

A third extremely important role Catholic colleges could assume has to do with their need to innovate and with the need for innovation in higher education generally. A number of private colleges, such as those in the Union for Research and Experimentation in Higher Education, place heavy emphasis upon experimentation. A few Catholic colleges have shown an interest in the union's and related programs, and, in a very few cases, have begun to participate in them.

Such experimentation is badly needed in the private sector. Public colleges are less free to innovate since they are tax supported, subject to legislation, and cannot be as selective in enrollment. Both sectors face the problem of meeting the increasingly sophisticated needs of young adults entering college today.

Special theology centers could be set up if the Catholic innovations were to be limited specifically to the religious sphere, but the concern of the colleges must go beyond this. In addition to fostering serious scholarship in the arts and sciences, Catholic colleges could encourage creativity by establishing centers for the creative arts, sponsoring creative writing workshops, and establishing centers for research, experimentation, and development in education.

It is not enough to point to a good art department here and there or to the few faculty who manage to be creative and scholarly in spite of lack of church support, to an evening lecture series, or to the modest research center established to attract a few faculty members who could not be retained by a college otherwise. Catholic colleges could make significant and needed contributions to education just as other private colleges are doing, but not without a searching reappraisal and drastic modification of the church's educational resources. At this point, we can touch only on a few problems that afflict Catholic universities and colleges.

We join others in asking why many Catholic schools should stress professional fields such as engineering and business. As a rule, it is difficult for Catholic colleges to compete in these fields with the larger public institutions and large, endowed private universities which can better afford the equipment and faculty necessary for superior programs. Catholic colleges can afford such equipment and staff only through large grants which are more likely to go to the major centers of the physical sciences. Even if more funds were available for technological, professional programs in Catholic colleges, would these programs be appropriate to the role of Catholic higher education? If Catholic colleges only reproduce curricula provided elsewhere and reproduce it poorly, then one might well question the need for separate "Catholic" colleges.

These questions of appropriate allocation of educational resources in Catholic educational institutions do not apply solely to the large Catholic colleges and universities that maintain professional schools. The limited resources also affect the role that small Catholic colleges assume in higher education. Most Catholic colleges enroll no more than 1,000 students; these small colleges usually are restricted in operating funds and therefore find it difficult to provide adequate curricula, facilities, and faculties.

In the context of the "opening" church system in a pluralistic, fast-changing society that requires creative intellectual endeavor, the small Catholic college must begin to reappraise itself as it seeks new and reasoned roles. In this light, the fact of its Catholic character is not necessarily a persuasive reason for its existence. As a prominent Catholic layman wrote in *Commonweal,* Catholic colleges in the past have been just good enough so that their graduates have learned enough that they do not want to send their children to the same kind of college.[5] And whether they are loyal graduates of Catholic colleges or disassociated Catholic graduates of secular colleges, the more enlightened and critical that Catholics become, the less likely will they be to favor Catholic schools which they consider lacking in educational quality. Unless the small Catholic colleges, and the large ones as well, modify their objectives and methods of operation, their role is likely to be only that of an arbor for a dying vine of Catholic education.

The Catholic college faces not only the problems posed by an evolving church and the increasing self-criticism and intellectual questioning among many of its members; it faces the physical, and particularly financial, problems that any small American college encounters. For that reason, if for no other, the Catholic colleges will be forced to reappraise themselves and their goals, weighing the costs of broadened spiritual and educational leadership as elite institutions against the

[5] Cogley (1963).

limited scope of the type of Bible college which reaches a few very devout students who are little inclined to scholarship.

There has been a wasteful duplication of facilities in Catholic higher education, occasioned in part by the lack of cooperation among the competing orders that maintain their own colleges. Almost every metropolitan area contains a number of small Catholic colleges, each of which has its own library and laboratories, struggles for adequate faculty, and replicates most of the curricula of the others.

Although the small Catholic colleges appear to pose special problems, there are indications that often the best of Catholic higher education is found among these colleges, particularly the women's colleges. Better and more coordinated planning and open communication among the religious orders and between the orders and diocesan operations will be necessary to develop truly elite institutions; in fact, these actions may be necessary to the survival of Catholic colleges.

Policies must be reviewed not just as they relate to their own orders but to other orders and to laymen. This includes taking stock of college administration—deciding whether there is special justification for having a priest as president and a board of trustees composed of priests. Colleges probably will be forced to weigh this question not only to attract financial support, but to attract good lay faculty members and good students who want to participate in the policies of their college. The examples of lay participation in Catholic college administration set in 1967 by the University of Portland, the University of Notre Dame, Webster College, and a few others, may have been unique at the time, but they may be essential for most Catholic colleges in the future.

There are a number of ways the best, and less than best, colleges can become better while surviving financially. They might form a cluster college system or establish small colleges on a large campus.[6] The previously mentioned Claremont Colleges are a cluster of relatively small liberal arts colleges and a graduate school located on a campus in southern California. Each college maintains its own autonomy, individuality, and specific goals while drawing strength from the others by sharing classes, faculty, and such key facilities as the library. The unprecedented action taken by Immaculate Heart College in joining the Claremont Colleges is a move of considerable significance and an example of the kind of forward thinking that is so sorely needed in Catholic higher education.

Cooperative ventures of this kind also could be formed among the

[6] See Martin (1967).

Catholic colleges or among Catholic and Protestant colleges where these groupings are geographically practical. In this way, a particular order or religion could maintain its individuality while enhancing its educational services by sharing with others. Some relocation of facilities will be necessary, and this will be expensive, but most major improvements in Catholic higher education will be expensive in one way or another.

Another possibility is the small college within the complex of a large college or university. A case in point here is Raymond College, a select liberal arts college which was established in part to bring catalytic qualities to the Methodist-founded and administered University of the Pacific. Additional satellite colleges now are attaching themselves to these units, and other examples of this kind of innovation are to be found in Monteith College at Wayne State University, New College at Hofstra University, and New Division at Nasson College. All of these colleges are undertaking concurrent research to evaluate the effectiveness of their programs.

A relationship of this kind could be initiated by Catholic colleges such as St. Mary's College in Notre Dame, Indiana, and the neighboring University of Notre Dame. St. Mary's College is a women's college already perceived by its students as outstanding for its scholarly climate on the basis of College and University Environment Scales data. Perhaps it could become a really enriching coeducational liberal arts college within the sphere of the University of Notre Dame to the mutual advantage of both institutions. The same could be true of Trinity College and Georgetown University or Catholic University of America, or San Francisco College for Women and the University of San Francisco. There was word in the spring of 1967 that the University of Notre Dame and St. Mary's College were considering such a union, as well as Marymount College and Loyola University of Los Angeles. Serious discussion has also taken place concerning the possibility of a liaison between Barat College of the Sacred Heart and the University of Chicago. Such liaisons could be set up throughout the country. They could go well beyond the loose interinstitutional cooperation that now exists among some Catholic colleges and undoubtedly would require reevaluation and willingness to compromise. However, the success of developments like the Claremont Colleges suggests that the value to be gained would warrant the compromise.

Several Catholic colleges might consider amalgamation to form major universities. Certain other Catholic colleges could be maintained as autonomous, self-contained institutions if they are good enough to warrant the respect and financial support given those private colleges of educational excellence. Another possibility is self-elimination if a college stands little chance to be anything but mediocre. Administrators in some schools may justify continued operation of their institutions on the basis that their relatively unselective recruitment and lower academic standards allow them to provide a Catholic college education to students who would have difficulty obtaining one otherwise. We propound, however, that financial and physical restrictions limit the number of students they can educate and so preclude undertaking this broad mission.

Educational improvement must be extended to the lower schools, seminaries, and novitiates as well, where formal Catholic education begins. If Catholic elementary and high schools do not foster intellectual, scholarly qualities among their students, then the Catholic colleges will be limited by this condition no matter what their intentions. By the same token, the schools cannot provide an enriching education if the seminaries and novitiates do not produce teachers with the intellectual qualities prerequisite for such an education.

Catholic colleges doubtless will continue to draw most of their students from those who have attended Catholic schools. However, financial and personnel difficulties and the possiblity of increased dissatisfaction of Catholics with their schools suggest that there may be fewer Catholic elementary schools. The lower years of Catholic grammar school are being eliminated in some places, and high schools are being closed elsewhere. Compounding the difficulty is that the number of religious teachers is diminishing when the student population generally is expanding. Therefore, more lay teachers will be needed even without a great increase of enrollments in Catholic schools.

To attract good lay teachers, Catholic schools must provide attractive teaching environments and adequate salaries. Financing the lay teachers will require a degree of commitment from Catholics that many will question if the schools do no more than provide the minimal education and religious training of old. At the college level, the talented professor with a good graduate education cannot afford to take a position in a mediocre college where he cannot fully realize his potential.

This situation has serious implications in conjunction with the findings of this study. The data reveal a pervasive operation of self-selectivity among Catholic college students. Generally, the better, more intellectual students are not attending Catholic colleges. The colleges are recruiting students who in many cases are intellectually restricted products of an intellectually restricted Catholic education.

If Catholic colleges hope to foster intellectual excellence, they will have to attract more intellectually disposed students in the future, and not simply academically able students, just as they will have to be more innovative in the education they provide for them.

A projected 80 per cent of Catholic students will be in secular colleges by 1970. Even so, church leaders are just beginning seriously to examine the pertinence of the Newman Apostolate, which provides an opportunity for religious development for students attending non-Catholic colleges. Catholics outside the Catholic colleges have received little attention from the church, which has expended its efforts on its own colleges. The greater loosening of the bonds, the greater openness to others, the increased communication and more intermarriage that we saw among secular college Catholics indicate that more and more Catholics will enter secular colleges and slip away from traditional Catholicism. Church leaders concerned with the religious training of its members might well consider how to reach these secular school Catholics, perhaps through concentrating the greater part of their educational efforts on programs in the Confraternity of Christian Doctrine, Newman Centers, and neighborhood or parish adult centers rather than in its parochial schools and colleges.

Since the Catholic colleges probably will continue to serve a small minority of students, the church would be free to bring an enhanced education to a few unabashedly elite schools and colleges where it could foster intellectual leadership in a religious context. Should the colleges continue to give an intellectually limited minority an unexceptional education, then questions must persist about the function of these colleges.

Prerequisites to educational excellence appear to be thorough self-study, analysis, and evaluation of objectives ahead, and subsequent commensurate action by the host of Catholic colleges. Since the Catholic colleges hold an important key to the church's intellectual life, their roles must be earnestly and continually examined. We are in agreement with the recent urging of the National Catholic Educational Association that the entirety of American Catholic higher education be involved in the evaluation of its effectiveness.[7] We propose that this evaluation consider examples of leadership in self-appraisal, self-improvement, and innovation cited in this volume. Many of the key programs that have been initiated have yet to mature or to demonstrate their worth. But the needs are such in all of Catholic higher

[7] Ford and Roy (1966).

education that these examples should be followed up and seriously evaluated and considered. Encouraging such educational leadership at other Catholic institutions would make possible unprecedented contributions to the intellectual life and educational excellence of the church and of the nation.

APPENDIX A

Construction and Validation of the
Omnibus Personality Inventory

The Omnibus Personality Inventory is an attitudinal inventory whose scales purport to measure intellectual, emotional, and dispositional personality traits. It was developed at the Center for Research and Development in Higher Education at the University of California, Berkeley, and in format resembles the Minnesota Multiphasic Personality Inventory and the California Psychological Inventory. The Omnibus Personality Inventory was designed primarily for research on college students and has indicated an impressive capability of distinguishing differences in intellectual and emotional attitudes and behavior among a variety of student groups.

The ensuing discussion applies to Forms C and D of the Omnibus Personality Inventory which were administered to the West Coast and National samples. The inventory has since been further revised and refined and a new manual is under preparation. The final Form F of the Omnibus Personality Inventory and the corresponding manual is scheduled to be available for circulation by the Psychological Corporation in 1967.

Validity and reliability data summarized for each scale are drawn from the *Omnibus Personality Inventory Research Manual* in all cases not otherwise specified.[1] Considerable validation data are based on correlations with other known, functional scales, such as those in the Minnesota Multiphasic Personality Inventory (MMPI), California Psychological Inventory (CPI), Allport-Vernon-Lindzey Study of Values (AVL), the Kuder Preference Record, the Myers-Briggs Type Indicator (MBTI), the Stern Activities Index, the Strong Vocational Interest Blank (SVIB), and the Opinion, Attitude, and Interest Survey (OAIS).[2] Other validation data are based upon various ratings and recognized performances such as prize-winning artistic endeavor.

---

[1] Center for the Study of Higher Education (1962).

[2] Among the references which discuss the various published instruments cited as possessing a validating correlation with the Omnibus Personality Inventory are: Allport, Vernon, and Lindzey (1951); Dahlstrom and Welsh (1960); Kuder (1957); Fricke (1963); Gough (1964); Hathaway and McKinley (1951); Myers and Briggs (1962); Stern (1958); Strong (1959); Weissman (1958); Williams (1964).

Five major factors have been identified as comprising the Omnibus Personality Inventory on the basis of Quartimax and Varimax rotated factor analyses: (1) tolerance and autonomy, or ideological open-mindedness and nonauthoritarianism; (2) psychological adjustment, including response set, as measured by the Repression-Suppression scale; (3) scholarly orientation; (4) masculine-feminine interests; and (5) social introversion. Only the first three factors are of concern in the present study. Several of the scales are intercorrelated, but each possesses its own unique variance, with the exceptions to be noted for the three autonomy scales. The intercorrelations of most of the scales comprising these factors, a measure of ability, and the Religious Concepts Inventory for the West Coast Catholic college freshmen and 1960 seniors and for the National Sample appear in Tables 56 and 57. Since scale descriptions and sample items were included when the scales were discussed in chapters 4, 8, and 9, only brief descriptions will be included here, in each case followed by a general summary of the validity data.

TABLE 56. *Intercorrelations and Reliability Coefficients of Psychometric Scales, West Coast Sample*[a]

	SCAT	RCI	RS	LA	IE	TI	TO	Co	Es	Na
SCAT	(—)									
RCI	.04	(.89)								
RS	.09	.15	(.93)							
LA	.11	.06	.76	(.82)						
IE	−.02	−.28	−.83	−.52	(.85)					
TI	.31	−.04	.17	.09	−.05	(.85)				
TO	.30	−.14	.08	.12	.09	.65	(.74)			
Co	.12	−.17	−.33	−.20	.55	.38	.38	(.71)		
Es	.18	−.01	−.13	−.19	.16	.59	.25	.39	(.80)	
Na	.27	−.22	−.09	−.05	.25	.30	.32	.35	.24	(.39)

[a] Number is 1,350. Reliability coefficients (KR 21) are in the diagonal parentheses; the coefficients are those listed by the Omnibus Personality Inventory Manual, except those on the RCI and Na scales which were computed on the total West Coast Sample. Test-retest reliabilities are noted following scale descriptions in Appendix A.

Autonomy (Au)

This scale measures nonauthoritarian thinking and a need for independence. It correlates with the Intuition and Perception scales in the Myers-Briggs Type Indicator (MBTI) related to nonauthoritarianism, and, as noted in the revised manual, it is also highly correlated (approximately .45–.60) with esthetic and creative inclinations,

TABLE 57. *Intercorrelations and Reliability Coefficients of Omnibus Personality Inventory Scales, National Sample*[a]

	TI	Es	Co	SM	Au	Na	RL	LA	IE
TI	(.87)								
Es	.69	(.80)							
Co	.51	.47	(.71)						
SM	.44	.32	.49	(.80)					
Au	.48	.37	.51	.82	(.82)				
Na	.44	.38	.45	.61	.70	(.51)			
RL	.18	.14	.35	.47	.53	.48	(.80)		
LA	.11	−.14	−.12	.24	.06	.02	−.02	(.82)	
IE	.16	.26	.59	.28	.39	.32	.47	−.32	(.87)

[a] Number is 4,313, which includes all high school graduates in the National Sample (college and non-college) who were tested in 1959 and 1963. Reliability coefficients (KR 21) are in the diagonal parentheses. All reliability coefficients are those listed by the Omnibus Personality Inventory Manual with the exception of the Social Maturity and Nonauthoritarianism scales, which were computed on the National Sample. Test-retest reliability coefficients are noted following scale descriptions in Appendix A.

independence of thinking, flexibility and intellectual quality as measured by a number of AVL, CPI, and OAIS scales. It is significantly related to measures of objectivity and (negatively) to measures of deference and abasement. It is negatively related to the SVIB Policeman and most business-oriented scales and positively related to such scales as Psychologist, Author-Journalist, Minister, Artist, Musician, and Social Worker. Students who consider that the main satisfaction of employment is the opportunity to be creative and original obtain a significantly higher score on Autonomy compared with other students who view job satisfaction in such terms as opportunity for advancement, security, and working with others. Students planning to attend graduate school score significantly higher on the scale than those planning to attend professional school or who report no plans for postgraduate education. The Autonomy scale correlates with instructors' ratings of "oral assignment presentation," "written performance," and "overall evaluation." (See also Social Maturity, p. 320.) Reliability: .80 (KR 21); .88 test-retest, Form Fx). 40 items.

Complexity (Co)

This scale measures orientation toward an experimental, inquisitive viewing of experience and toward tolerance for ambiguities. The scale correlates with the AVL Theoretical and Aesthetic measures, which distinguish creative individuals, and with the Myers-Briggs Intuition and Perception scales, which purport to measure a person's tendency to approach his environment with an open, receptive mind. In data to be published in the revised manual, this variable correlates highly with critical thinking and flexibility in problem solving, with the variety of perspectives with which one views a limited range of concepts, with measures of creativeness of personality, intellectual quality, and (negatively) with a need for order. Reliability: .71 (KR 21); .83 (test-retest). 27 items.

Estheticism (Es)

This scale measures diverse interests in artistic matters. The scale correlates highly with the AVL Aesthetic and the Kuder Literary scales. Data in the new manual show moderate correlations (approximately .35) between the Estheticism scale and creative disposition, the SVIB Artist scale, and the Kuder Musical scale (but not the Kuder Artistic scale). It significantly distinguishes art and humanities majors and students elected to an honors program. Reliability: .80 (KR 21); .90 (test-retest). 24 items.

Impulse Expression (IE)

This scale measures the extent to which a person tends to express his impulses in overt action or conscious feeling and attitude. High scores indicate proneness toward imaginative work and freedom of thought. It correlates negatively with CPI Responsibility, Socialization, and Self-control scales, presumably measurements of social conformity, and correlates positively with the CPI Flexibility scale. It distinguishes students highly rated by instructors for "oral assignment presentation," "written performance," and "overall evaluation" and distinguishes graduate students and prize-winning artists. In data to be published in the revised manual, this variable correlates significantly, although not highly (approximately .21), with measures of ability to comprehend and solve complex or unique problems. It correlates with scales indicating emotional disturbance and also correlates highly (and negatively) with measures of restrictiveness. Reliability: .91 (KR 21); .94 (test-retest). 75 items.

Lack of Anxiety (LA)

This scale measures freedom from unusual amounts of anxiety. The scale correlates negatively with schizoid tendencies; persons scoring high in Lack of Anxiety tend to score low in Schizoid Functioning. There is a moderate correlation with Impulse Expression and Social Introversion. Reliability is unavailable in the Omnibus Personality Inventory's preliminary research manual. The internal consistency coefficient computed on the total sample of Catholic college students is .61 (KR 21); computed on the normative sample in the revised manual it is .82.[3] Test-retest reliability coefficients obtained separately by the author and reported for two other samples in the revised manual range from .79 to .93, with a three-to-four-week interval between test administrations. 20 items.

Nonauthoritarianism (Na)

This scale, a refinement of the original California F scale, measures independence and freedom from authoritarianism and opionated thinking.[4] The scale correlates highly with CPI measures which distinguish achievement through independence, intellectual efficiency, flexibility, and with interest in occupations involving ideas. It correlates negatively with the Strong Vocational Interest Blank business occupation scales and significantly distinguishes professional social scientists and graduate students. The Nonauthoritarianism scale correlates very highly with the Omnibus Personality Inventory Social Maturity and Autonomy scales (see Table 57). Its highest loading, .64–.60, is on the first factor of the Omnibus Personality Inventory (autonomy and tolerance) compared with the Autonomy scale's loading of .77–.71 on the basis of unrotated two-factor analysis. (See also Social Maturity, p. 320.) Reliability information is unavailable in the manual. The coefficient computed separately on the National Sample (college students) is .51 (KR 21). The coefficient computed for a random sample of students in four colleges is .62.[5] The internal consistency reliability coefficient is relatively low, probably because of the small number and heterogeneous nature of the items composing the scale. Test-retest data with a three-week interval obtained separately by the author from a freshman psychology class at San Francisco State College in the spring of 1967 yielded a highly acceptable reliability coefficient of .92. 20 items.

Repression-Suppression (RS)

This scale is a measure of response bias—high scorers tend to be inhibited, prudent, and cautious as expressed in their attitudes toward self and others. They thus reject detracting items which express social alienation, unconventionality, or socially undesirable behavior. This scale correlates significantly and negatively with fantasied achievement, emotionality, and aggression. It correlates positively with the CPI Self-control, Sense of Well-being, and Good Impression scales and with the Edward's Social Desirability scale.[6] In research on the West Coast Sample reported previously, Catholic college students, secular

---

[3] The Lack of Anxiety scale is termed the Anxiety Level scale in Form F of the Omnibus Personality Inventory and its corresponding revised manual.

[4] The scale was devised by Christie and associates (1958).

[5] Center for the Study of Higher Education (1960).

[6] Edwards (1957).

college Catholics, and non-Catholics were not found to differ statistically in their responses to the Repression-Suppression scale. There also was no indication of response bias or an attempt to fake responses.[7] Reliability: .93 (KR 21); .82 (test-retest). 129 items.

Religious Liberalism (RL)

This scale measures tendency toward skepticism or rejection of religious beliefs and practices.[8] The scale correlates highly and negatively with the AVL Religious scale and the CPI Sense of Well-being, Self-control, Good Impression, and Responsibility scales. It significantly distinguishes groups of known religious orientation and degree of religious commitment, and correlates with the author's Religious Concepts Inventory (RCI) and Religious Practices Index (RPI), discussed in Appendix D. Reliability: .84 (KR 21); .93 (test-retest). 29 items.

Social Maturity (SM)

This scale, a 67-item abridgment of the 144-item Form C version, measures different dimensions of autonomy, openness, and flexibility, as well as some cultural interests. Because of the importance of the autonomy measures used in the present study and because of the importance of understanding the nature and interrelationship of the Autonomy, Nonauthoritarianism, and Social Maturity scales, several relevant sections of the research manual are quoted:

> Over a decade ago, Adorno *et al* (1950) reported some research on antisemitism, ethnocentrism, and anti-democratic political attitudes which indicated that these characteristics are functionally related within the "authoritarian" personality. Since then it has been found that related measures of authoritarianism also correlate with a great variety of social behavior. The Social Maturity scale was first developed in research on Vassar women as a measure of (non) authoritarianism that was relatively insensitive to political and religious ideology (Webster, Sanford, and Freedman, 1955). For inclusion in the *OPI* the SM scale underwent subsequent revision in an attempt to improve reliability, to reduce the correlation with measures of response set, and to increase the relevance of the content for subjects of both sexes attending a variety of colleges. The present revised form contains more items which reflect intraception, intellectual skepticism, and freedom of thought than was true of the SM scale contained in the VC *Attitude Inventory*. . . .
>
> A shorter version of the Social Maturity (SM) dimension was obtained also as a result of the general attempt to construct scales that were more independent, experimentally, by reducing item-overlap and similarity of content among several scales. Despite lower reliability, the correlation of these 40 items with SM remains amazingly high. At the same time, however, by comparison with SM, the Au items focus more upon the need for intellectual and social

---

[7] Trent (1964).

[8] The Religious Liberalism scale is termed the Religious Orientation scale on Form F of the Omnibus Personality Inventory.

autonomy and upon the desire for independence and freedom from restraint as imposed by social institutions.

In constructing the Au scale, more so than in the other revised shortform scales, major attention was given initially to removing selected items, especially those which also served in the following scales: TI, TO, Es, Co, and RL. The content of a large percentage of the remaining items warranted a final item analysis to determine which items functioned at the .01 level or better. Both the reliability (.80) of the 40 discriminating items and function of the scale across various groups were basic to the decision to use Au as a distinct scale. . . .

[Social Maturity] correlates highest with the Change scale (.45) in the *Activities Index*. In terms of *CPI* correlates, it correlates highest with Capacity for Status (.47) and Social Presence (.42) for men, and with Achievement via Independence (.49), Capacity for Status (.44), and Intellectual Efficiency (.43) for women. This measure polarizes several scales on the *Strong Interest Blank:* Psychologist (.60), Social Worker (.43), vs. Mortician (—.42), Purchasing Agent (—.47) and Banker (—.48). After correction for attenuation, SM was indistinguishable from NA [Nonauthoritarianism] in several college samples.[9]

Also, graduate students in all fields have consistently been found to score significantly higher on the Social Maturity scale than college students not attending graduate school. Reliability: .80 (KR 21, 67-item version); .79 (test-retest, Form C). 67 items.

Theoretical Orientation (TO)

This scale measures interest in science and tendency toward logical, rational, and critical thinking. The scale correlates highly with the AVL Theoretical scale and moderately with the Kuder Science scale. It significantly distinguishes professional social scientists rated highly for their creativity and originality, university students who are superior at solving problems which require flexible and adaptive thinking, and graduate students rated highly by their professors for their effectiveness and potential as future scholars. In data to be published in the revised manual, this variable correlates with measures of critical thinking in the field of social science and scientific reasoning. It is highly correlated with the Guilford-Zimmerman Thoughtfulness measure, indicating an interest in logical, critical thinking, and with the Activities Index measures of need for Understanding and Scientism, although it does not correlate with the OAIS science interests measures. It correlates at least moderately with the SVIB Psychologist, Physician, Mathematician, Engineer, Chemist, and (negatively) with the various business scales such as Banker and Real Estate Sales. Reliability: .74 (KR 21); .81 (test-retest). 32 items.

Thinking Introversion (TI)

This scale measures liking for abstract, reflective thought and an

⁹ Center for the Study of Higher Education (1962), pp. 22, 34, 37.

interest in a variety of areas such as literature, art, and music. This scale correlates highly with the Literary score in the Kuder Preference Schedule, the AVL Aesthetic and (negatively) Economic scales, with the Guilford-Zimmerman Thoughtfulness scale, with the Understanding score in the Stern Activities Index, and with occupations emphasizing ideas and interpersonal relations rather than with business and other practical concerns in the Strong Vocational Interest Blank. It significantly distinguishes graduate students rated highly by their instructors for their "power of assimilation and logic" and "written performance." Reliability: .85 (KR 21); .94 (test-retest). 60 items.

Composition of Research Samples

1. *West Coast Sample*

   College of the Holy Names, California
   College of Notre Dame, California
   Immaculate Heart College, California
   St. Mary's College of California
   San Francisco State College, California
   University of California, Berkeley
   University of Portland, Oregon

2. *National Sample (Communities of Graduating High School Classes)*

   Altoona, Pennsylvania
   Bakersfield, California
   Danville, Illinois
   Eau Claire, Wisconsin
   Freeport, Illinois
   Hutchinson, Kansas
   Joplin, Missouri
   Kalamazoo, Michigan
   Lorain, Ohio
   Muncie, Indiana
   Port Huron, Michigan
   Racine, Wisconsin
   San Francisco, California
   South Bend, Indiana
   Springfield, Missouri
   Zanesville, Ohio

3. *College and University Environment Scales Sample (Participating Catholic Colleges)*

   Alverno College, Wisconsin
   Barry College, Florida
   De Paul University, Illinois

Dunbarton College of Holy Cross, District of Columbia
College of the Holy Cross, Massachusetts
College of Notre Dame of Maryland
College of St. Benedict, Minnesota
College of St. Catharine, Minnesota
La Salle College, Pennsylvania
Loyola College, Maryland
Loyola University, Illinois
Manhattanville College of the Sacred Heart, New York
Marian College, Indiana
Merrimack College, Massachusetts
Misericordia College, Pennsylvania
Mt. Saint Joseph-on-the-Ohio College, Ohio
Mt. St. Mary's College, California
Newton College of the Sacred Heart, Massachusetts
St. Bonaventure University, New York
St. Louis University, Missouri
St. Mary's College, Indiana
St. Norbert College, Wisconsin
St. Peter's College, New Jersey
St. Xavier College, Illinois
Seton Hall University, New Jersey
Seton Hill College, Pennsylvania
Spring Hill College, Alabama
University of Scranton, Pennsylvania
Villanova University, Pennsylvania
Webster College, Missouri
Xavier University, Ohio

4. *Supplementary Samples*

Claremont Graduate School, California
Merritt College, California
St. Olaf College, Minnesota
University of California, Los Angeles
University of Notre Dame, Indiana

APPENDIX C

Statistical Analyses of Mean Differences and Change Scores

Significance of Differences between Correlated Means

To determine the significance between correlated means (or, as in the present study, the difference in mean scores obtained by the same group of students at different time periods), the standard error of the difference between the correlated means must first be determined.[1] The expression for $^{\sigma}M_D$ may be expressed:

$$^{\sigma}M_D = \sqrt{^{\sigma}\overline{X}_1^{\,2} + {}^{\sigma}\overline{X}_2^{\,2} - {}^{2r}12\,{}^{\sigma}\overline{X}_1\,{}^{\sigma}\overline{X}_2}$$

where $\overline{X}_1$ equals the mean of the group's pretest, $\overline{X}_2$ equals its posttest mean, and N equals the number of subjects in the group. Confidence limits are then expressed in terms of this standard error:

$$(\overline{X}_1 - \overline{X}_2) + t_{\frac{1}{2}} \propto {}^{\sigma}M_D \sqrt{1/N}; \ (\overline{X}_1 - \overline{X}_2) - t_{\frac{1}{2}} \propto {}^{\sigma}M_D \sqrt{1/N}.$$

The t values above are determined for a desired level of significance from a t table using $(N-1)$ degrees of freedom.[2] The probability is $(1 - \propto)$ that the true difference, $\overline{X}_1 - \overline{X}_2$, lies within the interval specified by the limits. When the two limits are of opposite sign, we accept the assumption that the difference is zero; thus the difference between the two means is not significant. If, however, both limits have the same sign, then the value zero does not fall between these limits, indicating that there is a difference between the means. The null hypothesis that there is no difference can thus be rejected at a specified level of significance according to the value chosen for t.

Significance of Differences between the Change Scores[3]

In testing the significance of differences in mean changes in Omnibus

[1] See McNemar (1955), p. 83.

[2] Dixon and Massey (1957), p. 128.

[3] The derivation of the analysis of the significance of differences between change scores is the work of Dr. Manford Ferris of the American Institute of Research, Palo Alto, California.

TABLE 58. *Significance of Difference in Mean Differences Presented in Chapters 5 and 8*

Sample and Scale[a]	$(\overline{X}_1 - \overline{X}_2) - (\overline{Y}_1 - \overline{Y}_2)$	Lower Limit	Upper Limit	Decision at .05	Lower Limit	Upper Limit	Decision at .01
West Coast Sample	Catholic vs. secular Catholic						
TI	0.18	−2.29	+2.65	Not significant			
TO	0.04	−1.43	+1.51	Not significant			
Co	0.14	−1.25	+1.53	Not significant			
Es	0.56	−0.73	+1.85	Not significant			
Na	0.84	−0.18	+1.86	Not significant			
RL	−2.76	−4.85	−0.67	Significant	−5.52	0.00	Significant
	Catholic vs. non-Catholic						
TI	0.30	−1.10	+1.70	Not significant			
TO	0.60	−0.20	+1.40	Not significant			
Co	0.00	—	—	Not significant			
Es	0.50	−0.20	+1.20	Not significant			
Na	0.10	−0.40	+0.60	Not significant			
RL	−1.55	−2.27	−0.83	Significant	−2.50	−0.60	Significant
	Secular Catholic vs. non-Catholic						
TI	0.10	−2.30	+2.50	Not significant			
TO	0.60	−0.80	+2.00	Not significant			
Co	0.10	−1.30	+1.50	Not significant			
Es	0.00	—	—	Not significant			
Na	0.80	−0.20	+1.80	Not significant			
RL	1.21	−0.90	+3.32	Not significant			
National Merit Scholars	Catholic vs. non-Catholic						
TI	+1.37	−1.24	+3.98	Not significant			
Co	−0.02	−0.90	+0.86	Not significant			
Es	−0.30	−1.28	+0.68	Not significant			
Fa[b]	+0.93	+0.22	+1.64	Significant	0.00	+1.86	Significant
National Sample	Catholic vs. secular Catholic						
TI	−2.16	−4.20	−0.12	Significant	−4.84	+0.52	Not significant
Co	−1.16	−2.16	−0.16	Significant	−2.48	+0.16	Not significant
Na	−0.39	−1.10	+0.32	Not significant			
SM	−2.31	−3.78	−0.84	Significant	−4.25	−0.37	Significant

TABLE 58—*Continued*

Sample and Scale[a]	$(\bar{X}_1-\bar{X}_2) -$ $(\bar{Y}_1-\bar{Y}_2)$	Lower Limit	Upper Limit	Decision at .05	Lower Limit	Upper Limit	Decision at .01
National Sample (Cont'd)	Catholic *vs.* non-Catholic						
TI	+0.5	−1.2	+2.2	Not significant			
Co	+0.1	−0.7	+0.9	Not significant			
Na	+0.1	−0.4	+0.6	Not significant			
SM	−1.8	−3.0	−0.6	Significant	−3.3	−0.3	Significant
	Secular Catholic *vs.* non-Catholic						
TI	+2.6	+1.2	+4.0	Significant	+0.8	+4.4	Significant
Co	+1.1	+0.4	+1.8	Significant	+0.2	+2.0	Significant
Na	+0.5	0.0	+1.0	Significant	−0.1	+1.1	Not significant
SM	+0.5	−0.6	+1.6	Not significant			

[a] TI, Thinking Introversion
TO, Theoretical Orientation
Co, Complexity
Es, Estheticism
Na, Nonauthoritarianism
RL, Religious Liberalism
[b] The measure of authoritarianism (Fa) administered to the National Merit Scholar sample that was a version of the California F scale (see Adorno and associates, 1950) and was scored in the opposite direction from the Nonauthoritarianism scale.

Personality Inventory scores obtained by the groups under study (Table 58) as noted in chapters 5 and 8, formulas were combined from several sources.

Let $\bar{X}_1 =$ mean of pretest for group 1
$\bar{Y}_1 =$ mean of posttest for group 1
$\bar{X}_2 =$ mean of pretest for group 2
$\bar{Y}_2 =$ mean of posttest for group 2
$n_1 =$ number of subjects in group 1
$n_2 =$ number of subjects in group 2

Let $\hat{\Psi} = (\bar{Y}_1 - \bar{X}_1) - (\bar{Y}_2 - \bar{X}_2)$. (1)

The formula[4] for the variance of the difference between these two means is:

$$\text{var}(\hat{\Psi}) = \text{var}(\bar{Y}_1 - \bar{X}_1) + \text{var}(\bar{Y}_2 - \bar{X}_2).$$ (2)

[4] Garrett (1958), p. 214.

The variance, however, of $(\bar{Y}_1 - \bar{X}_1)$, and similarly of $(\bar{Y}_2 - \bar{X}_2)$, involves the variance of the difference of correlated means. This formula[5] is:

$$\text{var}(\bar{Y}_i - \bar{X}_i) = \text{var}(\bar{Y}_i) + \text{var}(\bar{X}_i) - 2\text{cov}(\bar{Y}_i, \bar{X}_i)$$

$$= \frac{{}^s\bar{Y}_i{}^2}{n_i} + \frac{{}^s\bar{X}_i{}^2}{n_i} - 2r_i\frac{{}^s\bar{Y}_i{}^s\bar{X}_i}{n_i}. \tag{3}$$

Substituting (3) in (2) and using number subscripts, we obtain:

$$\text{var}(\hat{\Psi}) = \left(\frac{{}^s\bar{Y}_1{}^2}{n_1} + \frac{{}^s\bar{X}_1{}^2}{n_1} - 2r_1\frac{{}^s\bar{Y}_1{}^s\bar{X}_1}{n_1}\right) + \left(\frac{{}^s\bar{Y}_2{}^2}{n_2} + \frac{{}^s\bar{X}_2{}^2}{n_2} - 2r_2\frac{{}^s\bar{Y}_2{}^s\bar{X}_2}{n_2}\right).$$

Confidence levels[6] for $\hat{\Psi}$ with $n_1 + n_2 - 2$ degrees of freedom are:

$$\hat{\Psi} - t_{(\alpha/2, dt)} \sqrt{\text{var}(\hat{\Psi})} \text{ and } \hat{\Psi} + t_{(\alpha/2, dt)} \sqrt{\text{var}(\hat{\Psi})}.$$

When these two confidence limits are the same in sign, the value zero which would indicate no difference between the means of the change scores for the two groups does not fall between these limits, and we can thus reject the hypothesis of no difference at the level of significance chosen for t. When these limits are opposite in sign, we fail to reject the hypothesis that the difference between means of the change scores is zero, in other words, observed difference is not significant.

[5] Garrett (1958), p. 226.
[6] Hays (1963), pp. 314–21.

Construction of the Religious Practices Index

and of the Religious Concepts Inventory

Religious Practices Index (RPI)

This index represents a special coding and scoring of a cluster of six items in the student questionnaire devised by the author and administered to the West Coast Sample. It was designed to measure the degree to which a person practices his religion, apart from his religious attitudes or beliefs. As noted in chapter 8, the items assess the following: (1) frequency of church attendance; (2) comparison of the person's faith with his parents'; (3) frequency with which the person would attend church if under no obligation to do so; (4) frequency with which the person commits breaches against the tenets of his faith; (5) practice of the person's religious tenets compared to his friends'; (6) the extent of the person's disagreement with the dogmas of his religion.

A score between 1 and 3 has been assigned to each of the 6 Religious Practices Index item responses according to the schedule that may be found in Table 59. The most religious responses in respect to report of practices are scored 3; moderate or middle responses are 2; the least self-reports of religious practices are scored 1. The simple addition of the item scores constitutes the total score, with a range of 6 to 18.

The rationale behind the Religious Practices Index is that a summary measure of the extent of various religious practices constitutes more of an index of overall religious involvement in this sense than does the reliance upon a single item such as frequency of church attendance. This should be particularly the case in respect to Catholics whose weekly church attendance is obligatory according to church precept. This rationale appears justified by the item intercorrelations obtained by the Catholic college students and a sample of junior college students which may be found in Table 60. The items are more related to the total Religious Practices Index score than they are to one another, indicating that they represent distinct practices while contributing to a more comprehensive measurement of religious practices. And, as might be expected, Catholic students' feeling that they would attend church regularly, regardless of sanction, is more related to the total score than is their actual attendance.

TABLE 59. *Scoring System for Items Composing the Religious Practices Index*

Item	Response	Score
1. Your average attendance at religious services	Once a week or more	3
	Once a month or so	2
	Once or twice a year or less	1
2. Your religious faith compared to your parents'	More religious than they	3
	About as religious	2
	Less religious than they	1
3. Average attendance at religious services if left completely up to you	Once a week or more	3
	Once a month or so	2
	Once or twice a year or less	1
4. Frequency you feel you commit serious breaches against the moral tenets of your faith	Seldom or rarely	3
	Occasionally	2
	Frequently	1
5. The practices of the moral tenets of your faith compared to your friends'	More faithful than they	3
	The same as they	2
	Less faithful than they	1
6. Amount you seriously disagree with the principal dogmas of your religion	In no respects	3
	In some or a few respects	2
	In many respects	1

Total RPI score equals summation of item scores. Range: 6–18 points

Religious Practices Index validity data are not available other than through the findings of the present study. The Religious Practices Index correlates with two other religious scales, the Religious Liberalism scale of the Omnibus Personality Inventory and the Religious Concepts Inventory, discussed below (see Table 61). It also distinguishes Catholic and non-Catholic students attending Catholic colleges from those attending a public junior college (see Table 35).

The reliability coefficient, estimated on interitem correlations, is .73 for both the Catholic college students and approximately 100 junior college students used as a comparison group. Considering the minimal number of the items constituting this scale, and the deliberately heterogeneous nature of these items, the reliability of the Religious Practices Index would appear to be quite adequate. Nevertheless, this effort represents only a crude scale which might benefit greatly by elaboration and refinement of items. A particularly difficult task in this respect would be devising items of comparable meaning to persons of various religious faiths.

TABLE 60. *Religious Practices Index Item and Total Score Intercorrelations Obtained by West Coast Catholic College Students Shown with Item-total Score Correlations of Public Junior College Students*

	Catholic College Intercorrelations ($N = 1,174$)							Jr. College Item-total r's ($N=98$)
	1 Attnd	2 Par	3 Vol	4 Breach	5 Frien	6 Disag	Total	Total
1. Average attendance	1.00	.11	.51	.03	.14	.27	.53	.75
2. Faith compared to parents'		1.00	.17	.12	.10	.07	.53	.60
3. Voluntary attendance			1.00	.17	.19	.24	.64	.83
4. Breaches of tenets				1.00	.25	.17	.58	.22
5. Comparison to friends					1.00	.27	.53	.50
6. Disagree with dogmas						1.00	.48	.41
Total							1.00	1.00
r_{tt} (Spearman-Brown item-total estimate)							.73	.73

TABLE 61. *Intercorrelations of the Religious Liberalism, Religious Practices Index, and Religious Concepts Inventory Scales Obtained by 1,350 Catholic College Students, West Coast Sample*

Scale	RPI	RCI
RL		
Men	−.49	−.66
Women	−.29	−.40
Total	−.43	−.60
RPI		
Men		.44
Women		.18
Total		.36

Religious Concepts Inventory (RCI)[1]

The purpose of this inventory is to gauge religious attitudes as they are actually expressed; that is, in reference to specific religious con-

[1] This scale was devised by Dr. Elwin Farwell of Luther College, Decorah, Iowa, and James Trent. Dr. Roger Cummings, San Francisco State College, contributed several of the original items and subsequent validity data. His assistance is gratefully acknowledged.

cepts and feelings, beyond the general response of "favorableness" or "unfavorableness." Through the combined measurement of six sub-scales, the Religious Concepts Inventory indicates the person's position along a continuum from fundamentalist religious belief through liberalism to fundamentalist disbelief. The inventory may be found at the conclusion of Appendix D, p. 334.

A pool of nearly 250 items was assembled to reflect the different religious orientations. The items were derived from several sources: (1) the authors' knowledge of several sectarian theologies; (2) their contact with ministers from other religious sects as well as acquaintances alien to any religious sect; (3) their canvassing of the feelings and expressions of religious convictions of persons representing the gamut of religious attitude and orientation. This pool of items was reduced to a true-false questionnaire of 151 items and was administered in two sessions to over 200 students evenly distributed among the 5 criterion groups by their own report (inscribed by them on the inventory) and by the judgment of the test administrators.

Of the original 151 items, 55 were selected as most differentiating among the criterion groups on the basis of an item analysis. The minimum basis of an item selection was a 40 to 60 per cent contrast between extreme group responses. Forty-two of these items were then arranged after the Thurstone technique according to a fundamentalist-liberalism continuum on the 6 subject-content subscales of: (1) Bible; (2) Prayer; (3) Man; (4) God; (5) Sin; (6) Eternity. Each subscale contains seven items, only one of which is to be checked.

For each subscale a response to the most fundamentalist response in the direction of religious belief is scored 7. Depending on the alternating order of the subscale items, the item just preceding or just following the most fundamentalist-religious item is scored 6. Each preceding or subsequent item is scored a point less than its adjacent item more religious in orientation. The most fundamentalist response in the direction of non-belief is scored 1. Thus the score for each subscale ranges from 1 to 7. The total score used for analysis is comprised of the sum of the 6 subscale scores and therefore ranges from a possible 6 to 42.

The subscale items were arranged on the basis of the judgments of the authors and several staff members at the Center for Research and Development in Higher Education. These subscale arrangements were then matched against the judgments of eleven additional staff members at the Center. The mean rank difference correlation between the two groups of judgments may be found in Table 62, together with the mean rater coefficients for each scale indicating the amount of agreement among the second group of judges exclusively. The *rho* coefficients range from .93 to 1.00; the mean rater coefficients range from .65 to .88. All of the judges were either research psychologists or sociologists or graduate students with considerable training in these disciplines.

In addition to the materials presented in chapter 8, through research, as yet unpublished, at the Center for Research and Development in Higher Education, there is repeated evidence that the Religious Concepts Inventory distinguishes fundamentalist, orthodox, liberally religious, and liberally non-religious groups. A rank difference correlation

TABLE 62. Rho *Coefficients, Eleven Judges'* vs. *Scored Religious Concepts Inventory Ranking of Items, and Mean Judge Correlations Indicating Amount of Agreement among Judges on Arrangement of Items, by Subscale*

Subscale	*Rho*, Mean Raters' vs. Scored Rank	Mean Rater Coefficient
Bible	.96	.87
Prayer	.96	.86
Man	.93	.82
God	.96	.88
Sin	.93	.65
Eternity	1.00	.85

of .91 was obtained for 15 groups of seminarians and various college freshman classes ranked according to their fundamentalist-liberal mean position on the Religious Concepts Inventory and to a measurement of authoritarianism. Religious conservatism measured by the Religious Concepts Inventory has also been found to be highly related to conservatism in artistic taste and to conservative, authoritarian beliefs.[2] The RCI also correlates with the Religious Liberalism and Religious Practices Index scales (Table 61).

Religious Concepts Inventory reliability coefficients computed for various college groups including those in the present study have ranged between .89 and .93 (KR 21). In Table 63 may be found the subscale and total score intercorrelations for approximately 900 freshmen participating in the Study of Selected Institutions conducted at the Center for Research and Development in Higher Education. These correlations indicate an interrelationship among the 6 subscales. However, the correlations do not appear to warrant the use of one subscale in place of another or the use of any one subscale in place of the total inventory.

[2] Roy (1961).

TABLE 63. *Intercorrelations of Subscale and Total Religious Concepts Inventory Scores Obtained by a Random Sample of Freshmen Enrolled in Several Private and Public Colleges, Fall, 1958*

	Bible	Prayer	Man	God	Sin	Eternity	Total
Men (N = 608)							
Bible	1.00	.60	.61	.63	.62	.63	.82
Prayer		1.00	.54	.72	.61	.65	.83
Man			1.00	.63	.57	.56	.79
God				1.00	.60	.72	.86
Sin					1.00	.65	.82
Eternity						1.00	.85
Total							1.00
Women (N = 282)							
Bible	1.00	.53	.54	.50	.49	.55	.75
Prayer		1.00	.57	.70	.60	.63	.83
Man			1.00	.60	.50	.57	.79
God				1.00	.58	.65	.84
Sin					1.00	.54	.79
Eternity						1.00	.83
Total							1.00

RELIGIOUS CONCEPTS INVENTORY

INSTRUCTIONS: Please check only *one* major definition within each of the six major concepts listed below. Select the statement that most nearly agrees with your attitude regarding that concept. Place an X in the space to the left of the statement that you select in each group of seven. *Mark your responses on this sheet.*

A. *The Bible*

___ 1. The Bible is inconsistent, contradictory and exaggerated in value.
___ 2. The Bible is a collection of myths.
___ 3. The Bible is a great literary work expressing religious philosophy.
___ 4. The Bible is valuable because of its inspirational effect.
___ 5. The Bible is an account of man's experiences with God.
___ 6. The Bible is God's revelation written by inspired men.
___ 7. The Bible was dictated by God through the hand of man and is infallible.

B. *Prayer*

___ 1. Prayer is a direct approach to God which will always bring results if there is enough faith.
___ 2. Prayer is communication with God.
___ 3. Prayer is a means of bringing man into a proper relationship with God.
___ 4. Prayer may be communion with God but how it is effected is not understood.
___ 5. Prayer is a means of relieving anxiety.
___ 6. Prayer can be equated with strong wishes or desires.
___ 7. Prayer is only a superstitious practice.

C. *Man*

___ 1. Man represents no more than the highest order of evolution.

___ 2. Man is a biological organism with distinctive powers of memory and rational thought.

___ 3. Man is a psychological organism with spiritual needs.

___ 4. The nature and significance of man are not determinable.

___ 5. Man has both a body and a soul with the soul being the more essential.

___ 6. Man is the created object of God's love.

___ 7. Man is a descendant of Adam who was created from the dust of the earth.

D. *God*

___ 1. God is our creator and judge who observes everything that we do.

___ 2. God exists as a divine being.

___ 3. God exists as a supernatural power beyond man's comprehension.

___ 4. God probably exists but no one knows what he is like.

___ 5. The concept of God is a means of explaining the unknown.

___ 6. God is a projection of man's unconscious mind.

___ 7. There is no supernatural being.

E. *Sin*

___ 1. Sin is a religious concept used to create guilt feelings in man.

___ 2. Sin consists of behavior which is not culturally approved.

___ 3. Sin consists of a violation of the rights of others.

___ 4. Sin is a violation of one's conscience.

___ 5. Sin is a denial of our best nature.

___ 6. Sin consists of any thought, word or deed that interferes with a proper relationship to God.

___ 7. Sin consists of a willful participation in worldly acts that transgress Divine Law.

F. *Eternity*

___ 1. After physical death there will be a judgment in which each man is sent to heaven or hell.

___ 2. All men will some day be responsible for their relationship to God.

___ 3. Heaven and hell are symbols of our relationship to God after physical death.

___ 4. Probably man does not have a separate identity after death, yet he participates in a kind of immortality.

___ 5. Man's immortality consists in the influence that he leaves behind him at death.

___ 6. The concept of eternity is a manifestation of man's fear of death.

___ 7. Our present life constitutes the whole of our existence.

REFERENCES

Academic Senate, University of California, Berkeley. 1966. *Education at Berkeley, Report of the Select Committee on Education.* Berkeley: University of California Printing Department.

Adolfs, R. 1966. *The Church Is Different.* New York: Harper and Row.

Adorno, T. W., Fenkel-Brunswik, Else, Levinson, D. J., and Sanford, R. N. 1950. *The Authoritarian Personality.* New York: Harper.

Allen, M. K. 1955. Personality and Cultural Factors Related to Religious Authoritarianism. Doctoral dissertation, Stanford University, abstracted in *Dissertation Abstracts* 15:2324.

Allport, G. W., Vernon, P. E., and Lindzey, G. 1951. *Study of Values.* Rev. ed. Cambridge: Houghton Mifflin.

America. 1958. 98:590.

Astin, A. W. 1962. "Productivity" of Undergraduate Institutions. *Science* 13:129.

————. 1965. *Who Goes Where to College?* Chicago: Science Research Associates.

Astin, A. W. and Holland, J. L. 1961. Environmental Assessment Technique: A Way to Measure College Environment. *Journal of Educational Psychology* 52:308.

————. 1962. Distribution of "Wealth" in Higher Education. *College and University* Winter:113.

Ave Maria. 1966. The Silenced Priests. 103(2):2.

Becker, C. 1964. Consequences of Different Kinds of Parental Discipline. In *Review of Child Development Research,* M. L. Hoffman and Lois W. Hoffman. Vol. 1. New York: Russell Sage Foundation.

Bendig, A. W. 1956. The Development of a Short Form of the Manifest Anxiety Scale. *Journal of Consulting Psychology* 20:384.

Berelson, B. 1960. *Graduate Education in the United States.* New York: McGraw-Hill.

Berelson, B. and Steiner, G. 1964. *Human Behavior: An Inventory of Scientific Findings.* New York: Harcourt, Brace and World.

Blake, E. C. 1966. The Right to Break Unjust Laws. *San Francisco Chronicle,* February 19, p. 31.

337

Bland, Joan. 1959. Education for Dialogue. *Commonweal* 71:12.

Bogue, D. J. 1959. *The Population of the United States.* Glencoe, Ill.: Free Press.

Borromeo, Mary Charles (ed.). 1967. *The New Nuns.* New York: New American Library.

Broen, W. E. 1955. Personality Correlates of Certain Religious Attitudes. *Journal of Consulting Psychology* 19:64.

Brown, F. G. 1959. Measured Personality Characteristics of Liberal Arts College Freshmen. Doctoral dissertation, University of Minnesota, abstracted in *Dissertation Abstracts* 19:3009.

Butler, R. 1965. The End of the Newman Club. *Commonweal* 82:627.

Callahan, D. 1963. *Mind of the Catholic Layman.* New York: Charles Scribner's Sons.

————. 1965a. *Honesty in the Church.* New York: Charles Scribner's Sons.

————. 1966. Ethics and Evidence. *Commonweal* 85:76.

———— (ed.). 1965b. *Generation of the Third Eye.* New York: Sheed and Ward.

Cartter, A. M. 1966. *An Assessment of Quality in Graduate Education.* Washington, D. C.: American Council on Education.

Cass, J. 1967. Fordham University: Renaissance in the Bronx. *Saturday Review*, June 17, p. 52.

Catholic Voice. 1964. Oakland, California, August 14, p. 6.

Ibid. 1966. June 16, p. 8.

Center for the Study of Higher Education. 1960. *A Multiple Scale Inventory for Use with College Populations.* Berkeley: Center for Research and Development in Higher Education, University of California.

————. 1962. *Omnibus Personality Inventory—Research Manual.* Berkeley: Center for Research and Development in Higher Education, University of California.

Chardin, T. de. 1962. Letter written on board the *Cathay*, September 14, 1935, to his brother Joseph. In *Letters from a Traveller*, ed. B. Wall. New York: Harper & Brothers.

Christ, F. and Sherry, G. 1961. *American Catholicism and the Intellectual Ideal.* New York: Appleton-Century-Crofts.

Christie, R., Havel, J., and Seidenberg, B. 1960. Is the F Scale Irreversible? *Journal of Abnormal and Social Psychology* 60:151.

Coffey, W. 1963. Jesuit Education: Between Two Worlds. *Ramparts* 1 (5):10.

Cogley, J. 1963. Catholicism on the Campus. *Commonweal* 78:88.

————. 1966. Catholic Education—After the Council. *National Catholic Educational Association Bulletin* 63(1):49.

Cole, D. 1965. The Limbo of Minds Without Voices. In *Generation of the Third Eye*, ed. D. Callahan. New York: Sheed and Ward.

Commager, H. S. 1950. *The American Mind.* New Haven: Yale University Press.

Comment. 1966. Immaculate Heart College, September 26.

Commonweal. 1964. 80:223.

Ibid. 1966. 83:572.

Ibid. 84:44.

Ibid. 85:5.

Cox, H. 1965. *The Secular City.* New York: Macmillan.

Cross, R. D. 1958. *The Emergence of Liberal Catholicism in America.* Cambridge: Harvard University Press.

Curley, T. 1965. World War II: Dividing Line. In *Generation of the Third Eye,* ed. D. Callahan. New York: Sheed and Ward.

Dahlstrom, W. G. and Welsh, G. S. 1960. *An MMPI Handbook.* Minneapolis: University of Minnesota Press.

Darley, J. G. 1962. *Promise and Performance.* Berkeley: Center for Research and Development in Higher Education, University of California.

Davids, A. 1955. Some Personality and Intellectual Correlates of Intolerance of Ambiguity. *Journal of Abnormal and Social Psychology* 51:415.

Davis, Beverly. 1953. Eminence and Level of Social Origin. *American Journal of Sociology* 59:11.

Davis, Helen E. 1949. *On Getting into College.* Washington: American Council on Education.

Davis, J. A. 1964. *Great Aspirations.* Chicago: Aldine.

Dawson, C. 1959. Catholic Culture in America. *Critic* 17 (6):7.

―――――. 1961. Building a Bridge to Secular Culture. *Catholic World* 193:86.

Deedy, J. G., Jr. 1965. The Catholic Press. *Commonweal* 81:666.

Dewart, L. 1966. The Celibacy Problem. *Commonweal* 84:146.

Dixon, J. D. and Massey, F. J. 1957. *Introduction to Statistical Analysis.* New York: McGraw-Hill.

Donovan, J. D. 1964. *The Academic Man in the Catholic College.* New York: Sheed and Ward.

Downtowner. 1966. St. John's University, October 28.

Dreger, R. M. 1952. Some Personality Correlates of Religious Attitudes as Determined by Projective Techniques. *Psychological Monographs* 66(3): (Whole No. 335).

Dressel, P. L. 1959. *Critical Thinking, Attitudes and Values in Higher Education (Preliminary Report).* East Lansing: Michigan State University.

Drummond, E. J. 1956. The Spirit of Scholarship. *National Catholic Educational Association Bulletin* 53:64.

Dubay, W. H. 1966. *The Human Church.* New York: Doubleday.

Dunne, W. J. 1960. Personnel Policies for Sister College Teachers.

National Catholic Educational Association Bulletin 57:158.

Ederer, R. J. 1960. The Poor Professor. *Commonweal* 73:34.

Educational Reviewer. 1963. *A Survey of the Political and Religious Attitudes of American College Students.* New York.

Edwards, A. L. 1957. *The Social Desirability Variable in Personality Assessment and Research.* New York: Dryden.

Ellinger, R. 1965. Newman Jamboree. *Commonweal* 82:682.

Ellis, J. T. 1955. American Catholics and the Intellectual Life. *Thought* 30:351.

———. 1956a. American Catholics and the Intellectual Life—Some Reactions. *National Catholic Educational Association Bulletin.* 53:105.

———. 1956b. The American Catholic and the Intellectual Life. In *The Catholic Church, U. S. A.,* ed. L. J. Putz. Chicago: Fides Publishers.

———. 1960. American Catholicism in 1960: A Historical Perspective. *American Benedictine Review* March-June, 1.

———. 1962. The Catholic Layman in America Today. *Commonweal* 76:319.

———. 1965. Religion on the Secular Campus: A Prime Responsibility. *Southern California Quarterly* 47:357.

Emmet, T. A. 1965. *Proposal for a Center on Research and Development for Jesuit Higher Education in the United States and a Prospectus for Some Priority Studies to be Undertaken in 1966–1967.* Mimeographed. Commission on Higher Education, Jesuit Education Association.

Evans, J. W. 1967. Catholic Higher Education on the Secular Campus. *The Shape of Catholic Higher Education,* ed. R. Hassenger. Chicago: University of Chicago Press.

Farwell, E. D. and Warren, J. R. 1959. *Student Personality Characteristics Associated with Types of Colleges and Fields of Study.* Mimeographed. Berkeley: Center for Research and Development in Higher Education, University of California.

FitzGerald, P. A. 1966. Catholic Graduate Schools. *America* 115:510.

Flanagan, J. C., Davis, F. B., Dailey, J. T., Shaycoft, M. F., Orr, D. B., Goldberg, I., and Neyman, C. A. Jr. 1964. *The American High School Student.* Pittsburgh: University of Pittsburgh.

Fleming, T. J. 1963. The Crisis in Catholic Schools. *Saturday Evening Post* 236(37):19.

Fletcher, J. 1966. Love Is the Only Measure. *Commonweal* 83:427.

Ford, C. E. and Roy, E. L. Jr. 1966. *Study of Catholic Higher Education—A Working Paper.* Advisory Committee, National Catholic Educational Association.

Foster, J., Stanek, R., and Krassowski, W. 1961. *The Impact of a Value-Oriented University on Student Attitudes and Thinking.* Mimeographed. Santa Clara, California: University of Santa Clara, & Cooperative Research Project No. 729, Office of Education, Department of Health, Education & Welfare.

Freedman, M. B., Webster, H., and Sanford, N. 1955. Some Psychodynamic Correlates of Authoritarianism in Women. *American Psychologist.* 10:341.

Fricke, B. G. 1963. *Opinion, Attitude and Interest Survey.* Ann Arbor, Mich. OAIS Testing Program.

Fry, L. C. 1933. Religious Affiliation of American Leaders. *Science Monthly* 36:241.

Fugate, G. 1964. Where Are You Going? *America* 110:673.

Gallagher, M. A. 1957. A Study of the Concept of Discipline in the Field of Guidance. *Catholic Educational Review* 55:263.

Garrett, H. E. 1958. *Statistics in Psychology and Education.* New York: Longmans and Green.

Getlein, F. 1964. *The Trouble with Catholics.* Baltimore: Helicon.

Glass, G. J. 1961. Present Status of the Lay Teacher in Catholic Elementary Schools of Ohio. Master's thesis, Catholic University of America, abstracted in *Catholic Educational Review* 59:51.

Glazer, N. and Moynihan, D. P. 1963. *Beyond the Melting Pot.* Cambridge, Mass.: M. I. T. Press.

Glock, C. Y. 1959. The Religious Revival in America? In *Religion and the Face of America,* ed. Jane Zahn. Berkeley: University of California.

———. 1962. On the Study of Religious Commitment. *Religious Education, Research Supplement* 57:98.

Glock, C. Y. and Stark, R. 1966. *Christian Beliefs and Anti-Semitism.* New York: Harper and Row.

Goldberg, S. and Stern, G. G. 1952. The Authoritarian Personality and General Education. *American Psychologist* 7:375.

Gough, H. G. 1964. *Manual for the California Psychological Inventory.* Rev. ed. Palo Alto, California: Consulting Psychologists.

Greeley, A. M. 1962a. Catholic Scholars of Tomorrow. *Critic* 20 (5):24.

———. 1962b. The Influence of Religion on the Career Plans and Occupational Values of June, 1961, College Graduates. Doctoral dissertation, University of Chicago.

———. 1963. *Religion and Career.* New York: Sheed and Ward.

Greeley, A. M. and Rossi, P. H. 1966. *The Education of Catholic Americans.* Chicago: Aldine.

Gregory, W. E. 1952. The Psychology of Religion: Some Suggested Areas of Research of Significance to Psychology. *Journal of Abnormal and Social Psychology* 47:256.

———. 1955a. Authoritarianism and Authority. *Journal of Abnormal and Social Psychology* 51:641.

———. 1955b. Doctrine and Attitude. A Study of the Relationship between Religious Doctrines and Socio-Political-Economic Attitudes. Doctoral dissertation, University of Chicago.

Gremillion, J. 1964. *The Other Dialogue.* New York: Doubleday.

Gremma, Mary. 1959. No More Discipline Worries. *Catholic School Journal* 59:37.

Gropper, G. L. and Fitzpatrick, R. 1959. *Who Goes to Graduate School?* Pittsburgh: American Institute for Research.

Halton, T. 1961. The Priest as Critic. *Catholic World* 193:100.

Handlin, O. 1951. *The Uprooted.* New York: Grosset and Dunlap.

Hathaway, S. R. and McKinley, J. C. 1951. *Manual for the Minnesota Multiphasic Personality Inventory.* Rev. ed. New York: Psychological Corporation.

Hays, W. L. 1963. *Statistics for Psychologists.* New York: Holt, Rinehart and Winston.

Hazo, S. (ed.). 1963. *The Christian Intellectual: Studies in the Relation of Catholicism to the Human Sciences.* Pittsburgh: Duquesne University Press.

Heiss, Ann M. 1964. *Berkeley Doctoral Students Appraise Their Academic Programs.* Mimeographed. Berkeley: Center for Research and Development in Higher Education, University of California.

Heist, P. and Yonge, G. 1962. *Over- and Under-Productive Institutions.* Mimeographed. Berkeley: Center for Research and Development in Higher Education, University of California.

Herberg, W. 1960a. *Protestant, Catholic, Jew: An Essay in American Religious Sociology.* New York: Doubleday Anchor.

———. 1960b. Religion and Culture Today. *Commonweal* 71:667.

Herzfeld, Norma K. 1964. What's Wrong with Commonweal. *Commonweal* 80:293.

Highbough, Mary Assunta. 1961. An Analysis of the Teacher Education Program of the Benedictine Sisters in the U. S. *Catholic Educational Review* 59:404.

Hofstadter, R. 1964. *Anti-Intellectualism in American Life.* New York: Knopf.

Holland, H. K. 1959. What Public and Parochial Teachers Can Learn From Each Other. *Catholic Educational Review* 57:227.

Holland, J. L. 1957. Undergraduate Origins of American Scientists. *Science* 126:433.

Honingmann, J. J. 1954. *Culture and Personality.* New York: Harper.

Hruby, N. 1966. *Comparative Tabulations: One Possible Interpretation.* Chicago: Mundelein College.

Hyman, H. H. 1955. *Survey Design and Analysis.* Glencoe, Ill.: Free Press.

Jackson, D. N., Messick, S. J., and Solley, C. M. 1957. How Rigid Is the Authoritarian? *Journal of Abnormal and Social Psychology* 54:137.

Jacob, P. E. 1957. *Changing Values in College.* New York: Harper.

————. 1958. Does Higher Education Influence Student Values? *National Education Association Journal* 47:35.

Jacobs, W. J. 1964. New Things and Old Catholics. *Ave Maria* 99 (24):18.

Justin, Mary. 1957. An Ideal Classroom: A Surpervisor's Dream. *Catholic School Journal* 57:28.

Kane, J. J. 1955. *Catholic-Protestant Conflicts in America.* Chicago: Regnery.

Kastner, M. A. 1958. Some Practical Suggestions on Maintaining Discipline. *Catholic Educational Review* 56:476.

Kavanaugh, J. 1967. *A Modern Priest Looks at His Outdated Church.* New York: Trident Press.

Keating, E. M. 1963. Jesuit Education: A Layman's View. *Ramparts* 1(5):6.

————. 1965. *The Scandal of Silence.* New York: Random House.

Kelley, D. 1959. Use of Critical Wit in the Classroom. *Catholic Educational Review* 57:599.

Kelley, G. A. 1946. Catholics and the Practice of the Faith. Doctoral dissertation, Catholic University of America.

Kennedy, Mary. 1961. Faculty of Catholic Colleges for Women. *Catholic Educational Review* 59:280.

Kenniston, H. 1957. *Graduate Study in the Humanities.* Education Survey, University of Pennsylvania.

Khanna, J. L. 1957. A Study of the Relationship between Some Aspects of Personality and Certain Aspects of Religious Beliefs. Doctoral dissertation, University of Colorado, abstracted in *Dissertation Abstracts* 17:2696.

Kilduff, T. 1966. Presenting to Major Seminarians the Meaning of Celibacy in the Priesthood. *National Catholic Educational Association Bulletin* 63:75.

Kinnane, Mary. 1963. Catholic Students' Attitudes toward College Authority. *Catholic Educational Review* 61:294.

Kinsolving, L. 1966. The Religious World. *San Francisco Chronicle,* December 10, p. 33.

Kirvan, J. J. 1964. Newman and a New Era. *Ave Maria* 100(9):14.

Knapp, R. H. and Goodrich, H. G. 1952. *Origins of American Scientists.* Chicago: University of Chicago Press.

Knapp, R. H. and Greenbaum, J. J. 1953. *The Younger American Scholar: His Collegiate Origins.* Chicago: University of Chicago Press.

Kuder, G. F. 1957. *Manual for Kuder Preference Record—Vocational.* Chicago: Science Research Associates.

Küng, H. 1963. The Church and Freedom. *Commonweal* 78:343.

Kunkel, B. W. and Prentice, D. B. 1951. Colleges in *Who's Who in America. School and Society* 74:241.

Lally, F. J. 1959. The Function of the Catholic Press. *Catholic Mind* 57:421.

Lawler, J. G. 1959. *The Catholic Dimension in Higher Education.* Westminister, Md.: Newman Press.

Lazarsfeld, P. F. and Thielens, W. Jr. 1958. *The Academic Mind.* Glencoe, Ill.: Free Press.

Leavitt, H. J., Hax, H., and Roche, J. H. 1955. Authoritarianism and Agreement with Things Authoritative. *Journal of Psychology* 40:215.

Leclercq, J. 1961. *The Love of Learning and the Desire for God.* New York: Fordham University Press.

Lee, J. M. 1961. Professional Criticism of Catholic High Schools. *Catholic World* 194(1159):7.

―――――. 1965. Overview of Educational Problems in Seminaries. In *Seminary Education in a Time of Change,* eds. J. M. Lee and L. Putz. Notre Dame: Fides Publishers.

Lee, J. M. and Putz, L. 1965. Afterword. In *Seminary Education in a Time of Change,* eds. J. M. Lee and L. Putz. Notre Dame: Fides Publishers.

Lehmann, I. J. 1960. Some Socio-Cultural Differences in Attitude and Values. Paper presented at the Annual Meeting of the American Psychological Association.

Lehmann, I. J. and Dressel, P. L. 1962. *Critical Thinking, Attitudes, and Values in Higher Education.* Cooperative Research Project no. 590. East Lansing, Mich.: Michigan State University.

―――――. 1963. *Changes in Critical Thinking, Ability, Attitudes, and Values Associated with College Attendance.* Cooperative Research Project no. 1646. East Lansing, Mich.: Michigan State University.

Levinson, D. J. and Schermerhorn, R. A. 1951. Emotional-Attitudinal Effects of an Inter-Group Relations Workshop on Its Members. *Journal of Psychology* 31:243.

Litzinger, B. 1961. Multiplication and Division. *Commonweal* 74:37.

Long, Mary. 1956. Survey of Discipline Problems in the Elementary School. *Catholic Educational Review* 54:217.

Luke, Mary. 1965. The Council and Sisters' Renewal. *The Catholic World* 201(1201):41.

McAvoy, T. T. (ed.). 1960. *Roman Catholicism and the American Way of Life.* Notre Dame: University of Notre Dame.

―――――. 1963. The Composition of the Catholic Minority Today. *Notre Dame* 16:15.

McCabe, H. 1966. The Validity of Absolutes. *Commonweal* 83:432.

McCarthy, T. N. 1965. Are They All Made Out of Ticky-tacky? *Catholic Psychological Record* 3:1.

McCluskey, N. G. 1958. Catholic Education's New Look. *America* 99:574.

McDonald, D. 1956. Teaching the Teachers. *Commonweal* 64:345.

—————. 1960. Can We Keep on Paying for Catholic Schools? *America* 102:760.

McDonald, G. E. 1959. Some Starting Points in Reforming American Catholic Education. *Catholic Educational Review* 57:526.

McDonnell, K. 1960. After Four Centuries. *America* 103:13.

McDowell, J. M. 1960. Challenge to Catholic Education. *National Catholic Educational Association Bulletin* 57:223.

McGlade, J. 1953. *Progressive Educators and the Catholic Church.* Westminister, Md.: Newman Press.

Mackin, T. 1961. Does Controversy Belong on Campus? *Santa Claran* 10(1):3.

McNamara, R. J. 1963. The Interplay of Intellectual and Religious Values. Doctoral dissertation, Cornell University.

—————. 1964. Intellectual Values: Campus and Seminary. *Sociological Analysis* 25:200.

—————. 1965. *Profile of Student Attitudes and Values: A Comparative Study.* Jesuit Education Association Workshop.

McNamee, M. B. 1961. American Catholic Apathy to Art. *Catholic World* 192:352.

McNemar, Q. 1955. *Psychological Statistics.* New York: John Wiley and Sons.

Maguire, J. J. 1961. A Family Affair. *Commonweal* 75:171.

Majella, Mary. 1962. Enriched Program for Liberal Arts Students. *Junior College Journal* 33:100.

Mangan, T. P. 1966. Fostering an Intellectual Atmosphere in the Minor Seminary. *National Catholic Educational Association Bulletin* 63:173.

Mannion, J. B. 1966. A Dull New Day. *Commonweal* 84:519.

Martin, W. B. 1967. The Will To Be Different. *Saturday Review,* January 21, p. 68.

Maynard, T. 1960. *The Story of American Catholicism.* Garden City, N. Y.: Doubleday.

Medsker, L. L., and Trent, J. W. 1965. *The Influence of Different Types of Public Higher Institutions on College Attendance from Varying Socioeconomic and Ability Levels.* Berkeley: Center for Research and Development in Higher Education, University of California.

Mills, J. A. 1964. Faculties of Roman Catholic Colleges, 1948–1962. *National Catholic Educational Association Bulletin* 61(2):13.

Muckenhirn, Charles (ed.). 1965. *The Changing Sister.* Notre Dame: Fides Publishers.

Murphy, F. X. 1964. Vatican II Needs a New Approach. *Catholic Mind* 62(1182):25.

Mussen, P. H., Conger, J. J., and Kagan, J. 1956. *Child Development and Personality*. New York: Harper.

Myers, G. 1960. *History of Bigotry in the United States*. New York: Capricorn.

Myers, Isabel B. and Briggs, Katharine C. 1962. *Manual for the Myers–Briggs Type Indicator*. Princeton, N. J.: Educational Testing Service.

Nale, Mary A. 1961. Present Status of Lay Teachers in Selected High Schools in Pennsylvania. Master's thesis, Catholic University of America, abstracted in *Catholic Educational Review* 59:123.

National Catholic Reporter, Kansas City, Missouri, October, 1965 to August, 1967.

Neel, Ann. 1962. Asking Questions and Giving Answers: Two Approaches to the Teaching of Social Science. Unpublished seminar paper, Sociology Department, University of California.

Neuwien, R. A. 1964. Preview Report of the Study of Catholic Education. *National Catholic Educational Association Bulletin* 61(2):1.

————. (ed.) 1966. *Catholic Schools in Action*. Notre Dame: Univeristy of Notre Dame Press.

Newcomer, Mabel. 1959. *A Century of Higher Education*. New York: Harper.

Newman, J. H. 1872. "What Is a University?" In *Historical Sketches*. London: Basil Montagu Pickering.

Newsweek, 1961, 57(16):74.

Nichols, R. C. and Astin, A. W. 1966. Progress of the Merit Scholar: An Eight-Year Follow-Up. *Personnel and Guidance Journal* 44:673.

Noonan, J. T., Jr. 1965. *Contraception: A History of Its Treatment by the Catholic Theologians and Canonists*. Cambridge: Harvard University Press.

Novak, M. 1962. Catholic Education and the Idea of Dissent. *Commonweal* 76:105.

————. 1963. Nuns in the World. *Commonweal* 79:274.

O'Dea, T. F. 1958. *American Catholic Dilemma*. New York: Sheed and Ward.

————. 1959. Catholics at the Crossroads. *Commonweal* 70:493.

Office of the Vice President. 1966. *Comparative Tabulations of Mundelein College Student Questionnaire Responses: 1963–1966*. Chicago: Mundelein College.

O'Gara, J. 1961. The Empty Chair. *Commonweal* 75:306.

————. 1966. The Archbishop and the Sisters. *Ibid.* 85:47.

Ong, W. J. 1956. The Intellectual Frontier. In *The Catholic Church, U. S. A.,* ed. L. J. Putz. Chicago: Fides Publishers.

Pace, C. R. 1962. *CUES College and University Environment Scales*. Princeton, N. J.: Educational Testing Service.

————. 1963. *CUES College and University Environment Scales Technical Manual*. Princeton, N. J.: Educational Testing Service.

Pattillo, M. M. and Mackenzie, D. M. 1965. *Eight Hundred Colleges Face the Future: A Preliminary Report of the Danforth Commission on Church Colleges and Universities.* St. Louis: The Danforth Foundation.

Pauson, J. J. 1966. Duquesne: Beyond the Official Philosophies. *Continuum* 4:252.

Peterson, R. E. 1966. *The Scope of Organized Student Protest in 1964–1965.* Princeton, N. J.: Educational Testing Service.

Phillips, C. A. 1956. Teaching the Meaning of Good Law. *Catholic School Journal* 56:149.

Plant, W. T. 1958. Changes in Ethnocentrism Associated with a Two-Year College Experience. *Journal of Genetic Psychology* 92:189.

————. 1959. Changes in Ethnocentrism Associated with a Four-Year College Experience. *Journal of Educational Psychology* 49:162.

————. 1962. *Personality Changes Associated with a College Education.* San Jose, Calif.: San Jose State College.

Pleasants, J. and Bauer, B. 1946. Needed: Catholic Scholars of Any Kind. *America* 75:411.

Poole, S. 1965. *Seminary in Crisis.* New York: Herder and Herder.

Powell, L. C. 1967. Speaking of Books: The Horgan File. *The New York Times Book Review* 72(20):2.

Power, E. J. 1958. *A History of Catholic Higher Education in the United States.* Milwaukee: Bruce.

Ranck, J. G. 1955. Some Personality Correlates of Religious Attitude and Belief. Doctoral dissertation, Columbia University, abstracted in *Dissertation Abstracts* 15:878.

Reinert, P. C. 1964. The Responsibility of American Catholic Higher Education in Meeting National Needs. *National Catholic Educational Association Bulletin* 60(1):134.

Riesman, D. and Jencks, C. 1962. The Viability of the American College. In *The American College,* ed. N. Sanford. New York: John Wiley & Sons.

Riggs, D. R. 1967. Religion on the Campus. *The Rhode Islander,* May 21, p. 16.

Rogoff, Natalie. 1957. *College Board Members: A Comparative Analysis.* New York: Bureau of Applied Social Research, Columbia University.

Rokeach, M. 1960. *The Open and Closed Mind.* New York: Basic Books.

Rommetveit, R. 1955. *Social Norms and Roles: Explorations in the Psychology of Enduring Social Pressures.* Oslo: Akademisk Förlag.

Rosen, B. C. 1961. Family Structure and Achievement Motivation. *American Sociological Review* 26:574.

Rosen, B. and D'Andrade, R. 1959. The Psychological Origins of Achievement Motivation. *Sociometry* 22:185.

348   REFERENCES

Roy, J. P. 1961. The Relationship of Certain Religious Attitudes to Artistic Behavior. Doctoral dissertation, Pennsylvania State University, abstracted in *Dissertation Abstracts* 22:1.

Ryan, Mary P. 1960. Problem of Religious and Lay Teachers. *Catholic Educational Review* 58:248.

————. 1964. *Are Parochial Schools the Answer?* New York: Holt, Rinehart and Winston.

Salerno, Mary Dolores. 1966. Patterns of Interinstitutional Cooperation in American Catholic Higher Education. *National Catholic Educational Association Bulletin* 62(4):1.

Salzbacher, J. 1967. "Canon Salzbacher's Observations on American Catholic Colleges for Men, 1842." In *Documents of American Catholic History*, ed. John Tracy Ellis. Rev. ed. Chicago: Henry Regnery Company.

San Francisco Chronicle. April, 1961 to December, 1966.

San Francisco Monitor, 1959.

Santa Claran, 1961, University of Santa Clara.

Sarbin, T. R. 1954. Role Theory. In *Handbook of Social Psychology*, ed. G. Lindzey, Vol. I. Reading, Massachusetts: Addison-Wesley.

Schall, J. V. 1966. Censorship in the Church. *Commonweal* 83:601.

Scharper, P. 1960. American Catholics and American Culture. *Critic* 19(1):7.

Schrag, P. 1967. Notre Dame: Our First Great Catholic University? *Harper's* 234(1404):41.

Seidl, A. E. 1965. Those Expensive Lay Teachers. *Commonweal* 82:147.

Sheehan, Helen. 1957. The Catholic College and the Ph.D. *Catholic Educational Review* 55:258.

Shuster, G. N. 1962. *Schools at the Crossroads. Atlantic* 210(2):95.

Sister Formation Bulletin, 1964, 10(4):32.

Sloyan, G. S. 1960. Seminaries in America. 73:37.

Star, J. 1963. Trouble Ahead for the Catholic Schools. *Look* 27(21):37.

Stark, R. 1963. On the Incompatibility of Religion and Science: A Survey of American Graduate Students. *Journal for the Scientific Study of Religion* 3:3.

Stern, G. 1958. *The Activities Index: Preliminary Manual.* Syracuse, N. Y.: Syracuse University Research Institute.

Stewart, D. and Hoult, T. 1959. A Social Psychological Theory of the Authoritarian Personality. *American Journal of Sociology* 65:274.

Stotsky, B. A. 1955. The Authoritarian Personality as a Stereotype. *Journal of Psychology* 39:325.

Strodtbeck, F. L. 1958. Family Interaction, Values, and Achievement. In *Talent and Society*, eds. D. C. McClelland *et. al.* Princeton, N. J.: D. Van Nostrand.

Strong, E. K. Jr. 1959. *Manual for Strong Vocational Interest Blanks for Men and Women.* Palo Alto, Calif.: Consulting Psychologists' Press.

Struening, E. L. 1957. Dimensions, Distribution, and Correlates of Authoritarianism in a Midwestern University Faculty Population. Doctoral dissertation, Purdue University.

————. 1958. The Relationship between Authoritarianism, Prejudice, and Church Attendance in a Large University Faculty. Paper presented at the Annual Meeting of the American Psychological Association.

Suenens, L. J. 1963. *The Nun in the World.* Westminster, Md.: Newman Press.

Sutor, D. 1965. Mundelein Makes the Change. *U. S. Catholic* 31(2):28.

Sweeters, J. 1962. Education, Si! Controversy, No! *Santa Claran* 10 (2):6.

Sylvester, H. 1948. Problems of the Catholic Writer. *Atlantic Monthly* 181:109.

Tavard, G. H. 1963. Theology in the Catholic College. *Commonweal* 78:273.

Thistlethwaite, D. L. 1959*a.* College Environment and Development of Talent. *Science* 130(3367):71

————. 1959*b.* College Press and Student Achievement. *Journal of Educational Psychology* 50:183.

Thomas, J. L. 1956. *The American Catholic Family.* Englewood Cliffs, N. J.: Prentice-Hall.

Time, 1961, 77(17):37; 1963, 81(8):70; 1965, 86(21):118; 1966, 87(3):55; 1966, 88(4):65; 1966, 88(21):95; 1967, 89(22):56.

Trapani, Mary C. 1960. Status of the Lay Teacher in Catholic Elementary Schools of Four Southern Dioceses. Master's thesis, Catholic University of America, abstracted in *Catholic Educational Review* 58:268.

Traxler, A. E. 1957. *An Appraisal of American Colleges on the Basis of Men Graduates Listed in Who's Who in America.* Paper presented at the American Association for the Advancement of Science, December 29.

Trent, J. W. 1964. The Etiology of Catholic Intellectualism: Development of Intellectual Disposition in Catholic Colleges. Doctoral dissertation, University of California.

————. 1965–66. A New Look at Recruitment Policies. *College Board Review* 58:7.

Trent, J. W. and Craise, Judith L. 1967. Commitment and Conformity in the American College. *Journal of Social Issues* (In press).

Trent, J. W. and Medsker, L. L. 1967. *Beyond High School: A Study of 10,000 High School Graduates.* U. S. Office of Education Project No. 1328. Berkeley: Center for Research and Development in Higher Education, University of California.

Trombley, W. 1966. *Conflict in Catholic Education, Los Angeles Times.*

Tyrrell, Mary I. 1957. A Study of the Attitudes of Catholic High School Girls Versus Those of Public High School Girls toward Certain Phases of Home Problems. *Catholic Educational Review* 55:612.

U. S. Department of Health, Education, and Welfare. 1961. *Education Directory, Part 3, Higher Education.* Washington: U. S. Government Printing Office.

U. S. Department of Health, Education, and Welfare. 1966. *Education Directory, Part 3, Higher Education.* Washington: U. S. Government Printing Office.

Van Kaam, A. L. 1963. A Psychology of the Catholic Intellectual. In *The Christian Intellectual,* ed. S. Hazo. Pittsburgh: Duquesne University Press.

————. 1965. Religious Counseling of Seminarians. In *Seminary Education in a Time of Change,* eds. J. Lee and L. Putz. Notre Dame: Fides Publishers.

Velardi, Angelica. 1959. Aspects of the Preparation of Sister Teachers for Teaching in Secondary Schools. Doctoral dissertation, Fordham University, abstracted in *Religious Education* 54:462.

Victor, J. 1963. Restraints on American Catholic Freedom. *Harper's* 227(1363):33.

Voight, J. J. 1962. Nine Proposals to Better American Catholic Education. *Catholic School Journal* 62:87.

Wakin, E. 1963. *The Catholic Campus.* New York: Macmillan.

————. 1965. The Catholic College That Disappeared. *The Sign* 45:30.

Wakin, E. and Scheuer, J. 1965. The American Nun—Poor, Chaste, and Restive. *Harper's* 231(1383):35.

Waldschmidt, P. E. 1966. A New Role for Religious at the University of Portland. *The University of Portland Bulletin, Alumni Edition* 29(3):7.

Wallach, M. A. and Kogan, N. 1959. Sex Differences and Judgment Process. *Journal of Personality* 27:555.

Walsh, J. 1966. The Sacred and Secular in American Universities. *National Catholic Educational Association Bulletin* 63(1):251.

Walters, E. (ed.). 1965. *Graduate Education Today.* Washington, D. C.: American Council on Education.

Ward, L. R. 1958. *New Life in Catholic Schools.* St. Louis: B. Herder.

Warner, W. L., Meeker, Marchia, and Eells, K. 1957. *Social Class in America.* Gloucester, Mass.: Peter Smith.

Wayman, W. 1955. Attitude Change and Authoritarian Personality. *Journal of Psychology* 40:3.

Weber, M. 1963. *The Sociology of Religion.* Boston: Beacon Press.

Webster, H. 1958. Changes in Attitudes During College. *Journal of Educational Psychology* 49:109.

Webster, H., Sanford, N., and Freedman, M. 1955. A New Instrument for Studying Authoritarianism in Personality. *Journal of Psychology* 40:73.

Weigel, G. 1956*a*. Enriching the Intellectual Life of the Catholic College. *National Catholic Educational Association Bulletin* 52:7.

———. 1956*b*. An Introduction to American Catholicism. In *The Catholic Church, U. S. A.*, ed. L. J. Putz. Chicago: Fides Publishers.

———. 1957. American Catholic Intellectualism: A Theologian's Reflections. *Review of Politics* 19:275.

———. 1963. Religious Schools and Civic Harmony. *Catholic World* 196:351.

Weiss, R. F. 1963. Student and Faculty Perceptions of Institutional Press at Saint Louis University. Doctoral dissertation, University of Minnesota.

Weissman, M. P. 1958. An Approach to the Assessment of Intellectual Disposition among Selected High Ability Students. Doctoral dissertation, University of California.

Whiteman, P. H. 1962. *Attitudes Toward Child Rearing, Personal Characteristics, and Religious Group Membership.* Mimeographed. University of Wisconsin.

Whiting, Anita. 1962. Intellective and Non-intellective Factors in Selection of Graduate Students. Master's thesis, Claremont College.

Williams, Phoebe. 1964. The Relationship between Certain Scores on the Strong Vocational Interest Blank and Intellectual Disposition. Doctoral dissertation, University of California.

Wright, J. J. 1956. Introduction. In *The Catholic Church, U. S. A.*, ed. L. J. Putz. Chicago: Fides Publishers.

Wright, Patricia. 1964. *Earned Degrees Conferred 1963–1964 Bachelor's and Higher Degrees.* Washington, D. C.: U. S. Department of Health, Education, and Welfare, OE-54013-64 Misc. No. 54.

INDEX

Ability
   of Catholic and non-Catholic college
      students, 54–56
   of graduate and professional school
      students, 168
   and intellectualism, 35, 94–97, 100–101,
      104–5, 209–12, 221, 232
   measurement of, 40
   and religious orientation, 190, 194
Abortion; *see* Morals
Academic aptitude; *see* Ability; Intellec-
      tualism, and ability
Academic freedom
   in Catholic colleges, vi, 34, 267–72
   and religious commitment, vii
   in seminaries, 282
Academic standards, Catholic college stu-
      dents' perception of, 135–37
Acculturation of Catholics, 46, 48–52, 99,
      128–29
   and college attendance, 48–51
Activism, student; *see* Protests of students
Administration of Catholic colleges
   lay, 267–68, 271, 310
   lay-religious tensions in, 267–71
Adolfs, R., 149
Adorno, T. W., 28–29, 320
Affluence of Catholics, and intellectu-
      alism, 99
Agnostics, 179
Allport-Vernon-Lindzey Study of Values
      (AVL), 315, 317–18, 320–21
Alter, Archbishop, 298–99
America, 25, 27, 292–93
American Catholic Psychological Associa-
      tion, 266
American Council on Education, 267
American Federation of Priests, 283
American Men of Science, 25
Anti-intellectualism; *see* Intellectualism,
      lack of; Intellectualism, Catholic,
      lack of

Antioch College, 307
Anti-Semitism, 151–52
   among Catholics and Protestants, 294
   Church policy on, 294
Anxiety
   and intellectualism, 225–26, 228, 230–33
   measurement of; *see* Lack of Anxiety
      scale
   prevalence of, 7
Apathy, student, 155
   at St. John's University, 153
Apostasy, 255
   and intellectualism, 240–41
Aptheker, H., 272
Aquinas, St. Thomas, 299
Archbishop of Canterbury, 294
Association of Chicago Priests, 283
Astin, A. W., 31, 41–42, 153
Attitudes
   toward Communism; *see* Communism,
      attitudes toward
   family influence on, 156
   intellectual; *see* Intellectualism
   toward learning, 139–40
   religious; *see* Religious orientation
   see also Educational values; Occupa-
      tional values; Social issues
Authoritarian personality, characteristics
      of, 27–30
Authoritarianism
   in Catholic families, 13–14
   among Catholics and non-Catholics,
      29–31
   and intellectualism, 13–15, 27–30
   and religious orientation, 28–30, 333
   see also Autonomy
Authoritarianism scale, 74–75
Authority in Catholic colleges, 155; *see
      also* Administration of Catholic
      colleges
Autonomy
   in the Catholic church, lack of, 12–15

353